The Book of the Incipit

M E D I E V A L C U L T U R E S

Series Editors

Rita Copeland
Barbara A. Hanawalt
David Wallace

Sponsored by the Center for Medieval Studies at the University of Minnesota

Volumes in this series study the diversity of medieval cultural histories and practices, including such interrelated issues as gender, class, and social hierarchies; race and ethnicity; geographical relations; definitions of political space; discourses of authority and dissent; educational institutions; canonical and noncanonical literatures; and technologies of textual and visual literacies.

Volume 28
D. Vance Smith
The Book of the Incipit: Beginnings in the Fourteenth Century

Volume 27
Edited by Glenn Burger and Steven F. Kruger
Queering the Middle Ages

Volume 26
Paul Strohm
Theory and the Premodern Text

For more books in the series, see pages 297–99.

Contents

Preliminary

I wish I could begin somewhere else, but beginning means starting with a text. At least it does here, because there's no way to start talking about beginnings without getting drawn into the language that they shape and are shaped by. And I'm mainly interested not in the shape that texts have, but in the things that they do, in the things they make us do or not do, in the reasons they give us for doing or not doing things. In thinking about beginnings we also think about the plans they give, the initiatives they present to us, the courses of action to which they call us. But in allowing us to act, or to think that we are creatures of beginning, capable of action, they entangle us in the very promises they make to us. We have to act on beginnings, or we end up making new beginnings. And in acting on beginnings we're no longer beginning but pursuing something that unfolds despite us. We're becoming formed by those beginnings. I began to intuit the strange pulls of beginning growing up in a country in the process of becoming a former British colony, a place where the purported beginnings of empire assumed the monstrous form of origin myths that replaced the intrinsic histories that had actually been lived and histories that could only be experienced as a desperate, unwritten, very real desire to begin again. And ecstatic as that beginning eventually was, the country has come to experience a series of crises over what constitutes a real beginning, over the degree to which an origin must continue to shape political communities. What intrigued me most about the poem that's at the heart of this book is that it seemed to me profoundly aware of that insidious paradox of human action, and in ways that stretched far beyond the confines, the concerns, of shaping a literary text, into the predicaments of political action and individual salvation. Because we're beginning with a poem, we will be following the shape that necessarily follows from a beginning, and we'll have to understand how and why a literary work's shape follows from its beginning. But we'll also be seeing how a poem crucially about beginning develops ways of continuing to begin, even to construct a literary form that neglects the injunctions of almost every medieval compositional precept. But the question of whether a poem obeys or disregards conventions of literary form is not intrinsically interesting to us anymore, at least since we have begun to think more about the cultural, political, and social pressures on writing in the Middle Ages and since we have begun to think of formalism as a mode of understanding literature that is dangerously synchronous. Our objection to formalism, that it excludes history, rests on the legacy of the long autonomy sought by formalism in the past century, to take writing out of time, to assert that literature has a quirky ontology of its own. To the degree that we worry about ontology anymore, we worry about the ontology of the social, the way that human pressures inform the production of texts, a process we now understand as beginning well before the first words we read in a text and that now includes the workshops of medieval London, the circulation of goods in and out of the realm, and the desires to propagate or suppress ideas that mattered to more than the casual reader of vernacular romance.

In thinking about the way beginnings work and about the way a particular poem works as what we now would call a critique of beginning, a mode of analysis that shows how beginnings can undo their own initiatives, I want to focus on the way that books open, not on how and why they *remain* open. I suspect that much of the recent interest in discursive closure is underpinned by a desire to perfect a work as literary, to keep it immune from the world—in short, to think of a means to contemplate its formal perfection even when it seems to be pulling away from recognizable forms. In thinking about how medieval beginnings work, I want to keep coming back to the reasons beginnings emerge in the world or why we think they are important. Beginnings are two different things—or rather we think of them in two different ways: as the capacity to start something new, to make, to develop initiatives of our own, and as the events that determine us, that allow us to make sense of the way we got here—as origins. We think of them as either forms or actions, as things that circumscribe what we can do or that constitute our essential freedom, our capacity to act politically or ethically, even to resist. In the Middle Ages, these two aspects of beginning, their radical contingency and their comforting determinism, are even easier to confuse. As we will see, even political, or popular, initiatives were imagined and represented both in terms of beginning and in terms of recognizable forms of political or social behavior.

Beginning provides a way of imagining—a provisional form for—modes of thinking, acting, and reacting outside the confines of the text, beginning with the sanctioned forms of the written word, but, to the degree that the beginning remains a beginning, in a way that allows one to move beyond it, almost as if beginning were a talisman. And, as we will see in the first chapter, it was: a talisman for action, an acknowledgment of cultural form deployed in the service of exceptionality.

I ought to apologize for the philosophical registers of parts of this book, but I am not sure that those are my fault. It may seem bizarre for us to see scholastics wondering to what branch of philosophy a narrative belongs, and certainly strange that they should think that it belongs to philosophy in the first place, but this book has slowly placed itself there. I found while wrestling with the nature of particular beginnings in *Piers Plowman* that often the only way to make any sense out of them was to think about them philosophically—that is, to think about why they are there in the first place, to think about them through the work of real philosophers for whom beginning is a more or less articulated and conscious problem in their thinking, discovering often that the best way of understanding the nuances and urgencies of medieval treatments of beginning was to move forward to work we are accustomed to thinking of as less restrained, bound, or niggling than that of scholastic philosophy. The names of the medieval philosophers I draw on will emerge as the book unfolds, as will their particular engagements with the problem of beginning. It might not be clear even to readers familiar with the modern thinkers on whom I draw, however, that I am primarily interested in the ways in which they take up the problem of beginning as an aspect of their engagement with, or repudiation of, the phenomenological tradition—often at an earlier, more seminal stage of their careers than that at which we normally encounter them. I am interested, for instance, in the recognizably phenomenological trends in Heidegger's thinking, Derrida's early work on Husserl, and Deleuze's on Feuerbach as the most rigorous critic of the quasi-phenomenological Hegel of *The Phenomenology of Spirit.* Because of his insistence that Hegelian philosophy begins by positing its own presuppositions, Feuerbach is, says Deleuze, "among those who have pursued furthest the problem of where to begin." I would like to think, too, that this is as far as we can go: asking where to begin, a question that I think resonates without ever being quite answered, because it cannot be, in Langland's own epoch. For reasons that have much to do with the interest of phenomenology in beginning—indeed its *arete* as the science of the perpetual beginner—this book will diverge significantly from the most recognizable book on literary beginning in this generation—Edward Said's magisterial *Beginnings.* With the exception of A. D. Nuttall's book *Openings,* a more traditional literary study that occupies the critical equivalent of an analytical philosophical position in the study of narrative beginning, we seemed to have ended with Said's beginning, a beginning whose principles are manifestly and profoundly those of a Foucauldian structuralism. Similarly, the interest in closure so evident in the work of Frank Kermode, Barbara Herrnstein Smith, and Umberto Eco and, for the Middle Ages, in Rosemarie McGerr's *Chaucer's Open Books,* has brought home to us the practical indeterminacies of texts, but in ways that create closure of another kind: thinking about a work as open already defeats its work. In work that attempts to preserve the initiative of beginning, openness is a kind of dangerous termination: the death of the possibility that any action can come out of the beginning, the acknowledgment that we're doomed to suffer an inescapable literariness. The stunning recent work on rhetoric in the Middle Ages—particularly that of Rita Copeland and Jody Enders—has shown us how far beyond the mere shape of a text we need to go in order to understand why texts were begun and what they make impossible. In *Piers Plowman* we encounter a poem that engages with the problem of beginning on a level far beyond the rhetorical, taking up the problem as it was thought through at other stages of the trivium and quadrivium, in grammar, certainly, but also in logic, physics, and, above all, theology. And it thinks about beginning through modes of intellection that the medieval ages might have regarded as ephemeral, accidental, and provisional, through such objects and actions as the book, the mechanics of time-telling, ritual, and the forging of popular and alternative histories.

The kindness and interest in this project taken by a number of people only impressed on me further how insufficient my own beginning originally was. I'm especially indebted to Rita Copeland, Hoyt Duggan, John Fleming, Douglas Gray, R. Allen Shoaf, A. C. Spearing, and Michael Uebel for their ideas, guidance, and time. At particular points, I've received helpful encouragement or advice from Robert Adams, John Alford, Janet Bately, Janet Cowan, Jody Enders, Louise Fradenburg, David Hult, Claudia Johnson, Robert Kellogg, Kathryn Kerby-Fulton, Samuel Overstreet, Jane Roberts, and Steven Justice. For research support and hospitality I'd like to thank the United Kingdom Fulbright Commission, the University of Virginia Society of Fellows, King's College London, Magdalen College Oxford, Patricia Spacks, Robert Huskey, Galfrid Congreve, and Michael Gilsenan. I completed the manuscript at the National Humanities Center with the aid of a fellowship from the National Endowment for the Humanities and with the considerable assistance of Karen Carroll. People at the following libraries have helped tremendously: the Firestone Library at Princeton; Alderman Library at the University of Virginia; the Magdalen College Library; the Bodleian Library, Oxford; the Sterling Library at the University of London; and the Western Manuscripts Division at the British Library.

A version of part of the sixth chapter appeared in *Yearbook for Langland Studies.* I am grateful to John Alford for permission to reprint it.

And since this is a book about beginning, I should say that it began one evening when I placed side by side two stunning pieces about literary work and its predicament in the Middle Ages, one by Judson Allen, whose work on medieval literature remains some of the most provocative and intriguing out there, and the other by Anne Middleton, whose articles remain the best book yet begun on *Piers Plowman.*

INCIPIT

[It begins, from *capio,* take or seize, a purposive action, an "arbitrary" beginning, the beginning of a text]

A Fourteenth-Century Incipit

I am measuring the "too much" of the beginning of the fable.
—Michel Serres, *The Parasite*

Writing Out

Much of the writing in medieval London began in three streets next to Saint Paul's Cathedral. The ambiguity of the English past tense "began" in this beginning, the incipit of this book, shows already the difficulty we have in talking about beginning, in deciding whether we are talking about the origin of writing itself or individual acts of writing, what happens whenever pen is put to parchment. If this writing that begins in medieval London is not a uniquely original event, then we have to decide how to imagine those individual acts of beginning to write. They must be habitual to some extent, or we would not recognize them, yet they must be unique, or they would not be acts of beginning. The beginnings of writing in London in the fourteenth century might help us to answer this question, or to appreciate its complexity.

Many, if not most, of the books produced in London were copied and compiled in the district to the north and west of Saint Paul's, in three streets occupied by stationers, illuminators, and parchment makers. It is remarkable that by the fourteenth century none of these streets was known by its original name nor directly by the occupations of bookmaking so prevalent there, but by names that come from the beginnings of texts. Paternoster Row, the center of the book trade, was named after the opening word of the Lord's Prayer, while at its west end ran Creed Lane, named for the first word of the statement of faith in the liturgy, and Ave Maria Lane, named for the "angelical salutation," the "Hail Mary." These names do not come from stations of the procession of Corpus Christi, as many historians of London have argued, since they were being used before the appearance of the feast in England after 1310.[1] It is far more likely that they come from, or were propagated by, the work being done by the scores of book producers who lived in those streets, copying out texts that were frequently liturgical, but often vernacular narratives, romances such as those in the Auchinleck manuscript or generically hybrid works like *Piers Plowman*.[2] But if the books produced in this district were so diverse, then why should its streets be called by liturgical incipits? As elements of the liturgy they were instantly recognizable, but recognizable in a particular way—as the *beginnings*, the incipits, of parts of the liturgy, conjuring not just the texts they begin, nor even the very beginnings of these texts, but the recognizable, universal significance of beginnings themselves, the sign of beginning as the mode of writing itself.

These streets named for incipits show that the incipit itself is a condensation of political, religious, and textual beginnings. They show that inevitably and unconsciously the act of writing is imagined as, and represented as, the act of beginning to write. It is an act that, in certain senses, never ends, that never gets rid of the obligation to begin all over again. Having finished one book, these book producers had to begin another one, or even the same one, all over again. Beginning a book was necessarily fraught with anxiety. A book made on speculation could waste several months of labor and piles of expensive parchment if it did not sell. Even books made on order required the coordination of independent scribes and illuminators, the acquisition of an exemplar, and countless decisions about its shaping to suit the tastes of the person who commissioned it. Incipits furnish not only a sign that books are being made, but also that beginnings signify something in their own right. Beginning sometime in the thirteenth century, these incipits map part of London, giving their names to a central part of the city's topography, hinting at a powerful association between incipits and the making of books, beginning and shaping the world. And so they began to write, these makers of texts, writing texts that never came to an end, never fulfilling the impossible, compelling project of making a real beginning.

As the mapping of incipits onto the district of book producers suggests, in the Middle Ages a book was virtually equivalent to its beginning. In indexing systems that began to emerge in the thirteenth century, the first few words of a work were often used to identify the whole work, and this kind of metonymic citation is found from the abstruse world of scholastic writing to the far more pragmatic one of household administration.[3] We still identify medieval manuscripts in this way. But the incipit of a text did not just tag the work for the sake of convenience. They represented something more powerful, a principle that can almost exceed the importance of the text itself. The beginning was a model for reading a work, a model that became in the Benedictine Rule, for example, a fundamental principle, as Mary Carruthers points out: "'Begin at the beginning' was made a moral duty in the Rule because of its fundamental mnemonic importance."[4] The idea of an incipit, a textual beginning, was applied in different ways to composing other texts; almost any portion of text could become the incipit of a new text. Franciscan preaching manuals urged preachers to choose a single biblical phrase as a text, which was called the *thema* or the *principium*, the beginning, of the sermon. In many ways, as we will be seeing in the following pages, that *thema* was the most important part of the sermon. In medieval universities, the beginning of a scholar's career was formalized by a peculiar display of rhetorical ingenuity called the *principium*, in which he cited a text as an incipit, a speech that elaborately and ingeniously intertwined his name with the *thema* he had chosen. At least three times a day in each of the cathedrals and collegiate churches of England, one of the two leaders of the choir (also called "rulers" or *canonici hebdomadarii*) turned to a book called a *Tonale* to see how to begin the antiphon, which introduced the psalm. Only the beginning of the antiphon was normally sung before the psalm, and concluded after the psalm had been sung. The antiphon was a kind of musical incipit, and the *Tonale* highlights that function in several ways. The ruler beginning the antiphon needed to know how much of it to sing (to anticipate a phrase we will discuss later, to know "where this beginning ends") and needed to know the "mode" of its beginning so he could choose the appropriate antiphon to conclude the psalm. In one *Tonale* this arrangement by beginning is called *inceptio*.[5]

We can see how pervasive and important the incipit was in daily life in another common medieval practice. The most famous incipit of the

Middle Ages was often used as an ordinary, if somewhat ostentatious, opening to a conversation. A pleasant *in principio,* as Chaucer's friar demonstrates, lent even unsavory clergy an air of propriety. That incipit, the famous beginning of the Gospel of John, was used in various forms throughout the Middle Ages: it was inscribed on amulets; used as a charm against fever, demons, and ghosts; recited at extreme unction; and deployed against the Arian heresy, among others.[6] Such practices suggest that incipits constitute a kind of documentary ritual in everyday life in the Middle Ages, and that they also designate something exceptional, irreducibly powerful, in their very repetition. What is suggestive about the widespread use of the incipit of the Gospel of John is that it is an incipit itself about beginning, an incipit that doubles back on itself, pointing out the very importance of beginning. It could even be said to be an incipit that points out the importance of beginning a text, above all a text that concerns the archetypal relation between beginning and, as its remainder says, the word. This particular incipit, above all, points out the way that beginnings tend to be marked only by language, only by the moment at which the word begins to be used. Heidegger's reading of the word *logos* in Heraclitus makes the point more insistently. It is the *logos,* he says, that *makes* a beginning: Heraclitus uses it to mean both "word" and "collection," the "primal gathering principle."[7] This is the likely source of the influential Lacanian notion that individual beginnings coincide with the entry into language, an idea that medieval texts on grammar, rhetoric, logic, physics, and theology not only ascribe to but also work out thoroughly and systematically. All of the higher sciences were interested in the problem of beginning and, as we will see, found themselves having to think through it as fundamentally a problem of signification, of how to designate the instant at which something begins. As a result, grammar and logic become the instruments by which beginning is measured. The more precisely grammarians could describe the metaphorical action of language by describing the behavior of words that belong to what was called the syncategorematic kind, the more precisely physical movement and ontological movement (such as the so-called intension and remission of forms) could be measured. The beginning that language makes possible is at the frontier of late medieval intellectual exploration, and late medieval writers with any exposure to universities or cathedral schools could hardly have failed to be aware of the technical and abstract resonances of the beginnings they themselves wrote.

Even if we bracket out these influential and pervasive contexts, the beginning of a late medieval text is still a stunningly complicated Möbius wonder of reversals and negations. The practice of allegoresis involves what Rita Copeland has called a "deep recausing" of a text, in which a commentary on the text supplies "an anterior structure of reference" by inserting itself "as the originary point of the text" as it takes up and examines the question of the *intentiones scribentis, libri,* or *auctoris.*[8] What Maureen Quilligan has called an "initiating pun" signals a text's emergence out of its very implication in language, unfolding the consequences of its beginning.[9] Following Bernard Huppé's discussion of the polysemous meaning of the adjective "trielich" in *Piers Plowman* (which describes the tower at the beginning of the poem), she argues brilliantly that the subjects—and indeed the forms—of truth, treasure, and tripleness, perhaps the poem's most important themes, are punningly anticipated in that adjective. But the relationship, she argues, is stronger than mere suggestion. The so-called *Visio,* the segment of the poem most explicitly interested in just those terms, develops as a commentary on that incipient pun. The inchoate nature of the poem's narrative, she argues, is less a failure of poetic imagination than it is the emergent form of commentary. And that form, as Morton Bloomfield points out, is the trace of the original text: "The progression is in the work commented on—that is, *extrinsic to itself.* It expands from a fixed point... and then returns to the next fixed point outside itself in the work being explained."[10] But if that is true of a poem such as *Piers Plowman,* what text is it that furnishes it with its intermittent points of reference and, above all, its beginning? Quilligan suggests that the answer lies in the poem's own inception, the initiating pun itself, which she describes as an "intrinsic threshold text," a phrase that suggests the literary genesis of allegorical texts in their opening scenes, which "unfold as narrative investigations of their own threshold texts."[11] The initial object of allegory, in other words, is the mode of its own procedure. The unfolding *Visio* is a commentary that demonstrates how to read beyond the opening, but does so by providing, at the same time, the text that is to be read: the larger text of beginning itself.

If this is confusing, it demonstrates how complex the nature of such poems is. They begin on a threshold that is never quite crossed, a *limen* between the inner sense of the text and its extrinsic incentives. At most moments it is possible to look both ways, at the poem spinning out from its own points of verbal origin and at the traces of the poem's extrinsic beginnings. I say "traces" because such beginnings, by definition, cannot appear in a work. The three-fold "trielich," for instance, is the initiative for the poem's thematically episodic nature, which is a developing commentary on the word. But it is also *itself a commentary,* unfolding from a prior *poesis,* as a commentary on the tower that already appears "trieliche ymaked" at the beginning of the poem. That "initiating pun" does not make the poem so much as it meditates on what has already been made, what inducements there are or there have been to begin the poem.

The relationship between texts and the idea of beginning is a complicated one in the Middle Ages. A text not only exemplifies a particular beginning, but can also be thought of as a response to the problem of making a beginning. That is, every text is a liminal text, its beginnings both intrinsic and extrinsic to it, a problematic that is really just a dilation of the dilemma of human language itself. As the work of Giorgio Agamben shows, historical and structural linguistics alike are unable to explain the origin of language because language is "constitutive of the human." That is, the assumption that there is a human activity that precedes language, and one that invents it, is unintelligible because language *is* that activity of invention. It does not have a beginning or history prior to its emergence because it is "itself *historicizing,* and itself founds the possibility of there being any 'history.'"[12] Language is something both given and made, both natural and cultivated, a double inheritance whose "double signification" (in Emile Benveniste's phrase) is both the closed, recognized system of semiotics and the open, comprehended experience of semantics, carrying with it the continuous origin, the *arché* of Aristotle, that "is not a simple beginning that is left behind by what follows, but on the contrary, it never ceases to begin, that is, to govern that whose ever-bursting-forth inception it is."[13] As we will see, language must be used not only to describe these beginnings, but also to make them. Especially in written language, a beginning is a *limen,* wholly part of neither what precedes from it nor of what proceeds from it.

In the Middle Ages, beginning is not only an instant of time: it is a puzzle, a deeply compelling mystery. We cannot fully apprehend it, no matter how surrounded by beginnings we believe ourselves to be. Speaking about the most recognizable medieval incipit, that of the Gospel of John—

the famous "In principio erat Verbum"—Augustine says that the beginning is something that "the natural man does not perceive." Even John, the most philosophical of the Gospel writers, probably did not fully understand the beginning he had written: "perhaps not John himself spoke of the matter as it is, but even he only as he was able; for it was man that spoke of God, inspired indeed by God, but still man. Because he was inspired he said something; if he had not been inspired, he would have said nothing; but because a man inspired, he spoke not the whole, but what a man could he spoke."[14] Although the *incipit,* the beginning of a text, expresses the powerful idea of beginning, it does so in a necessarily fragmentary way: an incipit is only a portion of the whole discourse, a beginning that must continue in order to be understood, if it can be at all.

The idea that the beginning represented in a text somehow represents a real beginning, a beginning we all seem to long for, is something of a dream, a fantasy that hovers over the beginning of the medieval text. To associate it merely with the incipit is to anatomize it, to subject it to the temporality of language. It is another aspect of the vast dream of humankind, the dream that Boethius says we are always elaborating on, the dream of the beginning: as Lady Philosophy tells us, you "who are creatures of the earth, dream of your origin."[15] In the idea of beginning, we confront the nostalgic dream that constitutes the most essential aspect of our being, its desire to return to its origin. Conversely, the medieval dream offers a means of narrating the beginning that is the vanishing point of desire. The resources and techniques of the medieval dream vision offer us a way of thinking through the attempt to reunite the beginning and the Word in medieval narrative. More specifically, as we will see, the fourteenth-century poem *Piers Plowman* shows us how the incipit, or a series of incipits, is employed in what is essentially a series of dreams of beginning.

Beginning with one of the simplest, most understated beginnings of any long medieval poem, *Piers Plowman* is also the unusual medieval poem that begins again—not just once, but many times. By this I mean that it is a poem that not only inserts *a* beginning, as, for instance, Chaucer's *Troilus and Criseyde* does before each book, but also repeatedly reprises *its own beginning* at points that are constitutively new beginnings, and in such a way that they become new narrative initiatives, not just an interlude in an already developing narrative. Even the individual tales, or the beginnings of days or fragments, in Boccaccio's *De-*

cameron or Chaucer's *Canterbury Tales* are subordinated to a larger narrative framework whose initiative remains consistent, whose time is unchanged, whose development remains unhindered, subordinate to the original teleology of the initial opening. The new initiatives in *Piers Plowman,* on the other hand, are disruptive enough to the general framework of the poem that numerous readers of the poem have read it under the assumption that it is actually two poems, or (less radically) a poem written in two separable halves, the *Visio* and the *Vita.* As far as I know, it is also the only medieval dream vision that has more than one distinct, articulated dream, figuring a cognitive mode that itself reflexively concerns the very beginning of narrativity.[16] It is a poem obsessed with beginning, convinced of the simplicity of beginning, yet haunted by its complexity. It is a convincing demonstration of a principle that all medieval writers in the West knew well: that beginnings are inseparable from language, that the Word was there at the beginning.

Just as *Piers Plowman*'s radical rewriting of the beginnings deeply implicated in medieval culture cannot be fully understood unless we can understand what those beginnings are, we cannot understand the way in which these beginnings operate without considering the text in which they appear. In this book, I argue that the poem's distinctive feature—its composition out of multiple dream narratives—is what most provokes puzzlement over the poem, and precisely what thwarts attempts to construct sustained accounts of its function. Because each of those dreams has its own beginning, *Piers Plowman* is a medieval poem that massively concerns beginning, constructed as it is of multiple beginnings. This crucial feature alone makes it important to discuss *Piers Plowman* in terms of beginning—a thing, like Milton's reading of biblical beginnings, unattempted until now. This book will consider *Piers Plowman* as an extended meditation on beginnings, a subject that is of central importance not only for the maker of the poem, but also in fourteenth-century England. Why is it that at this moment a poem gathered together a number of the diverse discourses on beginning that were being produced starting at the end of the thirteenth century? What compelling pressures found their genius in a poem about the very problems these diverse treatises were interested in, giving the problem of beginning such extensiveness and harmonic significance? I will be examining what Bloomfield's and subsequent work on the importance of apocalyptic thinking for the poem leaves unexamined, that beginning has increasing narrative, political, and theological urgency for the Edwardian and Ricardian England in which *Piers Plowman* was being written.

In the following chapters I will examine the ways in which virtually no aspect of *Piers Plowman* is untouched by the effort to begin writing or to think about the consequences of beginning. I examine how the poet theorizes about and rehearses beginnings even while he is writing the work itself. Indeed, beginning comes to be the important topic from which the poet examines the consequences of writing the poem that dangerously impinges on his own life. Beginning also is a means by which the poet examines the lives of those around him, to contemplate social and subjective practices that are innovative in more than one sense. More than that, the poem's earliest readers seem to have intuited that it is a poem crucially concerned with the way in which textual beginnings are a fantasy of beginnings in real life. They were able to do this because the very form of the beginning carries with it a complex of unresolved and potentially powerful ideas. It is a form of invocation or of writing that is suggestive precisely because it is not fully realized. As Hannah Arendt has shown, the principles of action—by which she means any human activity that is not necessary for the most basic labor of living—and beginning are not only related, they are essentially the same. "To act, in its most general sense, means to take an initiative, to begin," a condensation of meaning that is implicit in the Greek word *arché,* meaning "to begin," which also means to lead and to rule. From the outset, Arendt argues, our condition is both to begin and to act: because "they are *initium,* newcomers and beginners by virtue of birth, men take initiative, are prompted into action."[17] The kinds of action that *Piers Plowman* enjoins, as we will see in the final chapter, are, finally and specifically, forms of beginning. In a more local way, the poem's forms of beginning, its images of the incipit, could be used, obversely, as injunctions to action. When a political philosophy could be gleaned from it, it was one that linked beginning and action in just this way.

As Steven Justice has shown eloquently, the rebels of 1381 followed a script that they compiled, in part, out of *Piers Plowman,* which gave them "a language and style, an imaginative model of rural articulacy that conferred on empirical language a conceptual utility and a public force."[18] John Ball, especially, misreads important moments of the poem in his sermons prior to the revolt, and the rebels' letters include the injunction "doþ wele and ay bettur," clear allusions to two of the most important figures of the *vita*'s attempt to define a salvific ethics.[19] As acute as Justice's argument is, even he may be too ready to argue that the rebels turn from the poem's model to other kinds of writing, from what he describes as the "skeptical shufflings" of *Piers Plowman* to documentary models, to develop a form of writing that could be coupled with action. For quite apart from the poem's audacity in developing a sophisticated conceptual vocabulary out of the language of everyday life, it also seems to have presented itself to the rebels as a compelling meditation on a problem their letters articulate, and which has never been commented on.

That problem is the problem of beginning. Each of the rebels' statements is constructed, as Justice has shown, as a letter, possibly written by the hands of several of the rebels themselves; the statements seem to assert collectively the power of writing itself, the emergence of the symbolic from unexpected quarters.[20] But what gives these symbolic assertions their force, what makes them work in the first place, is their form. That form is only recognizable from its incipits, from the gestures each letter makes at its beginning, declaring the name of the writer, "followed by a greeting, request, or command."[21] Two of the letters, the one by "Jak trewman" and one of John Ball's, even echo the incipits of royal letters patent, as Justice points out, and, possibly, of school texts dictated in cathedral schools and the Inns of Court: "jakke trewman doþ ȝow to understande..."[22] Trewman's letter, too, embeds an incipit, the beginning of the liturgical Psalm 132, in its text in a fashion that every reader of *Piers Plowman* will recognize: "no man may come trewþe to. but he syng *si dedero*."[23] If, as Justice argues, writing is a crucial site of contention and a means of self-declaration in the rising, then it is the form of the incipit that most clearly signals the importance of inscribed and potential literary forms to the rebels. It may not be too much of an exaggeration to say that one of the things at stake in the rising was not so much the place of the *ars dictaminis* in lay culture but the signifying form of the incipit itself. As we will see, such moments demonstrate that the incipit has a particular political and theological urgency in the fourteenth century.

More than that, the rebels' letters also are constructed around the problem of beginning itself. That is, the incipits they themselves use point not just toward the written forms of chancery and classroom, but also to a discourse on beginning embedded in the letters. Three of them enjoin action on their listeners or readers precisely because of the beginning that they represent, linking inception and completion, as in Jack Carter's letter: "make a gode ende. of þat ȝe haue begunnen."[24] These letters not only acknowledge the commensurability of beginning and action, but they use beginning as a sign of, and an inducement to, action. We will explore, in the next section, the relation between making a beginning and making an end. What is salient here, however, is the awareness that these letters trace, an awareness of the obligations placed upon their writers by the beginning that they have enacted in 1381, in their own lives, and in these letters.

A sermon preached by John Ball himself helps to show why, and how profoundly, these letters are concerned with beginnings. His infamous Blackheath sermon concerns the origin of what Chaucer's Franklin and the Wife of Bath refer to as "gentilesse," and the question of whether it is natural or conventional. We will be discussing Ball's sermon further in the fourth chapter ("Thema"), but it is sufficient for the moment to point out that the sermon shows that what is at stake in the designation and deployment of beginnings is the very status of the rebels and the definition of what actions are appropriate in the act of living, in judging how, exactly, to go about making a good end given the beginning that one already has. Thomas Walsingham rather cannily calls attention to the relation between the form and the philosophical subject of Ball's sermon. I will quote most of his account, because the description itself makes some fine but important distinctions about beginning.

> Continuansque sermonem inceptum, nitebatur, per verba proverbii quod pro themate sumpserat, introducere et probare, ab initio omnes pares creatos a natura . . . quia, si Deo placuisset servos creasse, utique in principio mundi constituisset quis servus, quisve dominus futurus fuisset.[25]

> [And continuing the sermon he had begun, he endeavored, by means of proverbial sayings which he took up for the theme, to introduce and to prove, [that] all were created equal by nature . . . because, if God had wished to create slaves, he would have established from the beginning of the world who would be a slave and who would be a lord.]

Walsingham not only calls attention to the sermon as an artifact of beginning ("sermonem inceptum"), he represents Ball using the full apparatus of homiletic beginning (which we shall examine more fully in the third chapter), starting with a theme that will shape the rest of the discourse ("introducere et probare"). The body of the sermon is about more important kinds of beginning: the beginning of human history ("ab initio") and of the world itself, created by God ("in principio"). Concluding, of course, that current social differences reflect neither the natural nor the "original" disposition of the world, Ball's sermon urges that such distinctions be collapsed so that things can conform to their beginnings. Ball's sermon, then, is a program for ensuring that the end and the beginning of things conform, in the way that a sermon's *thema* and *probatio* agree and in the way that humans might now conform to their true beginnings. Making a good end, then, is a matter fundamentally concerned with beginnings. It invokes an ideology based on origins, but also necessarily involving, if not flaunting, the medieval techniques of making textual beginnings—in the case of the rebels' letters and Ball's sermon, the incipit and the *thema*. The making of an end is compared with the obligation to act properly, but that obligation is produced by beginnings already made. Yet those beginnings slide from sense to sense, meaning anything from the beginning of the world itself to the beginning of a text. Those beginnings cannot really be separated.

That confusion, and the urgency with which people in the fourteenth century thought about beginnings, is a large part of the subject of *Piers Plowman* itself, a poem that stages successive beginnings, that mimics the attempt in the real world to anchor more important beginnings to texts, to discover how it was that beginnings keep coming back to language. As we see already in 1381, the earliest readers of *Piers Plowman* that we know of responded most vitally to it as a work about the form of beginnings, a work that imagines that beginnings can be suspended over the work—both literal and metaphorical—that they inaugurate.

This book, as a consequence, may seem periodically to be undertaking a formalist analysis of one poem, but the problem of form is anything but an abstract, disinterested exercise in the fourteenth century. It is, as we will see, one that is thought out in subtle and polemical ways, one that is urgent because it has such immediate political consequences. The single year 1388 provided a number of occasions on which the efficacy of social, political, legal, and theological forms was tested, revised, repressed, or reimagined. The most obvious of these is the Cambridge Parliament in September, in which the intensity of feeling over the matter of liveries and badges of affiliation masked, or displaced, a much graver and more massive concern over the ontology of social reality. In more extensive ways, the same problem lay at the center of the discussion over the Parliament's response to the earlier Statute of Labourers, a conspicuous failure that prompted the invention of a variety of documentary instruments and a close regulation of them, from seals to what Anne Middleton calls "internal passports,"[26] not to mention a concern over the form and power of statutes themselves. The ability of the English ruling assemblages to think through the problem of form in the practices of rule—or perhaps their helplessness in the face of it—is a large part of their response to the trauma and brutality of the February parliament, in which a number of the king's close associates were summarily tried and hastily and brutally executed, Thomas Usk, for instance, pulled down indecorously as soon as he had been hung and his head hacked off with about thirty blows.[27] Even at the inception of the parliament the anxiety that its final legislative form would not, in fact, be final is voiced by the petitions presented by the Commons, which asks the parliament to condemn as traitorous any attempt to reverse its enactments. But their petition worries more about the form of potential interventions than it does about the potential reversals themselves, and is anxious about the transformative power of what it calls "ymaginacioun et interpretacion." By foreclosing these acts, by representing imagination and interpretation as socially pathological, the petition vests considerable hope in the administrative force of the formal law and in the objective existence and efficacy of written form. The petition punctiliously observes this logic, defining such a traitorous hermeneutics only as that which is established "de record" and implicitly disbarring such acts of imagination and interpretation even for those whose charge is to uphold the peace of the realm.[28] Yet even this overdetermined protection was clearly not enough to allay worries over the indelibility of the work done by the parliament, for well after its conclusion the Lords and Commons asked Richard on June 3 to ratify "pro perpetuo inviolabiliter" the proceedings of the parliament.[29] It is likely that the very forms of this generalized anxiety over the durability of forms provoked an unsettling awareness of the power of legislative bodies to revise encoded forms. A final and more profound attempt to shore up the integrity of forms was the center of the primary activity on that day, when Richard renewed his vows of coronation at Westminster Abbey before the assembled magnates and other powerful men of the kingdom, after a mass and sermon. It is clear that this occasion was designed to mark, and indeed to publish, the rapprochement between Richard and the magnates, for they were also induced to renew their oaths of fealty. But the very means by which these symbolic and political links were reimpressed is simultaneously a powerful articulation of their contingency.

The sermon delivered just before these acts of renewal, preached by Robert Braybrooke, the bishop of London, concerned the form ("forma") and responsibility ("periculo") of oaths.[30] That the form of oaths themselves is ambivalent is seen already in the peculiar word that describes them: *periculum,* which here must mean the responsibility that they enjoin, the dangers that await those who do not keep them, and possibly the modes in which they are essayed. But the word also means, and means primarily in the English Middle Ages, "danger," even "ruin." Even if Thomas Favent, who wrote this account, does not intend to conjure up the instability of declarative forms, the renovation of oaths itself demonstrates their impermanence and susceptibility to revision. For if Richard's original oath *had* been effective the renovation would have been unnecessary. Indeed, the occasion of their renewal is also the occasion of their undoing. If Braybrooke's admonitions to adhere to the sanctity of the form of avowal had been strictly adhered to, then this second ceremony would not only have been unnecessary, it would have been self-defeating.

Some of the urgency and aporetic nature of the responses to this problem can be seen in the way in which Favent's account closes with this narrative of the renewal of inviolable oaths. Immediately preceding it is the conclusion proper of the account of the parliament and the executions of the men who had been appealed, which Favent sums up in grandiloquent but proverbial language: "Qui legis scrutare quomodo mala, malo inchoata principio, vix est ut ullo bono peraguntur exitu!" (You who scrutinize in some manner the evils of the law, barely begun with a bad beginning—hardly is it possible that they are accomplished with any good outcome!).[31] Clearly worried about the potential for a beginning to generate dangerously powerful alternative forms to those which should be dominant, Favent represents actions based on bad, unbegun beginnings as pathologically doomed. This is an interesting glimpse into the strong connection between beginning and form in the political imaginary of the fourteenth century, but even more striking is the way Favent goes on to demonstrate the continuing political and symbolic consequences of the very lesson he has just adduced. Rather than argue that Richard's reign is condemned to failure for the same reasons, he simply casts the renewal of oaths as a new, and more legitimate, beginning. The difficulties of Richard's reign stem from a beginning that is bad because the formal dimension of the oaths could not properly be upheld, since Richard was in his "minor estate" when he took them. Their invalidity, in other words, amounts to no beginning at all, an unbegun beginning, that makes a beginning that will be marked by, and that will mark, the forms of legitimate collaboration between a king and his subjects. It is clear, given such events as these, that the relation between beginning and form is hardly a disinterested one, precisely because of the urgency with which political and social actions took it up.

The eight months between the two 1388 parliaments may be the epicenter of a massive crisis of registration in the English social imaginary, glimpsed in such poems as *St. Erkenwald,* whose own moments of *peripateia* turn on the intervention of documents of widely varying legibility and authority, especially the illegible words found from the remote pagan past, demanding a response that can only be a response to their manifest form. As I will be showing throughout this book, we need to be aware of the cognitive horizons of such poems, the limits of their intelligibility, if we are to think more thoroughly through the manifestation of the particularly ideological form that beginning takes in medieval England. That is, the elusive form of beginning represents failures and contradictions in political and social projects as well, and the narration of attempts to invent beginnings traces the double movement of ideology to articulate precisely that which needs to be covered up. The problem of beginning is the problem of repression itself, a scene whose place is not registered in political or personal memory, but which still constitutes a founding moment. It is the point to which the work of symbolization returns but never fully represents. A beginning, in other words, never really recuperates its own arbitrariness. That is to say, beginning is perhaps the clearest form of what Slavoj Žižek calls the "pre-ideological 'kernel' of ideology," the real that "returns in the guise of spectral apparitions."[32] That is why beginnings can also be immanent, representing the potential for forms of all kinds—political, literary, narrative—to be unmade by being rebegun. And so rather than shore up the formalist limits of the text, meditating on the form of beginning declares its heterogeneity, its recursive dependence on unresolved forms of political contestation and representation. The poem is concerned not with the immanence of a form, but with the very form of immanence in a world where a beginning has not only been made but where we discover we *are* that beginning.[33] As Augustine said, "initium . . . ut esset, creatus est homo."[34] We must make beginnings because we are made as creatures of beginning ourselves, whose being and action are intimately bound up in it. We only belatedly make sense of our beginning, trying to imagine and then act on an end that may or may not be implicit in it.

The forms that beginning takes are a register of an abiding and deep interest in temporality in the fourteenth century, what Krzysztof Pomian calls "the most important age in the entire history of time,"[35] an interest in the resources that could be used to gauge the extent of actions and obligations, whether that included the increasing presence of mechanical clocks, their regulation by a central time, the first idea of the cosmos as a clock, times of the year when service was due to landlords, the movements of planets or of one color to another, the time since Troy had fallen, the historical genesis of "gentilesse."[36] As such, this concern with the forms of beginning is anything but an empty formalism disengaged from history and change. Forms of beginning are really meditations on temporality, meditations that are also rooted *in time,* in the pressing circumstances of times that make such meditations and their formal images necessary. For any meaningful work, in both senses of the word, in the fourteenth century must also imagine the form in which its injunctions can be achieved practically.[37] That is exactly why Dowel in *Piers Plowman* cannot take a precise form *within the poem,* for its only true form is as action. The sense in which the end of a text is only a beginning as long as it lacks its form in action is rivetingly clear in Julian of Norwich's *Shewings,* where she writes, or has written, at its end that her "booke is begunne be Gods gift and grace, but it is not yet performid"—that last word one whose double sense, of doing and of completing, perfectly conveys the intrinsic relation of action to form.[38]

But if all this is true, why have we now forgotten beginnings and their forms? To ask a more specific question, why has almost nobody thought about the importance of beginnings in a poem like *Piers Plowman* before? Because it is a basic claim about the way the poem functions, and a claim that entails a new way of reading the poem, it may be useful to try to explain why the poem has not been read this way before.

The poem has usually been read in terms of its endings, at least since Morton Bloomfield, whose immensely influential book *Piers Plowman as a Fourteenth-Century Apocalypse* has imbued many studies of the poem with an intractable sense of its endings. Bloomfield, indeed, argues that ending is the poem's crucial feature, that "the apocalyptic is the central concern of the poet and that only from this point of view can his main purposes and aims be understood."[39] Close readings of sections of the poem have ratified Bloomfield's conclusions. In reading the poem's ending, for example, Robert Adams situates the apocalyptic strains of the poem in a larger cultural preoccupation with endings: Langland "is not only aware, as were all medievals, of living in the world's last age; he is convinced that that last age itself is about to end, that its last period, the infamous tribulation, is beginning."[40]

Even where beginnings have been invoked in conjunction with *Piers Plowman* they have served merely as markers for its discourses on ending. Beginnings do involve endings, but not always as the initial terminus of an inevitable conclusion. At least one previous reader of the poem, and one of its most acute, has seen that beginnings must be part of any discussion of the poem's endings, and that beginning, in fact, is, from the middle of the poem on, one of its greatest enigmas. In arguing that the poem's disruptions mark its moments of greatest self-interrogation and that disruption itself is a crucial aspect of the poem's *modus procedendi,* Anne Middleton suggests that its recurrent endings disclose an original rupture, a beginning that has reached its terminus. After the Pardon scene, she argues, Piers becomes an "absent object of desire. Never again in the poem will the hope for a principle of love and truth incarnate and visible . . . be free from a kind of nostalgia, a lament for the lost order of time."[41] In the absence of a beginning, the lack of truly generative principles, we find what defines the mode of the poem as elegiac and nostalgic. If beginnings do play any part in *Piers Plowman,* they would seem to do it as harbingers of failure and cessation. Yet its disruptions pose the even greater problem of how to get over them, of the kind of work that will be necessary to work through, beyond, them.

In one sense, and a sense of which fourteenth-century scholastics were well aware, everything that has been written about *Piers Plowman*'s endings, or its apocalypticism, also has had something to do with beginning. Especially when endings are abrupt or unexpected, beginnings become entangled in unnatural endings, endings that provoke regret, nostalgia, and resistance. Defining beginnings can induce a keen awareness of what has ended, an awareness of belatedness and insufficiency. As Milton's Adam recognized, that awareness is the condition of historical time itself, unresolved by any project of recuperation: "For man to tell how human life began / Is hard; for who himself beginning knew?"[42] The inceptive project is both rigorous and durable, and its double operation plagues and characterizes efforts to construct human knowledge. As he was finishing the writing of *From the History of an Infantile Neurosis,* Freud noticed the same phenomenon. Patients, he says, often construct their clearest awareness of the inception of their neuroses, the *Urszene* or primal scene, when their analysis nears its conclusion.[43] It is the agency of primal repression, the traces of "archaic experiences,"[44] that links endings with beginnings. Middleton posits a similar psychic link between beginning and ending, tracing a "combative animus" that informs the poem:

> Its assertion disrupts expository discourse, propelling the episode to its terminus as an action and engendering a new occasion and ground for dialogue. This explosive disruptive power acquires in this way a crucial generative function: it supplies the "horizontal" motivating force of the poem as narrative, an impetus which counters the stasis of the purely expository. But it does not carry allegorical meaning of its own.
>
> This energy does not cease to be disruptive.[45]

Each of the poem's disruptions enables other beginnings, other attempts at reconstituting the lack that is dispersed throughout the poem. The termination of one dream allows another one to begin.

The link between ending and beginning is not merely an epiphenomenon of the apprehensive mind, not merely the result of trying to discern patterns when we suspect one is not really there. We can imagine that the link is more rigorous, something like a logical sequence or a formal principle. Yet doing even that is to treat the epiphenomena of beginning, or to treat beginning as an epiphenomenon itself, which I suppose it is. When we confront a work made up of beginnings, then, we will need to read its forms a bit differently, if not innovatively. As I will argue in this book, the inception of new episodes *does* "carry allegorical meaning of its own"; the crucial importance of beginnings to the formal structure, theology, and political phantasmatics of the poem suggests the powerful presence of what might be called, rather, an *inceptive* animus, the epiphenomenon of beginning—the anxiety of beginning that is manifest indirectly as indirection itself, as the reluctance to make closure, or as the irrepressible remnant of what comes before the beginning, which is made to end. The B and C Texts of *Piers Plowman* only end, after all, with a beginning: the start of the search for Grace. And beginnings always seem to be contaminated with a kind of violence, if not expressing themselves *as* violent intervention.

Freud, of course, was not the first to imagine that beginning and ending were linked, whether benignly or malignantly. An important project of fourteenth-century thought—particularly among academics with connections to Oxford, especially Merton College, including William of Ockham, Thomas Bradwardine, Walter Burley, and William Heytesbury—attempts to determine the limits of beginning and ending.[46] The ubiquity and authority of these treatises in fourteenth-century England, indeed, demonstrate that beginning is an important subject of intellectual discourse in Langland's time. Fourteenth-century English writers are not exclusively obsessed with apocalyptic endings. They think a great deal about beginnings, too, as the wide range of inceptive discourses from which I draw my arguments in this study will demonstrate.

Treatises on the limits of beginning and ending explain why a poem like *Piers Plowman,* which crucially concerns beginnings, has also been described in terms of endings. These treatises mostly concern the verb *incipit,* which is classified as a "syncategorematic" term because it belongs to a class of words that carry with them their own implicit negation. They draw on the terminist logic that dominated Oxford in the thirteenth century, a science that explored the logical problems underlying discussions of beginning. Recognizing that beginnings have limits, terminist logicians attempted to resolve the even more difficult problem of how to determine what those limits were, an enterprise that forced them to ask larger questions about anteriority, about what, if anything, comes before a beginning. The logician William of Sherwood imagines it as a negation, but in terms that show how unavoidably we associate priority with reality: "What begins to be ceases not to be. . . . What begins to be takes being into itself, and what takes being into itself casts out not-being, and what casts out not-being ceases not to be; therefore . . . what begins to be ceases not to be."[47] Although a logical absurdity, his description of beginning attributes a kind of being to nonbeing, even if only in the form of negative predication. It is an alternative to being, rather than its inconceivable annulment. Nonbeing is simply an ending, the cessation of a (non)event that makes beginning possible. Beginnings, in other words, must entail endings. One is merely the negative image of the other. The great grammarian Petrus Hispanus, too, recognizes that the relation between beginning and ending is, on some level, reciprocal: "'[B]egins' signifies the inception which is the beginning of the being or non-being of a thing. . . . 'Ends' signifies the cessation which is the term of the being or non-being of a thing. And they logically follow each other reciprocally, for what begins to be, ceases to not be; and what ceases to be, begins to not be."[48] But like all negative images, beginnings that are described in terms of ending, or endings that are described in terms of beginning, are not clear enough to be useful. As discussions of the poem in terms of endings demonstrate, beginnings emerge only as their murky negative, as an apparently less interesting alternative to the discourse of apocalypse, collapse, and termination that has fascinated so many of the poem's readers.

Syncategorematic treatises on *incipit* disclose an underlying principle of beginning and ending that accounts, perhaps, for this aspect of the poem's reception history. Walter Burley describes the "rule" by which a description of beginnings excludes a description of endings, and vice versa: "dare primum instans esse rei, in eisdem non est dare ultimum instans non esse rei . . . dare ultimum instans in quo res habet esse, in eisdem non est dare primum instans in quo res habet non esse" (to assign the first instant of the being of a thing . . . is not the same as to assign the last instant of a thing's being. . . . to assign the last instant in which a thing has being is not the same as to assign the first instant in which a thing ceases to be).[49] Petrus Hispanus's influential assertion that "given any kind of object the assigning of a first instant of its non-being excludes the assigning of a last instant of its non-being," which he had intended merely as an observation about the formal operation of logical categories, becomes in the fourteenth century a description of what physically occurs when a beginning is imposed, an early version of the Heisenberg indeterminacy principle that argues for the nonconvertibility of beginning and ending.[50] Other medieval logicians and physicists argue that it is uniquely beginning that must be imagined in this way, as an event whose complete ramifications are unknowable because its very procedure is one of annulment.

Some syncategorematic treatises on *incipit* explore just this radically disjunctive function of beginning. A standard definition argues that beginning excludes anteriority altogether: "the verb 'begins' eliminates *(privat)* the past."[51] As I shall argue in the next chapter, the inception of each dream in *Piers Plowman* emulates precisely this aspect of beginning: each dream is a rebeginning, a privation of the dream just past. More generally, we will see that beginnings are a privation of the past in a larger sense: as the annulment of history, of what must become the outside, the exterior, of an event to make the event unique—which is to say, intelligible, initiating, and historical.

Perhaps it is appropriate that a poem structured around the figure of the plowman should have a series of such obliterating beginnings. Ever since Cain killed Abel, plowmen have been associated with violence and rupture. But the violence that Cain inflicted on Abel is also linked to his foundation of the earthly city. His fratricide and his act of foundation are together considered the beginning of human evil:

> Generationem Cain, qui erat semen serpentis, velocius pullulasse, civitates et regna constituisse. Item, Cain reproborum, Abel autem electorum generationis principium fuisse.[52]
>
> [The kin of Cain, who was the serpent's seed, rapidly flourished, founding cities and kingdoms. For this reason Cain was the beginning of the unclean, Abel of the chosen.]

The plow links primal violence and foundation in a kind of double inscription. Beginnings and foundations appear only because what preceded them has been destroyed, or has become a tabula rasa. The double operation of plowing is both a metonymy of the beginning of civilization and, in Cain, as Michel Serres points out, the historical origin of civilization: "It wasn't a question of fertilizing and fecundating the earth through labor but rather of extirpating, suppressing, and banishing. Of destroying. The blade of the plough is a sacrificial blade, killing all the plants to make a clean space. . . . The ploughshare founded the city, and in the hollow of a furrow, a brother killed his twin."[53] Plowing does not always turn up the violent traces of its own history. It often is treated, however, as an important beginning that in some sense obliterates the past. Derrida, following Rousseau, finds that plowing inaugurates both civilization and its distinguishing mark, writing: "The furrow of agriculture . . . opens nature to culture (cultivation). And one knows that writing is born with agriculture."[54] Plowing, then, suggests both erasure and inscription, both beginning and rebeginning, a turning over of the earth to prepare it for new seasons and new cultivation.[55] It traces the beginning of civilization, of writing, of a new year—but it also works by obliterating previous traces. It is a powerful inaugural act, but powerful only because it also destroys.

The *modus procedendi* of plowing—a rebeginning that obliterates—also describes the way that *Piers Plowman* operates as a poem. The radical disjunction that characterizes beginnings in *Piers Plowman* is as unusual—if not as unprecedented—as the multiple inceptions of the poem's structure. As I have argued, the significance of these beginnings has been bafflingly overlooked. Indeed, the most recent theoretical work on beginnings, A. D. Nuttall's sweeping and magisterial *Openings,* uses *Piers Plowman*'s beginning to illustrate its compliance with the "natural" demands of the opening of a *visio*.[56] As I will show, however, even the poem's first beginning disrupts the generic conventions that govern most dream visions.

The poem opposes conventional medieval theories of beginning in several ways. The powerful beginnings that constitute the poem are, in several senses, original, lacking theoretical and narrative precedents. Nuttall's work on openings, however, might initially suggest useful ways of accounting for the phenomenon of *Piers Plowman*'s beginnings. Recognizing the homology between the classical distinction of "natural" and "artificial" openings and the beginnings of purely natural events, he explores the "tensions which exist between the formal freedom to begin a work of fiction wherever one likes and an opposite sense that all good openings are somehow naturally rooted, are echoes, more or less remote, of an original creative act."[57] With its multiple inceptions that each promises a stronger opening than the last, that each echoes the poem's original opening yet asserts its formal independence, *Piers Plowman* embodies more thoroughly than any of the works that Nuttall discusses the tensions between the kinds of beginning that he calls formal and natural.

The poem's ability to impose new beginnings suggests that such distinctions are heuristic, that the formality of an artificial opening necessarily simulates the validity and force of natural beginnings. As Nuttall says in connection with the surprisingly compromised beginning recounted in *Genesis,* "[A]n exclusively formalist account—an account which admits no concept of beginning other than that created by a fictive reading-*in*—will never be adequate for these canonical openings, for all their manifestly literary character."[58] Indeed, a powerful force in acts of beginning insists on reading them as form, attempting to make us complicit in obliterating the things that precede the beginning, the grounds of its possibility, in order to represent it as much as possible as a true beginning.

Imagining powerful natural beginnings tempts us into thinking that nothing precedes them. Despite his caveat, Nuttall ultimately reads beginning as a prescriptive form, attempting to obliterate the disjunctive features of beginnings altogether, arguing that their echo of the origin is more than accidental and provisional: "[E]very genesis involves a transformation, but there are real beginnings because in this way things which did not exist before came into being."[59] As I have already argued, however, the transformations that every genesis involves also produce a corollary anteriority, the necessary past that precedes every beginning. As the treatises on incipit demonstrate, an inception simultaneously designates the traces of an ending, shaping the form of history even while it claims to be eliminating the past.

On the level of narrative, the designation of the past as the deprivation of beginning and of beginning as the point of history's disappearance takes the shape of a formal principle. The compendious beginnings of *Piers Plowman* do not completely subvert the narrative expectations that the sections preceding them engender. Despite their apparently radical beginnings, they only incompletely expunge the past, the history of the dreams that precede them. The series of dreams, as every reader of the poem knows, constitutes an elusive but manifest continuity. The openings of several of the dreams in *Piers Plowman* chronicle the poem's attempts to achieve formal perfection in opening, yet elucidate simultaneously an archaeology of their belatedness and a semiosis of their power to effect a beginning, constituting a powerful critique of Nuttall's separation of formal and natural beginnings. They are strong and distinct echoes of "an original creative act," yet their location in medias res calls attention to their artificiality; indeed, their own success as beginnings compromises the durability of the poem's original creative act, its author's opening gestures at the inception of the poem itself.

The poem's critique of the imposition of a natural beginning on material that is invented and contrived by human agency is not one that must be inferred only from its structure. In the C Text, Imaginatyf responds to the dreamer's questions about the natural impulses that govern the universe by explicitly conflating the natural and the artificial: "Was neuere creature vnder Crist þat knewe wel þe bygynnyng / Bote Kynde þat contreuede hit furst" (C 14.159–60). An anticipation of Adam's explication in *Paradise Lost* of the epistemological difficulties that are involved in thinking about beginning, this passage also contests the effectiveness of artificial beginnings altogether. They are indistinguishable from natural beginnings: in the poem's imaginative regimen, Kynde—nature itself—is the only agency that can "contreue" a beginning.

Imaginatyf's insistence that an unmediated beginning is unknowable leads us to wonder what kinds of beginning *are* knowable, and what the differences among them are. The collapse of contrived and intrinsic beginnings into each other in Imaginatyf's figuration suggests the extravagant kind of beginning we usually refer to as an origin, a beginning that precedes human thought but that becomes one of its primary occupations. Foucault examines precisely this epistemological dilemma in *The Order of Things,* describing an indeterminacy in origins themselves that recalls the indeterminate aspects of beginning in the treatises on incipit. The attempt to delineate an origin, Foucault suggests, only discloses "man's radical finitude, the dispersion that at the same time separates him from his origin and promises it to him, and the insuperable distance of time."[60] Origins construct a greater awareness of belatedness and of the anteriority of events that necessarily precede human knowledge. Attempting to recover them precipitates a double temporal action: while our knowledge of them begins to bridge the gap between the present and the past, the origin recedes still further. Yet the apparent immanence of the origin encourages recuperative projects that promise to bring knowledge closer to its own inception, to its grounds of self-knowledge. Writing against what he calls the "ideal geneses" of eighteenth-century theories of representation,[61] Foucault argues that the recovery of the origin is driven by a reciprocating urgency and futility:

> [Man] is never contemporaneous with that origin which is outlined through the time of things even as it eludes the gaze; when he tries to define himself as a living being, he can uncover his own beginning only against the background of a life which itself began long before him.... when he attempts to define his essence as a speaking subject... all he ever finds is the previously unfolded possibility of language, and not the stumbling sound, the first word upon the basis of which all languages and even language itself became possible.[62]

For Foucault, the origin becomes a heuristic device, a mode or, in Deleuze's term, a "fold" that enables epistemological activity, the fantasized barrier that justifies the belief that is knowledge. It stands apart from what Foucault distinguishes as the "beginning," the terminus a quo of a temporal event. As I will suggest, this distinction provides a useful way of characterizing the inceptions of *Piers Plowman,* those beginnings that tantalizingly remind us that the poem is still beginning, that the poem's time is marked with each beginning, and that time itself is empty, filled and made by what happens at its beginning and end. The time that Langland has spent writing the first two versions (and perhaps all three) is marked as useless expenditure in C passus 5, but an expenditure nonetheless—"y haue ytynt tyme and tyme myspened" (93)—even while he is simultaneously ending the poem and dreaming about beginning it again.[63] In this inability to forget the immanence of a beginning even while the ostensible topic is conclusion we are faced with a poem that both signifies an origin external to it, and hopelessly absent from it, and *makes* an origin as it proceeds. This strange double movement may be a characteristic of all narrative, although to argue that would demand a far more ambitious beginning than this book already has. Let us, therefore, think just about whether this happens with language.

If the origin for Foucault can *only* be narrativized, then it is clear that he must think of it as it emerges along with the historical topic of linguistic study. And, indeed, Foucault's discussion of origins begins with his account of eighteenth-century grammars, which posit the origin of language as "the transparency between the representation of a thing and the representation of the cry, sound, or gesture... that accompanied it."[64] In his study of the ideologies of medieval grammar, in which the "primacy of origins is an important, indeed, the defining characteristic," Howard Bloch finds that the same transparency characterizes medieval accounts of grammatical origin.[65] The function of grammar is to reaffirm the linearity and rectitude of a signifying system; its legitimacy derives from its direct, although perhaps attenuated, denotation of an origin:

> To signify properly is, within the recuperative, semantically oriented grammar of the period between Donatus and Abelard, to recapture the essence of things before the Fall. The science of straight connections enables those who practice it to undo the dislocations—obliquities, circumlocutions, distortions—of sense that characterize the history of human speech, and hence to restore to each altered articulation its proper or original meaning.[66]

Piers Plowman, as I shall argue later, is pivotally concerned with the authority that is conferred by origins, the same kind of authority that underwrites etymological dictionaries such as Isidore of Seville's. Yet the poem's imposition of grammatical and genealogical metaphors often achieves a merely heterogeneous dispersal of meaning, nothing like the recuperated integrity of sign and thing that exists at the origin. Anima's parody of precisely that assumption, for example, is partly informed by a recognition that object and sign are split from each other. Anima upbraids Will for assuming that the names of bishops signify their substance directly and for wanting to know the "cause of alle hire names" (B 15.45), the material principle that informs linguistic reality. The poem's only explicit etymology, which comes later in Anima's speech, recapitulates an origin that makes manifest the effects of the Fall and the deficiencies of supposedly natural beginnings:

> [And] so it fareþ by a barn þat born is of wombe;
> Til it be cristned in cristes name and confermed of þe bisshop
> It is heþene as to heueneward and helplees to þe soule.
> Heþen is to mene after heeþ and vntiled erþe,
> As in wildernesse wexeþ wilde beestes.
>
> (B 15.456–60)

This passage confronts us with the abominable clarity of the origin, a moment of self-identity, a moment before difference—which is to say time—exists. That is, the being of things can be understood by the signs naturally conjoined with them, even understood as *being* those signs. The absence of modern quotation marks in medieval manuscripts helps contribute to the illusion. We cannot tell, for instance, whether "heþen" in this passage is the thing or the sign, nor, more generally, how to read decisively the passage's etymologies. They are all "true," intuitively and linguistically sound, but here a "true" etymology signifies (because it unfolds in a world that is now fallen) an origin that is ambivalent, even less than original. What is invoked here is the figure of a savage world that is originally fallen, a world that is incessantly fecund yet unregenerate and unregenerative, capable of "wexing," but only wildly, irrationally. The origin unexpressed here is the truly transformative one, the inception of salvation. Yet this fundamentally more important origin is also configured by language and, as a consequence, configured as belated and artificial. Christening marks this origin by delimiting the time of "hethenesse" ("so it fareþ," "Til"), a metaphorical cultivation of the wild places of this unregenerate origin. It might not be surprising that Langland here stresses the outward signs of the act of christening and their ritual and documentary legitimation ("name," "confermed of þe bisshop"), but it is hard to overlook the figure of plowing that runs through this passage in a poem that weighs plowing with such extraordinary originary force, extirpating as the poem is written the "vntiled erþe" of the heathen, beginning and cultivating a life that will have much more to do with writing and beginning.

Before we examine the forms that this cultivation will take, we need to resolve the problem of infinite regression that is suggested by the appearance of a beginner so late in the poem (in passus 15), whose tilling is what makes the poem necessary, and even what makes the poem itself. This problem is really just an example of one that interested a number of medieval physicists and logicians, who discussed it most directly in treatises about the logical quandaries of beginning. In asking whether motion can have a beginning, they realize that beginning itself is a paradoxical notion. The very impossibility of what Petrus Hispanus describes as the "infinitation of motion" suggests that beginning may not be a temporal or physical event:

> If someone is moving, he will be moving and was moving. Now if he was moving . . . it will be true in that instant in the past as well to say "He is moving." Therefore he was moving earlier at some other past instant. . . . Thus one can go on *ad infinitum* backwards and forwards, or in the past or in the future. Now it is impossible to go on *ad infinitum,* because infinite things cannot be transgressed. Therefore it is impossible that motion begins.[67]

Although he goes on to argue that motion is finite because all "sublunary motion begins and ceases," he continues to maintain that motion is infinitely divisible, and that nature itself is characterized by infinite regress and the lack of an origin. The generation of men, plants, and animals poses the same problem. One cannot posit a first man, he says, because that man would himself owe his existence to another man, and so on, in the same infinite regression that characterizes motion. For Petrus Hispanus, the only solution to this regression is to posit a beginning outside of the series, a beginning that differs from inception, a "principium quod est supra naturam ut Causa Prima, ex sua summa potentia potuit facere quidlibet ex nichilo, quod natura non potuit" (a beginning that is higher than nature, the First Cause, [which] can fashion whatever it wishes out of nothing from its supreme power, which nature cannot do).[68] This solution answers the ontological problem of motion's impossibility and of the impossibility of beginning. But it does not answer, perhaps, the ethical or phenomenological question of what we are to do ourselves with beginning, as creatures who are enjoined, and able, to make beginnings. For Derrida this question is not only related to writing, it is inseparable from it. There is something implicit in writing, he argues, that causes us to ask continually what it is, a question that really "means 'where and when does writing begin?'" While he argues in his magisterial work *Of Grammatology* that to ask this very question inscribes a metaphysics of presence that already assigns to writing an originary place, Derrida nevertheless asks it several times himself[69]—for if it is writing that adequates (as a medieval scholastic might say) a beginning, then the question is unavoidable.

Derrida's early work on Edmund Husserl's *Origin of Geometry,* indeed, is fascinated by this very question. Husserl had observed that writing makes historicity and historical becoming possible because it allows knowledge to be transmitted in a way that no longer depends upon participation in an event. It unmoors events from their immediate temporal contexts, making it, as he says, the "condition of the possibility of ideal objects."[70] It is Rousseau's, Lévi-Strauss's, and Saussure's denial of the necessity of writing in thinking at all, Derrida argues, that makes their exclusion of it deeply ironic. All three of them place their projects at critical moments at an origin of language and then explicitly write out, so to speak, the emergence of writing at the same time or even before it, the writing that makes language possible. Rousseau, for instance, argues that speech emerges as the degeneration of the world's natural music, in which melody is replaced by harmony and the "calculus of intervals was substituted for nicety of inflection."[71] The effectiveness of this calculation, a calculation that is the origin of speech, is determined by its ability to obliterate what it replaces, by its ability to forget its beginning. Since speech is the "first social institution," as Rousseau says (230), its beginning is natural. Even then, we could argue that this beginning is difficult but not impossible to articulate, except that Rousseau's argument hangs on the assumption that music has its genesis in speech, not simply in sound (195 ff.). Song, too, he argues, is a feature of intervals (that is, of harmony), a beginning he forgets in his apparent desire, as Derrida says, "to pretend that the 'fineness of inf[l]ections' and of the 'oral accent' did not already and always lend itself to spatialization, geometricization, grammaticalization, regularization" (201). Nevertheless, Rousseau's *Essay on the Origin of Languages* defines this original space clearly, a space in which we discover the act of calculation even (and especially, Derrida would say) at the beginning, describing precisely what Rousseau "*does not wish to say;* articulation and therefore the space of writing operates at the origin of language" (229). This is the operation that Derrida calls arché-writing, an originating movement of organization and determination that makes the beginning the effect of that writing, or that, to put it more clearly, makes the beginning writing.

In treatises on *incipit,* indeed, the real problem is actually the nature of the *word* "incipit" itself. Thomas Bradwardine, who had a knack for writing treatises on some of the most important fourteenth-century topics (free will and divine foreknowledge, the art of memory), begins his treatise on incipit by saying that its purpose is to clarify the significance of the *dictio* or *verbum* itself.[72] Even while these treatises try to analyze beginnings using the techniques of the new physics of motion, they begin and end with the nature of beginning as verbal. Bradwardine's analysis of the word "incipit," for instance, sounds something like arché-writing. Since motion is a number of successive intervals, he says, it is impossible to say that motion begins, since it cannot have a first instant without those successive intervals already in place.[73] And so the analysis of beginning returns to the problematic nature of the word itself, existing, and signifying, an impossible beginning, but a beginning that we know perfectly well must occur. The whole problem turns on the question of whether we can begin without the word. Coming to the problem through this route rather than through Rousseau's route of emergent nationalisms, Petrus Hispanus more clearly points out the impasse at the heart of Rousseau's meditation on the origin of languages: an origin cannot be part of the series, since it is subject to the same infinitation. This infinitation is articulated in Rousseau as the collapse of nature into society, their coterminous origination, and the denial of writing's own infinitation. By allowing an activity prior to nature, Petrus shows us two things: that this language is there with the First Cause, and that the only beginning that authorizes, so to speak, is one that is unmotivated, free, and voluntary.

In yet another way, this is a description of arché-writing. Without recourse to the First Cause outside the series, this wreck of sense at the beginning of anything human can only be understood as a repetition of something that is already there. Much of Freud's work, indeed, examines the close relation between repetition and the desire to return to an origin, a primordial state, or even the natural state of quiescence "inherent in organic life,"[74] a movement that is both telos and origin. Inherently conservative, this impulse is, says Freud, like the pleasure principle, which seeks to avoid unpleasant states of excitation, whether they are "Lust" or "Unlust." Yet this impulse is, Freud comes to realize, more basic than the pleasure principle. The act of repeating scenes, which he had earlier thought was a form of repression, he now regards, in *Beyond the Pleasure Principle,* as a basic need: "[T]here really does exist in the mind a compulsion to repeat which overrides the pleasure principle."[75] It is this compulsion to repeat that emerges as the death instinct, the *Trieb* that cannot be recalled yet must be remembered, a repetition that is never fully the same. It is in the nature of repetition, as Deleuze argues in his first major work, to unfold "within the conditions which make possible an idea of repetition" *and* beyond them in the concept of difference (since something cannot be said to "repeat" if it is precisely the *same* event or thing).[76] The conceptual acts behind repetition, he argues, are so complex that repetition can only find its origin in the unconscious, which, by definition, can have no awareness of the present that is being staged in the form of representations to the conscious mind, but "carries out the passive [synthesis] of an original time."[77] That is, while it knows nothing about time (to paraphrase Freud), the unconscious helps us to construct a notion of time by containing the notion of a "before" that we know nothing about, a before that we tend to identify as a temporal origin, the inception, as a back-formation, of what we recognize as a temporal series. Yet precisely because "originary time" is located in the unconscious this way, it does anything but merely disappear.

This is a third sense in which arché-writing appears at the beginning of things. It is, as Derrida says, the "structure of an originary repetition," an origin that comes about only because a second event resembles a first, which only then *becomes* the first. We could invert this and say that writing is the originary structure of repetition, because it produces the incipit that "remains external to something which is repeated and must be supposed primary."[78] As Allen Frantzen elegantly puts it in his important study of the work performed by origins—in Foucault's and Said's sense of the term—in modern Anglo-Saxon scholarship, "The structures built around the origin are built around nothing more than the idea of origin that they have themselves created."[79] Heidegger analyzes repetition as necessary to the very function of beginning, or, rather, the structure of beginning: "Since it is a beginning, the beginning must in a sense leave itself behind." The only way a beginning can be preserved, or the only way that it is prevented from concealing itself entirely once it has appeared—the only way we can know anything about it—is by repeating, by drawing again from its own source. More to the point, we can only know about a beginning by repeating it ourselves: "it is only by repetitive thinking *[denkende Wiederholung]* that we can deal appropriately with the beginning."[80] This arché-writing, this beginning, is only possible, in other words, as both an act of origination and repetition, as simultaneously an act of invention and of memory.

Heidegger's important readings of Heraclitus call attention to what, after the fact, we conceive of as the antithetical impulses behind the genesis of the *logos,* the origination that is also a memory, the *arché* that is also an archive. In Heraclitus, *logos* corresponds to the German word *Sammlung,* a collection, a gathering, what Heidegger calls the "primal gathering principle."[81] The *logos* signifies, or *is,* the beginning of things, gathering *(legein)* things while it necessarily and concomitantly neglects others in an action that is simultaneously display, a seizing, inception *(Anfang),* and concealment: the *logos* is "die ursprüngliche, Ursprung verleihende, im Ursprung einbehaltende Versammlung als das Wesen des Seins selbst" (the original, imparting origin, withholding the gathering in the origin as the nature of Being itself).[82] What is important for Heidegger in beginning is this antithetical movement in the *logos,* selecting while it is neglecting, revealing while it is veiling something else—whatever is not collected in the gathering that is the word. This difficulty lies at the heart of his phenomenology of disclosure *(erschliessen, aletheia),* since the gathering that *is* disclosure is necessarily also a concealment *(verschliessen, lëthë).* At the beginning, there is always something that is left out, forgotten—in fact, it is the beginning that causes the concealment or forgetting. This is why memory remains a crucial part of beginning. Memory is, in a sense, produced, led forth, in the act of beginning, because something is forgotten initially. In Freudian terms, this is why repetition *(Weiderholung)* is necessary: because an act that cannot or will not be fully remembered remains incomplete, and its beginning must continue to be repeated. Heidegger, as we have seen, has his own reasons for arguing that a beginning must be repeated in order to function as a beginning. But an even deeper sense that beginnings remain implicit in all actions pervades his work—not simply because a beginning involves obscurity and forgetting, but because beginning in its antithetical complexity is, in a sense, the object of thought itself. As Reiner Schürmann says, commenting on *Being and Time,* an initial *failure* to understand is the very thing that makes philosophical thinking "authentic," a beginning that continues to characterize "the always inceptive experience that is thinking."[83] Thinking, as much as writing, is an act of beginning: "[I]nitially being makes itself known as *logos* and thereby discloses itself as what is to be thought *originarily.*"[84] That is, thinking and writing do not only have an origin, they are an origin, a beginning, that they continue to make: "Thinking and writing *[Dichten]* are . . . originally *and* 'beginningly' the same."[85] These respective enterprises, although vastly different, are the same insofar as they are works of beginning, incipient projects that remain inceptive.[86] Saint Bonaventure imagines the beginning *(principium)* more broadly, but also as immanent and persistent: because of its imperfection, he says, the individual "constantly needs its *principium,* and the first *principium,* because of its clemency, ceaselessly pours itself out into the creature."[87] What kind of writing, informed by what principles, could be true to this kind of constant beginning except one that reminds us of its principles, repeating its beginning ceaselessly? The inextricability of thinking and writing, especially of poetry *(Dichten)* is especially, doubly, true for *Piers Plowman,* a poem that traces throughout its complex and repetitive genesis in three major versions the actions of beginning to think, thinking in order to begin, beginning in order to write, and writing in order to begin. The obsessiveness of this endeavor, even if we knew nothing about its compositional gestation and revisions, would be signaled by its chronic intrigue with dreams, particularly the strangely repetitive, recurrent structure that they take in the poem. If, as Derrida concludes in *Of Grammatology,* the "scene of the dream is the scene of writing,"[88] then the dream, haunted by and directed toward the *eschaton* (especially in the Middle Ages) is also where the *arché* appears in all its contradictions, and where, especially in *Piers Plowman,* writing begins.

The form of the dream itself is the means by which *Piers* imagines the potential of pure beginnings, enacting them as the poem unfolds. Its reiterated dreams literally make possible new beginnings. But they also suggest, unfolding as they do in a poem vexed by the status of origins, the metaphysical nostalgia voiced by dreams. Most medieval theories of the "true" dream (as opposed to the "false," physiologically or demonically induced dream) argue that its content teaches the dreamer about a future event. Both Steven Kruger and A. C. Spearing have shown compellingly how the ambiguous nature of dreams—they can be simultaneously true and false, objective and subjective—is a powerful analogue for the work that fiction performs in the Middle Ages. But dreams derive some of their power also from their resonance with origins. As Kruger points out, the very presence of true dreams recalled, in Platonic dream theory, the celestial origin of the soul: "Dreams, arising in the activity of the soul, partake fully of the range of qualities of the soul (and the universe). Dream, soul, and universe are all, in some sense, coextensive."[89] Chaucer's translation of *The Consolation of Philosophy* nicely shows the ambiguity of origins in dreams: "ye men," Lady Philosophy tells Boethius, "dremen alwey youre bygynnynge, although it be with a thynne ymaginacioun."[90] Dreams are the condition of a humanity that not only longs for its origin but imagines that it can, in the dream itself, create the origin anew. That is, the dream is not just an index of the complexity of fiction, of the ability of humankind to create works reminiscent of the real, but of its ability to create the real itself. If dreams not only remind us of our origins, but in a sense *are* our origins, then they are more real than our waking lives. In one of his earliest works, an introduction to Ludwig Binswanger's *Dream and Existence,* Foucault argues that the dream is just such a point of radical origin: "By breaking with the objectivity which fascinates waking consciousness and by reinstating the human subject in its radical freedom, the dream discloses paradoxically the movement of freedom toward the world, the point of origin from which freedom makes itself world. The cosmogony of the dream is the origination itself of existence."[91] The double nature of *Piers Plowman*'s beginnings suggests a similarly paradoxical movement. As a series of beginnings, they signify the failure of the previous one to make a true beginning. The work must be started over again. But as beginnings, each one signifies the potential of the origin resonating in the form of the dream that begins over and over again. The fictionality of the poem's dreams is not so much the function of their ambiguous veracity but of their ability to signify true making, a *poiesis* that is also an *arché*. The dreams in the poem, in other words, link the potential of origin and of the most potent kind of fiction, the fashioning of the world itself.

But *Piers Plowman* also suggests that a beginning can be created by metaphorically deleting whatever marks it as complex and compromised. A beginning can be made simply because whatever went before it is no longer there. This kind of beginning, in fact, is perhaps the closest to an ideal and orthodox beginning in the poem, since it concerns penitential activity itself. What makes penitence so close to an ideal beginning is precisely the fact that it has nothing to do ultimately with human agency, except that the beginning must be willed. Contrition, as Will himself observes, blots out the sinful past:

> . . . a baptiȝed man may, as maistres telleþ,
> Thoruȝ contricion [clene] come to þe heiȝe heuene—
> *Sola contricio [delet peccatum]*—
> Ac [a] barn wiþouten bapteme may noȝt be saued:
> *Nisi quis renatus fuerit.*
>
> (B 11.80–82a)

Baptism and contrition effect disjunctive beginnings, beginnings that can delete the past. Rebirth can only be described as a new beginning, an inception that cannot be characterized in terms of ending. These radically disjunctive beginnings do not depend on prior events. Each one constructs its own occasion, effacing the deviations and instances of falling away that precede it, imposing an original purity. Anyone who desires it can

> ... be clene þoruȝ þat cristnyng of alle kynnes synne.
> And if vs fille þoruȝ folie to falle in synne after
> Confession and knowlichynge [and] crauynge þi mercy
> Shulde amenden vs as manye siþes as man wolde desire.
> (B 14.185–87)

The desire for origins is here replaced by a reiterative desire, a desire that reconstitutes new beginnings. Patience's description of penance characterizes the penitential life as a series of disjunctive beginnings that has close affinities with constructivist notions of identity as a performative perpetual beginning, "generated," as Kimberly Benston says, "from performance to performance."[92]

The close affinities of penance and reiterative beginnings have produced two of the most convincing accounts to date of *Piers Plowman*'s *modus procedendi*. As Robert Adams has said, the penitential life is characterized as a "continuously renewed pilgrimage."[93] Interrogating the categories of identity—or subjectivity—in *Piers Plowman,* David Lawton describes penance as a "continual and life-long training course," and characterizes Haukyn's "collapse of selfishness into emotion" as "one of the many necessary new beginnings."[94] Although he stresses the reiterativeness of penitential action rather than its disjunctiveness, he argues that penitential discourse in the poem resists the poem's other discursive tendencies "by continuing its process within a repeated pattern of fall and reconstruction along precisely the same lines as before; and it therefore offers a strong challenge to any discourse that would alter the process of its construction."[95] Although this account comes close to being a description of a repetition compulsion, it hints at the powerfully disjunctive tendencies contained in the poem's structure.

In his study of the penitential contexts of the poem, Nick Gray connects the inceptions that penitence and inscription represent in the clearest account yet of the poem's beginnings. The reversals and new starts of the poem echo the extended process of revising the poem itself, an enterprise that itself is characteristic of the *renovatio* that penitence enables: "[T]his pattern . . . echoes the penitential view of man—of man engaged in a lifelong struggle with sin in which there is no final victory, a lifelong cycle of striving to be free from sin, of raising oneself up through penance only to lapse, to lapse again and again."[96] The beginnings that recur in *Piers Plowman* are fundamentally ethical, the mode in which the motion from the beginning of things is conveyed. That trajectory is not always easy to trace, but the poem is enabled by a deep sense that beginning is possible, that inception is situated neither in an absent origin nor in an infinite repetition without difference. Every beginning must be new, or they could not be beginnings, and we would not define our lives by them.

Reading In

The rest of this book will trace an inward movement, starting with its earliest readers' attempts to make sense of the poem's beginnings and ending with the poem's own discussion of what its readers need to do in order to make beginnings themselves. The poem encourages its own readers, in other words, to make their own idiosyncratic beginnings—at least, if its readers pay close attention to the clues the poem leaves to its discussion of beginning. It is not surprising that the poem does not itself describe this program anywhere, since its writer is clearly struggling with the problem himself even as he writes the poem. But the effort to understand the complexity and ubiquity of beginning—at least in this poem—imitates their real complexity.

I am not trying to argue that the poem traces an increasingly elaborate or subtle kind of beginning as it unfolds, as one reads through the poem for the first time, becoming entwined as if by Spenser's Error in an ensnaring interiority. I am suggesting, however, that a poem like this, which is clearly meant to be read multiple times, to be ruminated over, engenders in its reading the slowly unfolding awareness that the poem's writer has about the compelling and complex nature of beginning and its importance. Carruthers identified just this mode of reading not only as one appropriate to the poem, but also as one of its important subjects, a mode meant to be imitated as the poem is more completely understood, and indeed as the poem's protagonist achieves fuller understanding. In the scene where Piers tears Truth's pardon, she argues, "Will has not yet realized that the problem of doing well is related to the problem of interpretation. . . . The problem of *intus legendum,* of inward reading, is as pertinent to works as it is to words, for true works express an inner spiritual meaning just as true words do."[97] This *intus legendum* in a poem so crucially about beginning also consists in discovering the inner beginnings of words and works, the intrinsic points at which true language and proper living can be begun. It is the poem's genius to extend the sense of "work" to include the poem itself, as well as the very labor of reading it.

This program is quite clearly a part of the revisions Langland made to the poem in the twenty to thirty years he probably worked on it, and I will be discussing all three versions of the poem to show how the subject of beginning is elaborated during those several decades. While I am convinced that the final version, which I believe to be the C Text, is the version most clearly concerned with beginnings, I have not discussed only that version because of the conviction, entailed in the other one, that understanding beginnings is a necessarily ruminative process, an *intus legendum* that is a continuous activity, not a decisive, authoritative act. The poem's rebeginnings appear not only in the course of the developing story itself, but also in the poet's attempts to begin the whole thing all over again, to make a fresh start without writing a wholly different poem. Each version of the poem, from the A Text through the B Text and the C Text, in other words, contains beginnings that are not only related to the other beginnings in the same version, but also to the beginnings at the same point in preceding and successive versions of the poem. Within the text of the poem (I mean here the "text" in its most abstract sense, the Platonic hypertext that we begin to know after having read all three versions), the poem's beginnings have both a synchronic and a diachronic relation to each other. I will be discussing, therefore, both the beginnings that appear while one reads a particular version of the poem and the beginnings that the poet's writer makes in the course of producing three distinct versions of a poem that crucially concerns beginning. Because readers are likely to be most familiar with the B Text, however, I will be using it as the primary point of reference, except where beginnings—and references to them—in the A or C Texts differ from those in the B Text.

Both the revisions made to the poem and the shape of the final two versions trace definitions of beginning that are increasingly private, subjective, tropological, spiritual—what I will be referring to as "intrinsic." As Joseph Wittig shows in his important 1972 article demonstrating that the poem takes an "inward turn" from B 9 onward,[98] the concern with interiority is precisely the point of the B Text revisions. John Bowers has shown how the addition of what is commonly called the *Vita* extends the significance of the central figure of Will to include *voluntas,* the will itself, the faculty that permits individual action, as opposed to Will, the character dreaming about how to live in some version of the social world of the fourteenth century. Whether it was in response to the poem's uncomfortable function as a social document after 1381 or whether it was simply part of the poet's unfolding conception for the poem, the final version of the poem mutes its critique of the external world and inscribes a greater degree of subjective interiority even before the inward turn of the *Vita,* most famously in the so-called autobiographical passage in C 5, a passage that Middleton has described as an account of the poem's own genesis.

That passage, as readers of the C version will remember, is famously concerned with the poet's position in the world, situating him neither wholly in London nor in "opelond" (5.49), and wholly occupied neither in prayer nor in productive writing. As I will show in the "Thema" chapter, the new passage in C 5 uses the perplexed relation between writing and living to raise the question of just what kind of beginning it is that the poem's writer can hope to make at this point. What is at stake is the question of the things renounced in making a new beginning—a life of diffuse geographical location in which the writer is engaged in spiritual activity, but (since he is a chantry priest) for the sake of other souls, or a life in which his elaboration of his subjective experience through writing puts him at risk of losing his soul. Neither promises to be a wholly efficacious beginning.

Nevertheless, the passage imagines both alternatives as specifically textual beginnings. Will's own project will succeed, he hopes, because books allow you to make a new beginning by placing a "los at a leef at the last ende" (5.94), turning the page to begin the project anew. Something more than the start of a new passus or a new section is inferred here—the image invokes the book as the figure of *principium,* a beginning that is more than a marker of a stage in a continuum. That image may be something of a textual fantasy, imagining that the book can make beginnings *on its own,* that its beginnings are wholly independent, isolated not only from other texts but from the world itself: the book's beginning marks the "los" of the real, too. But the possibility that a book or a poem can do that is, as we will see, a powerful and compelling fantasy in this particular poem.

The "real" use of textual beginnings in the C 5 passage may seem initially to offer a more straightforward account of the use of writing in the fourteenth century. Will tells us that, as a chantry priest, his "work" is to "labore with" liturgical texts:

> The lomes þat I labore with and lyflode deserue
> Is *pater-noster* and my prymer, *placebo* and *dirige,*
> And my sauter som tyme and my seuene psalmes.
> (50–52)

It is clear that the passage stretches the concept of work beyond its likely meaning. It forges an allegorical practice of labor from texts. More specifically, it forges that practice from the beginnings of texts—from their incipits, most notably the incipit *pater-noster* that, coming a line after the invocation of Will's London situation, unavoidably recalls the production of books, which turns out, after all, to be the real subject of the C addition. The disingenuous—or ingenious—way in which this section imagines allegorical labor forged from the incipits of texts offers us a passing allegory of the work the poem itself is engaged in: the work of making something from the beginnings of texts, a labor, literally, of beginnings. In this section, however, unlike the section at the end of the new C passage, those beginnings are curiously external, located in texts other than the one that is really at stake at this moment and used for the cure of souls other than the writer's.

Here we get a glimpse of one of the curiously troubling aspects of textual beginnings. They also invoke other beginnings, situating a text not as a beginning ex nihilo, but as an artifact that owes its beginnings to other beginnings. Incipits, as this chapter has suggested, begin in the real world. They mark a text's break with the real, but also help—at least in the Middle Ages—to position that text in the world, to allow its public to determine its significance. They also are, in the most artificial sense, the point at which it must begin.

This last point may sound banal, but it is precisely the point of an important distinction made in medieval scholastic prologues. All beginnings, regardless of their manifold forms, could be categorized in the Middle Ages as belonging to one of two kinds—a *principium extrinsecus* or a *principium intrinsecus,* a beginning that starts independently of a thing or that originates from within it.[99] This is a distinction maintained by Derrida in his essay on Husserl's *Origin of Geometry,* where he points to Husserl's distinction between science *as* its "written work," which "represents a set of external arrangements," and Husserl's continuing phenomenological project, which insists on "writing as the *intrinsic possibility* and *intrinsic condition* of acts of objective cognition."[100] We have just examined the poem's own contemplation of both kinds, in the passage from passus 5 of the C Text. The ending of that passage suggests that writing *can* have a *principium intrinsecus,* while the first part of the passage betrays the nature of the incipit as a *principium extrinsecus.*[101]

This book is structured by that passage from extrinsic beginnings to intrinsic beginnings, attempting to show how a program of inward reading is bound up with the discovery of intrinsic beginnings. It starts with the most external beginnings of all, the beginnings that *Piers Plowman*'s earliest readers detected in it, the literal incipits they assigned to it in the attempt to give it intelligible beginnings, and ends with the poem's attempt to develop a theology of beginnings, envisaging the virtually impossible figure of the truly intrinsic beginning. The chapters between these extrinsic and intrinsic beginnings will examine, first, the kinds of beginning that can be given to a poem according to rhetorical theories in the Middle Ages, beginnings that may begin in the poet's mind but that are still external to the poem. The following chapter concerns beginnings that can be defined more ambiguously—as either *principii extrinsici* or *intrinsici*—the figures, the tropes, of poetic beginning that the poem uses, figures that normally describe external beginnings, but that describe the poem's own beginnings even while the poem is being constructed. The remaining chapters concern beginnings that are increasingly intrinsic to the subject of the poem and, even more importantly, to its readers. These concern images of political and dynastic beginning, which form a meditation on the possibility of beginning at all in the world of time. These beginnings, we will see, depend crucially on memory, on acts that are intrinsic not only to the event, but to the observer of the event, to anyone who wants to extricate sense from a beginning. Beginnings that apparently concern others, unfolding in public spheres, involving acts as public as coronations or documents as communal as charters, actually involve beginnings that are intrinsic to the selves involved, who either make their own beginnings or, in recalling beginnings, remake them. Finally, we will see that the poem's theology of beginnings rests on a concept of beginning that is not only intrinsic but radically so—the poem, in effect, enjoins the individual to make beginnings that have already begun in him or her. And so this book will follow that inward movement, reading for the desired beginning of the book, the location of effective and potential beginning. At the same time, however, we will be moving away from beginnings that are intrinsic *to the text* toward beginnings that are extrinsic to it, beginnings that are increasingly difficult to articulate because they are difficult to locate. To remind readers of this opposing movement, each of this book's chapters is labeled with the name of the kind of medieval beginning to which it most closely corresponds, names that designate beginnings that are increasingly less intrinsic to a text but more intrinsic to the ideal principle *(principium)* of beginning. These labels will also indicate that each of these chapters is, in a sense, another beginning to the book. Rather than calculate the distance from this book's beginning with traditional chapter numbers, each chapter will remind us that we must always, as Hunger says, "Go to oure begynnynge."

INITIUM

[A going in, a commencement, an entering upon;
a beginning without necessary implications of agency]

Incipits and the Intentions of Vernacular Writing

Euery bygynnyng hys harde, and euery
thyng hath a bygynnyng.
—From a medieval schoolbook

The Influence of *Ordinatio* on Beginnings

As massive *summae* of theology and digests of law began to be produced regularly in the thirteenth and fourteenth centuries, new ways of organizing books had to be invented. Single works contained a range of topics that could not conceivably be contained in the mind. Indeed, works like *distinctiones* and concordances, which gave a preacher everything he needed to know about important words in order to construct a sermon, clearly were not intended to be read sequentially. They exploited, in fact, some of the innovations that helped to organize larger and more complicated works. Readers could turn to indexes that would refer them to marks in the margins of a relevant passage. They could open commentaries they had not read and find the material they needed by considering an intertextual reference system. Knowing that distinction 30 of book 2 of Peter Lombard's *Sentences* discussed philosophical relation, they could easily find William of Ockham's own discussion of it in the corresponding, marked, section of one of his commentaries.

Such systems of *ordinatio* made it easier to navigate around difficult or bulky texts. They also created certain expectations for the shape of texts. Poems like *Piers Plowman,* whose structure still perplexes modern readers, provoked a certain response from its earliest scribes. Trying, futilely, to make it conform to a rational textual schema, they applied conventional schemes of *ordinatio* to it. These various schemes show clearly that scribes attempted to construct ways of negotiating a poem that thoroughly resists conventional *ordinatio,* even though it frustratingly invokes such principles of organization. The poem's design is radically different from that of other fourteenth-century texts, and scribes who try to invent an *ordinatio* for the poem reveal just how difficult and unprecedented is the poem's peculiar use of beginnings, and how that use is modulated by the practices of other late medieval beginnings.

The form of *Piers* sets it apart from any other vernacular poem and probably from any other poem of any kind in the Middle Ages. It is, of course, possible that similar poems were written in the roughly thousand years that make up the Middle Ages, but if they were, they remain obscure or they vanished without a trace. It is certainly the only major poem that contains more than one dream, and its separate dreams make it unique among Middle English dream visions.[1] Some readers of the poem, indeed, have argued that it is at least two entirely separate poems, a *Visio Petri Ploghman* and a *Vita de Dowel, Dobet, and Dobest.* Samuel Moore draws the conclusion that the "colophon which in all of the MSS stands at the junction between the *Vision* and the *Vita* shows that the A Text was regarded as consisting of two poems."[2] Skeat suggests that "altogether a new poem" begins at passus 8 of the B Text[3] and that the two parts of the A Text are "really *two* poems, each perfectly distinct from the other, with different titles and separate prologues."[4] More recently the notion of a *Piers* anthology has been discredited by George Kane, who points out that all the rubrics treat the work as a single poem, and Robert Adams, who argues that it is precisely the rubrics that seem to divide *Piers* into multiple works that are the least reliable indications of the original design of the poem. Both have shown convincingly that the *Visio* and the *Vita* are parts of a unified whole.[5] But even if the scribal rubrics that we can trust attest to the poem's "unitary character,"[6] they also attest to the difficulty that scribes had when they encountered a poem that abruptly begins again, something that runs completely counter to the principles of conventional *ordinatio.* The new beginnings in the poem may not inaugurate entirely new works, but they challenge the ingenuity of scribes who assimilate them into the body of the poem.

The poem's reordering of the traditional protocol of beginning extends throughout the body of the poem, but begins at its very start. Its truncated waking prologue and its abridgment of the narrator's voice *in propria persona* at the beginning of the poem make it difficult to define what, precisely, *is* the opening of the poem. It is difficult to determine where, to reverse the problem that John But's continuation of the A Text poses, "this beginning ends." As we will see, this is perhaps the most difficult question we can ask of the poem. Here, at *this* beginning, we have a chance to observe the poem's early readers struggling to make sense of what they may believe at that point is only a local problem. Most *Piers Plowman* manuscripts simply begin the poem with no formal incipit or title; the first rubric usually appears with the first passus. Two B Text manuscripts, BL Add. 35287 and Bodl. Laud Misc. 581, devise an identical *ordinatio* for the opening of the poem that delineates a clear beginning. Both manuscripts offset the first ten lines of the poem to allow space for a historiated *I* that runs the length of the ten lines; both manuscripts leave a space the width of a line before continuing against the ruled margin with the explicit beginning of the dream, "Thanne gan I meten..." (B Prol. 11).[7] Such dispositions of the opening are decisive scribal responses to a beginning whose boundaries are unclear or conflicting, an attempt to forge a deliberate incipit for a poem that is plagued by the inability to really begin.

Some manuscripts, however, suggest that their scribes were already coming to terms with the poem's peculiar passion for beginning. The attempt to define the body of the poem in terms of a series of beginnings is clearest in two manuscripts: MS Antiquaries 687 (M of A) and the Westminster manuscript (W of A) are the most extreme examples of the A Text tradition, which divides the poem into two discrete parts with their own titles. Both designate passus 9 not merely as the first passus of the *Vita,* but as a formal prologue: M has "hic incipit prologus de dowel, dobet & dobest"; W has "Sequitur prologus de dowel dobett & dobest."[8] Another manuscript of the A Text, Douce 323 (D of A), seems to follow this pattern, while adding an ambiguity of its own. The rubric at passus 9 conforms to type, marking the start of the *Vita,* but the rubric at passus 10, which reads simply "Primus passus in secundo libro," retrospectively designates the preceding passus as a prologue, while challenging the usefulness of the codicological conventions that provide *Piers Plowman*'s *divisio textus*. The word *liber* reappears in the poem's *explicit,* where it clearly describes the entire poem.[9] While the ambiguity of the word may enable a deliberate scribal strategy—dividing the work simultaneously into two dependent parts and into two independent poems—the scribe may simply not have resolved the problems of disposition that the beginnings present.[10] The manuscripts of the A and B Texts offer little clear information about the relationship between the formal incipits and the poem's new beginnings. Scribal rubrics acknowledge the subsequent beginnings, but they do not always neatly subordinate what follows into the larger whole. Perhaps the most intriguing manuscript comment in this light is at the top of the first folio of the poem in the B Text manuscript BL Add. 35287: "Assit sancta Maria principio meo."[11] It seems to comment both on the difficulty of the poem's beginning and on the problems connected with beginning that the poem raises. As that reader knew, and as we are coming to see, sorting out the poem's beginnings is not an easy task.

A more complicated scribal response is to mark the poem as constituted by two or more beginnings, which several manuscripts in effect do by providing parallel schemes for the *ordinatio* of the poem. The Westminster manuscript, whose rubrics accentuate the disruption that the new beginning of passus 9 creates, also numbers each passus, beginning with the prologue and continuing through passus 23, which it numbers as "Capi xxiiij & ultimo."[12] This disposition reaches its most complex form in several of the B Text manuscripts, which simultaneously number both the passus from the beginning of the poem and the passus within each division of the poem, as in passus 16: "Passus sextodecimus et secundus de dobet."[13] All of these manuscripts designate with a formal incipit new divisions within the poem that prompt changes in the numbering of subordinate sections. Two of them—L and W—begin numbering the first full passus after the one introduced by an incipit, implicitly turning the preceding passus into a prologue. But the rubricator of one C Text manuscript—the second part of the "Z Text" manuscript—carefully warns readers that a prologue will not follow the rubric: "hic explicit passus vii^{us} & ultimus de Dowel / *Iam* incipit passus primus de Dobet."[14] The concern that this rubricator takes to show the reader what begins where, and when it begins, is a smaller instance of the problem that faced the poem's scribes, who had to grapple with the *ordinatio* of a poem that seemingly began again several times. The internal incipits are not the signs of a stable, certain disposition, but of a deep uncertainty over what to do with beginnings themselves. The poem's multifold inception prompts an *ordinatio* made up of multiple incipits, but these merely highlight the difficulty of consolidating multiple beginnings into a coherent disposition. The Z manuscript rubricator's deliberate marking of a precipitate beginning warns the reader who might expect for the start of the search for Dobet a more explicit or elaborate beginning. The incipit at that point literally creates a beginning, imposing an inception at just the point where the C Text divides passus 15 into two parts: the dreamer's protestation to Liberum Arbitrium that there is no one who has never borrowed or begged "[a]nd ȝut oþerwhile wroeth withouten eny synne" (C 17.3). The rubricator draws attention to the importance of a new beginning even where the poem itself does not: at a point, indeed, where the C Text revision emphasizes the continuity of the poem's disposition.

The arrangement of the dreams themselves, as several critics have argued, is perhaps a more reliable indication of the poem's disposition than the scribal rubrics.[15] Some critics, indeed, have arranged the dreams into thematic groups, arguing that the dreams follow a clearly articulated sequence that discloses a moral or epistemological development.[16] Fewer, however, have been interested in the deployment of the dreams as more than merely markers of an unfolding, internally regulating, design.[17] Indeed, since each dream has its own clearly defined beginning, a beginning that usually imitates the beginning of the whole poem, the dreams themselves challenge any attempt to make the poem conform to an articulate, readily discernible, disposition. As James Weldon observes, each dream "has its separate prologue and epilogue, and in terms of formal properties constitutes a separate dream vision poem."[18] Each threatens the formal unity of the entire poem because each also bears the traces of principles that organize independent dream visions, principles that govern the disposition of a whole work, not of parts that are subordinated to the whole.

The Intention of Ending

The technique of *ordinatio* depends on that very knowledge of the whole, which is what medieval writers knew as the *causa finalis,* the end, or the intention, of a work. Another important way in which the poem's first readers tried to come to terms with its unusual preoccupation with beginnings was, by a logic that at first appears perverse, to try to make sense of the poem's endings. The final cause, in Aristotelian terms, is an extrinsic principle that determines the final shape that, in a work of art, already exists in the maker's mind—his initiating intention. According to the principles of medieval narrative design, the ending of a work bears a crucial relation to its beginning. By examining how a poem ends one can not only determine the shape of the whole, but can also, more importantly, recover the writer's intention for the work. These early attempts to make sense of the shape of the poem show that the problem of the poem's form is one of its longest-standing hermeneutical problems. They also show that these problems are one of the poem's most profound subjects. The possibility of a guiding, preordaining intention—the problem of the poem's own genesis—is the form of the poem itself.

A work's beginning and end are linked most profoundly in the conceptual stages of medieval composition, precisely because they are contained by the intention of a single mind, even if that single mind is the invention of a work's readers. Indeed, as Rita Copeland has argued, this mode of reading, in which the original work of invention is supplanted by *inventio* redefined "as hermeneutical inquiry," is motivated both by exegetical directives, the increasing importance of the *"modus interpretandi,"* and by the decline of primary forms of rhetorical invention in favor of secondary modes of description.[19] It is more useful, as a result, to think of medieval works as having an intentionality (the "intentio huius libri," as one form of the *accessus ad auctores* puts it), a tendency that is articulated in terms of its beginning or ending, than to think of the medieval concern with intention as having anything to do with a recuperation of what we think of as *authorial* intention, since that is usually ratified by the evident directives of end or beginning. The interanimation of intention, beginning, and end concerns the directives implicit in the word *intention* itself—to reveal what things strain or stretch toward, to hold something in tension. Thinking about beginnings means thinking about what they intend, toward what ending they tend, and also means thinking about the tension that unites them, as Edward Said suggests:

> Formally, the mind wants to conceive a point in either time or space that marks the beginning of all things (or at least of a limited set of central things), but like Oedipus the mind risks dis-

> covering, at that point, where all things will end as well. Underlying this formal quest is an imaginative and emotional need for unity, a need to apprehend an otherwise dispersed number of circumstances and to put them in some sort of telling order, sequential, moral, or logical. Very frequently, especially when the search for a beginning is pursued within a moral and imaginative framework, the beginning implies the end—or, rather, implicates it; this is the observation around which Aristotle builds the *Poetics*.[20]

As Rosemarie McGerr has argued, the disclosure of intention seems fullest at the conclusion of a work, and medieval compositional precepts often suggest that "no element in a text takes on its full significance until it is viewed in terms of the text's end."[21] And it is the immanent pressure of this final disclosure that motivates the placement of this "end," in a more Aristotelian sense, at the beginning of a text as well, to give it just that formal unity of intention. Several medieval works demonstrate the beginning's implication of the ending by literally imitating the relation between beginning and end. Some university sermons conclude by restating the opening *thema,* and at least fifteen Middle English poems use their opening lines as their concluding lines.[22] Indeed, as A. C. Spearing has pointed out, Holy Church's speech in passus I exemplifies the circular structure recommended by the *artes praedicandi:* "[I]t is organized not about a narrated action or even a logical argument but about a text or *thema:* 'Whanne all tresours ben tried . . . treuthe is the beste.' Holychurch begins with this *thema,* circles round it citing Scriptural *confirmationes,* and eventually returns to the point at which she began."[23] Holy Church's speech is a model of homiletic construction, using principles that, as Spearing demonstrates, seem to shape the rhetorical strategies of other parts of the poem. But even if parts of the poem use principles drawn from the *artes praedicandi,* the poem as a whole seems almost deliberately to violate such principles. It does, indeed, end with a beginning, but not the same beginning that opens the poem: it ends with the start of a quest for Grace, not the start of a wandering tour to hear "wondres." The last line of the poem describes a beginning, but a beginning that stops short of revealing any useful information about the conception of the poem or the effect of the dream upon the narrator. The dreamer merely begins to awake; he does not summarize the facts of the dream or recount its ethical effect. The beginning that ends the poem does not reveal the teleology of the poem's beginning, disclosing the end toward which everything has been directed. The ending of the poem tells us as little about the poem's compositional gestation as its beginning does, a coyness, deliberate occlusion, or aphasia that is thoroughly uncharacteristic of dream poems and poems with devotional topics.

Such works often return at the end to the point of the work's conception, divulging the unity that the mind of the author imposes on the work. Robert of Basevorn describes as "subtilis et curiosus" (subtle and ingenious) the "assimilatio finis principio" (the assimilation of the end in the beginning) and implies that what Said identifies as the "emotional need for unity" underwrites the pleasure inherent in such simplicity of form: those writers of sermons "curiosissime faciunt qui *simpliciter* idem principium et finem habent" (are most ingenious when they simply have the same beginning and end).[24] Other works demonstrate even more clearly at their endings than at their beginnings the desire to recuperate the conceptual beginning of the work, to formulate the intention of its author. The accepted definition of a letter's conclusion, according to Ludolf of Hildesheim, is a statement explaining its author's intention.[25] Scholastic prologues link intention with ending by using the terms *intentio scribentis* and *finis* interchangeably.[26] The English prologue to the *Legendys of Hooly Wummen,* indeed, defines intention almost entirely in terms of the "finis":

> The final cause declaryth plenly
> Of the work begunne the cause why;
> That is to seyne, what was the entent
> Of the auctour fynally, and what he ment.[27]

The passage distinguishes between "intentio" and "finis" by suggesting implicitly that the "entent" looks toward the end of the work: "fynally" means "the final cause," which is the "auctour's" intent for the *end.* The "entent" of the author is his "end" in writing, both his purpose and the conclusion toward which the beginning of the work is projected. By distinguishing meaning from intent, the passage suggests that intention might not simply be the ethical purpose; it might also be the projected design of a work.

For most medieval works, intention comprehends not only their end but also their order. Order is not imposed on a work while it is being written down, but created in the first stages of its mental conception: Bene of Florence, in his rhetorical handbook, says that copious eloquence follows from the *ordinatio*.[28] The prologue to a scientific text by Walter Burley, a commentary on Aristotle's *De generatione et corruptione*, itself an interesting meditation on the problems of physical beginning, is a good example of the close relation between *intentio* and *dispositio*: "In prohemio huius libri proponit Philosophus suam intencionem, dicens quod intendit in hoc libro determinare causas universales" (In the prologue of this book the Philosopher proposes his intention, saying that he intends in this book to determine the universal causes).[29] Burley's statement of intention determines both the form of the prologue, since its main subject is intention, and the form of the work itself. The work that follows becomes the manifestation of the intention that Burley "proponit" in the prologue. Other writers pay close attention to the relation between the purported intention and the form of a work, as Alistair Minnis observes: "Nicholas Trevet and Thomas Waleys . . . would criticise a *divisio textus* which, in their opinion, obscured instead of clarified the *intentio auctoris*. For example, in the prologue to his commentary on Seneca's *Declamationes*, Trevet wonders aloud if the present *divisio* is contrary to the mind of the author *(mens auctoris)*."[30] The Merton mathematician and astronomer John Ashenden states even more explicitly the relation between his own intention and the form of the work in one of his prologues: "Intencio mea in hoc libro est compilare sentencias astrologorum" (My intention in this book is to compile the observations of the astrologers).[31] Rather than expounding his intention in terms of an ethical, morally edifying, purpose for the work—what Alexander of Hales calls an *informatio affectum*[32]—or situating his intention for the work within the categorical demands of the order of human sciences,[33] Ashenden relates it as a drive toward clarification of form, toward *ordinatio*. His prologue makes intention and form virtually identical: his intention is his *modus procedendi* ("compilare"), which becomes the *forma tractatus* itself.

The close relation between a work's form or its conclusion and its *intentio* determines the form that later writers use to complete an unconcluded work: many use the devised conclusion to restate the circumstances of the work's composition or to attempt to reconstruct the *mens auctoris*. Caxton's conclusion to *The House of Fame*, for example, summarizes the narrator's reaction to the dream:

I sodeynly awoke anon tho
And remembryd what I had seen
And how hye and ferre I had been
In my ghoost and had grete wonder
Of that the god of thonder
Had lete me knowen and began to wryte
Lyke as ye have herd me endyte
Wherfor to studye and rede alway
I purpos to doo day by day.[34]

The early responses to A Text of *Piers Plowman* also concern the problem of the poem's underlying *intentio.* In providing conclusions for the A Text, readers of the poem attempt not only to disclose the poem's moral purpose, but also to devise an ending that is the fulfillment of a goal intended from the beginning, a "summational fiction" that is authorized by its beginning intention.[35] "Intention," indeed, is sometimes a category constructed by an audience, and can even make authorial intention irrelevant. Jean de Meun's digressive continuation of *The Romance of the Rose* cannot, for example, have been part of the design of the poem intended by Guillaume de Lorris.[36]

Unfinished works provide particularly good examples of an audience's appropriation of a writer's intent. The author's intention is frequently gauged by the effect that his work ought to have upon an audience. On the one hand, the interest in a work's effect defines all rhetorically based works, but some medieval commentators discuss *intentio* in ways that make it difficult to separate author from audience. The form of a work becomes almost as much a product of the audience's *intentio* as it does of the author's *intentio.* Indeed, the transition from classical rhetoric to medieval exegesis as the dominant model of hermeneutics, as Copeland argues, involves the powerful conflation of the *modus inveniendi* and the *modus interpretandi,* a change that not only authorizes the audience to understand a work from the perspective of its writer, but also allows the writer to understand his or her work as initially interpretive. In his *Commentum in Theodulum,* Bernard of Utrecht seems to suggest that *intentio* imparts a retrospective order to the constituent parts of a work, much as the impulse toward *ordinatio* prompts compilers to construct a new order for the elements of a diverse body of material or for a disordered exemplar.[37] The disposition of the work is governed by the intention that lies behind both its original construction and its reception: "The intention is a disposition *(affectus)* of the soul concerning a matter *(materia)*, or a discourse *(oratio)* which especially directs the soul in reading a book."[38] In Chaucer's prologue to the *Legend of Good Women,* as Copeland argues, the question of *intentio* is bound up with the invention of the text itself, constituting what she calls a "prospectus" to the *Legend.* Chaucer's narration of the principles he pursues in the subsequent work and the reasons he adduces for doing so amount to an analysis of the *dispositio* of his own work in terms of the *intentio* of the *auctor,* who happens to be Chaucer himself in the process of *inventio.*[39] The intention of both reader and writer guides the deployment of the work's material, and a work can be read more effectively if the reader is aware of the intention that informs it. The predisposition of a work can be recovered by observing its parts, its orderly arrangement disclosing the *archetypus* that existed in the author's mind before the work was deployed on the page. The successful conclusion of a work signals the effectiveness of the work's antecedent plan, the fulfillment of the author's intention.

The ending of the A Text of *Piers Plowman* betrays the inconclusiveness of its *archetypus,* the incompleteness of its compositional gestation. The two successive revisions that followed the A Text, and which supplement the poem considerably, demonstrate in retrospect that the primal conception of the work did not include its final form. The A Text and B Text, could not, according to standard medieval definitions, have descended from the same origin: the form of such different works could not be comprehended in the same beginning. If supplementarity necessarily obscures an origin, displacing the beginning by becoming the beginning itself,[40] the incompletion of the A Text nevertheless encourages Langland, and other writers, to supplement it by returning to its beginning. Langland's substantial revisions and supplements to the poem eventually produce versions that no longer seem to proceed from the same origin. George Kane suggests that in conjoint A and C manuscripts the juncture will always be evident because the traces of wholly different beginnings and archetypes remain: "On comparison with the corresponding passages in the accepted versions, the C-Text portion of these manuscripts proceeds as if from another beginning."[41]

Some of the earliest reactions to the A Text were to use its beginning to make a suitable ending, a strategy that would both produce a clear design, a *certus ordo,* and reveal the *intentio* of its author. One of the first manuscripts that completes the poem by returning to its beginning is the Westminster manuscript, whose marginal commentator concludes the poem with what Anne Middleton describes as a "reprise-in-reverse of the opening lines of the poem":[42]

And when I was wytterly awakyd I wrote all thys dreame
And theys mervellys þat I met on mawlverne hyllys
In a sesoune of sommer as I softe nappyd
For þe people after ther power wold persen after dowell
That þe tresure moost tryed and tryacle at neede
now god gravnt hys grace to make a good ende
And bryng vs all to þe blysse as he bowghte vs on þe Roode.[43]

The Westminster manuscript concludes the poem with a conventional closing gambit recommended by preaching manuals, what Robert of Basevorn, quoting Boethius, refers to as the only remaining vestige of the "traditus ordo" in modern discourses: "Repetunt proprios quaeque recursus, nec manet ulli traditus ordo, nisi quod fini junxerit ortum stabilemque sui fecerit orbem" (They all seek their own way back, nor does the traditional order remain for any of them, except where the beginning is joined to the end and it makes of itself a stable whole).[44] By reinscribing the poem's beginning at its conclusion, the Westminster commentator reconciles *Piers Plowman* with at least one kind of traditional literary order.

The Westminster commentator's impersonation of the narrator's voice also suggests that more than a pleasing circularity of form is needed to complete the work. The commentator sets out to supplement the author's own intention, beginning with the disclosure of the author's activity of writing about his experience, a disclosure that never appears in the A Text and that is only cursory in the other two versions. The first of these disclosures, indeed, is anything but conclusory, since it begins passus 19, and leads directly to one of the poem's rare moments of waking activity: "Thus I awaked and wroot what I hadde ydremed, / And dighte me derely and dide me to chirche" (B 19.1–2). The second disclosure ends the same passus and sounds very much like its beginning: "And I awakned þerwiþ and wroot as me mette" (B 19.481). Chaucer's conclusion to *The Book of the Duchess* is, by comparison, a compendium of information about the author's state of mind and his attempts to represent his experience adequately:

> Thoghte I, "this is so queynt a sweven,
> That I wol, by processe of tyme,
> Fonde to putte this swevene in ryme
> As I can best"; and that anoon.—
> This was my sweven; now hit is doon.[45]

Piers Plowman's lack of any such formal conclusion and its refusal to draw local and simple correspondences between the activities of dreaming and writing, or between ending a dream and ending a poem, elicit responses such as John But's and the Westminster commentator's.

The Westminster conclusion projects authorial intention over the poem's landscape, attempting to throw into relief features of the poem that will reveal its design, its *archetypus*. The distillation of the Dreamer's experience elicits a distillation of the important themes of the poem. Two successive lines in the conclusion offer keys to the structure and themes of the *Vita*—the people who "persen aftir dowell" are adequate representatives of the interests of the second half of the poem—and the *Visio:* the "tresure moost tryed and tryacle" encapsulates the economic and spiritual concerns that several critics argue are the main concerns of the *Visio*.[46] The conclusion, in other words, attempts to account for the disposition of the poem by reconstructing the intention behind the poem. It cuts a missing piece to shape, showing the poet setting out to write the beginning of the poem, an event that never appears in the poem itself.

The conclusion's attempt to portray the poet in the process of invention suggests that the poem's prehistory, the construction of its *archetypus,* holds some clues to the structure of the poem itself. But as such scribal responses to the poem show, both the *intentio* and *dispositio* of the original conception can only be discovered by recreating, or creating, them. The perplexing formal problems of the poem, its narrative disjunctions and multiple beginnings, owe something to the adequacy, or inadequacy, of the design mapped out before the poem was set to paper. A. J. Colaianne suggests that the poet deliberately rejects a preconceived plan for the poem because he "cared more about clarification than anything else [and] could not allow such a plan to carry him along."[47]

Colaianne's explanation does not differ greatly in kind from the Westminster conclusion's account of the poet's activity: he also attempts to reconstruct the poet's intention as a means of accounting for the disposition of the poem:

> In the *Apology for Poetry* Sir Philip Sidney comments on the importance of "foreconceit"—his term for an idea as it develops in the mind of the poet before the actual process of composition. For Sidney the poet must have this whole conception before he can write. It may be that "foreconceit" or the absence of it explains some of the most disturbing features of Langland's narrative.... The result of the absence of foreconceit is not simply formlessness, but, as Muscatine has observed, a kind of narrative disintegration.[48]

Medieval writers insisted even more strongly that a work must be preceded by a completed design. Geoffrey of Vinsauf's admonition that a work be "prescribed" in a "certus ordo" before pen is set to paper is the most famous advice on an aspect of composition that rhetoricians since Cicero have seen as the most important stage of composition. Indeed, Sidney's notion of foreconceit owes more to Geoffrey of Vinsauf than to classical rhetoricians.[49] But the attempt to reconstruct the intention of the poem's author by responding to problems in the poem's form, a strategy that both Colaianne and the Westminster commentator use, doubles back on itself. The Westminster commentator's conclusion creates a literal circularity, returning to the beginning of the poem to reveal its retrospective design; Colaianne argues that the poem is not governed by a single design because a single design is not evident.

The usual indices of authorial intention are unusually elusive in *Piers Plowman*. More than the poem's apparent incoherence of design points to an obscure preconception. In comparison with other dream visions, as John Bowers says, the dreamer's waking thoughts in *Piers Plowman* bear unusually little relation to the events of the dreams: "[In other poems] the waking narrators have their minds focused upon the subjects that will be explored within their dreams. This is probably not the case with Will. Unlike other poets, Langland tells us nothing of Will's thoughts at the moment he falls asleep, and the Dreamer's confusion over what he sees suggests that his mind was elsewhere entirely."[50] Rather than suggest simply, as Bowers does, that this inattention is the consequence of Will's *acedia*, Middleton argues that the narrator's secession from a conventional active role allows the poem to explore the relation between authority and experience, the complex nexus between words, works, and will. The poem deliberately obscures the marks that conventionally guide the reader's *intentio*, the traces of the intention behind the work, what scholastic prologues sometimes call the "intentio huius libris."[51]

> Neither at the beginning nor at any point in the poem does the composer present himself as managing the act of narration. . . . It is not simply that he makes no attempt to present the poem as a performance or book, but that in his declining to do so the composition as such vanishes; it becomes indistinguishable from the experiencing of it by the audience. The literary fiction is that there is no fiction, no design or "foreconceit."[52]

By beginning without a formal prologue, the poem only succeeds in raising questions about its author's conception for the poem, questions, as we will see, that the poet himself tries to answer. Most scholastic prologues include information about the "intentio auctoris" or the "causa finalis" of the work; many non-Aristotelian prologues attempt to locate the work within the larger body of human knowledge or to acknowledge the models for the work.[53] Middle English alliterative prologues are often phrased in the voice of the poet, as in *Winner and Waster*'s opening lament over the decline in patronage and in the standards of literary production. Such openings also implicitly situate the following work in a literary tradition, either resisting it or ascribing to it. The *Wars of Alexander*'s recitation of a generic catalog in its opening lines is one manifestation of the beginning impulse to subscribe to anterior conceptions:

> Sum is leue to lythe þe lesyng of sayntis
> . . . sum has langinge of lufe lay[e]s to herken,
>
> . . . .
>
> Sum couettis & has comforth to carpe & to lestyn
> Of curtaissy, of knyȝthode, of craftis of armys,
> Of kyngis at has conquirid & ouircomyn landis;
> Sum of wirschip, iwis, slike as þam wyse lattis,
> And sum of wanton werkis, þa þat ere wild-hedid.[54]

As Said suggests, declarations of this "dynastic" sort, using figures of political potency and continuity, are a necessary corollary of beginning any work.[55] *Piers Plowman*'s lack of such declarations is one aspect of the poem's evasion of formal statements of purpose or form at its beginning, the first evidence of its concealment of design or foreconceit. Rather than try to resolve the problems raised by the beginning, John But—the author of perhaps the most extensive conclusion of the poem[56]—tries to resolve them by displacing them to the end. His conclusion is apparently informed by the preconception that the poem is concerned with the formal problems of ending, and by completing its ending he attempts to fulfill the projected design of the poem. He expiates the author's reluctance to "present the poem as a performance or book" or to negotiate the poem's place within a tradition by showing at the ending the poem's assumption of place within the corpus, the "oþer workes," established by its now dead author: "Wille," he says,

> . . . wrouȝthe þat here is wryten and oþer workes boþe
> Of peres þe plowman and muchel puple al-so;
> And whan þis werk was wrouȝt ere wille myȝte a-spie,
> Deþ delt him a dent and drof him to þe erþe.
>
> (A 12.96–99)

John But's conclusion, like the Westminster commentator's, also attempts to resolve the formal problems for which the poet's concealed intent offers no guidance. Middleton points out that passus 12, which she argues is But's own composition, offers a rapid précis of the preceding events of the A Text and a proleptic summary of the second half of the B Text, which resolve some of the intellectual problems that the A Text poses but does not solve.[57] But's proprietary concern over the ending of the poem suggests that the ending he makes is also the resolution of the poem's form. A good ending will be faithful to the poem's beginning intention, and Middleton argues that But attempts just that act of authorial faith or rectitude in attempting to incorporate the poem's larger intention, an intention that seems not to dictate Langland's own subsequent additions to the poem: "In assimilating Will's story to the exemplification and promotion of pious practices he saw as the pervading intent of Langland's 'works,' John But must remain committed to the narrative enterprise of spiritual romance that Langland himself begins to dismantle and reassemble in the two long versions."[58] By using the poem's ending to fulfill what he believes to be its original intention, But's extemporization consummates the formal tendencies of the poem and retrospectively discloses the intention underlying the poem, making a beginning that *would have been* effective for the ending he is now making. In declaring his own name so explicitly, however, But suggests that his intention for the poem and the original poet's might not be perfectly congruous, miming himself as the poem's executor as he dispatches a poem whose failed execution had ended in the death, real or fictive, of its author and of the poem's initiating intention. But's conclusion does not attempt to simulate the intention behind the poem as thoroughly as does the Westminster conclusion, but it does largely concern his own intention in writing the conclusion:

> And so bad Iohan but busily wel ofte,
> When he saw þes sawes busyly a-legged
> By Iames and by Ierom by Iop and by oþere,
> And for he medleþ of makyng he made þis ende.
> (A 12.101–4)

As Middleton points out, But's conclusion invites the reader to determine the extent of his contribution: "The question of where 'þis ende' begins is posed by the literary form John But claims for it: it is not a scribal *explicit* but a tribute in kind, a 'makyng' about a making, an act of both literary criticism and literary imitation."[59] The problem of delimiting the beginning of the nonauthorial portion of passus 12 blurs into the question of what form the continuation takes.[60] The conclusion reprises the central architectonic problem of the entire poem: the relation between its beginning and its form. By appropriating the function of the maker who begins a new work, John But's conclusion also reiterates the important question of what relation the beginning of *Piers Plowman* has to the rest of the work. An even more fundamental question for the poem than where John But's ending begins is where the beginning ends.

The scribal attempts to resolve the inconclusiveness of the poem's form by reiterating its beginning are conventional responses to a poem that seemed to lack both conclusion and clear intention. Scribal responses attempt to reassert a preconception for the poem that should have been contained in its beginning. The poem seems not to have been preceded by a foreconceit, a *prehabita dispositio,* because its literal beginning does not ordain its disposition.

In a very important sense, the beginning of *Piers Plowman* never does end. Even the poem's writer, most startlingly, enacts his own fictive making of poetic intention in the C Text addition to passus 5, a passage that is increasingly coming to be read as the poem's summational fiction, its most rigorous account of the poem's discursive placement. Above all, that concern with placement involves the discovery, or rather, in the rhetorical and mnemonic senses, the invention, of some form of intention prior to the unfolding of the poem. Reason and Conscience, Will's tropological interlocutors, push him either to admit that his work is a kind of wasting, an unethical expenditure of time and social capital, or to define it once and for all as a redemptive or recuperative project. But what emerges most persistently in this late addition to the poem is the poet's absolute, inextricable relationship with his writing, a relationship clarified at this point by Will's rejection of other vocations in favor of the one that can only be justified by its execution—the continuation of the poem. So the economy of *this* writing is the economy of the entire poem, a poem whose completion is predicted by its writer's total competence to write it. In short, the passus 5 passage amounts to the most harrowing, deprecating, and politically charged statement of intention for any poem in Middle English.

In fact, far from being a belated attempt to justify the work of the poem, the passage is actually a brutally compendious statement of the form that authorial predisposition must necessarily take. As we will see, this crucial dispute establishes the question of the poem's intention, its *causa finalis,* as its most important one, threatening to put an end to any further writing. Or, perhaps more accurately, to prevent any writing from happening—for this passage is above all an originary fantasy of the poem's inception, although a belated origin precisely because the question of what intention presides over the dislocations of this poem is one that we now know, after having read the A and B versions, to be the very question that is being asked throughout the poem as its condition of possibility, as the mode of its inception—and as the inception itself of its own formal mode. The very thing that forces *Piers Plowman* into such a dilatory, recursive mode is its incapacity for origination, its incapacity to reflect the *causa finalis* that should appear at its beginning and end, but whose absence hovers everywhere over the poem, threatening it with the making of something other, with a termination that is merely inert rather than final and conclusive. This is why such a powerful account of the poem's own perlocutionary modes of intention can be inserted at this juncture, between the first and second dreams, just where the poem first declares its intention of beginning again, or declares its intention to continue (as Conscience urges, "ȝe, and continue") to be a poem that has not yet really begun.

EXORDIUM

[Beginning of a speech or sermon; literally the warp of a web, from *exordior,* to lay a warp, to begin to weave]

Making Beginnings

Disposition and Inscription

Are we that higher or the participant
newcomer, the thing of beginnings in time?
—Plotinus, *Ennead* 6

We have seen that texts in the Middle Ages begin well before the moment marked by the incipit. Part of the work itself is the conceptual history of the poem, the kinds of mental discipline, exercise, and design that lead to the performance of the idea in language. This mental prehistory is perhaps more important, of course, for the writer of a work, or for rhetoricians, than for its audience. For all practical purposes, the work begins with its incipit, a moment that is just as charged with significance and just as complex as the act of "inventing" the work in the first place. The beginning of a work is supposed to follow a recognized protocol, one designed to have a particular effect on its audience. As with the stage of invention, this stage is also deeply concerned with the ethical nature of a poetic work; the difference, however, is that the literal beginning involves its audience, rather than its maker, in an ethical relationship with the work. As I did in the previous chapter, in this chapter I will show how *Piers Plowman*'s apparent violations of some of these basic precepts actually demonstrate their profound importance even for this most egregious of medieval poems. In the terms of medieval compositional practice, by failing to make manifest the intention behind its form *Piers* makes its form a fundamental part of its subject. By failing to get past the beginning, the poem makes beginning the formal principle of the poem. In order to show how deeply such a poem could be concerned with its making in terms of beginning, it would be useful to discuss the importance of discussions of the literal beginnings of works in rhetorical treatises, what amount to medieval theories of the incipit.

DISPOSITION: BEGINNING AS MAKING

Medieval theories of composition maintain that the most important aspect of a work's disposition is its beginning, that a work is, for most purposes, practically written when a beginning is finally made. On the most obvious level, a work cannot hope to succeed unless it has a good beginning, because it needs a foundation on which to build the edifice. Echoing an idea that seems to begin with Hesiod ("Dimidium operis totius principia occupant" [Beginnings take up half of the entire work]), the author of the thirteenth-century compendium of rhetorical theory called the *Candelabrum* offers one of the most explicit medieval statements of the potency of literary beginnings:

> [S]i principium, quasi fundamentum quoddam, bonum fuerit et perfectum, totum sequens edificium roboratur. Nam principium est totius rei pars potentissima.
>
> [If the beginning, as a kind of foundation, is good and perfect, the entire subsequent edifice is given strength. For the beginning is the most powerful part of the whole thing.][1]

But the *Candelabrum* more directly derives the traditional lament over the difficulty of beginning a literary work from Horace than from the tradition descending from Hesiod.[2] The *Candelabrum* emphasizes not the effort that a beginning demands, but the power it wields over the rest of the work. The beginning, indeed, is the most powerful part of the work: if the beginning is good (or even perfect), the rest of the work is strengthened. The beginning of a work ought to provide the clues for understanding the work that follows. Biblical commentators, as I have shown, treated this principle as axiomatic. But prescriptive treatises on the composition of works urge authors to pay especially close attention to the way in which they begin the work. Almost all rhetorical treatises discuss the necessity of using some form of the Ciceronian exordium to render the audience *benivolens, attentus,* and *docilis.*[3] Dictaminal treatises offer exhaustive formulae for the protocol of exordia, showing the proper form to use to make every kind of audience as well-disposed as possible. Preaching manuals are slightly less prescriptive, usually suggesting that the best place to win over the audience is at the beginning of the sermon. Both Ranulph Higden and Thomas of Chobham, indeed, apply the principle of the rhetorical exordium to the structure of a sermon, pointing out that an effective sermon will begin with a proem or prologue that will produce the ideal Ciceronian audience.[4] In his section on *dispositio,* Thomas points out that a beginning should be strong because the audience expects to be impressed at the outset. A weak beginning will cause the audience to despise the whole work:

> Oportet enim in principio collocare ualidiores rationes quas habet et ualidiores auctoritates quas habet ad persuadendum et dissuadendum quod intendit, et postea subiungere infirmiores rationes in medio.... Auditores enim si in principio audierint probabiles et necessarias rationes uel ualde motiuas, facilius credent et intendent quod sequitur. Si autem tepide et inefficienter inceperit predicator, de facili contempnunt sermonem.

> [It is appropriate to gather in the beginning the more valid reasons and authorities that he has for persuading and dissuading what he intends, and later to adjoin the weaker reasons in the middle... for if the listeners hear the likely and necessary reasons, or the strongly persuasive [ones], in the beginning, they will more easily believe and direct their attention to what follows. If, however, the preacher begins tepidly or unpersuasively, they will easily despise the sermon.][5]

The author's anticipation of the audience's reaction dictates the shape of the material: the beginning should collect together the authoritative and persuasive points of the following discourse. All of these *artes incipiendi* agree on the same basic point: that a work that has a weak beginning—whether it is weak structurally, rhetorically, affectively, or performatively—will probably not end successfully. Its structure—to explicate the image that the *Candelabrum* uses—will not be fully articulated, all of its various segments joined. And most important, it will not effect the necessary beginning in its audience, starting the process that will allow the audience to make the discourse its own. These prescriptions are, of course, ideal; they describe what every successful medieval work is supposed to do. Many medieval works, of course, fail by these standards, or such prescriptions would be unnecessary. Many of these failures, virtually by definition, are ignorant of the advice dispensed in manuals like these—especially, perhaps, vernacular works that are clearly uninfluenced by the learned Latinity of the university or church. But what are we to make of a work that violates these very precepts when it is a work that meditates profoundly on the very problem of beginning works, especially when it exhibits a canny awareness of the rhetorical stakes in beginning?

What are we to make, that is, of *Piers Plowman,* a work whose compositional history, at least as far as we can make sense of it, is one of unsuccessful endings? It is a poem whose first ending, that of the A Text, was so inconclusive that it took an addition nearly as long as the poem to bring it to another ending. And even that was not sufficient, so we have a third version of the poem that makes major structural changes that betray, at least in terms of medieval compositional practice, the effectiveness, intelligence, or competence of its own beginning. As we have seen, one of the great mysteries of a poem that turns out to be fascinated with beginning is why it should have a beginning that seems so muted, truncated, and unspectacular.

The answer perhaps is that the poem's beginning does not end where we think it does. This is true in several senses. Its beginning does not end at the points we might normally designate, and its beginning does not end when it should have, in the poet's mind well before the parts of the work were arranged in writing, and even while the poem is being written. In a strange way, but one recognizable in medieval rhetorical theory and in much traditional Western philosophy, the poem could be said never to begin.

The poem's first dream is partly concerned with the very conception of the poem: it is partly the narration of its own invention. Like Boethius's vision of humankind, who "dremen alwey [their] bygynnynge,"[6] the dreamer dreams about the beginning of the poem, well after the literal beginning has passed. The first part of the first dream becomes a dream of the beginning, a dream about what should have already taken place—the process of invention. Only after the dream has begun does any indication of the scope of the poem appear. Some of the changes that Langland made to the C Text suggest that he had, by the time he had completed and then rewritten the poem, completed more of that initial work, invented more of what he had to in order to begin the work adequately. In the C Text a moralized summary of the themes of the poem a kind of précis or thema—replaces some of the topographical details of the waking moments in the A and B versions, which accompany a figurative and literal wandering through a landscape whose significance we are still to discover. The C Text is much more emphatic and conclusive:

> Al þe welthe of the world and þe wo bothe,
> Wynkyng as hit were, witterliche y sigh hit;
> Of treuthe and tricherye, tresounn and gyle,
> Al y say slepynge as y shal [ȝow] telle.
> (C Prol. 10–12)

The C revision considerably shortens the waking introduction to the poem and provides a more didactic beginning. The dreamer realizes the significance of much of the vision before Holy Church needs to explain it to him. As soon as he sees the tower, he remarks, "y trowe, treuthe was thereynne" (C Prol. 15). The work of invention (literally, of finding and discovering), even when it is performed by characters in the poem, proceeds much more efficiently and cannily in this version. But even remarks like this hint at the process of constructing the poem or discovering the significance of the experience of the dream. Langland's reiteration of the fact of sleeping in lines 10 and 12 suggests that the mode of the dream itself is at least as important as its content. In none of the versions does he say anything about the dream before he describes falling asleep and beginning the actual dream. In the C Text the summary is part of the dream, not part of the beginning of the poem.

In the first two versions the discovery of the range of the poem is less explicit, but the first lines of the dream nevertheless describe the process of discovery. The conception and the significance of the dream unfold as the dream progresses. Indeed, in the A and B texts the dream begins with a kind of cognitive dissonance. The dreamer is at first unable to tell where he is:

> Thanne gan I meten a merueillous sweuene,
> That I was in a wildernesse, wiste I neuere where.

> [Ac] as I biheeld into þe Eest, an heiȝ to þe sonne,
> I seiȝ a tour on a toft trieliche ymaked,
> A deep dale byneþe, a dongeon þerInne
> Wiþ depe diches and derke and dredfulle of siȝte.
> A fair feeld ful of folk fond I þer bitwene...
> (B Prol. 11–17)

The beginning of the dream emphasizes the dreamer's passivity, situating him in a world not of his own making. He describes the "tour," for instance, as "trieliche ymaked," an object in his own dream that declares another maker. The dreamer emphasizes the act of looking, and the profusion of adjectives in the passage suggest the intensity of the impression the sights make upon the dreamer's senses: the "dongeon," for instance, is "dredfulle of sighte." The significance of the vision is impressed upon the dreamer's senses before it is impressed upon his intellect. Holy Church's first words to him express astonishment that he is not awake: "sone, slepestow?" (B 1.5). At critical junctures of the opening vision, the poem carefully emphasizes the poet's passivity, his constricted response to the beginning of his own poem. Its significance is unclear to him; he must appeal to Holy Church to explicate his own experience: "mercy, madame, what [may] this [by]meene?" (B 1.11). The dreamer experiences the unfolding of the poem's conception simultaneously with the reader.

Indeed, as Holy Church suggests, the poem's conception may precede even the life of the dreamer:

> "The tour on þe toft," quod she, "truþe is þerInne,
> And wolde þat ye wroȝte as his word techeþ.
> For he is fader of feiþ, and formed yow alle..."
> (B 1.12–14)

The dreamer must conform his work to the word that is already disposed by Truth, who shapes not only the work of human lives, but human lives themselves.

The beginning of the first vision narrates, in part, the process of the poem's invention, the discovery of its conception. Although the poem's beginning itself is careful to obscure the traces of that conception or to attribute it to the prior generative power of Truth itself, the topography of that beginning conforms to the directions mapped out by rhetorical manuals. The beginning of the dream discloses its entire extent, the oppositions of "treuthe" and "tricherie" that the C Text proclaims. In the A and B Texts the magnitude of the poem is suggested, but in topographical terms—the "tour on a toft," the "deep dale" and "depe diches" of the "dongeon," the "fair feeld ful of folk" between them. The poem's scene of action is nevertheless clearly circumscribed at the beginning, with the field of folk, the primary concern of the rest of the poem, poised between the two structures that contain the two opposing principles of the poem, the "fader of feiþ" (B 1.14) and the "fader of falshede" (B 1.64). The beginning of the dream applies almost literally the advice that several rhetorical manuals give on constructing the "praedispositio" of the poem. The *Candelabrum* advises writers to "premeasure" the extent of their material in their minds before writing; Geoffrey Vinsauf advises writers to let the "interior compass" of the mind circumscribe or "precircle" the whole extent of the material.[7] In *Piers Plowman* the material is circumscribed after the poem has already begun.

Similarly, the poet's passive discovery of the scene imitates, though with significant dilution, the act of poetic invention itself, the process of discovering suitable "topics" for discourse, which many writers pointed to as the most important phase of a work.[8] Indeed, the verb the poem uses to describe the dreamer's discovery of the field of folk is a literal translation of the verb "invenio": "A fair feeld of folk *fond* I þer bitwene . . ." (B Prol. 17). The same verb is used only a few lines later to describe the inventions of the false minstrels, the "[i]aperis & iangleris," who "[f]onden hem fantasies" (A Prol. 35–36). In the C Text the sense of "invention," of discovery, is even clearer: "mynstrels . . . [f]yndeth out foule fantasyes" (C Prol. 35–36). The minstrels in the Prologue present the first critique of the dreamer's own enterprise, but they also reveal the indeterminacy of the poem's own beginning. The poet does not apply the verb that he himself uses to describe poetic making until the poem is well under way. Even then "finding" appears in a peculiarly passive sense, unlike the aggressive activity of the C Text minstrels, who actively "fyndeth out" their work. Unlike them, and unlike almost every other medieval poet or rhetorician, the poet-narrator of *Piers* is still in the act of discovering his material, engaged in the process of invention after the poem has already begun. The poem's literal beginning precedes its own prehistory, its invention and predisposition in the poet's mind.

That aspect of the poem's beginning, at least, situates it almost perfectly as the Derridean supplement, the beginning that must account for its own origin.

More precisely, perhaps, it is a critique of the supplement, which is to say, a kind of Derridean project, since Derrida's point was that the supplement masks the impossibility of origin. The poem's beginning demystifies the unexpressed forces that characterize a work's beginning in the Middle Ages. What is strange about the poem, in medieval terms, is its eagerness to define its own inception as something external to it as a written artifact, even while it mimics the actions of inventing a beginning. The peculiar impasses that surface in its conception of beginning show the very strangeness—the alien character—of the rhetorical beginning, a beginning that is integral to the work's structure, meaning, and completion, but a beginning that does not appear in the work itself. It is, despite the metaphors of integration that the manuals invoke, still a *principium extrinsecus,* a beginning out of nowhere, a beginning that is imposed on the *materia* yet to be shaped.

But if the invention of a work, its fundamental beginning, is a *principium extrinsecus,* where does *that* beginning start? As the word *invenio* implies, the process of constructing a work must begin somewhere else in order for it to be discovered or rediscovered. The answer that rhetorical theories in the classical and medieval ages give is that the process begins in the act of living itself. A well-ordered life, an exemplary life, constructs the mind as a well-ordered place in which to store the knowledge acquired in living properly. It is for this reason that the Middle Ages connects poetry with ethics.[9] The "invention" of a work is connected with ethics in at least two ways: it is a task that because of its very difficulty takes on ethical dimensions—it is a kind of labor that acquires all of the moral force of real work—and it is something that can be done properly only by someone who has disciplined his or her mind in a particular way, a way suited for the composition of moral instruction, a way that is, in every sense of the word, ethical. The difficulty in beginning a work, in other words, mirrors the difficulty of living properly. The possibility of *recte scribendi* depends quite clearly on *recte vivendi.*

Medieval discussions of beginning comment again and again on the difficulty that writers experience when they begin a work. The writer of a fifteenth-century textbook on rhetoric and grammar begins a collection of proverbs with one that comments on its own position, and also appears to summarize the writer's own experience: "Euery bygynnyng hys harde, and euery thyng hath a bygynnyng."[10] The proverb offers a poignant glimpse into the unexpressed struggles that occur in a work's prehistory, the decisions that writers must make before they can begin a work. Writers can appear anxious to distance themselves from the work's beginning, and even relieved to cover the traces of the trauma that the beginning inflicts. One of the earliest versions of this proverb appears in a homily by Chrysostom, in which he looks anxiously past the opening of the work to its main body: "Semper principium & exordia sunt difficilia. haec ergo jaciamus tanquam fundamenta, & deinde omnia expedita erunt ac facilia" (The beginning and exordia are always difficult. Therefore let us lay out these things like foundations, and then everything will be ready and easy).[11] Even when they become stock observations, such proverbs record the psychological turmoil that beginnings induce because they are the foundation of the rest of the work.

The frequency of such comments suggests that almost everyone who wrote treatises on composition shared, or understood, the tribulations of beginning. But even compilers of collections recognized that beginnings are difficult precisely because they are the most important part of a work. One particularly popular proverb, one that appears at the beginning of several such collections, comments succinctly on both of these aspects of beginning. It points out that beginnings demand at least half of the work of writing, and that they determine at least half of the written work itself: "Principia tocius operis dimidium occupare dicuntur" (Beginnings are said to occupy half of the whole work).[12] As a poem that is largely constructed from beginnings, *Piers Plowman* applies this proverb more literally, and more pervasively, than most medieval works. The difficulty that medieval writers clearly associate with the beginning of a work is, in *Piers Plowman,* a difficulty that occupies the entire poem. The poem remains entangled in its inception, a record of the immanence of its own beginning and also, incidentally, a record of the immanence of beginning in other medieval works.

Medieval theories of composition, indeed, suggest that the most important phase of a work's execution is its conception, sometimes referred to as "invention." In a passage that made its way into numerous rhetorical treatises, the *Rhetorica ad Herennium* stresses the primacy and difficulty of this phase of composition: "De oratoris officiis quinque inventio et prima et difficillima est" (Invention is the first and most difficult of the orator's five tasks).[13] Medieval rhetorical treatises insist almost as strongly as do Romantic theories of artistic conception that the work begins in the author's mind,[14] and consequently deny that a work should have any further beginnings. The formulation of a work in the mind determines its fate, and an author who lacks a sufficient plan will produce a deficient work. Rhetorical manuals such as the *Candelabrum* often advised writers to prepare themselves adequately before beginning a work, because the foundation, or the beginning, of good writing is a wise mind: he who lacks "knowledge of things" will also lack words.[15] The same manual recommends reading "nobiliores libros" extensively to allow idea and form to knit together in the "uterus" of the mind before the birth of the discourse: "[M]ateria intra mentis uterum concepta pariter et formata, iam sine deformitate aliqua sermo nascatur ingenuus" (When the material has been both conceived and formed within the uterus of the mind, one's own discourse may be born without any deformation).[16] The integrity of the entire work depends upon its mental gestation, the adequacy of its beginning in the mind. But this attention to what happens before a work is even written shows how beginning must be an ethical act, an action that begins before the act of inscribing anything, a discourse that participates in an integrity that exists before writing ever started.

THE WILL TO BEGIN

But what about the *principium extrinsecus* that the poem's literal beginning makes on the rest of the work? How can we think about works whose beginnings fail blatantly and engagingly? In medieval terms, the answer to these questions takes us even further into the domain of ethics, because much of the medieval discussion of beginning is intimately bound up with questions of personal disposition, of ethics, as well.

Preaching manuals treat the beginning as a fundamental part of the work. They point out that the selection of the *thema* is perhaps the most important aspect of a sermon, since it is the beginning of the sermon in several senses:[17] it usually stands first in the completed sermon,[18] and everything in the sermon should develop naturally from it. Thomas Waleys offers a straightforward syllogism for the principle that the *thema* is the proper beginning of a sermon: "*thema* debet esse materia sermonis. Unde *thema* graece idem est quod *materia* latine. Materia vero debet esse fundamentum et rei principium" (the *thema* must be the *materia* of the sermon, for *thema* in Greek is the same as *materia* in Latin. The *materia,* indeed, must be the foundation and beginning of things).[19] Because the theme is so important in shaping the sermon, most preaching manuals are primarily concerned with the procedure of selecting a thema and dividing it properly. Indeed, the art of preaching may involve little else. As John of Wales points out, the *thema* contains the whole sermon: "[T]hema quasi tocius operis fundamentum . . . in quo omnia dicenda virtualiter contineantur" (The *thema* is as the foundation of the whole work . . . in which all things that are to be said should be virtually contained).[20] John's definition of the thema is also a concise definition of the relation between beginning and disposition in medieval compositional theory: the disposition of a work depends radically upon its beginning. Preaching manuals, having defined the thema as the beginning or foundation of the sermon, generate from it a trope that shows the deployment of the whole sermon from a single source: "[E]x themate procedunt diuisiones tanquam ex radice. ut patet in arbore" (from the theme proceed the divisions as from a root, as is evidenced in a tree).[21] An anonymous sermon combines the tropes of construction and development to describe the function of the thema:

> Unde, quia thema est quasi radix totius sermonis et per ipsum fundamentum stabilita totius aedificii fabrica consurgit, et sicut ex uno et eodem stipite hinc et inde nascuntur ramuli, sic ex eodem themate membra sermonem integrantia propagantur.
>
> [Therefore, because the theme is like the root of the whole sermon, and from the same foundation rises the stable fabric of the whole edifice, and, just as from one and the same trunk branches are born here and there, so from the same thema parts integrating the whole sermon are propagated.][22]

The elements of a well-constructed work will concord with each other because of their common beginning, the harmonious disposition of the parts of a sermon, for example, deriving from a single origin. The beginning, not the parts, of a work imparts its unity. As Judson Allen observes, *dispositio* in rhetorical manuals is really the treatment of the beginning of the work. The section on disposition in the *Poetria nova* is really about the types of beginning: the natural or the eight kinds of artificial.[23] Indeed, the art of selecting a beginning is really the art of imparting order to one's material. In a section entitled *De arte inchoandi,* John of Garland's *Parisiana poetria* shows how the order of a work depends upon the point at which the writer chooses to begin narrating his material, after the work of invention and mental ordering has been completed:

> Post inuentionem et electionem materie sequitur de inchoatione et disposicione ipsius.... Si continget forsitan materiam esse poeticam, tunc possumus ordiri materiam aut secundum principium naturale aut secundum principium artificiale.
>
> [After the invention and the selection of the material follow the inception and disposition of the same.... If the material happens to be poetic, then we can order the material according to either a natural beginning or an artificial beginning.][24]

Although advice on disposition can be subtle and elaborate, in rhetorical manuals it nevertheless ultimately collapses into the single concern of inception. A work is ultimately ordered by its beginnings. The formal shape of a work is not decided by the progression of its parts or their architectonic relation to each other, but rather by the beginning that the writer chooses at the outset. The beginning dictates the disposition of the work. As Allen puts it, "Dispositio... most properly occupies itself with beginnings, because it is from the beginning that all else hangs—medieval poems, like modern newspaper articles, depend on their headlines."[25]

We can read this project backward and discover the most important aspects of a work's disposition by examining its beginning, since it records the traces of invention, declares the author's intention, and contains the most valid points of the argument. And, as Rita Copeland has established, for the later Middle Ages features of a work's order such as its disposition were seen as part of a continuum that included *inventio.* The beginning, indeed, establishes the foundations of the edifice of the entire discourse; it is the root of the diverging, but orderly, branches of the work.

But while many of these manuals demonstrate that the inception determines the disposition, almost none even contemplates the possibility that the inception might literally become the disposition. No medieval theoretical work, in other words, adequately describes the form of *Piers Plowman,* a poem whose disposition is composed of repeated beginnings. The poem embodies perhaps the most extensive demonstration in medieval literature that the disposition depends radically upon the beginning: its order *is* beginning.

Few treatises acknowledge the possibility that a work could embody several beginnings. The nearest approximation I have found, in fact, comes from a discussion of *inventio* rather than *dispositio.* In his *Ars praedicandi* Thomas Waleys seems to suggest that a preacher can impose a beginning for a sermon different from the one that he originally conceived, or even impose a new, "higher" beginning once he arrives at the thema. Having discovered

> quod debet esse fundamentum totius introductionis, non credat praedicator quod necesse sit ibi inchoare introductionem. Immo, hoc erit in sua potestate. Nam, habito fundamento, potest, si vult, ibi inchoare et procedere versus thema introductionem. Et expedit sic facere. Tamen, hoc non obstante, cum ad thema pervenerit, potest, si vult, cogitare de altiori principio et, stante tota deductione quam excogitavit et invenit, altius inchoare.
>
> [what must be the foundation of the whole introduction, the preacher should not believe that it is necessary to begin the introduction there. On the contrary, this will be in his power. For, once he has the foundation, he can, if he wishes, begin there, and proceed to the introduction [of the] theme. And that is what he ought to do. With this out of the way, when he reaches his theme he is able, if he wishes, to think about a loftier beginning and, when the entire *deductio* that he has excogitated is in place, to begin in a higher place.][26]

This passage offers an exemplary account of the *modus agendi* of *Piers Plowman,* with its evident willingness to conceive of better beginnings and impose them on the emerging structure of the work. But Thomas Waleys does not attempt to account for the form that such a strategy would engender, and his suggestion does not appear in other preaching manuals. The only other discussions of multiple beginnings appear in Hexaemeral works, which present them as a heterodox threat to the primal unity of divine creation and the unity of the church itself. Boniface VIII implicitly admits that multiple beginnings would threaten his authority, and condemns any belief in them as heretical. His bull *Unam Sanctam* argues that those who question the divine origin of papal authority directly challenge divine authority, since

> [q]uicunque igitur huic potestati a Deo sic ordinatae resistit, Dei ordinatione resistit, nisi duo, sicut Manichaeus, fingat esse principia, quod falsum et haereticum iudicamus, quia, testante Moyse, non in principiis, sed in principio caelum Deus creavit et terram.
>
> [whoever, therefore, resists this power, established in this form by God, resists God's ordering, if he imagines that there are two principles, as Manichaeus did, a thing we judge false and heretical because, as Moses testifies, God created the heavens and the earth not in the beginnings but in the beginning.][27]

Boniface appeals to heterodoxy to reach the reductio ad absurdum of the argument against absolute papal authority; no sensible person would argue that God or institutions have multiple beginnings. His apparently irrelevant invocation of the Mosaic account of creation underlies an unspoken assumption that multiple beginnings always violate unity. The beginning of the world is the exemplary account of all beginnings, and the only beginning to which any subsequent event ought to be or can, in any theologically or philosophically serious way, be traced.

In his *Hexaemeron,* which provides one of the likely sources for the passage in *Unam Sanctam,* Robert Grosseteste demonstrates more explicitly how all beginnings can be reduced to a single beginning. The first book of the *Hexaemeron,* which is essentially an exposition of the first line of Genesis, "[I]n principio creavit Deus celum et terram," criticizes philosophers who follow the lead of Plato and Aristotle in proposing that the world had multiple beginnings.[28] In what Grossesteste himself calls a "distinctio principii,"[29] he attempts to demonstrate the difference between what beginnings, as grammarians might say, signify "realiter," and what they signify "accidentaliter." Since several things are signified by the word *principium*, it may be possible to talk of beginnings, but that convention is really only the result of applying linguistic distinctions to philosophical accidents. All beginnings refer back to a single, fundamental beginning:

> Simpliciter autem principium omnium dicitur divina virtus ut primum movens et efficiens omnia. Omnes autem hii dicti intellectus principii[30] coacervantur in hoc nomine "principium," cum dicitur: *In principio fecit Deus celum et terram.*
>
> [Moreover, simply expressed, the beginning of all things is said to be the divine virtue, that is, the first moving and the maker of all things. But all these terms for the meanings of beginnings are lumped together under this term "beginning" when it is said: "In the beginning God made the heaven and the earth."][31]

Medieval thinking generally abhors multiple beginnings for a similar reason: they threaten order and intelligibility. Grosseteste admits the existence of several kinds of beginning, but argues that they coalesce into a single kind. He produces a unified field theory of beginnings by suggesting that, while accidental kinds of beginning signify different accidental things, they all signify the First Beginning, the "principi[um] temporis" (the beginning of time).[32] He subordinates the beginning principle of the work of art, too, to the first principle of divine creation: it is merely one of the many kinds of mundane beginning that are possible: "Dicitur eciam ars 'principium' artificii" (*ars* therefore is said to be the "beginning" of artifice).[33] Even the work of art has implicitly a single beginning. By "ars" Grosseteste seems to mean the conception or the requisite skill to undertake a work,[34] an art of beginning that is necessary to all art. A new beginning carries with it a new teleology of perfection also, the principle of a wholly different work than the one already begun. For a new beginning to be effective it must either make anew or fill in for a beginning that is inadequate or absent altogether. The Wycliffite observation about the foolishness of those who attempt to supplement the original ordinances of Christ applies equally to those who attempt to impose subsequent beginnings: "[W]isere men moten ordeyne first, & lesse wis moten worche þer-aftir."[35] Langland's procedure in *Piers Plowman,* in which he must necessarily "worche þer-aftir," not only makes his activity "lesse wis" than it should be, but also opposes some of the fundamental tendencies of political, ecclesiastical, and literary theory. Paradoxically, it does so in order to examine the ethical demands that writing can make in a way that conventional medieval form precludes, despite its alignment of poetry with ethics. Most medieval poetry is deeply interested in the response of the individual will to its implicit doctrine, but that response is something that can only be represented in the margins of a poem, in commentaries that gauge the effect of the poem on the reader's faculties. *Piers Plowman* exemplifies and makes even more explicit these perennial concerns of medieval rhetorical practice by locating these marginal concerns at the center of the poem. The marginal topic of the will and the "threshold" topic of beginning—of the incipit—are not only central, but bound up with each other in a way that hints at their fundamental interdependence in other medieval works.

The will is a recurring topic in classical and medieval rhetorical theories of beginning and in prologues to commentaries on authors. Cicero's argument that the purpose of the exordium is to capture the good will of the audience becomes one of the standard medieval definitions of the purpose of a work's beginning, particularly in dictaminal treatises. By the twelfth century, indeed, most dictaminal treatises referred to the exordium simply as the *captatio benevolentiae*.[36] Some of these works suggest that the *captatio benevolentiae* is an aspect of the *forma tractatus:* it determines the disposition of the words in order to influence the disposition of the audience. As an anonymous treatise suggests, the securing of good will depends upon the fit ordering of the words: "Beneuolentie captatio est quedam apposita uerborum ordinatio recepientis animum conpetenter alliciens" (The capturing of good will is a certain appropriate ordering of words that successfully entices the mind of the recipient).[37] The beginning act of capturing the good will assumes, at times, the importance of *dispositio:* it can determine not only the order of the subsequent work, but also its *forma tractandi,* as it does in an anonymous commentary on Statius's *Thebaid:*

> Et notandum quod satis ydonee quasi quodam prefatione prescribitur breviter partiendo in tria, scilicet in propositionem, invocationem, et narrationem, prohemiorum officia eleganter exequendo. Nam lectores benivoles, dociles, et attentos facit. . . . Nam tunc quoddammodo manifestatur modus tractandi, et in modo tractandi sunt semper lectores benivoli.

> [And it is worth mentioning that it is suitable that almost every preface be briefly outlined by being split into three parts—that is, into the proposition, invocation, and narration by elegantly following the functions of introductions. For it makes the readers well-disposed, docile, and attentive.... For thus the *modus tractandi* is made clear in some way or other, and readers are always [made] well disposed through [the disclosures of] the *modus tractandi*.][38]

In later medieval theory, the *captatio benevolentiae* has consequences that extend well past the beginning of the work. As prologues to biblical commentaries often point out, the scriptural modes of discourse proceed by example rather than argument, since they appeal to the will rather than the intellect. Bonaventure's comments are representative: "Quia enim haec doctrina est, ut boni fiamus et salvemur; et hoc non fit per nudam considerationem, sed potius per inclinationem voluntatis; ideo Scriptura divina eo modo debuit tradi, quo modo magis possemus inclinari" (For this is the teaching: that we should become good and be saved; and this does not come about through mere consideration, but rather through the inclination of the will. Therefore divine Scripture ought to be handed on in this way, whereby we may better be able to be swayed).[39] The inclination of the will is the primary concern of Scripture, which as a whole performs the same role that an opening *captatio benevolentiae* does in rhetoric.

Some preaching manuals consolidate the two methods of informing the will, making the capturing of the audience's good will at the beginning of a sermon the beginning of the progress of the will toward salvation.[40] As Alain of Lille puts it,

> praedicator debet captare benevolentiam auditorum a propria persona per humilitatem, et a rei quam proponit utilitate, dicendo, se iis proponere verbum Dei, ut fructum faciat in mentibus eorum, non ad terrenum emolumentum, sed ad provectum et profectum eorum ... ut eorum animi informentur.

> [the preacher must capture the good will of the listeners by his own character through humility and by the usefulness of the matter that he puts forward, by preaching, if he is presenting to them the word of God, in order to produce fruit in their minds,

> not for earthly gain but for their advancement and progress to inform their minds.][41]

Alain grafts classical rhetorical doctrine onto a theology of voluntarist salvation, making the opening *captatio benevolentiae* the metaphorical root of a tree that brings forth the fruit of a perfected will. His strategy has certain affinities with the opening of passus 18 in the C Text, in which Liberum Arbitrium captures Will's good will by laughing and leading him "forth with tales" to the Cor-hominis, where the Tree of "Trewe-love" grows. The fruit, which comes forth from the blossoms of "Benygne-speche," is the perfected will achieving "Werkes / Of holynesse, of hendynesse of help-hym-that-neodeth, / The whiche is callid *Caritas*" (C 18.12–14). As in Alain's treatise, the journey to the tree begins with the favorable disposing of the will (in this case by Liberum Arbitrium, an aspect of the will itself) and ends with the fruition of the redeemed will.

"Benynge-speche" inaugurates the *captatio benevolentiae* of Charity's project, as the adjective "benynge" itself suggests.[42] The rules that regulate the methods of *captatio benevolentiae* in the exordium, indeed, define what this "benynge speche" might be and the nature of courtly language equally well.[43] The language in an exordium should be elevated but not unintelligible; it should be pleasant and not harsh; and it should not be arrogant.[44] At its most effective, the language of a good exordium will disarm its audience. It may even become a means of exploiting the audience, of diverting their good will toward bad purposes, just as we see happen in passus 2 of the A Text with Meed, who is "a-maystred with . . . myri wordis / That heo graunteth to goo with a *good wille*" (A 2.124–25).[45] The language at the beginning of a discourse is itself morally neutral: what determines its effect is the intention of the speaker, as the Samaritan in Will's later dream suggests:

> . . . þere nys sik ne sory, ne noon so muche wrecche
> That he ne may louye, and hym like, and lene of his herte
> Good wille, good word [boþe], wisshen and willen
> Alle manere men mercy and forȝifnesse . . .
>
> (B 17.350–53)

The speaker's will is what selects and modulates the language he uses. *Piers Plowman* seems to dramatize this twofold aspect of the will in the inception of a discourse by having Liberum Arbitrium lead Will to the Tree of True Love. Liberum Arbitrium's method demonstrates that the "benigne" words of an exordium may even include straightforward narrative: he captures Will's good will in precisely the same way that Ranulph Higden recommends capturing an audience's good will at the beginning of a sermon—by telling a tale "insolitum et subtile et curiosum" (unusual, subtle, and skillful).[46] Ranulph's description might also, of course, fit the tale of *Piers Plowman* itself. As a tale cast explicitly in the mode of poetry, it operates primarily upon the affections.

Patience's riddle, which is especially "insolitus et subtilis et curiosus" and which the Doctor of Divinity calls a "disours tale" (B 13.172), captures, for one, the good will of Conscience, who argues in turn that the will or intention behind the discourse helps to inform the audience's will. The riddle, he claims, informs the will more effectively than does the Doctor's brand of scholastic argument:

> For al þat Pacience me profreþ proude am I litel.
> Ac þe wil of þe wye and þe wil of folk here
> Haþ meued my mood to moorne for my synnes.
> The goode wil of a wight was neuere bouȝt to þe fulle,
> For þer [is] no tresour [þerto] to a trewe wille.
> (B 13.189–93)

As James Simpson points out, the "effect of the prophecy on Conscience is affective: through the goodwill, if not the clear sense, of the speaker, his own will is, he says, moved to 'moorne for my synnes.'"[47] The riddle, that is, creates a rhetorical model that the poem itself falls short of. *Piers Plowman* does not declare its own intention clearly enough to capture the good will of its chief protagonist, whose main activity is the search for the proper mode to inform his will. The poem's precipitous beginning offers few clues to its intention for Will's disposition. Indeed, as John Bowers has argued, a large part of *Piers Plowman* concerns its chief protagonist's refusal to exercise his will, his willingness to accede to acedia.[48] The poem begins much more rapidly than comparable dream visions, with the narrator of the C Text sliding into a slumber after only seven lines. The body of *Piers Plowman*, not just its beginning, narrates the attempt to influence the will. But the poem itself associates the will with a particularly active beginning: the creation of the world, when God "bigan al of his gode wille" (C 20.221). Its failure to represent "good wille" at the beginning, its failure to observe the conventional gestures of capturing the will, intimates that the poem will be at least partly concerned with the failure of the will.

Both the language and form of the poem, as Simpson has shown, relate to the topic of the will. Like Joseph Wittig, he argues that the formation of the will, which is the central psychological and theological drama of the poem, is closely linked to the formation of the poem itself: "As the formal modes of the poem change to 'inform' the will ('ad informationem affectus'), so too . . . does the poem itself take its own, poetic form."[49] Simpson's examples of this "poetic form" are primarily local instances of mimetic expression (such as Patience's riddle), which demonstrate the *modi revelativus, exhortativus,* and *parabolicus,* or the form of the *quaestio* in the Meed episode, which interrogates the way in which categories of authority are defined.[50]

But the relation between the formation of the will and the formation of the poem itself becomes the subject at other points of *Piers Plowman.* The Prologue in the B and C Texts impugns minstrels specifically because they "[Fonden] hem fantasies" (B Prol. 36), although they are capable of exercising their wills "to werken if [hem liste]" (B Prol. 37). The making of poetry becomes a kind of sloth, the negation of the real work toward which the will should be directed. The passage containing the confession of Sloth in the C Text, indeed, challenges the validity of poetry by linking it to a deficiency of the will. The "braunches þat bryngeth man to sleuthe" (C 7.69) include those who have "no likynge to lerne ne of oure lord to here / But harlotrie and horedom or elles of som wynnynge . . . [they] wol not here but wordes of murthe" (C 7.74–78). Those who prefer entertaining to edifying matter are slothful because they do not exercise their wills when they ought to. In the light of Will's own apology to Imaginatif for the making of the poem, that it is an entertainment that interposes itself between cares (B 12.20–24), the indictment of "murthes" as slothful raises profound problems for the form of a poem that is fundamentally concerned with the reformation of the will.

On the highest level, however, the disposition of the poem itself interferes with the disposition of the will. Merely by making the poem, Langland suggests, he may be invalidating its moral purpose. Episodes that concern the informing of the will lead directly to perplexing questions about the form of the work itself, as in the confession of Sloth or Imaginatif's questioning of Will. The disrupted episode, which Middleton sees as characteristic of Langland's mode of composition, often involves such questions about the work's utility and form, but it also has important implications for the body of the work. The poem's successive beginnings are the responses to such moments of disruption, and they themselves constitute the form of the work, its *forma tractatus.* One of the subjects of the poem in that sense is the conditions of its making, but it is a subject that profoundly involves the will, just as every classical and medieval work that is aware of its own beginning involves the will of its audience. What distinguishes this poem, perhaps, is the degree to which the conventional appeal to an audience initiates an extended meditation on the ethics, and not merely the form, that such an appeal makes both possible and compelling. We will see, in the next chapter, that the intimate link between the compositional problems posed by writing (or beginning) a work and the ethical problems posed by engaging in the act of writing is represented in several ways through the Middle Ages. None of these figures will be surprising, because what the poem does is not surprising at the local level, at the level of a particular beginning. What is surprising is the way that these figures of beginning massively pervade the entire poem, in just the way that the customary form of a medieval beginning pervades the entire poem.

THEMA

[Theme, topic, subject; position of heavenly bodies at the moment of birth; the beginning of a sermon]

The Book That Makes Itself

There is no difference between what a book talks about and how it is made.

—Gilles Deleuze and Félix Guattari,
A Thousand Plateaus

It should be abundantly clear by now that, in terms of its use of beginnings to order the poem, *Piers Plowman* is a complicated and aberrant text. Yet its preoccupation with beginnings reiterates its location in history as a textual product of the High Middle Ages; it is a poem that, like most others, mirrors the outward world, the world that is itself a divinely authored book. If *Piers Plowman* is a book about the world, however, it is a world far stranger than those in other medieval books. Its peculiar *ordo* certainly does not reflect the measured calculus of Augustine's and Boethius's architectonically minded creator. Its rebeginnings suggest less a divine, authoritative fiat than divagation and deviation.

The poem's structure of reiterated beginnings counters a dominant image of the book in the Middle Ages: the tree. Medieval encyclopedias, in fact, point out that the word "codex," which originally meant a tree trunk, recalls the book's origin as a collection of wooden tablets. The material of the book, in other words, is homologous with the material of the tree. But the book and the tree are also alike in form: the codex is like a tree, says Hugh of Saint-Victor, because it contains a "multitudinem librorum quasi ramorum" (a multitude of books as if of branches).[1] The implicit metaphor of a central trunk with radiating branches is, in many ways, the most important aspect of the analogy. Cassiodorus makes absolutely clear the connection between a strong investment in the authoritative beginnings and origins that are signified by the *radix* and installed by the foundational operations of the book. For him, as for Langland, grammar is the "grounde of alle," and an intriguingly overdetermined discussion of that beginning elides with the account of the book's origin we have been discussing:

> Intentus nobis est de arte grammatica, sive rhetorica vel de disciplinis aliqua breviter velle conscribere; quarum rerum principia necesse est nos inchoare; dicendumque prius est de arte grammatica, quae est videlicet origo et fundamentum liberalium litterarum. Liber autem dictus est a libro, id est arboris cortice.
>
> [It is our intention to write some things briefly about the subject of grammar, both about rhetoric and about individual disciplines. We must first sketch the beginnings of these things; first, we must write about the subject of grammar, which is surely the origin and foundation of liberal arts. For a book *[liber]* comes from the *libro*—that is, from the bark of the tree.][2]

Although the book contains multiplicity, it does so by means of constraint and subordination, literally restraining it. Branches refer back to a central trunk or to a single origin that mediates that multiplicity. In this passage, the tree is the image of subordination to the discursive domain of Grammar, that pedagogical tyrant of the symbolic order who is memorialized in dozens of illustrations and carvings holding a switch over the backs of unwilling students. That the influence of the book begins in literally physical discipline is only the most visible sign of the book's disciplinary influence. Even discussions of material practices outside the bounds of the book refer back to the symbolic field of the book. Colloquies on the occupations, such as Aelfric's, interrogate the linguistic development of the students using them, not the range of practices developed by the workers being described. As I have been suggesting, the tree is perhaps the dominant image of the book's own linguistic development, a model of *ordinatio* that helps to organize texts as diverse as Hugh of Saint-Victor's *De arca Noe morali* and *The Parson's Tale*.[3]

As I will argue in this chapter, the rebeginnings of *Piers Plowman* engender a radically different notion of the book, one that, in fact, does not depend upon the central metaphor of the *radix* at all. The poem undoes the connection between the book and the tree, reformulating the link, indeed, between the book and the world. As such, it is perhaps best described as rhizomatic, a kind of writing that develops on its own initiative, independent from a mooring in an authoritative origin. As Gilles Deleuze and Félix Guattari say, almost perfectly describing the procedure of *Piers Plowman,* a "rhizome may be broken, shattered at a given spot, but it will start up again on one of its old lines, or on new lines."[4] In *Piers Plowman,* the originary and originating elements of the tree-book break loose; they form the developing domain of the book, a domain that equally, and infinitely, implicates social and textual formation. Undoing the arborescent development of the book, it also undoes the means by which the book integrates individuals into preassigned places. The poem implicates its subjects, rather, in beginning and becoming.

Piers Plowman is not a book about the world but a book about beginning the world. Its important subjects are inextricable from the gestures of beginning and rebeginning. By the same token, the book's gestures of beginning are the same thing as its own most important topics. As the epigraph for this chapter says, there is no difference between what a book talks about and the way it is made. Some of the poem's important figures of beginning—most notably the plowman and Will (or the will)—not only represent but are produced, in the root sense of the word, led forth, by the poem's deep desire to begin significantly, to mark the important instant of beginning, but also to make the instant the point of signification itself. This fundamental contradiction is played out in the figures associated with beginning, figures who contain the contradictions of activity and inactivity, hope and hopelessness, and responsibility and nostalgia that are summoned up by the possibility of beginning again.

This contradiction is written across the body of the poem itself. The new beginnings are both a part of the disposition of the work and the primary obstacles to the completion of its disposition. The ruptures in the work's form are its essential mode of epistomological disclosure, and its inchoate form is the symptom of Langland's fundamental question:

> "What must I do to be read?" It is the surface of Langland's work, with all its fissures and new starts, both as a story and as a much-revised text, that reveals to us his implicit answers to this practical question. . . . What we learn by following the lit-

> eral level... is not what Langland set out to display, a conception of truth or of Christian well-doing, but his idea of "making."[5]

The narrative ruptures of the poem call attention to the narrativity of beginning, to the profound association of beginning and writing. Apart from the questions the poem raises about the form that the ethical life should take, it raises questions about the possible forms that a poem can take. Each new beginning signifies an attempt to begin the poem again, to resow the germ that fails to become a completed form and that also reproduces the incontrovertible power of beginning. In this chapter I will be discussing some of the powerful medieval images of beginning that are also linked with beginning the work of writing. In most medieval works these images appear in prologues as signs of the literal beginning of the work. In *Piers Plowman* they appear throughout the work and suggest its ceaseless concern with a moment that most texts are able to leave behind.

Imaginatif's famous indictment of Will in passus 12 of the B Text partly concerns this aspect of the poem's *modus procedendi,* implying that the state of the poem is the consequence of a guiding intelligence that, as a Wycliffite said of those who "ordeigne after," is "lesse wis" than it ought to be. Imaginatif accuses Will of neglecting his salvation for the sake of his writing: "þow medlest þee wiþ makynges and myȝtest go seye þi sauter, / And bidde for hem þat ȝyueþ þee breed, for þer ar bokes y[n]owe" (B 12.16–17). The unfolding disposition of the poem compromises the order that Will's life ought to have, interposing itself between Will and the imperatives of Christian ethics. As Imaginatif points out later in the passus, "[p]atriarkes and prophetes" also indicted earlier men of learning for holding the "selkouþes [marvels] þat þei seiȝen" in high esteem:

> ... hir wordes [ne] hir wisdomes [w]as but a folye;
> A[s] to þe clergie of crist counted it but a trufle:
> *Sapiencia huius mundi stulticia est apud deum.*
> (B 12.137–38a)

As the writers of medieval romances point out, making a record of "selkouþes" is often their impetus for committing them to parchment.

Imaginatif's severely Platonic critique of the writing of poetry concerns especially the marvelous and legendary subjects that were the particular province of alliterative poetry. His critique includes, of course, the poem in which he appears, whose beginning tells us that a "ferly" [a wonder, a marvel] prompts its writer to start it. He is implicated in the foolishness of the bookish who allow the making of books to interfere with the ordering of their lives. Like those who have altered the ordinances of the church, those who become entangled in the wisdom of this world create disorder by attempting to impose order on their material. They are working "aftir" the true ordinance has been established. "Making" implicitly opposes the dictation of the Holy Spirit, who should be the true exemplar for the writing of books: "Alþouȝ men made bokes [þe maister was god] / And seint Spirit þe Samplarie, & seide what men sholde write" (B 12.101–02).

Imaginatif's critique implies that Will is undertaking a work that is extraneous, that merely repeats other material: "þer are bokes y[n]owe / To telle men what dowel is" (B 12.17–18).[6] But these books, tellingly, fail to make an appearance in the rest of the poem, which is plagued by the search for Dowel. The book of the poem is, in some sense, the book for which the poem is searching. The poem echoes, in its multiple and elaborately staged beginnings, the only beginning that is not troubled by inconclusion and disorder. But its repeated beginnings suggest more than an optimistic project of subcreation. They also suggest the provisional, disordered nature of what the poem is undertaking. The poem's concern with the formal and moral integrity of "making" is an aspect of its own interrogation of the category of literature in relation to sacred writing. Underwriting the poem's search for the imperatives that govern the well-ordered Christian life is a preoccupation with the problems that the poem itself raises for the poet, a troubling awareness that every human beginning is both a triumph and a failure.

To a significant degree, the beginnings of each major section of the poem show the dreamer attempting to make a truly good beginning, to get beyond these problems. But they also show him becoming increasingly entrapped by beginning, by a greater awareness that beginning again merely disrupts the poem's ethical and narrative impulses. The figure of Will, so prominent in these rebeginnings, enacts the predicament of the poem's intention, willing to begin a work but unwilling to begin it just once.

THE MAKING AND UNMAKING OF WILL

If the first beginnings in *Piers Plowman* depict the entanglement of Will in the body of the poem, showing him falling into the slumber of acedia as he "babbles" over his prayers, subsequent beginnings record Will's further attempts, and almost immediate failures, to properly align his will with the active demands that the promise of salvation makes. Further, the soporific power of "babbling" suggests a recurrent theme in most of these beginnings—the failure of "Will" to manage the noise of the world, a noise that lulls him to sleep and is the proximate cause for the resumption of the poem. Each resumption, that is, begins with a staging of the poem's own beginning as the search for a technique by which to manage the noise of the world, a technique that will be neither *turpiloquio* nor mere "mynstralcye." The action of "Will" at these moments of resumption suggests that the management of the poem, too, is at stake, as the immediate, declared object of this particular will, which is responsible for managing the noise of the world in the form we have before us. As we discover later in the poem, in passus 17 of the C Text, to be precise, the will is also partially responsible for the predicament of the narrator at these points. In that passage one of the reflexes of the complicated subject of the will, Liberum Arbitrium, narrates the great evangelical imperative but interpolates his own observation about the involvement of both the will and of language in it:

> *Ite in universum mundum,* sethe ȝe wilne þe name
> To be p[astor]s and preche the passioun of iesus,
> And as hymsulue saide so to lyue and deye:
> *Bonus Pastor animam suam ponit pro ouibus suis &c.*
> Hit is reuthe to rede how riht holy men lyuede,
> How they deffoule[d] here flesche, forsoke here owne wille,
> Fer fro [k]uthe and fro kyn euele yclothed ȝeden,
> Baddeliche ybedded, no boek but Consience
> Ne no rychesse but þe rode to reioysen hem ynne.
> (C 17.191–198)

The *imitatio Christi* demands a repudiation of the individal will—or more precisely, a translation of it, in which a new will is assumed, traced in the passage from the desire for simple designation ("pastors" or "prelates," as Pearsall has it in his edition) to the performance of the word, to "preche the passioun of iesus," narrating Christianity's constitutive act of willing passivity. The passage also provides a kind of conspectus of the various acts with which "Will" begins his assumption of the word, from the guise of the shepherd to wandering in the world. Liberum Arbitrium describes the consequences of setting aside one's own will to undertake God's will. The beginnings of the poem's dreams imitate these consequences closely, but they are largely the result of Will's volitional deficiency, the result of his refusal to act properly. Although these beginnings chronicle the poem's successive attempts to dispose the will successfully, Will comes dangerously close to forsaking his own will for no purpose. Liberum Arbitrium's vision of the ideally disposed will may provide a model for Will to follow, but the beginnings of the dreams also allow precisely these signs to be interpreted as a lack of will, as the volitional deficiency that John Bowers argues is one of the poem's fundamental themes. If grammar in the Middle Ages was sometimes defined as the imposition by the will of sense on noise, then the typical beginning of *Piers Plowman* narrates a failure of will that describes an auditory rather than a grammatical, or narrating, subject, with its incapacity to manage its own emergent discourse, collapsing into slumber, allowing itself to be delighted, distracted (taken from its own *tractus*) by the bird song he hears, and fantasizing (or allowing us to fantasize) that it "made" him sleep—a denial of his volition, but also an implicit fiction of his own "making" of story and self. Yet this initiation of the third vision is disingenuous, if the cases of Rousseau, Saussure, and Lévi-Strauss are emblematic of a general desire to hear sound at the beginning of things. Everything else about this poem tells us that we continually need to have recourse to grammar, "the grounde of alle," yet at the inception of one of its greatest moments of self-disclosure, that of the "kynde name" of Will, we are distracted into thinking that we are also hearing the "kynde" sounds of the world in the background shaping, if not precipitating, the poem—a fantasized account of the poem's own origination as a version of the mythic origin of language out of natural sound. But the poem's pretense of impetuousness and susceptibility at the inception of the dreams, especially because that initial scene comes increasingly to be associated with the immediate topic of the will in the dream, is the result of a carefully forged series of impostures that playfully echo and are echoed in the variously self-canceling and self-reinforcing intersections of the dream, the dreamer, the narrator, and the poem.

The dreamer's persistent itinerancy, which may remind us of the conventional openings of *chansons d'aventures,* feebly enacts the commandment from Liberum Arbitrium's passage to go forth into the whole world. In the Prologue he tells us that he has gone "wide in þis world," not to preach, but "wondres to here" (B Prol. 4). Even there his traveling is ludicrously far from an evangelical campaign and close to pointless errancy: by line 7 he is "wery forwandred." He is unable to sustain even his wandering for very long at the beginning of the second dream: "Ac er I hadde faren a furlong feyntise me hente / That I ne myȝte ferȝer a foot for defaute of slepynge" (B 5.5–6). In passus 8, Will continues to go "widewher... walkyng myn one" (B 8.62–63), although the passus opens with him engaged, for the first time, on a specific search: "I romed aboute... for to seke dowel" (B 8.1–2). From that point on, the wandering at the beginning of dreams signifies less an aimless desire for "wondres" than the agitation of his own mind, the tumultuous wondering in which he engages. The "ferlyes" that have befallen the dreamer have transmuted him into a "freke þat [fey] were" (B 13.2), whose walking is characterized by his presumed mental state:

> And I awaked þerwiþ, witlees nerhande,
> And as a freke þat [fey] were forþ gan I walke
> In manere of a mendynaunt many yer after
> (B 13.1–3)[7]

In passus 18 Will gives almost no information about the location or duration of his wandering: "Wolleward and weetshoed wente I forþ after / As a recchelees renk þat [reccheþ of no wo], / And yede forþ lik a lorel al my lif tyme" (B 18.1–3). Like the figure of "Rechelesness" itself, the beginnings that portray Will as a lunatic wanderer are deeply ambiguous. On the one hand, they expose Will's lack of purpose, his *curiositas* over "wondres" lapsing into a mere mimicry of the action of roaming around seeking curiosities. On the other hand, these beginnings chronicle Will's increasing alienation and detachment from the world. Like the holy men of Liberum Arbitrium's passage, Will is "[b]addeliche ybedded." Only in passus 5 of the C Text does Will dream while in bed. Elsewhere, he begins his dreams where he can: "[v]nder a brood bank by a bourn[e] syde" (B Prol. 8); "vnder a lynde vpon a launde" (B 8.65); in church, "In myddes of þe masse" (B 19.4). Like the Son of Man, Will has nowhere to rest his head.

Although these beginnings really say more about Will's sloth than they do about his asceticism, they reiterate the theme of alienation that inaugurates many of the dreams. The dreamer is solitary, ostracized by society or shunning it. The initial setting of the dreams themselves often intensifies this alienation: "I was in a wildernesse, wiste I neuere where" (B Prol. 12). In passus 8, this wilderness becomes the wilderness in which he finds himself wandering *before* he even begins to dream. And in passus 11 the dreamer is carried away ("I was ravysshed right there—for Fortune me fette") into a *regio dissimilitudinis,* the "lond of longyngge." It is both the image of his interior faculties and an evocation of the whole mundane state of exile, a place that Chaucer's *Balade of Good Conseil* describes with the word that Langland uses: "here is no home; here nys but wyldernesse."[8] Except for the beginning of passus 5 in the C Text, Will, again like Liberum Arbitrium's holy men, is "fer fro kyth and kyne." As Bowers points out, the wilderness may reflect the fundamental disorder and aridity of Will's own spiritual life, and his "lack of fear upon entering it suggests that grave problems also reside in his failure to estimate the danger of the place and to recognize the aptness of his receiving, personally, these visions of public corruption and spiritual chaos."[9] One of the ethical problems that informs the poem itself is precisely the will's improper disposition at the beginning.

Indeed, Will's own deliberate self-presentation at the beginning of dreams is both precipitate and indistinct. Almost all of the beginnings show Will assuming an identity largely dictated by the clothing he describes. For the most part, those beginnings recount how Will goes about, like Liberum Arbitrium's holy men, "euele yclothed," beginning the entire poem, indeed, dressed as a hermit. The dreamer apparently intends his accounts of the clothes he wears at the beginnings of dreams to establish his identity. But in most cases the identity he assumes displaces his actual identity. His observation that he is "yclothed as a Lollare" in passus 5 of the C Text, for instance, probably does not mean that he actually is a Lollard, especially when he goes on to describe how he is "lytel ylet by" by the Lollards and "lewede eremytes" themselves. Indeed, this last category of false religious suggests that his identity at the beginning of the poem also involves dissimulation. Many of the other descriptions of his identity at the beginning of dreams are imprecise, phrased, like the two descriptions in the Prologue and passus 5 of the C Text, as analogies: "*as* a freke þat [fey] were" (B 13.2); "in *manere* of a mendynaunt" (B 13.3); "[w]olleward and weetshoed . . . *as* a recchelees renk" (B 18.1–2); "*lik* a lorel" (B 18.3). These analogues of identity objectify the dreamer's true identity as completely as do the descriptions of his clothing. Both kinds of description reveal little biographical information about the dreamer, but they establish his character at the inception of each dream. Even where the descriptions are particularly imprecise—does "in manere of a mendynaunt" mean that he wears a beggar's rags but does not beg, or simply that he begs?—they disclose a disparity between the subjective, "kynde" identity of the dreamer and the identity he assumes. Each dream begins with an act of impersonation, with an authentic, undisclosed identity displaced by a feigned identity.

The second line of the poem's beginning is probably the most dramatic example of Will's impersonation. It describes his attempt to acquire for himself an explicit disposition: "I shoop me into [a] shrou[d] as I a sheep weere" (B Prol. 2). The word "sheep," however, makes this identity as multivalent as many others that he assumes. Skeat argues that it means "shepherd," pointing out that almost all the C Text manuscripts have the reading "shepherde" and adducing several examples where the word "shepe" clearly means "shepherd."[10] But nowhere else in the poem does the word mean "shepherd"—the B and C texts even use the word "shepherd" itself several times, while the only time the word "sheep" appears elsewhere is in a hypermetric line in the B Text, from which George Kane and E. Talbot Donaldson drop it altogether in their edition (15.361). So the use of the word to mean "shepherd" is unusual, if not unprecedented: the only example the *Middle English Dictionary* cites is from *Piers Plowman*, and all of Skeat's examples are later than the B Text of *Piers Plowman*. But in the beginning of the poem it is clear that "shroudes" and "sheep" are in apposition with "habite" and "heremite," and equally clear that the word "sheep" is part of a complex of concerns about the role and nature of the prelacy, especially in Anima's extended disquisition in B 15 on the incongruities between priestly names and activities.

When read backward from the C Text, the obliterated and altered lines of the B Text in this passus amount to a spectral commentary on the nominating actions of the rebels of 1381, at least as they are understood in their letters. John Ball's assumed name, which he makes it quite easy to decode, of John Schep in Walsingham's letter makes explicit, or literalizes, the possibilities that are delicately balanced in Langland's reference to "pastors" and the *bonus pastor*—that is, that priests are like shepherds. But by assuming a name that inaugurates a different set of tensions Ball seems to have recalled the very tensions of the *Piers* passage between the value of naming and doing that is so much a central part of the passus in which "Piers þe Plowman" is finally named explicitly as *"Petrus id est Christus"* (15.211a). In that letter only, Ball's feigned name of John Schep is accompanied by a set of names that, as Steven Justice points out, signify labor: "johan þe mullere and johan carter." But they are also accompanied by "johan nameles," a walking oxymoron, but an oxymoron as "schep," the "som tyme seynte marie prest of ȝork," is an oxymoron, unless, of course, John Ball wanted, quite exceptionally, "schep" to mean "shepherd." But given the concatenated and sophisticated references to *Piers* in his letters, this can only mean that he is intentionally echoing the opening of *Piers*. But he is also apparently echoing the echoes of that opening in *Piers* itself, playing off of the self-concealing opening that raises right away the problem of *kynde* naming that is the larger reflex of the more specific problem here of the congruency of prelacies and their names. For John Ball has literally taken the name of *pastor*, but in the curiously antithetical form of the word that appears at the beginning of the poem. The other names that he conjures in his letter, it is true, signify manual labor, and implicitly a utopian agrarian community, but what may be more to the point is that he is conjuring names at all, and names that must be parsed and construed in ways that could, if pursued far enough, yield a miniature summa of late medieval grammatical theory, as indeed B 15—the passus that announces that grammar is "þe ground of al"—as a whole does, with its analogies of impression, marking, grammar (the "ground of al"), etymology, calculation, and grammatical construction itself, and its closing one in which the incipient faith of the heathen is based on the incipit of the Creed. The questions of the ontological and social status of names is obviously a pressing one in these letters generally as it is in the rising as a whole, and as it is in B 15. We can see how interested the passus is in the difficulties of naming properly, of understanding what a word signifies, of knowing how to act on written language, if we consider some of the changes Langland made to the passus *after* the rising had run its course.

These changes help to show how extensively the roots of John Ball's letters run into the heart of *Piers Plowman*'s interests and anxieties about its own status as an action of written language, as a form that is not yet performed. It further removes itself from the language of action in the letters by reining in the free-ranging play on the words "pastor" and "schep." In the otherwise authoritative C manuscript Huntington HM 143, the crucial name for prelates, "pastor," has been changed to "prelate" (C 17.192), and the hypermetric line "Shipmen and shepherdes þat wiþ shipe and sheep wenten" (B 15.361)[11] has been changed to "by þe seuene sterres" (C 17.95 in Pearsall) or "oþer witty peple" (Russell and Kane). One could argue that these changes are part of the same motive to render the C Text more politically inert, detaching the poem from more intimate association with John Ball's declaration of clerical status and his assumption of the tactics of the poem's complex acts of impersonation, except that the C version still begins with the impersonation of a "shep," whatever that should be taken to mean. But one change in the passus does signal the reviser's awareness of the poem's propensity to be read as a text about the political consequences of literacy and of the intertwined concerns of grammaticality and prelacy in this passus.[12] That change has everything to do with the poem's sensitivity to its own forms of circulation, to the ways in which it might be read—consider, especially, the beginning of passus 5 in the C Text.

The specific complaint in passus 15 of the B Text about the decline of grammaticality is directed against "þise newe clerkes" who cannot "versifie faire ne formaliche enditen, / Ne nauȝt oon among an hundred at an Auctour kan construwe" (373–75). Given the poem's later self-location in Cornhill, the use of grammaticality as a lightning rod of social turbulence is not only self-reflexive but also pitched toward and possibly originating from the center of grammatical studies in London. Saint Paul's itself is known to be a center for grammatical disputation, and disputation specifically concerning the scansion and construal of *auctores,* involving the teachers of grammar and metricists living in London. Many of them lived in the vicinity of the cathedral—and therefore of the producers of books. At least one of the circle was known as Anthony de Monte Granario: in other words, Cornhill, where another "magister docens primitivam scientiam" lived—as did William Langland.[13] The specificity and formality of the poem's allusion to grammatical study at this point, then, is not surprising, although it may be surprising to learn of the urgent presence of a clerical audience not only for the poem but in it as well. What is surprising is that in revising the poem Langland has excised a reference to the other kind of text that provides a challenge to clerical literacy: "a lettre in any langage but in latyn or englissh" (376). Given the circulation of letters in the guise of clerical authority before the rising, it is possible that the satirical reference came to take on a specificity that Langland had not intended. The language that is conspicuously missing in this line, however, is French, a language not normally marked out as distinctively learned or abstruse, at least not any more than Latin was. Nor was French a much more suitable subject of grammatical study than English was at the end of the fourteenth century. Who, then, could Langland have meant by "þise newe clerkes," if not those in London formally teaching grammar or those (almost certainly) who worked for the Chancery, Exchequer, and King's Bench, all of which used French widely? The reference to Latin and English, and the exclusion of French, is almost certainly a pointed reference to the languages used in the Court of Common Pleas, the place where subjects of the king could take action against each other. In a move designed to make the process accessible to a larger part of the commons, a legislative initiative as early as 1362 required that its languages be restricted to English (in which pleas could be made) and Latin (in which the proceedings would be recorded).[14] This leveling gesture, presumably made so that more learned (and more powerful) participants could not befuddle their opponents by using French, did little to lay to rest an evident widespread hatred of the Court of Common Pleas. During the 1381 rising, most of the recent records of the court held in the Temple Church were burned by the rebels, as were a number of books and records owned by apprentices of the law living in the New Temple. This apparently improvised and incipient site of legal pedagogy for Common Pleas also became its earliest memorial, for these apprentices were killed by the rebels.[15] In an act of discriminating literacy of the kind that Justice has argued occurred extensively throughout England during the rising, the rebels had given that line in *Piers Plowman* a force that far outstripped the poem's relatively mild criticism of clerks who neglect the dictates of implicit and prescribed form, the immanent topic of grammaticality as a form of imagining and representing the rectitude of the world that they could, and should, have imbibed in the evidently lively world of London grammar.

So in his final revision of the poem Langland turns away from a dangerously broad world of circulating documents in which his own poem is turned outward to become a different work than it should have been. His complaint in the C Text at this point is directed much more specifically to the world immediately encompassed by the poem and against appropriations of the poem in the larger world. Now, he complains, among these "newe clerkes" there are hardly any who can "versifye faire or formallych endite / Ne construe *kyndelyche þat poetes made* (109–110; my emphasis). Rather than encompassing the *auctores* of the grammar school, the line concerns more *this auctor,* this poet, whose own poem had been construed so *unkyndely* and so massively by someone whose name was such a precise echo of the *unkyndely* name with which the poet himself begins the poem. In turning to those who can read the poem naturally, decoding its *kynde names,* Langland has revised this juncture of the poem into a compressed manifesto of the naturalness, the essentiality, of form. This one change suggests that the reason behind the other changes he has made in the poem is not so much to insist on a more regressive, reactionary, or conservative politics as it is to favor, if not compel, a closer scrutiny of the form of what he has written—that is to say, diverting us subtly but insistently to an intrinsic reading of his poem.[16]

And insist he does: the very first action in the poem—its first verb—is an intrinsic and imbricating act, but one that is inseparable from the unveiling, unfolding poem. "I shoop me into shroudes"—an initiating action that begins the shaping of the poem while plunging us into a world of dizzying inclosures and disclosures, of the double hermeneutics of implication and explication, of *Auflösung* and *Lösung*. What makes the poem unravel is also the ways in which it is raveled up in the integument of fictional impersonation, an integument that is constantly questioned—"what art [þ]ow?"asks Will of the "þouȝt" that has been pursuing him for seven years, his own thought confronting and challenging him in his own poem—and redefined, as (once again) in the beginning of C passus 5, where the integument of "making" is offered as a rationale for the avoidance of the larger and more politically and ethically pressing injunctions of "work." Elsewhere in the poem the verb "shapen" refers to deliberate and singular acts of creation, usually tinged with ethical and theological senses. When Gluttony decides, against allegorical type, to repent, he addresses his contrition to the "lord [þat] aloft art and alle lyues shope" (C 6.424). In a conjunction that suggests an even more intimate link between "shaping" and ethics, Wit laments that excessive drinking has prompted God to "forsaken hem þat he shoop to his liknesse" (B 9.67).[17] With these later senses echoing in our minds, we might imagine that Will's first action in the poem suggests both a deliberate act of creation and the disposition of an individual life. As I have suggested, however, what Will does create is an identity that is neither clearly in God's "liknesse" nor shaped by God himself. The ambiguities that his assumed identity engender suggest that it is anything but clearly shaped. Indeed, the act of "shaping" into "shroudes" portrays an act of dissimulation and disguise. Will has not so much shaped as abdicated his true identity. His "shroudes" are literally a fictional integument, the contrived veil of an undisclosed truth. The poem's very beginning shows its creator in the act of concealing his identity, burying his intentions in the opening lines of the poem. The poet's precipitate inauguration of the poem, his seemingly unmotivated act of concealment in "shroudes," effaces his own intention for the poem, his motivation for writing it. Instead, he submits his activity almost immediately to the dissimulation of the fictive guise.

This insistence on a complex fictionality that insists simultaneously and pervasively on truth, "the best treasure," marks the beginning of most of the successive dreams in the poem. Each of these echoes, without quite acknowledging, the opening of the poem, and in its separate way invokes the competing imperatives that lie behind the designation and disclosure of beginning. The mere presence of these dreams invokes the specter of a more devastating set of problems having to do with beginning, and, to a lesser extent, the more practical ones of what to do with patent beginnings that are manifestly ambiguous as beginnings. The introduction to the third dream in the poem, the beginning in which Will asks his own thought "What art þow?," is described in two A Text manuscripts as a separate prologue.[18] Portions of this "prologue," indeed, explicitly echo the beginning of the poem's ur-prologue. The time in both is "somer seson"; the first two lines provide details of the dreamer's clothing; in the ur-prologue the dreamer "went wide in this world," in passus 8 he "wente widewher"; the dream that follows both is described as "merveillous"; and in both cases the dreamer "lened" while he enjoyed the sensory stimuli of looking and listening that lull him to sleep.[19]

But the echo of the poem's opening in the third dream is more a revision than a reprise. It disrupts the narrative of discovery (concerning the identity of Dowel) by imposing a new beginning after the beginning of this passus, using a conventional alliterative dream *incipit,* and echoes the poem's first beginning. The strangely segmented echoes of the first beginning here (lines 1–2, 62–69) implicitly discount, both logically and formally, the validity of the dreamer's own experience:

> Blisse of þe briddes abide me made,
> And vnder a lynde upon a launde lened I a stounde
> To lythe the layes tho lovely foweles made.
> Murthe of hire mouthes made me ther to slepe;
> The merveillouseste metels mette me thanne
> That ever dremed [dr]ight in [doute], as I wene.
> (B 8.64–69)[20]

Once again, we are confronted with the poem's own fantasy of its origin as a seamless part of the natural sound of the world, its desperate and thwarted desire to supersede even the necessity for *kynde* naming and its problematics in a fictional narrative by equating language with nature itself. The natural sounds that here precipitate yet another dream are nearly the same sounds that cause the dreamer to fall asleep the first time, although their source is quite different. The "[m]urthe" of the birdsong in passus 8 is literally the agent of the dreamer's slumber: it "made me ther to slepe." The causal link between sound and sleep is not as clear syntactically in the Prologue, but it is nevertheless direct: "as I lay and lenede and loked on þe watres / I slombred into a slepyng, it sweyed so murye" (B Prol. 9–10). The "murye" sound of the brook itself, like the sound of "murthe" that the birds make, causes the dreamer to fall asleep. The same quality of sound—indeed, the same sound in the words for that quality—inaugurates each dream.

The poem's appeal to mimetic legitimation here is reinforced, if not undercut, by its simultaneous imitation of the poem's first beginning. The romance setting here is also a conventional opening: the gesture of pausing to listen to birdsong begins numerous *chansons d'aventures* and Middle English poems.[21] Such openings recapitulate the action that grammarians pointed to as the beginning of any meaningful discourse: the imposition of intellectual significance on the welter of natural, inarticulate sound, on what *Winner and Waster* describes as the "dadillyng of fewllys."[22] Sound is the natural material of language, but is inchoate until the intellect shapes it. The mind is, as the *Ars Meliduna* puts it, the "causa institucionis vocum" (the cause of the disposition of voices).[23] The imposition of order upon sound suggested to Priscian analogies with the foundation of political dynasties, but most grammarians treat the intellect's foundation of meaningful discourse only implicitly as a colonizing activity, frequently describing it as an *imponens* [an imposition].[24] The sound the dreamer hears is not merely an accident of observation, a consequence of happening to be in the right place at the right time: it is part of the background noise of the poem, the metonymy of the making of the poem itself. As Michel Serres has argued, it is noise that provokes us to attempt beginning in the first place, whether it is the beginning of cities, classes, concepts, or poems. We return to noise in order to silence it, rationalize it, convert it into sound, even if it falls short of the *harmonium mundi*. It is a constant provocation, and a meaningful beginning made from it is really more a cessation of multiplicity than the origin of a form.[25] Driven by medieval grammar's understanding of itself as the management of noise, by the appearance of natural noise that is the dominant trope of beginning in alliterative poetry, and by the larger imperative that Serres discusses, the successive beginnings of *Piers Plowman* return to this noisy site of origination (what Serres punningly refers to as a para-site). The beginning of passus 8 shows the dreamer playing a greater part in the creation of that poem. The dreamer's intellect begins to impose order on the beginning; he is less passive than he was in the beginning of the poem. In the beginning, indeed, the soporific effects of the "murye" sound of the brook steal upon him unobtrusively, almost by a kind of synesthesia: the alliteration of "as I lay and lenede and loked on the watres" (B Prol. 8) stresses his act of looking at, rather than listening to, the water, whose sound, almost as an afterthought, sends him to sleep abruptly in the next line: "I slombred into a slepyng, it sweyed so murye" (B Prol. 9).

In passus 9 the dreamer is engaged much more actively in the beginning events. This time he concentrates directly on the sound that will lull him to sleep—the "[b]lisse of the briddes." In most A Text manuscripts and in some of the B Text manuscripts, the dreamer stops not merely to listen, but also to "*lerne* þe laies þat louely [foulis] maden" (A 9.57). The dream is precipitated by a tutelary act, by the dreamer's desire to imitate what he hears. The dreamer is not merely listening to "layes," he is composing one himself.

The beginning of passus 8 records the activity of beginning a poem much more explicitly than does the diffident beginning of the entire poem. This new beginning, indeed, is ostentatiously, and perhaps self-consciously, "better" than the first beginning. In the Prologue, the dreamer describes the opening dream merely as a "merveillous swevene" (B Prol. 11); in the beginning of passus 8 he describes the dream to come as "[t]he merveillouseste metels . . . That ever dremed [dr]ight" (B 8.69–70). The topos of "outdoing" is a conventional opening gesture,[26] but its claims here only challenge the claims that the opening of the poem itself makes. Poems rarely try to outdo themselves. Such challenges to the validity of earlier experience, couched in the same terms used to describe that earlier experience, are more characteristic of anxious influence than of the dilation of one's own creation.[27] The different beginnings in *Piers Plowman* challenge not only the integrity of the claims that the narrator or the poet himself makes, but also the integrity of the poem's structure.[28] The beginning of passus 8 challenges the status that the beginning of the Prologue acquires simply by coming first. If the third dream is actually the "merueillouseste," the merely "merueillouse" dream of the Prologue is now simply the first dream of a series, and not the entire poem.

The introduction to the second dream in the A and B Texts subordinates the dream neatly into the scheme of the larger poem, but the revised introduction in the C Text emphasizes the discontinuity of beginnings. The B Text does not substantially revise the A Text, which actually emphasizes the continuity between the dreams by having the dreamer wake at the beginning of passus 5 and fall asleep shortly after to begin the next dream. The few steps he takes ("er I hadde faren a furlong"; B 5.5) suggests that the next passus will literally begin near the ending of the last passus. The dreamer's waking paces parallel the nearly uninterrupted progression of the fourth passus to the fifth. Indeed, the dreamer briefly regrets, for he is only briefly awake, that he was unable to continue the previous dream: "Thanne waked I of my wynkynge and wo was withalle / That I ne hadde slept sadder and yseiȝen moore" (B 5.3–4). The nostalgia for the vanished dream that absorbs him "with-alle" induces him to return in the next dream to the primal scene of the poem itself. The dreamer presents this second dream as a supplement to the first, reiterating that it is a recent member of a lineage already established by what has been said "bifore": "[Th]anne [mette me] muche moore þan I bifore tolde, / For I seiȝ þe feld ful of folk þat I bifore tolde" (B 5.9–10). Indeed, at this point the C Text stresses the filiation of the second dream even more insistently, recapitulating the poem's other important opening scene:

> Thenne mette me muche more then y byfore tolde
> Of þe matere þat me mette furste on Maluerne hulles.
> Y saw þe felde ful of folk . . .
>
> (C 5.109–11)

But despite the recurring references to the priority of the matter of the previous dream, this beginning, like the beginning of the third dream, implicitly challenges the status of the first dream. It responds to the dreamer's expressed desire to improve upon his previous experience, to sleep "sadder," to see more. The qualifier that appears in all three versions, "moche more than I bifore of tolde," implies that the second dream comprehends not only additional material, but also the entire material of the first dream. This dream is quantitatively better than the first: it embodies an intensity of experience and a plenitude of "matere" that the first one does not—"muche more."[29] It, too, makes a better beginning than the beginning of the entire poem.

Indeed, the beginning of the second dream is more disruptive than it might at first appear. As Bowers says of this waking episode, "Nothing in the sequence of the dream-action requires this break. . . . Elsewhere Langland is able to juxtapose far more disjointed actions without interrupting Will's sleep."[30] In the C Text the disruption is even more apparent, with the dreamer awaking in Cornhill from a dream that he had begun on the Malvern Hills. That this disruption is part of the deliberate design of the poem, and not the result of incomplete revision, is suggested by the C Text's own innovation: it reiterates the locale of the first dream's beginning "on Maluerne hulles." The C Text revision also introduces a temporal disjunction by having the dreamer awake "[i]n an hot heruest" (C 5.7), rather than in the "somer seson" that begins both the first and the third dreams.

Motivated as this change may be by a glancing but important allusion to concerns over the provision of laborers during the harvest—a concern that runs through the Statute of Laborers and its reflex in the legislation of the Cambridge Parliament of 1388—the misalignment of times in the C Text only accentuates a disjunction that was already present in the A and B Texts. The C Text "interpolation," indeed, is built around the principle that beginnings make disjunction possible. Despite the first word of the passus, "Thus," which makes this passus a consequence of the preceding one, the new section is constructed as an entirely new beginning, one that Anne Middleton has described as a mythic, fantasized account of the poem's own beginning. It discloses the information about the dreamer's situation that is more typical of the beginning of a long dream vision than is the beginning of the Prologue. Much of that information has little to do with what precedes it: the Cornhill location, the information that he is married, his Lollard dress, the information about his attacks on Lollards themselves.[31] The strong image of domesticity that begins the passage provides a more plausible beginning than the almost immediate alienation that begins the poem. The dreamer wakes to find "Kytte and y in a cote" (C 5.2), his "true" self situated in a locus of familial identity, not wandering across the Malvern Hills impersonating a hermit. Although it is one of the few rebeginnings that does not involve impersonation, it also includes the highly problematic figure of turning losses to good account, which indicts the whole enterprise of beginning over again. It also furnishes us with the potential geography of the poem's heterogeneous beginnings, in "London and opeland bothe" (C 5.44, Pearsall). More troublingly, it suggests that beginnings are useful because they allow anything damaging, any loss, to be obliterated. The dreamer compares the hazards of his life spent as an unbeneficed cleric, laboring over his psalter and prayerbook, and perhaps his poem, to the hazardous ventures of speculative trade ("chaffare"), in which bad investments are set aside by the winning of a "bargayn" (96). More specifically, the dreamer compares such a "bargayn" to a profit that will allow losses to be forgotten by the turning of a new page in a figurative account book, a codicological beginning that becomes a figure for the beginning of a new life, or at least a "tyme" that will turn all of his time "to profit" (100–101). Whether this is at all possible is something that both Reason and Conscience are probably more skeptical about, but this fairly disruptive new beginning in the poem does substantially concern the kinds of beginning that the incipit itself makes possible, the power to make and unmake, to recall and obliterate, that is contained in the opening of a new text.

The dreamer's description of the tools of his trade in this very passage is a description typical, perhaps, of the texts that the average fourteenth-century priest used, but also redolent of the passage's concern with the ways that textual beginnings help with recall or forgetting, or the ways that they impel one to work or allow one to evade it: "The lomes þat y labore with and lyflode deserue / Is *paternoster* and my primer, *placebo* and *dirige*" (46–47). The dreamer's labor, in other words, is defined by a set of incipits (the opening words of, respectively, the Lord's Prayer, an antiphon from vespers, and an antiphon from matins), a set that defines him as a priest, but that also places him in an uncomfortable position in relation to the ethics of labor that is the primary subject of this interpolation. This interpolation's interest in the topics of both the incipit and labor suggest that the connection between the two is deeper than it may at first appear, especially given the almost casual way in which it switches between them, as if the beginning of writing has always been associated with work. As we have seen already, there is a profound sense in which that is true, particularly in medieval rhetorical theory. But it is also true that the inception of writing is represented in the Middle Ages, and in *Piers Plowman,* by some of the quintessential figures of manual labor.

Hunger and Sweat: the Labor of Beginnings

As Ernst R. Curtius has noted, poets often compare writing to manual labor: "Many a man wrote poetry groaning and sweating and could say of himself, like the author of the Second Book of the Maccabees (2,27) 'Nobis quidem ipsis, qui hoc opus suscepimus, non facilem laborem, immo vero negotium plenum vigilarium et sudoris multi assumpsimus' [As for ourselves indeed, who assumed this work, we have taken on a difficult labor, a business full of sleepless nights and much sweat]."[32] Most of Curtius's examples portray sweat as a metaphor for the making of poetry, a metaphor, more particularly, for the labor entailed in beginning a textual work.[33] In *Piers Plowman,* the figure of Hunger links beginning directly with hard manual labor, arguing that man's role in the world began "*In sudore* and swynk" (B 6.233) and that contemporary problems like poverty and hunger (insofar as they are caused voluntarily) can be solved by calling to mind that beginning:

> Go to oure bygynnynge tho god the world made,
> As wyse men haen wryten and as witnesseth Genesis,
> Þat sayth, "with swynke and with swoet and [swetande] face
> Bytulye and bytrauayle trewely [ȝ]oure lyflode."
>
> (C 8.239–242)

The beginning that Hunger enjoins Will to return to is also a textual one. In *Piers,* Genesis is the text that brings forth the rest of human history: it is "the engendrour of us alle." Genesis is important because it records the beginning of the world, but also because it is the beginning itself, history being played out in its emerging form. The A and B Texts emphasize the potency of this beginning by attributing to Genesis generative powers: it is the giant that is "the engendrour of vs alle." The C Text appears to relegate Genesis to the role of a witness to creation, preferring to concentrate on the significance of the event rather than of the record. The "bygynnynge tho god the worlde made," the C Text suggests, is a more authoritative, and therefore less complex, beginning than the B Text's personification of Genesis as the progenitor "of us alle." In the C Text, Genesis merely records the inception of secular history, the beginnings of the conflicts that concern Hunger and Will in the present. In the two earlier versions, however, the poem collapses the act of creation and the beginning of the Book into the same event. Referring to the Bible's beginning is the same act as returning to the beginning of the world. That beginning is mediated by the text itself, which not only records the beginning of history, but *is* that beginning. The "swynk" and "swoet" that appear in Genesis as the consequence of the beginning of history also refer to the difficulty of the act of beginning itself. The sweat that in the earlier versions is the sign of contemporary labor conditions becomes an attribute of the witnesses to beginning; they are the signs, not only of the beginning of labor history, but of the beginning of texts.

"[S]wynke" and "swoet" in this passage from *Piers Plowman,* too, describe both the making of a livelihood and the making of a text. With characteristic ambiguity, the poem asserts two things at once: that the winning of a livelihood, the beginning that Genesis and other writers record, is accompanied by hard work and sweat, and that beginnings are difficult. If the third word of line 241, "with," is an adverbial complement, then the emphasis is on the difficulty of saying something about the beginning, the labor with which any act of beginning—of labor, of saying, of writing, of going to the beginning itself—must be made. This is one beginning in which the poem's persistent desire to say something sufficient to make its actions equivalent to labor, to the real work it should be undertaking, may have begun to imagine the point at which thinking and doing come together in a *principium* that is also a principle, a concept while it is also an action. But even while it tries to follow the forceful imperative of going to the beginning, the poem unravels, as if to ensure that it will have the material, other beginnings. The verb "sayth" in the passage has three possible subjects: God, "wyse men," and Genesis—each of which may also be the topic of the sentence. The passage alludes to three rhetorical beginnings (the "fiat lux" of the beginning of the world, the writings of "wyse men," and the witness of Genesis) that also record the beginnings of labor history, the "swynk and swoet" of all subsequent human endeavor. As the C Text revision shows, a single, authoritative beginning—however summational a fiction it may be—cannot sufficiently account for the complexity and difficulty of textual beginnings. Even the poem cannot simplify the problems of beginning. The C Text passage starts with the beginning of the world itself, but does not completely displace the originary force of the giant that is Genesis. Going to the beginning of such a mediated account of beginnings is far from simple, and the syntax of the passage itself is an example of the discursive tendency that counteracts attempts to recreate simple beginnings. The passage is a microcosmic instance of the larger influence that beginnings exert over the entire poem. By continually "going to a beginning," by introducing new beginnings, the poem associates the labor of beginning with the evolving problem of its own form, binding its work and its inceptions inextricably together. The act of beginning is a metonymy and the very condition of the act of writing the poem.

The apparent by-products of the scheme of writing as it is defined in the Middle Ages involve, in a strangely inverted way, the problematics of the form of the work and of the role of work itself in writing. It would seem that beginning is the antidote to sloth, the kind of work that could best engage the will. Yet, as we will see, the plan of the poem also suggests that beginning can obstruct the will precisely by appealing to it directly, by making its ethical ground too obviously the abstract and somewhat unreal world of poetry. This convergence of both projects of beginning a work in the Middle Ages—to begin it mentally and to assert a beginning that will allow the total plan to unfold—in the body of the poem makes its *forma tractandi* and its *forma tractatus* equivalent. As Judson Allen argued, the equivalence of the two allows the poem to narrate the process by which the will is ordered. In arguing that the poem enacts the progress of the will toward salvation and that the poem's structure encourages its readers to imitate the progress of Will, Allen finds certain parallels between Aegidius Romanus's description of the literary characteristics of *Canticles* and those of *Piers Plowman*. Aegidius had argued that the aesthetic effect of the structure of *Canticles* edified the soul: "[F]orma tractatus, quae talis debet esse, quale requirit modus agendi, immo quia ipse ordo capitulorum ad invicem bene intellectus animam demulcet et delectat, non inconvenienter forma tractatus per dulcedinem intelligitur" (the *forma tractatus,* how it should be, what manner of handling it requires, or rather, since the order of the chapters itself in turn soothes and delights the soul, it is not unfitting that the *forma tractatus* is understood as sweetness).[34] Allen points out that Aegidius equates the book's *forma tractatus* with its *forma tractandi:* "[T]he literal ordering of [the] text's material corresponds exactly to the order of that mental process whereby that material was invented and made significant. The result of this equation of the modus agendi and the forma tractatus is that the modus agendi becomes itself the subject, rather than or in addition to, the agent, of the book. The book is about its own making."[35] Allen's argument that the two aspects of the *causa formalis* in *Piers Plowman* are identical is richly suggestive, although he makes no real attempt to describe the *forma tractatus* of the poem.[36] The poem, most importantly, makes the rhetorical appeal to the will not only a figure of the properly ordered human will, but also the means by which it is ordered. Joseph Wittig and James Simpson have argued that both the trajectory and the poetic modes of the poem parallel its unfolding articulation of an affective theology, a theology that makes Will's actions both the central concern of the poem and its primary ordering principle.[37] Wittig's survey of the poem's unfolding definition of the will suggests that the subject of the will itself creates the poem's *forma tractatus.* The narrowing of the poem's dramatic scope from the opening vision of the field of folk to the final tropological scrutiny of the individual soul is caused, Wittig argues, "by the controlling argument of the poem: that all reform is rooted in the reform of the individual human will." The design of the entire poem prompts its reader to imitate the actions that the central argument dramatizes: it "serves as a central device in the poet's rhetoric; for the reader, empathizing with the frustrations of the dreamer and identifying with his protestations, is finally led to apply to himself the experiences of the *persona*."[38] The poem's affective appeal is engendered by the structure and subject of the poem itself—the human will. Conversely, the affective appeal, as it is defined in rhetoric, provides the occasion and form for the poem's extended meditation on the will. Even more pointedly, the means by which the poem engages in this meditation is through its dominant trope of writing, a trope that undercuts even its own attempts to anchor its activity in the plenitude of the natural world of sound, for what the poem is doing is anything but natural.

Plowing and the Beginning of Inscription

The evasion that characterizes the poem's beginning has serious implications for its status as the morally edifying work that it was taken to be.[39] As poetry, and poetry that seems particularly conscious of the rhetorical principles that govern the construction of poetry, its placement *sub ethice* suggests serious implications for its deeply problematic and dissimulating opening.

Writers on rhetoric and poetry allegorize both a work's beginning and its title as the domain of the work itself. The beginning is a work's most powerful part because it holds the key to the rest of the work. The title, which some *accessus* to authors treat as a work's true beginning, is important because it is a brief indication of the nature of the work that follows[40] or because it illuminates the work itself. Several writers explain this etymologically: an anonymous *accessus* to Sedulius, for instance, explains that the "term *titulus* comes from Titan, that is, the sun . . . just as the rising sun gives light to the whole world, so the title illuminates the work that follows."[41] The work, by implication, will be obscure and difficult if it does not have a title. As Peter Lombard explains, the title is like a key that gives one entrance to a house; the titles of the Psalms, he says, clarify one's understanding of their subject. The first psalm's lack of a title, indeed, posed a problem for commentators, which they usually resolved by discussing its formal function in the order of the entire Psalter. Bruno the Carthusian attempts to answer the question by suggesting that the psalm serves as the title to the entire Psalter.[42] Peter Lombard appends Bruno's rather tentative conclusion to his own ingenious synthesis of answers to the problem that had been suggested by commentators from Jerome to Cassiodorus:

> Hinc primo psalmo, ideo titulus non apponitur, quia psalmus iste principium est et praefatio, et caput libri, sicut in sequenti dicitur: *In capite libri scriptum est de me:* et de illo agit, qui est omnium principium, id est, de Christo, qui non habet principium. Ideo itaque titulo caret, ne titulus praescriptus, libri caput et initium videretur; vel etiam ideo quia iste psalmus, quasi titulus et prologus est sequentis operis.
>
> [For this first psalm a title is not attached, because that psalm is beginning, preface, and the head of the book, just as it is said in the following: "It was written about me at the head of the book"; one is dealing with that one who is the beginning of all things, that is, Christ, who does not have a beginning. Therefore it lacks a title, lest a written title seem to be the head and beginning of the book; or even for the reason that that psalm is, as it were, the title and the prologue of the work that follows.][43]

Lombard makes the first psalm's lack of a title the key to its content and function in the rest of the Psalter. The beginning of the Psalter, which seems to lack the most fundamental attributes of the power that it should wield over the rest of the work, imitates the content of the work that follows. Like Christ, the first psalm has no beginning. But Lombard's underlying fear that a title would arrogate the priority of Christ also divulges the extent to which he thinks beginnings can shape the content of the subsequent work. A formal beginning to the first psalm would usurp the authority of the person of Christ, the true subject of the Psalms.[44] The first psalm's lack of a title evades the usual formal constraints of beginning even while acknowledging that they exist, creating for the entire Psalter an echo of the divine attribute of its subject, a beginning without a beginning.

Peter Lombard's solution to the problem of the Psalter's beginning applies to the problems associated with *Piers Plowman*'s beginning: like the Psalter, it has a beginning that seems abrupt, that lacks the clear *titulus* and signs of an authoritative inception. *Piers Plowman*'s beginning, like the Psalter's, declares the importance of its ultimate subject, "Piers þe Plowman, *Petrus id est christus*" (B 15.212). And like Lombard's commentary on the Psalter, *Piers Plowman* consistently describes that subject in relation to beginnings.

Faith's description of Christ mirrors the attribute of pure origin that commentators on the Psalter mention. One of Christ's attributes, indeed, is negative. He never had an inception: he "was euere wiþouten gynnyng" (B 16.187). As I will note in the next chapter, *Piers Plowman* evokes the doctrine of the *genitor ingenitus* at least four times in the poem.[45] But the poem also describes the incarnation as Christ's assumption of a beginning. Christ's first miracle is the point at which "bigan god of his grace to do wel" (B 19.110). The poem does not directly examine the idea of the temporal inception of divine works much more fully than this, holding back from a formulation of divine procession that would directly contravene orthodox doctrine. The poem has no such compunctions with the figure it constructs whom it at one point equates with Christ: Piers Plowman.

The poem several times associates Piers Plowman with beginnings, and particularly textual beginnings. Behind this association lies an association between plowing and the act of beginning, or the act of textual inception.[46] Piers Plowman, as much as Christ, is a figure who stands at the beginning of good works in the poem. He initiates, for instance, the plowing of the half acre that becomes the poem's most potent, and transient, image of a utopian society where all humankind labor together. And the plowman is generally imagined in the Middle Ages as an originary figure, particularly as a figure of the inception of doing well. Rabanus Maurus, in a widely circulated definition, describes the plowman as the inception of good works.[47] Shortly after the idyll of the half acre, the poem adduces another connection between plowing and beginning. I have already mentioned Hunger's admonition to Piers himself to "go to oure bygynnynge," which the B Text suggests is the book of Genesis itself, "the engendrour of us alle" (B 6.232, C 8.239–40). Piers's return to the beginning principles of the text that founded the imperatives of human life echoes a traditional association between plowing and the foundation both of human society and of writing itself. The book of Genesis, Hunger tells Piers, contains the command that institutes plowing as the basic activity of the human economy: "*In sudore* and swynk þow shalt þi mete tilie" (B 6.233). Commenting on Rousseau's *Essay on the Origin of Languages,* Derrida further explores the conjunction between writing and the foundation of society that Hunger calls attention to, the *arché*-writing that appears along with the invention of the social economy:

> It is a matter of *writing by furrows*. The furrow is the line, as the plowman traces it: the road—*via rupta*—broken by the plowshare. The furrow of agriculture, we remind ourselves, opens nature to culture (cultivation). And one knows that writing is born with agriculture which happens only with sedentarization.
>
> How does the plowman proceed?
>
> Economically. Arrived at the end of the furrow, he does not return to the point of departure. He turns ox and plow around.... Writing by the *turning of the ox—boustrephedon*—writing by furrows was a movement in linear and phonographic script.[48]

As Curtius points out, the comparison between the "dressing of a field" and writing is at least as old as Plato, and the metaphor of "plowshare" for "pen" appears first in Isidore.[49] Isidore's etymology of the word "versus" also owes a direct debt to plowing:

> Versus autem vulgo vocati, quia sic scribebant antiqui aratur terra. A sinistra enim ad dexteram primum deducebant stylum; deinde convertebantur ad inferiora et rursum ad dexteram versus, quos hodieque rustici versus vocant.
>
> ["Verses" are called such in common speech because the ancients used to write just as the earth is plowed. For they used to draw the pen first from left to right, then they would turn around at the line below, and then again turn to the right, which even today country people call *versus*.][50]

In Middle English writing, as well, plowing is associated with the cultivation of narrative. Perhaps the most obvious example is Chaucer's Knight, who apologizes at the beginning of his tale for having to abridge his material: "I have, God woot, a large feeld to ere, / And wayke been the oxen in my plough."[51] In *Piers Plowman,* indeed, a knight is invited to try his hand at plowing, and his response provokes a quibble that echoes the conjunction between labor and textual inception. Piers had just completed a brief discourse on the division of labor and on his own duty to aid others. "'By crist!' quod a kniȝt þoo, '[þow] kennest vs þe beste, / Ac on þe teme trewely tauȝte was I neuere'" (B 6.21–22). The "teme" may refer either to the oxen in the yoke or to the *thema* of Piers's brief sermon on labor.[52]

The quibble appears again in passus 19, although this time the primary meaning of the word is explicitly textual, rather than agricultural:

> Grace gaf Piers a teeme, foure grete Oxen.
> That oon was Luk, a large beest and a lowe chered,
> And Mark, and Mathew þe þridde, myghty beestes boþe;
> And Ioyned to hem oon Iohan, moost gentil of alle,
> The pris neet of Piers plow, passynge alle oþere.
> (B 19.262–66)

The "teeme" here is much like the *thema* of a sermon, the most important of the biblical books that should furnish the *fundamentum* or *principium* of any sermon.[53] In this second episode of plowing with a "teeme," another biblical book emerges as preeminent. Like Genesis, it is an "engendrour" of sorts, since it also deals with beginnings—the book of John. Although *Piers Plowman* does not explain why John should be the "pris neet of Piers plow, passynge alle othere," most commentaries on the book explain in their prologues both why it surpasses the other Gospels and why the eagle is the most fitting symbol of John:

> [I]nter haec quatuor [Evangelia] praecellit Evangelium Joannis. . . . Nam Joannes aquilae, quae caeteris avibus altius volat . . . comparatur, cum Domino ad coelum volat, ejus divinitatem altius caeteris intuendo. Unde dicit Augustinus enim adeo alte coepisse, quod si altius intonuisset, nec totius mundus eum capere potuisset, dicens: *In principio erat verbum,* etc.[54]

> [Among these four [Gospels] the Gospel of John stands out. For John is compared to the eagle, which flies higher than the other birds, who flies to heaven with the Lord, his excellence in contemplation higher than the others. Wherefore Augustine says

> of him that he began so loftily that if he had resounded any more loftily, not even the whole world would have been able to restrain him.]

The book of John is literally "passynge alle oþere," the preeminent and foremost "neet" of the team, because it is about beginnings. It deals with what is anterior to all of the other Gospels: the institution of the beginning by the Word. Many commentators find in that beginning a similarity with the beginnings that human authors make. The divine Word is first ordained in the mind and then expressed outwardly, just as prescriptive writers urge their audiences to do:

> Verbum autem duo significat, sicut et *logos* Graecum, cui aequipollet, scilicet mentis conceptum, et oris prolationem. Mens enim prius intus concipit, quod postea oris prolatione manifestat.[55]
>
> [*Verbum* signifies two things, just as does the Greek *logos,* to which it is equivalent—that is, a mental concept and a production of the mouth. For the mind first conceives within itself what it afterward makes manifest by a production of the mouth.]

By emphasizing the priority of John in Piers's plow team, Langland draws attention to the inception of the Word itself. Piers's act of plowing, especially in such an allegorical context, reverberates with perhaps the most common metaphorical association of plowing: the sowing of the Word of God in the human heart.[56] The preachers who undertake this task must imitate the procession of the divine Word itself, first conceiving the discourse in their minds, and then giving it verbal utterance. The Gospel of John anchors this twofold operation in the most fundamental beginning possible: the Word that was with God. This is the beginning that Piers is enjoined to imitate, the beginning that places John ahead of all the beasts in his plow. The eagle symbolizes the height of the beginning of the book of John, a beginning higher than all the other Gospels. Like John of Wales, who suggests that preachers should attempt to "cogitare de altiori principio" when composing a sermon, the successive beginnings of *Piers Plowman* repeatedly attempt to figure forth the inception of the divine Word recounted in the book of John, the highest beginning imaginable, but also the book that provides the

Middle Ages with its most recognizable incipit, and its most compelling reminder of the primal gathering together of word and beginning.

Plowing may provide a compelling model for a *principium intrinsecus* that is uncovered in the course of the poem, a beginning that starts in the external world but that turns out to have been implicit in, or intrinsic to, the poem. But the emergence of the intrinsic beginning nevertheless raises some troubling questions. For one thing (to read the allegory *literaliter*), the plow must be hitched to the figures of successful beginning, following, not developing, the allegorically referenced beginning of the Gospel of John. Although the gospel offers a powerful model of beginnings that are intrinsic simply because they unfold in language, it is a model that does not appear in the poem until close to its conclusion. For it to be a *principium intrinsecus* for the poem in which it appears, the plow must retrace its course, doubling back on its own writing. It is the ongoing search for Grace, the search that closes the poem, that provides Piers with this allegory of intrinsic beginning—one that is identical to the appearance of language in the world—a beginning that appears too late in the poem to begin it, an inception that is belated, "passing," as the poem says, "all other," appearing after the poem's proceeding has already passed its beginning by a considerable way, much as Thought appears only halfway through the B version, seven years after Thought says he had begun following, "sewing," Will. For the poem to start with that beginning, it would need to obliterate itself, extirpating, as a plow does, everything that has gone before. No—extirpating, as the written word does, the *littera,* the mud and mire *(limus),* that is spread, poured out *(litum)* in its very proceeding, so that it can make its mark, so that writing can begin.

ORIGO

[Rising of heavenly body, daybreak, coming into being, birth, ancestry; related to *ordo,* a row of things, an order of things]

Genealogy

Engenderment and Digression

> *If the book could for a first time really begin, it would . . . long since have ended.*
>
> —Maurice Blanchot, *The Writing of the Disaster*

And so the book has still not begun. That is, its beginnings still emerge from the world outside the book, gesturing toward the ways in which one might make a beginning if one were to begin the book all over again, or gesturing toward the other beginnings that make this one possible. That is to say that we are still discussing the *principium extrinsecus,* the beginnings in the book that are not its own, but that provide it with its authoritative models of beginning. Yet the book also investigates beginnings that appear explicitly as figures that resist undoing and extirpation: the figure of genealogy, the articulation of continuity itself. It could even be said that genealogy constitutes the intervention of the dead in the work of beginning, undoing the obliteration of death in a schema that makes genealogical beginnings all the stronger. That is, it undoes death by foreclosing individual beginnings, by circumscribing the arena in which the will can be exercised. To the degree that patrimony, heritage, and occupation determine who we are, the inscription of genealogies also prevents us from making absolute beginnings in our lives. It is not the dead who construct genealogies, of course: it is those who want to stake a claim over the living.

In *The Laws,* Plato argues that rule is fundamentally legitimated by its beginning, a principle that is true in terms of both his political philosophy and etymology: "[O]nly the beginning *(arché)* is entitled to rule *(archein)*." As Hannah Arendt points out, the fate of political philosophy in the West was to forget this basic homology, losing an "authentic understanding of human freedom" along with the elaboration of arts of rule.[1] It is arts of rule, in fact, that call forth elaborated genealogies as a way of commemorating a beginning that can no longer be made. Indeed, they are useful precisely because they foreclose other potential beginnings. But when genealogy is explicitly linked to the practice of rule, the making of other beginnings is powerfully subversive of both political stability and genealogical formations. This is precisely what happened in England in 1381.

In Walsingham's account of John Ball's famous Blackheath sermon, political dissent takes the explicit form of genealogical contestation, framed as a discourse about beginnings. As I have already pointed out, it is an account that is powerfully interested in the discursive forms of beginning, citing the predicative point of departure, the *thema;* the term used in texts and in contemporary physics and logic to describe something already begun, the *incipit;* the term used in rhetoric, *introducere;* and two terms that at first glance seem to be used interchangeably but that ultimately point to the deep ambivalence of genealogical beginnings, *initium* and *principium.* It is worthwhile quoting the passage in which these two terms appear:

> [A]b initio omnes pares creatos a natura, servitutem per injustam oppressionem nequam hominum introductam, contra voluntatem Dei; quia, si Deo placuisset servos creasse, utique in principio mundi constituisset quis servus, quisve dominus futurus fuisset.
>
> [From the beginning all were created equal by nature, servitude introduced by the unjust oppression of unworthy men, contrary to the will of God; for, if it had pleased God to create slaves, he would certainly have in the beginning of the world established who was to be a slave and who was to be a lord].[2]

Steven Justice, who compellingly shows that the sermon draws on Wit's allusion to "kynde" in B 9, stops short of discussing the important differences between what seem initially to be equivalent instances of beginning in the sermon. Especially when they appear in conjunction, the two words *initium* and *principium* refer to vastly different notions of beginning. The word *principium* usually refers to the beginning of the world, precisely the same moment that Ball and Walsingham refer to as "in principio mundi." The word *initium* refers to the subjective beginning that each individual makes, a form of beginning that resonates powerfully through the discourse of the rebels' opposition to hereditary gentility. Augustine sums up the difference between the two in a succinct and lucid definition of the stakes of beginning in *The City of God*, his great work on the theological and cultural work of foundation. Distinguishing between the beginning of the world *(principium)* and the beginning of an individual life, he argues that humans were created in order that just such a beginning could come into being: "[S]o that such a beginning might be, man was created, before whom there was nobody."[3] Justice's argument that the phrase "out of o man" a few lines later in the same passage "generates the phrase *a principio [sic]*" could be supplemented by the observation that the phrase "ab initio" (the one Walsingham actually uses) is rooted in another cluster of ideas in the same portion of the poem. Ball is not drawing from just that section of passus 9. The passus contains the poem's earliest definitions of Dowel as a kind of beginning; even more specifically, it defines Dowel as just the kind of radical, individual beginning the rebels' writing advocated. In line 96a, Wit defines Dowel, in fact, as an *initium*, the "inicium sapiencie" that is "dred of God." The rebels' critique of genealogical formations is predicated on precisely the observation, and perhaps directed by the poem's unfolding awareness of subjective beginnings, that such formations constitute neither natural nor intrinsic beginnings. As we will see, part of Langland's revision of the B Text involved just this topic from B 9, which is given a more explicit, personal, and urgent treatment at the beginning of passus 5 of the C Text. Both passages are, in fact, the poem's most extended discussions of the poem's ethical status, in which the writer is confronted by interlocutors representing the cognitive faculties—Wit and Imaginatif in B 9, Reason and Conscience in C 5. And in both passages the poem's exploration of its own cognitive scene of production takes the form of a critique of genealogy.

But why should the interrogation of writing take this particular form, a form that gestures toward entrenched notions of lineal power and continuity? It is more than likely that the poem's remarkable subject of beginning is taken up in this guise because it offers a model of discursive continuity that was also susceptible to revision. The poem exploits the internal inconsistencies of this lineal, genealogical model in an oblique attack—far more oblique than others in late-fourteenth-century England—on the discursive forms that could prevent its more compelling project of fashioning radical, independent beginnings.[4]

Ball's representation of genealogical beginning as an unnatural formation is a canny appropriation of generalized assumptions about the continuity of forms of beginning in the Middle Ages. By linking the *initium* with *natura,* Ball highlights the origin of genealogical forms of governance as unnatural and, by extension, illegitimate. He also reminds us, whether deliberately or not, that it is an extrinsic form of beginning. Robert Kilwardby, Marsilius of Inghen, and Thomas Aquinas are just three of the many philosophers who point out that only nature can have an intrinsic beginning. What is more, they say, unnatural and therefore extrinsic beginnings are also violent ones.[5]

That the rebels' program is remembered as being a violent one is an accident, in the medieval sense of the word, for it was motivated by a serious conviction that intrinsic beginnings needed to be perpetuated. What *Piers Plowman* does with its meditation on genealogical beginning may have inspired the rebels in a more pervasive and consistent fashion than might be suggested in Justice's discussion. For the poem is acutely aware of the violence implicit in genealogical formations, a violence that hovers over the beginning in several implacable forms. The first of these is in the very form of the poem's project, the *forma tractandi* of beginning itself, which produces a poem that, as we saw in the previous chapter, complicates the authoritative model of the medieval "root-book" by equating its method of proceeding with both its ruptures and its most important topics. But in doing so it also complicates an important medieval mode of historical understanding, the genealogical imagination, by simultaneously extending and undermining it. Like the arboresecent book, genealogy arranges its objects of inquiry according to the model of the tree. That model shapes historical inquiry as a radical pursuit, trimming away the branches of the stemma to expose the trunk and *radix.* As it does with most well-established medieval epistemological models, *Piers Plowman* both exemplifies and undoes genealogical figuration. Because of its immense importance in the poem, I will be discussing it in the next two chapters.

This chapter will show how the genealogical inflections of several important figures in the Middle Ages and in the poem—especially those of paternity and Cain—demonstrate that beginning is simultaneously characterized by continuity and divisiveness. Michel Serres has shown how the two alternatives structure Livy's account of the founding of Rome. It would be better to refer to the *foundings* of Rome, since foundation is an act that is inaugurated, and continued, by obliteration and destruction, starting with the *translatio imperii* from Troy to Rome. These alternatives underpin Livy's account, which traces not a single point of origin, but a series of beginnings that are already dispersed and multiple; as Serres puts it, "[I]n the beginning is bifurcation." This dispersal at the beginning of things means that no foundation can be really adequate or final and that every writing of history not totally committed to a vision of the radical contingency of things must also unwittingly rewrite, and in the process remake, foundations. How are we to read, then, histories that are committed to excavating the foundational origin of cities, cultures, institutions, or forms of living? Serres suggests that we do so not by reading them as histories sanctioned by a singular act of foundation, but as histories *of* foundation, as narratives of the very acts that constitute foundation.[6] They are narratives that, in short, tend to reveal the heterogeneity of historical beginnings. Reading in this way is closely akin to what Foucault, borrowing from Nietzsche, calls genealogy. Its aim is to reveal the presence of extrinsic beginnings in beginnings that seem to be intrinsic, that seem to be unmediated and singular. As Jürgen Habermas puts it, "[G]enealogy is not supposed to search for an *origin*, but to uncover the contingent *beginnings* of discourse formations."[7] While most medieval genealogies certainly work by reinforcing familial authority, Nietzsche has shown how they also carry along with them the seeds of their own contingency. More precisely, such foundational histories could be said to trace as well the constitution of their own narrativity, the beginnings that become represented as authoritative by the unfolding genealogy itself and consequently become little more than simulacra of a truly intrinsic beginning. The fiction that is implicit in the authoritative beginning is thus most crucially an act of forgetting, an obliterating of the extrinsic features that really authorize it or that undermine it, of the dispersed motives and unnatural violence that must be forgotten in creating a pure origin. A poem too scrupulous to forget this, *Piers Plowman,* in its investigation of acts of foundation, attempts to represent, as it must, the transcendent beginning that is God, even while it reveals the messiness involved in affirming human acts of beginning, the gestures that highlight both their divisiveness and the means the poem uses to shore up their genealogical, original authority. The autobiographical passage in the C Text is an exemplary instance of both of these imperatives.

That passage shows how genealogy can become an activating fiction, the idealized stemma that organizes the imaginary beginnings of identity and language, or of kinship and grammar.[8] It begins by producing an idealized image of paternal influence that underwrites the poem's own use of language and that helps to explain its own desire for uncontaminated beginnings. The passage concludes, however, with the poem's most vociferous defense of its performativity, a defense that foregrounds the divisiveness of beginnings. The oscillation between those two projects is perhaps explained by a split inherent in the image of the father. As Lacan argues, paternal authority is itself performative, and the symbolic capital implicit in that "paternal metaphor" is lost when that authority is actually exercised, exposing its fallibility and contingency: when the "Legislator presents himself ... he does so as an impostor." More concisely, Lacan argues that the paternal metaphor can only function as a *metaphorein,* a language or symbolism always split from its referent: his answer to Freud's question "What is a Father?" is simply "It is the dead Father."[9] This paternal and linguistic dialectic operates, as *Piers Plowman* shows, in a range of discourses on foundation. The split that makes the first murderer also the first founder of cities is one that informs every beginning, including the ones that the writer of *Piers Plowman* attributes to himself.

The C Text passage begins with the dreamer in Cornhill, describing, for the first and only time, his domestic situation, living with his wife "in a cote" (C 5.2). The initial integration of the dreamer and his family signals one of the important topics of the following "autobiographical interpolation": the relation between beginning and lineage. It begins in a scene of domesticity and continues with a defense of the roles prescribed by genealogy. Those roles also provide the dreamer with a defense for his occupation:

> For sholde no clerke be crouned but yf he come were
> Of frankeleyns and fre men and of folke ywedded.
> Bondemen and bastardus and beggares children,
> Thyse bylongeth to labory and lordes kyn to serue . . .
> (C 5.66–69)

One's role is determined by filial beginnings, not by a beginning that one can choose freely. And the purity of that beginning determines one's degree of freedom, the degree to which one can choose at all, a self-replicating lineage of spontaneity. The violation of the protocol of human procreation, on the other hand, produces not radical freedom but servitude, a point that a marginal notation opposite lines 64 and 65 in one manuscript makes with undisguised vitriol: "basterds fit for slauerye."[10] Following the prominent appropriations of the poem in 1381, Langland announces a more pointedly deterministic notion of genealogy, as the determining factor in the answer to the question that plagues much of the B Text version of the poem: how to regulate work. And the subtle distinctions about the reasons for labor are swept aside, too, in this vision of a genealogically determined world. The limits of labor, the work one must perform, are determined not by the relentless, unanswered question "What must I do to be saved?" They are determined by the social facts that attend one's birth. The dreamer suggests, too, that the inception of even a life lived in the pursuit of intellectual truth can be traced up a line of biological causation. He attributes the impetus behind his education to his father and other relatives: "My fader and my frendes foende me to scole" (C 5.36).[11] So far, then, the passage endorses a reactionary revision of B 9's open-ended ambiguity, its endorsement of a poem that, like its author, is in search of its beginnings.

The strong insistence on lineage at the beginning of this section is another facet of the strong, disjunctive beginning of the second dream. As Edward Said points out, citing Vico, the "family metaphor of filial engenderment, when it is extended throughout the whole of human activity, Vico called *poetic;* for men are men, he says, because they are makers, and what before everything else they make is themselves."[12] What Langland has created in the interpolation is precisely a prospectus—only slightly less comprehensive than the vision of the field of folk itself—of the metaphor of "filial engenderment," which produces, among other things, his own life account as a maker of poetry.[13] The images of unimpeachable lineage and integration that make up the beginning of the second dream present a poet who is entitled to his occupation by virtue of his beginnings. The filial integrity of his pursuits becomes the main subject of the poem precisely at the point of its greatest disjunction to that point. Indeed, despite the obvious discrepancies of time and place, the poet draws attention to the second dream's filiation, to its own descent from "þe matere þat me mette furste on Maluerne hulles."

This second dream is motivated by the attempt to link the making of selves to the making of poetry, and it covers the disruptions to the poem's narrative and thematic continuity by interrogating closely the ramifications of genealogy, the continuity that disrupts itself. Despite appearing at a point in the poem where it is strictly unnecessary, the beginning of the second dream attempts to present itself as an integrated part of the whole, as a logical, lineal consequence of the preceding dream. The images of familial and genealogical legitimacy underwrite Will's defense of his life and of his "making." He presents the violation of lineal obligations in contemporary society as the impulse behind his satire and, indeed, behind all of his writing:

> Ac sythe bondemen barnes haen be mad bisshopes
> And bar[o]nes bastardus haen be Erchedekenes
> And so[þ]ares and here sones for suluer han be knyhtes,
> And lordes sones here laboreres and leyde here rentes to wedde
> . . . .
> And monkes and moniales þat mendenantes sholde fynde
> Imade here kyn knyhtes and knyhtes fees ypurchased,
> Popes and patrones pore gentel blood refused
> And taken Symondus sones seyntwarie to kepe,
> Lyfholynesse and loue hath be longe hennes
> And wol til hit be wered out [or] oþerwyse ychaunged.
> Forthy rebuke me ryhte nauhte, resoun . . .
>
> (C 5.70–72)

Will's discussion of the abuse of lineage is more than a digressive outburst. It demonstrates his conviction that he is one of those whose natural role is to "synge masses" or, most especially, to "sitten and wryten" (C 5.63). The logical flourish that begins the last line, "[f]orthy," suggests that Will believes that the rest of the passage is an unassailable demonstration of his own integrity. He suggests, implicitly, that he is discharging his own duty, unlike those who transgress the laws of natural order. But the very compendiousness of the catalog of transgressors demonstrates that Will has also become a chronicler of the widespread feats of usurpation and discontinuity about him.

Conscience's critique of Will's activity sweeps aside Will's elaborate apologetic for his "making," for his elaborately constructed beginning. Conscience simply points out that, as a beggar, Will has violated the very principles behind his defense (C 5.90–91). Will's response presents a radically different view of beginnings, and one that is perhaps closer to the track of the poem itself:

> "So hope y to haue of hym þat is almyghty
> A gobet of his grace and bigynne a tyme
> That alle tymes of my tyme to profit shal turne."
> "Y rede the," quod resoun tho, "rape the to bigynne
> The l[y]f þat is louable and leele to thy soule." "ȝe! and
> contynue," quod Consience . . .
>
> (C 5.99–104)

A profitable beginning will compensate for all the other unprofitable beginnings that Will has made. It will, in a literal sense, redeem the time. The language of the profit economy supersedes Will's elaborate defense of the necessity of inherited roles. The pursuit of the perfect life hinges not upon fulfilling one's hereditarily appointed role, but upon making a profit. Will's definition of personal redemption in economic terms is strange indeed, following his lengthy denunciation of the social consequences of economic cupidity and his resentments over simony and land transactions outside of knightly groups. As Will himself points out, trade enables merchants to acquire social status, even though they may not have hereditary status. Merchants can make new beginnings that compensate for their lack of pedigree, the noble beginnings that create noble occupations. In the fourteenth and fifteenth centuries, indeed, heralds guarded against the threat that merchants, in particular, posed to the privilege or "worship" that noble beginnings confer. As one heraldic treatise points out, "[H]eroudes were ordeyned to take hede that merchants shulde bere no armes though they had neuer so grete Riches."[14]

The explicitly pecuniary beginning that Will discusses directly opposes the vision of genealogical continuity that seems to motivate his writing, or at least the beginning of this passus. Will's beginning here breaks cleanly with the past. To "bigynne a tyme" is to establish temporal limits, to mark off one time from another. In a certain sense, the beginnings in *Piers Plowman* do just that. In the C Text, what had been the beginning of passus 5 in the B Text emphasizes much more strongly the anteriority of the previous dream: "Thenne mette me muche more than y *byfore* tolde / Of þe matere þat me mette *furste* on Maluerne hulles" (C 5.109–10). Although the second dream is clearly related to the first, it also clearly takes place at a different time. New beginnings create a temporal disjunction that confirms the loss of what has come before—witness the dreamer's nostalgia for the second dream at the beginning of the third dream—but new beginnings also offer hope that that very loss will be restored, that "alle tymes . . . to profit shal turne." The passage also describes the making of the poem itself, describing the writer of the poem as someone who has

> ay loste and loste, and at þe laste hym happed
> A bouhte suche a bargayn he was þe bet euere,
> And sette al his los at a leef at the laste ende,
> Suche a wynnyng hym warth thorw wordes of grace.
> (C 5.95–98, Pearsall)

Each new beginning that the poem makes reinforces a loss; it must inevitably come after an ending. Anne Middleton points out that what she describes as the poem's "episodic endings" create "a marked and lamented loss to narrative continuity."[15] The lament is at this point presumably shared by its composer: the narrative continuity of the poem itself has been "ay lost and lost." The ideal beginning that Will describes reinforces that discontinuity even while it affirms the relation between ending and beginning. As the syncategorematic treatises on "incipit" from the fourteenth century establish exhaustively (and exhaustingly, if one has to follow the entire argument), a beginning also marks the ending of what precedes it.[16] Part of the meaning of the passage seems to be that the poem's successive beginnings also delimit the endings of previous sections. A beginning relegates the "loss" to the past, to the previous division of the poem: the poet can "set al his los at a leef at the laste ende." The poet, that is, inscribes his "los" on the page that will contain not the final end, but the previous, "laste" ending, because of the new beginning that a new "leef" will contain.[17] It is a perfect image of the poem's own method of proceeding. It also demonstrates how beginning must be an obliteration, even while the technology of that obliteration—the leaves of the book—and the familial sponsorship of the writer's learning are vestiges of the grammatical and genealogical stemma.

The poem's self-critique has a tendency to branch out in this way, as we have seen before with the similar prophetically tinged lament over the neglect of grammar in passus 15 of the B Text, a complaint that necessitates a deflection in the C Text back to the incipient formal world of the poem. The revision of passus 5 in the C Text is more difficult to apprehend in these terms, since, as Anne Middleton has shown, its response is directed to a world that had become nearly as discursively complex as this poem has. In particular, its attention is focused on an especially knotted complex of social ideas—labor, residency, social quiescence, political allegiance, practices of affinity—that themselves are mediated through questions of documentation and registration.

In attempting to locate every segment of the population in relation to a productive occupation, the Cambridge Parliament of 1388 implicitly but powerfully returns those who do not fit into its comprehensive list—specifically the beggars who are unable to serve—to their origins, if they are unable to remain where they are, to "the hundred, rape, or wapentake, or to the towns where they were born." This legislative procedure is perfectly echoed in the poem at precisely the juncture where Langland is interrogated over the elusiveness of his profession and is sent literally back to his beginning—to this passage, which is imagined as the moment of the poem's inception. And just as the answer to the social disjunctions chronicled in the passage is the Cambridge Parliament's program of territorial and habitual beginning, the poem's answer to its own disjunctions at this point is one of persistent narratological beginning, to "bigynne / The lyif," to turn the page at this juncture, to begin another dream. And yet the return to his beginning here fails, because it is in the very beginning that we find the failure of place, the initial wandering that can only be heterogeneous in *this* beginning, too, with its author living "in London and opeland bothe." And we find, again, the same initial failure of the project, so that when Langland must appeal to the beginning that should authorize him, he must literally write it in, and write it in near the end of the poem's career. That initial intention—which we could now describe as incipient failure because it is configured here as a series of failures related to inception and as the initial failure to state the poem's intention—is what haunts the poem's disjunctiveness throughout. Middleton eloquently describes this scene in C 5 as the fictive account of the poem's own beginning, a fantasized "confrontation with his powers and talents that formed and articulated the *first intention* of the work, as well as the sense of sanction for it that purportedly *allowed* the generation of what became the poem."[18] Perhaps more cannily, this account also allows a social and political sanction for the poem's lack of initiating intention, since it becomes as futile and nostalgic a project at this point as its more ambitious counterpart in the texts generated by the Cambridge Parliament. But what the passage does above all is to cast the poem's formal problem into social and political terms, to make the failures of *intentio finalis* into an etiology of social and discursive instability in the late fourteenth century. What Langland seems to have realized, if Middleton's argument about the Cambridge Parliament as the context for this revision is right (and needless to say I think it is), is that a lack of intention, the insistence on the immanence of beginning, is the most provocative response to a politics that insists on beginning—or origin—as a point of conformity, for the ability to begin is the ability to reform and resist the governance of extrinsic forms. What remains to be seen is how this is practically possible, especially with intrinsic forms, such as paternity, that seem, almost by definition, to be incapable of being revised.

Principles of Paternity

As we have seen, the genealogical model ratifies the authority of beginnings and foundations but also exposes the machinery of the fiction that maintains it. In a poem whose central activity has been characterized as the search for Truth[19] but whose central drama is the spectacular complication of both epistemology and social and political imagination, beginnings become an important index of the installation of authority at almost every level. Indeed, the searches for truth and beginnings in the Middle Ages are implicated in each other. A. J. Minnis has shown how the categories of truth, authority, and priority are virtually identical in scholastic prologues.[20]

As a kind of dilated scholastic prologue itself, *Piers Plowman* further conflates these purportedly basic, foundational, principles. As I have already suggested, the image of the father is important in various ways for the poem's discussion of beginnings and foundations. Medieval writers often used the figure of the father as an abstract principle of beginning, an image of both authority and precedence. In his article "De generatione prosopia" in his encyclopedic *De universo,* Rabanus Maurus uses the distinction between kinds of beginning, "initium" and "origo," to explain the principle of paternity manifest in the figures of the *paterfamilias* and God the Father:

> Pater est, a quo initium nascitur generis. Itaque is paterfamilias vocitatur.... Multis modis in Scripturis pater positus reperitur:... naturaliter pater dicitur, ut Deus pater omnium, a quo sunt omnia, quia ab eo omnia originem habent.
>
> [The father is he from whom is born the beginning *[initium]* of the family *[generis]*. Therefore he is called the *paterfamilias....* The father *[pater]* is found placed in many modes in the Scriptures:... he is called father in its natural meaning, as God is the father of all, from whom all things come, because from him all things have their origin *[originem]*].[21]

Every *gens* must have a beginning, must begin somewhere, and that beginning is memorialized in part of the very definition of *gens,* in the term *paterfamilias.* Although the radical difference of the kind of beginning made by God is suggested by Rabanus's use of the word *origo* to refer to divine actions, the term *pater,* nevertheless, has sufficient intrinsic authority and impetus (unlike, apparently, the word *initium*) for it to be applied unaltered, if in a more capaciously metaphoric manner, to God himself.

In general, Langand's use of the word "father" is accompanied by terms that make clear that the word implies something more like a principle (indeed, a "principle" in the sense of *principium*) than just an antecedent biological relationship. Langland elaborates on the idea of God as "pater omnium" by emphasizing the absolute degree of priority that God possesses. The passage from the Good Samaritan's extended comparison of the Trinity to a fist is really a definition of the principle of paternity:

> So is þe fader a fol god, the furste of hem alle
> . . . And he fader and for[m]eour, þe furste of alle thynges—
> *Tu fabricator omnium.*
>
> (C 19.132–34a)[22]

The poem associates paternity with God and the creation of the world in at least three other places, two of which use this passage's collocation of "fader" and "formeour." The first is Holy Church's description of the occupant of the "tour on the toft," in which the poem shows how inextricably linked are the notions of truth, paternity, and priority: "Treuþe is þerinne. . . . he is fadir of feiþ & fourmide ȝow alle" (A 1.14). The second is Wit's exegesis of the poem's other great allegorical image of God: "Kynde . . . is creatour of alle kynnes [beestes], / Fader and formour, [þe first of alle þynges]" (B 9.26–27). The third is Faith's anticipation of the Good Samaritan's Trinitarian discussion: "The firste [person of the Trinity] haþ myȝt and maiestee, maker of alle þynges; / *Pater* is his propre name" (B 16.184–85).

For a poem as preoccupied with beginnings as *Piers Plowman* is, the linking of paternity and priority is another way to articulate the profound power and complexity of beginnings. Wit's discussion of Kynde (the second of the passages here) describes God as the principle of beginning that lacks a beginning itself:

> "Kynde," quod [he], "is creatour of alle kynnes [beestes],
> Fader and formour, [þe first of alle þynges].
> And þat is þe grete god þat gynnyng hadde neuere."
>
> (B 9.26–28)

It is a strange and complicated version of Rabanus's suggestion that the biblical principle of paternity is drawn from nature, a nature that imparts beginning and paternity to something else—the mundane world. The principles of beginning drawn from the natural world are paradoxically drawn from beyond it, from a principle that, in fact, has no beginning. Wit associates paternity and the beginning of nature with Kynde, but goes on to point out that the paternity of God is not drawn from anything; what makes God distinct from his creation is the principle that he "gynnyng hadde neuere." Langland's probable source for the idea, the Athanasian Creed, also associates divine paternity with pure origin, the absence of a beginning: "Pater a nullo factus, nec creatus, nec genitus" (the Father fashioned from nothing, and was neither created nor born).[23] Despite this absence, God is the principle of beginning itself, the image of paternity as origin, the "fader and formour of al that is maked."[24] As the *Cursor mundi* puts it, with epigrammatic terseness, "þouȝe he bigan al oþere þing / him self hadde neuer bigynnyng."[25] Beginning, then, does not begin where we think it does—or rather it begins there precisely because we think so. The tautological formulation of divine beginnings points to their location in history itself, to an immanent impossibility in the very nature of beginning. These original contradictions, in fact, are characteristic of what could be called the paternal sanction of language.

Rabanus Maurus's encyclopedia *De universo* imagines God as the vanishing point of language, paternity, and origination, but specifically as the unseen, ungenerated father who founds language and through it everything else. Christ, he explains, is called the word *(verbum)* through which the Father founded *(condidit)* and ordered *(iussit)* everything that exists. Once again, we should note that the salient problem is not one of paternity but one of language, the conflated state of inceptions and their designations. Lacan has usefully described this impasse as the very condition of language, summarized in what he calls the "paternal metaphor." This has little or nothing to do with a real father (in fact its unreality is its main attribute), describing instead the symbolic identification of the impulse, or the permission, to be *like* a father. At the same time, however, a primordial interdiction, that of the horror of incest, prevents one from being *too* much like the father. This basic structure of permission and interdiction makes, or causes, the emergence of law. In terms of the formation of the subject, this means that language plays a constitutive, not merely memorial, role. In other words, the subject is always the subject of beginning, but unable to determine whether that beginning has the quality of an *initium* or a *principium*. This problem is one of the reasons for *Piers Plowman*'s interest in the problem of time in language—for time is the enigmatic symptom of the initiative of language. Heidegger describes the symptomatology of the time in which we find ourselves the situation of *gewesenheit,* of *having been,* which arises out of an awareness of the future. What this means is that a beginning appears when something in its future makes sense of it *as a beginning,* and the temporal relation between them takes the form of memory. It is the historiographical memory that produces beginning, as we will see in the next chapter. *Piers*'s beginnings posit points of pure origin, yet the poem also recognizes the very impossibility of a true beginning, at least as a response adequate to mere humans. As the poem itself demonstrates, beginning implicates the subject fully in time. Rather than develop the tautology of such formulations, it continues to insist on acts of historical recuperation and memory.

Piers Plowman, in effect, reverses the trajectory of the line just quoted from the *Cursor mundi,* concentrating, instead of on the ineffable primordiality of God, on the beginning of all other things. The C Text ensures that we see its impetus toward the beginning of mundane time by revising such moments as the comparison of the Trinity to a fist. "For god þat al bygan in begynnynge of the worlde / Ferde furste as a f[u]ste" (19.113–14). What this clarifies has less to do with Trinitarian theology than it does with the necessity of thinking theology through beginnings, with the immanence and interference of time even when the most abstract and homogeneous principles are being invoked. It is as if we cannot think about a principle without also thinking about it as a *principium,* and, of course, the times that must follow from it. As we will see in a moment, the poem at one point describes even God's creation of beginnings as being mediated by a concept, a principle: God "gynnyng hadde neuere but þo hym good þoȝte" (B 16.194). What is different about divine beginnings, however, is the relation between thinking and the *principium.* Unlike us, God can think before he begins; for him, a principle is not yet a beginning. Our predicament of beginning is seen in the way in which this passage cannot invoke that idea without resorting to the language of beginning and temporality, which is to say, in our understanding of the nature of inception, without resorting to language.

Elsewhere in talking about the Trinity the poem makes just such an attempt to go beyond the constraints of language and time by flaunting the aporetic nature of Trinitarian language.

> That oon dooþ alle dooþ and ech dooþ bi his one.
> The firste haþ myȝt and maiestee, maker of alle þynges;

Pater is his propre name, a persone by hymselue.
The secounde of þa[t] sire is Sothfastnesse *filius*,
Wardeyn of þat wit haþ; was euere wiþouten gynnyng.
(B 16.183–87)

Invoking concepts of priority and enumeration while collapsing them into a homologic repository—one not available in Modern English, in which "one" is the same as "own"—the passage exploits the ambiguity of the word "sire," which, read one way, represents the apparently nonsensical, yet orthodox, idea that the Son is the Father, and read another way suggests that the Son *and* the Father participate in, and might be understood in, the discursive registers of fourteenth-century English principles of dominion.

This possibility is suggested by the poem's more explicit uses of the temporality of beginning to suggest an adequation between God's time and man's time. In more conventional descriptions of the Trinity, the question of beginning is the point at which language and human institutions disappear, leaving us able to say only, as Peter Lombard does, "[D]icitur Pater principium, et Filius principium, et Spiritus sanctus principium, *sed differenter*."[26] What is especially canny about Langland's appropriation of this gesture of ineffability is that he uses beginning as a mark of difference, and a difference that is the symptom of time, of fallenness. The C Text consistently extends this critique of beginning, pursuing its logic even to a point at which human time does (did) not exist:

Dauid in his daies dobbed knyghtes,
Dede hem swere on here swerd to serue treuthe euere.
And god whan he bigan heuene in þat grete blisse
Made knyghtes in his couert creatures tene,
Cherubyn and ceraphyn, suche seuene and anoþer,
Lucifer, louelokest tho, ac litel while it duyred.
(C 1.101–6)

The C Text places a section that in the B Text concerns the ethics of knighthood, and particularly the injunction to follow Truth, just before this passage, rather than between the accounts of David's foundation of knighthood and God's "beginning" of heaven.[27] This revision clarifies the relation between acts of foundation and the establishment of, quite literally in the B Text, "ordre" (B 1.104)—a word replaced in C by "knyghthed" (C 1.98). While these changes might seem trivial and unmotivated, taken as a whole they create a narrative in which human agency is less closely associated with abstract principles and God is more closely associated with the principle that is the beginning itself. The C Text account of the fall of Lucifer extends the abstract resonances of divine beginning in other ways. It emphasizes Lucifer's flight to the North as a deviation from a place of perpetual beginning:

> ". . . why wolde he tho, þat wykkede Lucifer,
> Luppen alofte *[in lateribus Aquilonis]*
> Thenne sitten in þe sonne syde þere þe day roweth?"
> (C 1.112–14)

Earlier emphasizing Lucifer's impatience with his situation—he "litel while it duyred" (C 1.106)—the passage brings to bear the insistence of temporality on a creature that is now fallen, using such adverbials of time here as "tho" to remind us that Lucifer cannot act outside of time. Nor can he remain with the beginning, the continually beginning day in the East, the *origo* that suggests a perpetual, always rising beginning *(oriens)* rather than the contingent, dispensable action of Lucifer. But is it possible to understand this *origo* as a beginning without thinking in terms of the fallenness of time, declining, falling away from, as we think about it, that *oriens*?

Despite the poem's own observations that God "was evere withouten gynnyng," the Good Samaritan's discussion of the first person of the Trinity suggests that the poem does implicate God in beginnings, and therefore in time. Indeed, Langland several times states the incarnation in this way, as a beginning for a God who gave everything else its beginning:

> . . . god þat bigan al of his goode wille
> Bicam man of a mayde mankynde to saue
> And suffrede to be sold to se þe sorwe of deying,
> The which vnknytteþ alle care and comsynge is of reste.
> (B 18.212–15)

This is an unusual statement of the doctrine of *kenosis,* the self-emptying of God in the incarnation. God's acceptance of mortality concludes, as it must, in death, but it is a death that Langland (or Peace, who is speaking here) states in terms of a beginning. In quite an unexpected sense, particularly at a point in the poem when one would expect any beginning to refer to the resurrection, Langland suggests that beginning is the condition of mortality and that the incarnation is characterized by God's submission to a beginning.

The beginning of Christ's earthly career is described in terms that implicate not only death in beginning, but also eternity. The poem's account of the Marriage at Cana includes the usual interpretation that the transformation of water into wine represents the transformation of the Old Law into the New,[28] but it emphasizes that the beginning of Christ's ministry is really the involvement of God in a beginning:

> ...þer bigan god of his grace to do wel
> . . . .
> So at þat feeste first as I bifore tolde
> Bigan god of his grace and goodnesse to dowel;
> . . . .
> ...þere comsede he do wel.
> (B 19.110, 115–16, 123)

If the fall of the angels historicizes Lucifer, this account of the beginning of Christ's ministry historicizes God. Conscience's account frames the incident in terms of beginning: the activity of a being without a beginning has been assigned, because of the incarnation, an identifiable, historical inception. Faith's similar account of the incarnation seemingly points out, however, that the beginning in which God is implicated does not compromise His eternally unchanging nature:

> ...god, þat gynnyng hadde neuere but þo hym good þo3te,
> Sent forþ his sone as for seruaunt þat tyme
> To ocupie hym here til issue were spronge,
> That is children of charite, and holi chirche þe moder.
> (B 16.194–97)

This passage again concentrates on the involvement of the incarnation in time, pointing to the moment at which God ordained it—"þo," "þat tyme." Although it seems to implicate only the Son in that beginning, the passage may come as close to the borders of orthodoxy as the previous one. It certainly comes close to self-contradiction. The easiest reading for the first two lines here is probably "God never had a beginning; but when it seemed good to him[29] he sent forth his son." There is no causal connection implied between the first two clauses. If, however, "but þo" is taken as a coordinating conjunction, the second clause qualifies the first: "God never had a beginning, except (or unless) when it seemed good to him [and] he sent forth his son."[30] The passage challenges its own statement of the conventional commonplace of the *genitor ingenitus,* which appears in three other places in the poem,[31] with the assertion of a divine, incarnational beginning.

Despite the averral that God the Father is *sine principio,* the poem's insistence on equating paternity with beginning implicates that very absence of beginning with beginning. The attraction of the equation between fatherhood and beginning distorts even apparently orthodox statements of the idea. As a proverb found in several medieval schoolbooks says, "[E]uery thynge hath a begynnyng."[32] The poem cannot seem to avoid assigning even to archetypal paternity a beginning of some sort. Faith's description of the incarnation chronicles an essentially emerging, incipient paternity: "[God] sent forþ his son . . . / To ocupie hym here til issue were spronge, / That is children of charite, and holi chirche þe moder."[33] Paternity marks a kind of beginning, a point from which new dispensations begin, and from which genealogies spring. But beginning is not always entailed in archetypal paternity, as the Chester Cycle demonstrates:

> I ame greate God gracious,
> which never had begyninge.
> The whole foode of parente is sett
> in my essention.[34]

The play presents what Julia Kristeva calls Trinitarian theology's "unprecedented affirmation of symbolic paternity"[35] as the abstract principle of parenthood. The verb "sett" reaffirms the underlying idea that God's essence is unchanged by creation, that his essence is not physically or ontologically involved in biological generation or genealogy.[36] His "essention" contains the "foode of parente"; he is not literal parenthood itself.

The Chester Cycle's elegant balance of the abstract principle of parenthood and the absence of a beginning is not sustained in *Piers Plowman*. The poem's reiteration of the presence of a beginning betrays its preference for searching out the temporal roots, the beginnings that may compromise the attractive fiction of origin. Even Holy Church's proclamation of her lineage uses the idea of a God without beginning more to declare the integrity of her own beginnings than to articulate the idea of God as pure origin:

> I ouȝte ben hyere þan she; I kam of a bettre.
> My fader þe grete god is and ground of alle graces,
> Oo god wiþouten gynnyng, and I his goode douȝter.
> (B 2.28–30)

Paternity, at least for Holy Church, is a point of beginning from which moral attributes ("graces," "goode") spring. But history thwarts the aim of beginning, to start without an origin. The problem with Wrong, as she points out, is that he is literally a false founder, the "Fader of falshed, [he] founded it hymselue." A parodic point of pure origin, he also points out the problematic nature of moral genealogy, as Holy Church defines it, which Langland will be exploring and attempting to redress throughout the poem. Holy Church's nearly totemic assertion of beginning does little to address the problem that it raises: how to distinguish between good beginnings in the formal sense and good beginnings in the moral sense. That is still family matter—a problem that the poem takes up in the form of good and bad genealogies.

ISSUES OF BEGINNING

Piers Plowman may struggle to preserve the absolute distinction between beginning and origin—a distinction described by Edward Said.[37] But in preserving the distinction between the ideal image of God as pure origin, the poem also shows how the aim of earthly, secular beginnings is thwarted by their very inception. And even accounts of origin are plagued by our inability to avoid repeating things in beginning them.[38] Repetition becomes a complex figure of individual action in *Piers Plowman*. Repetition represents tropological beginnings that mirror an original event, in the same way that Eve's eating of the apple in the garden is, tropologically, the genesis of individual concupiscence. At the other end of the scale is the kind of beginning that explicitly seeks to reject the problems associated with a beginning by making it a "necessary fiction." This is the kind that Said names "adjacency," characterized by the "lateral and dispersed rather than the linear and the sequential."[39] By exploring how these beginnings are even more fully implicated in history—and indeed how they found history itself—Langland attempts to create the crucial category of a beginning that is technically good, yet one that does not make manifest the power of beginning in its totality. Langland examines this kind of beginning in the fall of Lucifer, the "lateral and dispersed" descendants of Cain, discussions of miscegenation, and the figure of untimeliness itself.[40]

In the poem, Cain is a figure that counters proper beginnings. His progeny compromises the development of legitimate beginnings. The principal discussion of Cain's significance appears in a passus whose main topic is the significance of beginning as creation. Most of the passus is Wit's answer to Will's initial question, "'What kynnes þyng is kynde?" (B 19.25). The answer, as we have seen, defines Kynde clearly in terms of beginning and creation, the "Fader and formour" who "gynnyng hadde neuere" (B 19.27–28). After a brief account of the creation of man in God's image (32–52), Wit goes on to describe ways in which man either imitates or undoes the beginning that God made. The discussion of Dowel, for instance, fundamentally establishes Dowel as a figure of beginning, the first in a triadic scheme of salvation.[41] In the A Text, Thought clearly articulates a definition that the subsequent versions obscure but do not erase:

> . . . þat is dred of god, dowel it makiþ.
> It is begynnyng of goodnesse god for to douten.
> Salamon it seide for a soþ tale:
> *Inicium sapiencie timor domini.*
>
> (A 10.79–82)

Thought's association of Dowel with "inicium" and "dred of god" places Dowel at the beginning of the penitent life—the "lyif þat is louable and leele" that Reason counsels Will to "bigynne" in the C Text.[42] But Thought goes on to locate "Dowel" at the beginning of some of the most influential human institutions—particularly marriage.

Dowel inheres not just in the beginning of moral reformation but also in the foundation of beneficial human institutions. The world "stant" upon the institution of marriage; wedded people are the "rote of dowel" (A 10.133–34), and from this "rote" come

> Boþe maidenis & [mynchons], monkes & ancris,
> Kinges & kniȝtes, & alle kyne clerkis,
> Barouns & burgeis, & bondemen of tounes.
> (A 10.136–38)

Thought argues that those who do not contribute to the order of society are those who have bad beginnings, of whom the archetype is Cain: "Ac fals folk & feiþles, þeuis & leiȝeris, / Ben conseyuid in cursid tyme as kaym was on Eue" (A 10.139–40). Despite arguing earlier that penitent behavior is the foundation of society, Thought now points out that the seeds of social anarchy are not the consequence of individual moral actions but of the beginnings that individual lives have. Beginnings do not necessarily engender evil outright; they may be detrimental simply because they come at the wrong time. As Thought points out several times, Cain "muche bale wrouȝte" because he was "in cursid tyme engendrit" (A 10.148).

Cain becomes a figure of evil not because of his later actions, but because of the actions of his parents. His life begins at the wrong time. Langland borrows from a tradition beginning with the apocryphal *Vita Adae et Evae* that locates the conception and birth of Cain in a period of penance enforced on Adam and Eve after their expulsion from Eden, which they violate by conceiving Cain.[43] The C Text echoes the tradition: "Withouten repentaunce of here rechelenesse a rybaud þei [Adam and Eve] engendrede" (C 10.215). The A Text more generally associates Cain's conception with the curse placed on Adam and Eve, and their exile from paradise:

> An aungel in angir hiȝte h[em] too wende
> Into þis wrecchide world to wonen & to libben
> In tene & trauaille to here lyues ende;

In þat curside constellacioun þei knewe togideris,
And brouȝt forþ a barn . . .
(A 10.144–47)

Augustine implicitly blames the strains of evil perpetuated by Cain on Adam's condemned beginning, not on Cain's subsequent transgressions.[44] The *Cursor mundi* goes even further in attributing Cain's depravity to his origins, making him the offspring of the devil:

. . . caym was þe fendes fode
Was neuer wors of modir born
þerfore was he after for lorn.[45]

The *Cursor mundi*'s particular way of linking beginning and consequence summarizes the shape of Thought's discourse. Thought begins to discuss the dire result of Cain's engendering in "cursit tyme," and his insertion of Psalm 7:15 at this point assumes an almost proverbial force: "*Concepit dolore & peperit iniquitatem*" (A 10.150).[46] The B Text adds a line here that makes the lesson even clearer: "And alle þat come of þat Caym come to yuel ende" (B 9.126). This is a historical and theological warrant for the proverbial principle that no good can possibly come from a bad beginning. And Cain is imagined in the poem as the progenitor of all bad beginnings.

While commentators normally interpret the Cain legend morally, treating Cain as the symbol of excessive attachment to earthly possessions,[47] Thought interprets the legend almost literally, making Cain the ancestor of all evildoers. Indeed, he suggests that all who descend from Cain, or who marry into Cain's lineage, are condemned:

Alle þat comen of þat caym crist hatid aftir,
And manye mylions mo of men & wommen
[þat] of seth & his sistir siþþe forþ come
For þei mariede hem wiþ curside men of kaymes kyn.
(A 10.151–54)

The Cain legend contains not just tropological but also "historical" truth. Thought's treatment of Cain's lineage is an instance of what Ruth Mellinkoff has suggested is "a long tradition in England of popular belief in real descendants of Cain."[48] The B Text strengthens the suggestion that Cain's iniquity is conveyed along genealogical lines by adding a passage on the sins of fathers:

> Here abouȝte þe barn þe belsires giltes,
> And alle for hir [fore]fadres ferden þe werse.
> The gospel is hera[g]ein in o degre, I fynde:
> *Filius non portabit iniquitatem patris et pater non portabit iniquitatem filij.*
> Ac I fynde, if þe fader be fals and a sherewe,
> That somdel þe sone shal haue þe sires tacches.
> Impe on an Ellere, and if þyn appul be swete
> Muchel merueille me þynketh; and moore of a sherewe
> That bryngeþ forþ any barn but if he be þe same
> And haue a Sauour after þe sire; selde sestow ooþer:
> *Numquam collig[unt] de spinis vua[s] nec de tribulis ficus.*
> And þus þoruȝ cursed Caym cam care upon erþe.
> (B 9.146–156)

Thought's denial of the witness of "the Gospel" (actually Ezechiel 18:20) is also a denial that each generation makes a new beginning. Cain's descendants perpetuate his bad beginning, unable themselves to start over.

Cain is the figure of a beginning that cannot be shaken, the progenitor of a legacy that poses a threat to Seth's offspring, the "sons of God."[49] Cain is traditionally the founder of institutions that threaten the integrity and stability of divinely ordained institutions, the progenitor of the Saracens that threaten Christendom,[50] the builder of the earthly city that opposes the city of God,[51] the founder of the orders of friars that threaten the established church,[52] and the originator of opposition to the natural law.[53] *Piers Plowman* presents Cain as a genealogical threat, a figure who stands at the beginning of a long line of malefactors. God presents the flood to Noah as an opportunity to cleanse the legacy of Cain, to erase the beginning that is commemorated in Cain's descendants: "That I [man makede now] it me forþynkeþ: / *Penitet me fecisse hominem*" (B 9.133–33a). The flood will "[c]lene awey þe corsed blood þat Caym haþ ymaked" (B 9.139). Cain's act of genealogical creation challenges and compromises the divine creation of man. The numberlessness of Cain's descendants violates the primordial order established in the beginning of the world, replacing the primal act of creation with an infinity of instances—"manye mylions mo." His numberless offspring threaten to displace the conjoint unity of "trewe wedded libbynge folke" (B 9.110), whose descendants manifest the enduring unity of their origin: they "out of o man come" (B 9.114). The blood that Cain has "ymaked" is the metonymic figure of a physicality that threatens to overrun the entire world, obliterating the traces of original creation by the sheer ubiquity of its presence.

The passus's initial formulation of the paradox of divine creation, the production of physical being out of the act of speech ("þoruȝ þe word that he [warp] woxen forþ beestes"; B 9.32) anticipates this later account of the undoing of creation in the form of a flood that will destroy primarily beasts, the images of Cain, the creator of a progeny that represents both bestiality and pure corporality: the flood will

> Clene awey þe cursed bloed þat of Caym spronge.
> Bestes þat now beth shal banne þe tyme
> That euere þat corsed Caym cam on þis erthe.
> (C 10.227–29)

Cain's rival creation is transmuted into an undoing of creation. The flood cleanses the genealogy that is the record of Cain's inimical beginning and replaces it with the unity that had been threatened, with the initiation of new genealogical lines: "onliche of vch kynde a payre . . . shal be with þe ysaued" (C 10.232–33). The potential of genealogical creation is rescued from the flood that destroys its unfettered consequences.

The episode of Cain in the poem dramatizes the elemental power of beginnings and the way in which the poem uses genealogy to define the consequences of beginning. Creation and making are not morally neutral acts and may even, as the Cain story suggests, verge on destruction. The lesson about making that Wit attempts to teach Will here may anticipate Imaginatif's attack on making in B 12; if so, it is a much darker refraction of Imaginatif's comparatively bland warning that it might be better for Will to read his Psalter. The Cain episode suggests that there is an irredeemable gap between material making and divine creation, larger than the gap that Elaine Scarry finds characteristic of biblical narratives of creation. Genealogy is also an image of the undoing of creation, not merely a rival to divine, verbal creation.[54] It is not only the kin of Cain that unleash destruction and horror on the world: it is also the institutions founded by Cain himself, the father of civilization and murder. We may never know whether the two acts can be separated, yet that is precisely what the work of establishment, building, history, beginning sets out again and again to discover, hoping that its principles will not undo it.

CONDITORA

[Foundation, making, storing in the memory, burying, hiding, closing the eyes of a corpse, originating, composing, writing]

The Archive of Grammar

Beginning and Documentary Remembrance

[T]he city is never completely founded. It is the same for us—I mean for knowledge.

—Michel Serres,
Rome: The Book of Foundations

The previous chapter argued that familial beginnings, those imagined as stemming from the family or as being somehow analogous to the engendering of a family, are a compelling form of intrinsic beginning. But they are a kind of beginning that is not sustainable, resting on the absence of the progenitor, the obliteration of the familial origin in the emergence of successors, of new forms, of new progenitors. If the *familia* itself is not a stabilizing principle, if its structure can be revised by the very form it uses to represent itself—genealogy—then what resources are available to fix the beginnings of human institutions in history? What social practices are there that might reinforce the consolidating principles of language? Outside of the more or less central institutions of the Chancery and the Exchequer the principal popular investment was probably in the charter, an investment that we might regard as fetishistic. The famous story of the 1381 rebels at Saint Albans who demanded from the abbot an "ancient charter" with capital letters of gold and silver indicates the economic and historical desires embodied in the charter.[1] It is a written instrument whose obvious antiquity signifies an older, and therefore more authoritative, establishment, and an instrument whose value for the amendment of the political economy is instantiated in the lavish and numismatic materiality of the text's ornamentation. At least, that is the value that the charter is *imagined* to have.

At the other disciplinary and discursive extreme lies *grammatica,* a practice associated less with the imaginary than with the symbolic or, more precisely, with the superego. Beginning with acts of literal discipline in which students are compelled to memorize the rules of language, *grammatica* concerns itself with the transmission and refinement of the laws that regulate words and the relations between them. By enforcing these laws, both at its inception in the classroom and at the level of the university, *grammatica* extends the work of memory and animates the principles of language with a deliberative force of their own. As we will see, grammar is an important instrument—because it is one of the few available—for social analysis. In *Piers Plowman* we see, if not more clearly, then with more detail, just how grammar can be used to think through, to analyze, the implicit problems of the political economy. With the problem of "meed"—reward—the poem brilliantly and to a degree not seen elsewhere in Middle English literature turns to an exacting and precise discussion of grammatical principles, analyzing the problem as a problem of designation—deciding what to call reward and what bribery. That is to say, it analyzes the problem as a linguistic and grammatical problem, its incipient political economy also, and primarily, an economy of language.

The Principial Charter

Meed is important because it unfolds, is understood, in a language that has social consequences. It is an initiating pun that produces not merely a narrative but also a counternarrative, and in choosing which narrative relates its intrinsic origins most accurately, one needs to take into account the dangers intrinsic to language, the specific consequences of such an initiating pun. What the poem's meditation on the valence of meed—reward—asks us to consider, in other words, is the question of how intrinsic language can be prevented from overwhelming the world as its consequences unfold. The practice of assigning reward is a practice that can potentially redeem the incipient, originating function of language, in a practice of management that is articulated in terms of language, what is also called *recte scribendi*. But it is a practice that is, as we will see, inseparable from those of *recte legendi* and *recte vivendi* also. What the C Text ultimately does with the complex, imbricated discussion of meed and language is to imagine the possibility that a public practice of memory is possible, a practice that depends on the commemoration of the intrinsic principles of social foundation, in a daring attempt to construct a memorial grammar, a grammar that manages and regulates the acts of memory that are already implicit and necessary in language, reward, and social formation.

Texts that depend on the establishment of a beginning for their authority are used in *Piers* to explore the means by which a beginning can be established or the points at which its claims break down. As Anne Middleton argues, the poem's frequent appearance in manuscripts devoted to legendary or historical material suggests that it appealed primarily to its readers' "practical historical imaginations." As a work itself concerned largely with historical beginnings and foundations, *Piers Plowman* appeals to an audience interested in the relation between priority and authority:

> For the "fit" audience of *Piers,* penetrating to historical precedents and foundations of both temporal and spiritual imperatives is a habitual way of thinking, a means of resolution, and a source of deeply invested emotion. [*Piers* occurs] among shorter works whose central metaphoric device is one or another form of the written instruments by which possessions and offices were transferred and diplomatic relations sustained—charters, letters, wills. . . . *Piers* belonged among works in which the quest for salvation and the examination of the foundations of possession were mutually metonymic.[2]

But the relation between history and salvation is not as simple as the poem's own metonymic texts suggest. The best examples of the complex ways in which a beginning must be narrated in order to assert any spiritual or political authority are perhaps the poem's several charters, precisely because they make the connection between spiritual and historical authority seem too simple.

Charters and Beginnings

The poem's first extensive charter, that of Meed's marriage to Favel, raises the question of whether the mere incorporation of a different mode of writing can constitute a true beginning. The answer to this question produces perhaps the most complex discussion of beginnings in the poem, refracted through the lenses of grammar, genealogy and political theory. The A Text most clearly associates the charter with beginnings, but the B and C Texts, as they so often do, extend the implications of the association, probing further into the questions about beginnings and foundations that the charter raises.

The A Text prefaces the charter with the first of many clear echoes of the beginning of the poem itself, a return to the visionary landscape of the prologue, with its plenitude of people and professions:

> þer nas halle no hous to herberwe þe peple,
> þat iche feld nas ful of folk al aboute.
> In myddis a mounteyne at mydmorewe tide
> Was piȝt vp a pauyloun proud for þe nones,
> And ten þousand of tentis teldit beside
> Of kniȝtes of cuntr[e], of comeres aboute,
> For sisours, for somenours, for selleris, for beggeris,
> For lerid, for lewid, for laboreris of þropis . . .[3]
>
> A 2.38–45

It is difficult to tell whether this recapitulation of the opening vision is a completely new beginning or a revision. The second vision offers provocative similarities to the first, without quite resolving the problem of how the allegory, topography, or time of each relates to the other. In both passages in the A Text a structure on a hill, whose significance is not immediately apparent to the dreamer, dominates the scene. Both visions begin at about the same time of day: in the beginning of the poem, the dreamer "beheld in to þe Est an heiȝ to þe sonne" (A Prol. 13), in what is really a short *chronographia* of "mydmorewe tide." The phrase "feld . . . ful of folk" is less riddling, recalling more explicitly the initial scene of the poem, with its panoramic sweep of the professions of all humankind.

The B Text preserves the relation between the Prologue and this scene, though not the specific echoes, by substituting for the "feld . . . ful of folk" the line that follows it in the Prologue: "Of alle manere of men, þe meene and þe riche" (B Prol. 18, B 2.56). But the signs that this passage recalls the beginning of the poem indicate, also, that the passage is not a mere echo of the beginning. The field of folk is no longer aligned between two opposite poles, but crowded around an unchallenged center of activity, the "[proud] pauyloun." The setting supplants the fundamental conflict undergirding the opening vision, the allegorical opposition of Truth and Wrong. Indeed, the passage largely supplants the allegorical references of the opening with the language of knightly romance. It appeals more to a taste for courtly edifice than to an appetite for tropological edification, with its "pauyloun proud for þe nones" and "ten þousand tents." The setting is a staple of knightly romances, and the principal action of at least two that probably precede *Piers Plowman, Sir Landevale* and *Winner and Waster,* begins with the discovery of a pitched "pauyloun." This revision of the beginning of *Piers Plowman,* or this rebeginning that makes a plausible opening for a courtly, secular romance, forms the setting for a charter that attempts to forge new secular ties.

The B Text echo of the Prologue blunts the social resonance of the phrases that describe the field of folk, restricting the categories to simply the "meene and þe riche." This restriction makes it clear that the new beginning that the charter forges is concerned mostly with wealth and excludes most of the theological and political institutions that appear in the beginning of the poem. As the charter itself declares, "Mede is ymaried moore for here goodes / Than for any vertue or fairnesse or any free kynde" (B 2.76–77).

While the declaration of the charter invites comparison with the beginning of the poem, it rejects exact identification with it. As a new beginning, the scene has affinities with the kinds of beginning that Edward Said has found characteristic of modern writing: "[S]uch a beginning *authorizes;* it constitutes an authorization for what follows from it. With regard to what precedes it, a beginning represents . . . a discontinuity."[4] As the remarks of Theology and Conscience reveal later, the effort to create discontinuity is precisely the motivation behind the charter. A corollary of Said's observation might be that discontinuity also represents beginning: the charter's deliberate suppression of Meed's lineage and of her prior betrothal enables the fiction that the charter really does represent a beginning. That beginning, in turn, has a large part to play in the charter's construction of the fiction of authority, from the opening legal formula *Sciant presentes et futuri* (B 2.74a, C 2.80a) to the absolute infinitives[5] that make its first half what E. Talbot Donaldson describes as an "enabling instrument."[6] The poem's incorporation of the charter acknowledges the importance of a beginning even in the way it describes the act of its declaration:

> Symonye and Cyuylle stonden forþ boþe
> And vnfoldeþ þe feffement that Fals hath ymaked.
> [Th]us bigynnen þ[e] gomes [and] greden [wel] heiȝe.
> (B 2.72–74;[7] also A 2.54–56)

In having Symonye and Cyvylle "bigynnen," the poem makes of the act of declaration a gesture of beginning.[8] The reading of the charter links, at least provisionally, authority and authorship, foundation and beginning. The charter appears set to forge a new secular compact that bears no relation to the moral and theological antecedents of the poem.

A charter cannot make legitimate what is already dubious—as the account of the Donation of Constantine itself shows in *Piers Plowman:* "*Dos ecclesie* þis day haþ ydronke venym / And þo þat han Petres power arn apoisoned alle" (B 15.560–61). An opponent of Wyclif's uses the example of charters, in fact, to impugn Wyclif's identification of authority with antiquity: "Magister meis est illius opinionis, quod antiquitas Scripturae maximam auctoritate facit; unde aliae scripturae, quanto recentiores, tanto sunt falsiores; sicut exemplificat in cartis, in quibus facta mentione de donationibus dicitur, do hoc, vel istud, tibi, et haeredibus tuis in perpetuum. Et certum est quod hujusmodi donatio effectum promissum habere non potest" (My master is of the opinion that the antiquity of Scripture is the strongest argument regarding its authority. Therefore other writings are less authoritative in proportion as they are more recent. This is exemplified in charters, which say, with reference to gifts, "I give this, or that, to you and your heirs forever." And it is certain that a gift of this kind cannot have the promised effect).[9]

But charters might also fail to achieve their purpose precisely because newer compacts do not necessarily invalidate older ones. The granting of a charter does not obscure the moral imperative, at least in Langland's poem, of searching out its antecedents.

The late-fourteenth-century charter is a paradigm of the perplexed relations between authority, temporal priority, and civil dominion. It appears in such a form most prominently in the Wycliffite debates over possession, blended, not surprisingly, with the strains of apocalypticism that feature so heavily in antimendicant polemic.[10] In the passage from

De civili dominio to which John Kynyngham may be referring, Wyclif himself argues that charters cannot fulfill their object, that of granting perpetual ownership, because civil dominion cannot survive the Antichrist, much less the Day of Judgment.[11] Indeed, the controversy over the charter of enfeoffment in *Piers Plowman* touches on many of the problems raised in the debate over poverty and possession. The text from Luke 10:7 that Theology quotes in his denunciation of the marriage, "Dignus est operarius [mercede sua]" (Schmidt B 2.123), was, as Penn Szittya observes, one of those "in the forefront of the controversy over evangelical poverty."[12]

These discussions also focus on the kinds of beginning that charters record. Wyclif questions the efficacy of charters elsewhere in *De civili dominio* on the basis not of their effect but of their antecedents. Discussing the Magna Carta, he argues that the authority of charters and civil compacts derives from their accordance with divine law.

> [N]o mennes lawis ne chartirs maad of men han strengþe but in as myche as goddis law conferreþ him; for what is ony chartre or any lawe worth, but ȝif God conferme it by his lawe? & so þis grete chartre wolde moue by Goddes wyll, þat kyngis & here rewmes schulde mayntene þe churche by þe ordenaunce of god.[13]

This argument lies very much in the mainstream of the concerted attack against endowment and possession.[14] The primary appeal here, however, is not apocalyptic but nostalgic, the implicit argument not that beginnings confer an inherent authority, but that origins need to be recovered. Both sides of the argument over clerical dominion in fourteenth-century England, in fact, argued from what they regarded as the divinely instituted origins of their positions, rather than from a history of human compacts.

The debate over the right of mendicants and clergy alike to hold property might be called a contest of "ordenaunce." Some debate amounted to name-calling, a struggle over whether the speaker of a particular phrase, the phrase that occurs partially translated in *Piers Plowman* (B 15.560, C 17.223), "hodie infusum est venenum in ecclesia," is an angel or a devil.[15] The real debate revolved around the question of whether the church ever had been temporally endowed, and whether the ordinance of endowment could be invalidated by a previous endowment. The principles behind the debate are precisely the same as those behind the argument over Meed's charter of enfeoffment. Uthred de Boldon attempts to resuscitate the legend in *De perfectione vivendi,* arguing that the endowment of the church marked the beginning of its greatest growth: "*[diabolus]* publice in aere clamauerit . . . 'hodie infusum est *[venenum]* in ecclesia' . . . ipse mendaciter appellat 'venenum' quod est ecclesie optimum alitum" (The devil cried out publicly in the air, "This day has poison been poured into the church" . . . but he falsely calls "poison" what is the best nutriment of the church).[16] For him, the Donation of Constantine merely reified a right of dominion that had begun in the apostolic church.[17] His argument depends heavily on appealing to the precedent set by the apostolic church, but his chief concern is to justify the ordinance created by the Donation of Constantine. Favel and Gyle in *Piers Plowman* share Uthred's emphasis on the contract as empowering instrument, although they attempt, with a blatant duplicity that Uthred does not share, to ratify both the charter and Meed's betrothal by bribing notaries and witnesses.

The poem rejects the charter in ways that closely parallel the fourteenth-century polemic against the temporal endowment of the church. Both manifest an underlying conviction that a prior "ordenaunce" makes a stronger claim to authority than does a more recent disposition. This conviction may simply become an effort to separate *Ursprung* from *Entstehung,* a sacred origin from an historical beginning,[18] but it also demonstrates the extent to which the validity of an institution is weighed by examining its beginnings. Medieval guild charters, for instance, are sometimes a virtual celebration of the historical fact of beginning:

> þe ordenaunces of certeyn persones weryn be-gunnen in þe Cite of Norwyche, in yer of grace a thousande thre hundred and syxti, þe ȝer of regne of kyng Edward, þe thridde after þe conquest, xxxiij.[19]

The authority of an institution stems from the historical validity of its foundation. But the validity of an institution is often weighed against the authority of its beginning. Both anticlerical polemic and *Piers Plowman* use genealogical succession as an analogy of the faithfulness, or unfaithfulness, of an institution to its beginnings. They portray an institution's deviation from its beginnings as a blemish on an original purity. A Lollard tract against clerical possession blames secular lords for perpetuating a betrayal of the church's beginnings: "Lords should not sue her predecessouris and progenitours in her foly dedis and oþis þat þai han made to mayntene þis mischeuous peruertynge of cristis ordenaunce."[20] The tract depicts the conflict between competing "ordenaunces" (the original disposition of the church and the oaths sworn by secular lords) as a chronicle of divergent genealogies. The temporal, fleshly genealogy that inclines a lord to endow the church with worldly goods supplants the spiritual genealogy that is the true record of the church instituted by Christ. Legitimate familial descent literally entails another kind of illegitimacy or, as the tract calls it, a "peruertynge."[21]

The genealogy of illegitimacy becomes a virtual topos in Lollard criticisms of the church. The betrayal of the church's original "ordenaunce" does not simply become a rupture in apostolic succession. It becomes the "peruertynge" of a line, a betrayal of lineage. The priest who deliberately deceives his congregation, for example, is accused of miscegenation, not of malfeasance.[22] Betrayals that are represented as incestuous beget illegitimate strains, as the tract known as the "Twelve Conclusions of the Lollards" suggests:

> Qwan þe chirche of Yngelonde began *[incepit]* to dote in temperalte aftir hir stepmodir þe grete chirche of Rome . . . feyth, hope and charite begunne *[inceperunt]* for to fle out of oure chirche; for pride with his sori genealogie of dedly synnes chalangith it be title of heritage.[23]

This passage shows clearly that a beginning and an origin are not identical. Here, each beginning is a departure from an original "ordenaunce," first when the church in England swerves from its original lineage, and then when the ecclesiastical virtues desert the church. This last event is framed as a conflict of rival genealogies, the arrival of the genealogy of "dedly synnes" that supports pride's claim to the church, "of heritage." The polemicist's description of the threat to the church leads him to confer an unwilling legitimacy on pride's claim to primacy. A genealogy is more than a neutral record; it is also an empowering instrument.[24] Pride's "heritage" and the title to which he lays claim threaten to make these beginnings not just disruptions but important episodes in the founding of an institution. As Foucault observes, genealogy furnishes a significant threat to the integrity of versions of institutional foundation: "The search for descent is not the erecting of foundations: on the contrary, it disturbs what was previously considered immobile; it fragments what was thought unified; it shows the heterogeneity of what was imagined consistent with itself."[25] Genealogy is the contested record of rival versions of foundation. The desire to penetrate to the "historical precedents and foundations of both temporal and spiritual imperatives"[26] in *Piers Plowman* is projected in some mutually antagonistic ways. Perhaps the greatest of these contests is over the lineage of Meed, whose "heterogeneity" is only confirmed by her mixed lineage.

The Archaeology of Meed

Despite the precise and vehement genealogies that Holy Church and Theology ascribe to Meed, they do not settle the question of Meed's essential characteristics. Neither Holy Church nor Meed disagrees, presumably, with the use of genealogy as an index of status and even of moral inclination, but neither of the genealogies they offer provides an authoritative answer. Genealogy fails almost as badly as the debate in passus 3 to assign a role to Meed. As James Simpson points out, "There seems to be no authority from within the text who can fix the meanings of 'mede.'"[27] Perhaps the greatest measure of Meed's multivalence is the irresolvable ambiguity of her lineage.

It is clear from even the brief accounts in the A Text that the question of the meaning of Meed will not be answered on genealogical grounds. Yet Holy Church and Theology base their opinions of Meed almost entirely on appraisals of her lineage. Holy Church's objection to Meed's higher standing in the "popis paleis" suppresses her own allegorical nature—she fails to point out that the palace is also a synecdoche for the Church itself—to investigate Meed's and her own genealogical antecedents:

> . . . wrong was hir sire;
> Oute of wrong heo wex to wroþerhele manye.
> I auȝte ben hiȝere þanne heo for I com of a betre.
> (A 2.19–21)

Theology uses the same method to censure Meed's marriage. Like Holy Church, Theology does not approve of Meed's actions, and he also judges them not by their issue but by the forebears of Meed and her partner, Fals:

> . . . mede is molere of [me]endis engendrit
>
> . . . .
>
> fals is a faitour [and] feyntles of werkis,
> [And] as a bastard yborn of belsab[ubb]is kynde;
> And mede is a mulere, [a maiden of gode];
> She mi3te kisse þe king for cosyn 3if he[o] wolde.
> (A 2. 94–97)

Neither of the genealogies offered of Meed in the A Text impugns her lineage, but they ineluctably restrict the freedom of her actions. Neither Holy Church nor Theology questions Meed's own legitimacy, but each of them suggests that Meed's lineage confers illegitimacy on her actions. She is not debarred from the pope's court, despite her descent from Wrong, but her status there is higher than it ought to be. Holy Church's objection to the undue influence of Meed in "þe popis paleis" is based on her lineage: "heo is preuy as myselue; And so shulde [heo] not be for wrong was hir sire" (A 2.18–19). On the other hand, the status that her lineage gives her in the king's court prevents her from marrying without the king's consent, particularly preventing her from "disparagement" with the patently illegitimate Fals.[28]

But the different genealogies that appear in the A Text do not create irreconcileable images of Meed. Neither version impugns her legitimacy, and neither debars her from participation in "popis paleis" or king's court. The only difference in the two versions is the degree to which her lineage entitles her to involvement. Holy Church complains that the degree of Meed's involvement with the pope is not legitimate; Theology complains that the degree of Meed's involvement with the king makes other involvements illegitimate. In either case, her actions are judged according to her heritage. The A Text avoids a direct confrontation between the two pedigrees. Neither invalidates the other, and they are disclosed in two entirely different settings. But the "meaning of 'mede'" cannot easily be answered by examining her lineage: Holy Church uses it only as a mark of difference, a sign of a status that is only lower *in re-*

lation to herself. She does not reveal what Meed's lineage signifies in the nexus of the papal court.

In the C Text, Holy Church tracks Meed's malign influence from the nonspecific "lordis aboute" (A 2.17) to the center of secular power itself, "to lordes þat lawes han to kepe, / In kynges court, in comune court" (C 2.22–23). The central difference between the accounts of Meed shifts from subtle, if only partially articulated, appraisals of the legitimacy of her actions to appraisals of her own legitimacy. Holy Church includes an extensive account of Meed's genealogy and a more explicit judgment of her genealogical status:

> In þe popes palays he is pryue as mysulue,
> Ac sothnesse wolde nat so for she is a bastard.
> Oon fauel was he[re] fader þat hath a fykel tonge
> And selde soth sayde bote yf he souche gyle,
> And mede is manered aftur hym as men of kynde carpeth:
> *Qualis pater talis fili[us] &c.*
> For shal neuer breere bere berye as a vine,
> Ne on a croked kene thorn kynde fyge wexe:
> *Bona arbor bonum fructum facit.*
>
> (C 2.23–29a)

Holy Church's claim that Meed is a bastard changes entirely the relation between the two genealogies. They become competing registers of truth. Indeed, Theology betrays a kind of agonistic anxiety in the C Text version by asserting three times in four lines[29] that Amends is Meed's mother. Theology does acknowledge the genealogy that Holy Church records, and even extends it one generation back, but answers the problem this raises by simply reasserting his own version of the genealogy: "Althow fals were here fader and fikel-tonge her belsyre / Amendes was here moder" (C 2.124–25). His condemnation of Fals does nothing to settle the matter of Meed's legitimacy, for it only clarifies what is entailed in Holy Church's charge that Meed is a bastard: "Fals is faythles, the fende is his syre, / And as a bastard byȝete was he neuere" (C 2.146–47). Theology accepts the genealogy that Holy Church describes, but insists that his version carries more authority.

It is difficult to see why Theology should be convinced by his own proposal. He does not address the claim that Holy Church makes directly, nor does he say why Meed should be legitimate simply because her mother is Amends. His claim rests, apparently, on the implicit assumption that Amends confers legitimacy on Meed because of her gentle birth. But even a father's "gentle" blood is not enough to confer legitimacy on its own. Trevisa's translation of Higden's *Polychronicon* defines a bastard as "he þat is i-gete of a worþy fader and i-bore of an unworþy moder."[30] Higden's definition rests on an assumption that does not enter into either genealogy: that the parents are not married. It was a commonplace of medieval law that legitimacy could be conferred on a child if its parents were married after its birth; the only point of contention was whether that child would be barred from entering the priesthood.[31] Children could also be legitimated *(fait muliere)* by royal order.[32] Legitimacy does not necessarily involve genealogical considerations.

Allegory, of course, does not have to conform to rules of verisimilitude, and Meed's status need not be bound up in fourteenth-century legal realities. But Langland does grant an unusual degree of influence to genealogy. Indeed, Holy Church's C Text statement of Meed's parenthood is less a simple record than it is a defense of the power of genealogy to determine moral disposition. The statement adds an observation to the Latin tags in the B Text that gives Holy Church's argument some apparently empirical support: "For shal neuer breere bere berye as a vine, / Ne on a croked kene thorn kynde fyge wexe" (C 2.8–9). The insertion, in effect, emphasizes the conveyance of natural characteristics from one generation to another, the influence of biological heritage on morality and even manners, "as men of kynde carpeth." The C Text passage is the converse image of the associations that writers traditionally made between moral allegory and genealogy. The verse "Bona arbor bonum fructum facit," from Matthew 7:17, is almost always interpreted as an allegory of the human soul willing either good or evil. The fruit is human works, the product of the will.[33] The associations of the passage are predominantly tropological, not genealogical, having more to do with a Tree of Good and Evil than with a Tree of Jesse. Similarly, apart from its usual association with Trinitarian theology and the Athanasian Creed,[34] the phrase "Qualis pater, talis filius" had more to do with the assumption of genealogical characteristics by those with moral traits in common than with the use of genealogy to explain moral predilections. Isaac of Stella, for instance, says of those who choose not to hear God's Word that they are "[v]ere filii Adam, ut qualis pater, talis filii" (Truly sons of Adam; like father, like sons).[35] Langland uses the phrase to underpin Holy Church's claim that genealogy informs morality, not that genealogy can be used as an analogy for moral lineage. An even more revealing instance of the power the poem attributes to genealogy is in Wit's disagreement with the gospel:

> The gospel is herea[g]ein in o degre, I fynde:
> *Filius non portabit iniquitatem patris et pater non portabit iniquitatem filij.*
> Ac I fynde, if þe fader be fals and a sherewe,
> That somdel þe sone shal haue the sires tacches.
> Impe on an Ellere, and if þyn appul be swete
> Much marueille me þynkeþ . . .
>
> (B 9.148–53)

The poem appeals to experience in order to demonstrate the potency of genealogy, even contradicting biblical observations. Indeed, the C Text revision of the passing strengthens the argument for biological determinism. The revision concentrates on the passage of temporal goods to the son when they are forfeited by the father and attributes the contradiction of the gospel to "Westm[in]stre lawe" (C 10.239), not to personal observation. But the passage attempts to pass off the gospel text by suggesting that it is a "glose" that "hydeth þe grayth truth," a truth that a new reference makes plain: "Bon[a] Arbor bonum fructum facit" (C 10.244a).

Yet, as I have argued, genealogy does not resolve the questions surrounding Meed. Indeed, Wit's argument itself makes the value of genealogy dubious, since part of his function in the epistemological drama of the later part of the poem is to illustrate imperfect understanding.[36] The conflicting genealogies for Meed that Langland has considerably supplemented in the C Text do not impart any further authority to genealogy. It is difficult to see why the poem should prolong such an impasse, unless genealogy encompasses other issues. As I have suggested, genealogy is also an analogy of the adequation between institutions and their beginnings. The question of Meed's lineage, and of Meed's legitimacy, is really another mode in which the poem examines the legitimacy of beginnings.

The various revisions of the passage raise and suppress references to beginning in much the same way as the three versions of the reading of the charter. In the A Text, Holy Church follows her brief account of Meed's lineage with a pun that suggests that Meed's actions are a kind of beginning: "Gile haþ begon hire so heo grauntiþ alle his wille" (A 2.24). Despite her affiliation with Wrong, Meed does not fully become a threat until Gile has "deceived" her,[37] diverted her from her original course. In other words, he becomes a sort of progenitor, begetting for her a new beginning. In the B Text this passage is replaced by Holy Church's own pedigree: "Mi fader þe grete god is and grounde of alle graces, / Oo god wiþouten gynnyng, and I his goode dou3ter" (B 2.29–30). She declaims her own purity by tracing her lineage to a point of no beginning; her actions do not threaten to become new beginnings themselves. God, she says, "haþ yeuen me mercy to marie wiþ myselue" (B 2.31). She, unlike Meed, does not intend to forge a new beginning that will threaten a prior "ordenaunce." Even Theology in the C Text acknowledges that new beginnings threaten the ordinance of Holy Church: "That 3e [Simony] nymeth [and] notaries to nauhte gynneth brynge / Holy churche" (C 2.142–43).

Genealogy in passus 2 may be only an analogy of the problems associated with beginning. Indeed, the real key to Meed's nature may lie in her relation to beginnings, not in her genealogy, which may be only a metaphor of the presence of beginnings.

MEED'S BEGINNINGS

Theology's argument that Meed is legitimate because she is descended from Amends rests on the ideological strength of genealogy itself, but it acquires its greatest force by erasing the traces of genealogy, by going back to the beginning. "Amends," whose Latin ancestor *emendare* implies the correcting of a mistake or even the removal of a bodily blemish *(mendum)*,[38] allegorically removes the blemish that Wrong inflicts on Meed's lineage. Meed is legitimate not because of the mere fact that she descends from Amends, but because Amends restores an original legitimacy or purity. Amends is one facet of the poem's great theme of restitution, which encompasses both earthly economics and the penitential system,[39] the (re)payment of "quod debes." Repayment is bound up in penance, as a later passage in the C Text says: those will be forgiven who "repenten and restitucion make, / In as moche as they mowen amenden and payen" (C 19.205–6). Amends returns sinners to a state of grace, and institutions to the "clennesse of her firste fondation," as Richard Fitzralph says.[40] *Piers Plowman* usually uses "amends" in both senses simultaneously, as in passus 5 of the C Text: "Ac þer shal come a kyng... And amende ȝow monkes, moniales and channons, / And potte ȝow to ȝoure penaunce, *ad statum pristinum ire*" (168–71). Amends recovers both a personal and an institutional integrity that have been obscured by fraudulent genealogies, by figures such as Wrong and Fals, whose genealogies bequeath a rival beginning to Meed. Amends erases genealogies that obscure an earlier beginning.

But Meed, as an allegorical figure of payment and reward, does not always manifest her descent from Amends. Theology's declaration of her lineage does not resolve the problem of her status. Nor does Conscience's attempt to distinguish two kinds of Meed, one associated with Amends and the preservation of purity ("*sine macula,*" "of o colour"; B 3.237a–38), the other with Wrong and hereditary blemishes ("Swich a meschief Mede made þe kyng to haue / That god hated hym for euere and alle his heires after"; B 3.278–79). Conscience's conclusion shows that the two aspects of meed are as difficult to disentangle as Meed's lineage: "þeiȝ we wynne worship and wiþ mede haue victorie, / The soule þat þe soude takeþ by so muche is bounde" (B 3.352–53). But the genealogical analogy does suggest an aspect of Meed's nature that the extended grammatical analogy in the C Text explains further: Meed's nature is defined to a great extent by what precedes it. Meed has become dangerous in the Pope's court because she is preceded by Fauel (in the C Text) who creates distrust: he "selde soth sayth bote yf he souche gyle" (C 2.26). Meed is illegitimate there, "manered after hym," because reward and payment in such circumstances cannot bring about "worship"; it can only be "derne usurie." Meed is not illegitimate because of the use to which it is put, but because of the conditions that prevail when it is used. The genealogies that both Holy Church and Theology offer are not taxonomic devices, classifying the nature of a meed that is determined and stable. Indeed, the genealogies contribute to much of the confusion surrounding meed, since their conflicting accounts make the meaning of meed less fixed. But the genealogies do suggest that meed's history is an important aspect of its meaning: what the two genealogies have in common is an interest in tracing meed to particular historical, and usually institutional, roots. The genealogies of Meed are records of historical beginnings, not extrahistorical classifications. Meed's genealogies do not determine its meaning apart from the circumstances in which they unfold. The conflicting genealogies merely suggest that every use of meed can produce its own genealogy; the nature of meed is historically or institutionally conditioned, and its genealogies are the record of meed's various uses.[41] The meaning of meed is determined by the circumstances under which the giving and receiving of meed begins. When meed is preceded by guile, it does become an avaricious force that disrupts social order.[42] And unless meed is preceded by a willingness to honor bonds that have already been established, it rapidly gives rise to guile:

> withouten hure moder amendes mede may [nat] be wedded.
> For truethe plyhte hure treuthe to wedde on of here douhteres,
> And god graunte[de] hit were so so no gyle were . . .
>
> (C 3.123–25)

Meed cannot be allied with Truth—who stands both for God and for the bonds that hold society together[43]—unless it is preceded by a willingness to restore relationships founded on Truth. Theology's version of Meed's genealogy is correct as long as the giving and receiving of meed takes place in a relationship founded on "truth."[44]

Conscience's lengthy attempt to clarify the nature of meed in the C Text is merely an elaboration of the principle that the genealogical analogy unfolds in passus 2: that meed's meaning is determined by what precedes it. Conscience's new distinction between an illegitimate meed and a legitimate meed (which he now calls "mercede") rests, fundamentally, on chronological distinctions—on the beginning that each has.[45] In the C Text, meed becomes an illegitimate exchange that is founded on a bad beginning, a kind of false start: "Mede many tymes men ȝeueth bifore þe doynge" (C 3.292). As Robert Adams points out, this distinction "judges propriety of recompense by looking at the chronological sequence between the deed and the reward."[46] The important point of that chronological sequence is its beginning; it is the point that determines the legitimacy of both reward and of the men who use it. Those who begin a relationship by giving or asking for meed are "nat trewe" (C 3.299). They supplant the trust or "truth" that is the proper foundation of relationships. They make meed illegitimate by beginning relationships with reward, and subvert natural and legal relationships: instituting meed at the beginning is "nother resoun ne ryhte ne [I]n no rewme lawe" (C 3.294). Meed should not be implicated in a beginning at all. It becomes a clear sign of duplicitousness and untruth when it comes "bifore þe doynge," marking the ethical traits of those who use it: "Gylours gyuen byfore and goode men at þe ende" (C 3.303). Legitimate meed (or mercede) originates at the end, not the beginning, of relationships.

But the C Text's association of meed with an illegitimate beginning does not invert the importance of beginnings in the poem; it does not simply use endings to resolve the problem of reward. The C Text penetrates even further to the foundations of historical foundations to discover legitimate beginnings. The C Text's second major addition to the discussion of meed, the grammatical analogy, is perhaps the poem's most definitive statement of the fundamental importance of beginnings in human institutions and of their complexity. Langland's description of the grammatical concept of direct relation, in particular, suggests that social relations and individual being derive their meaning from their foundation or, more precisely, from the exercise of discerning, imagining, or remembering a beginning.

Remembering the Beginning of Language

The grammatical analogy in the C Text suggests that it is the habits of historical recuperation themselves that form the most powerful constitutive bonds of society, and that these are always mediated by language. The analogy's close affinities with late medieval philosophical realism suggest that the work it envisions is the process of a realist or materialist epistemology, the work of making history itself. Louis Althusser's discussion of the Marxian theory of the process of knowledge focuses on what he calls the "work of elaboration," an epistemological process that "beckoned both to labor, practice, and the display of truth [but more specifically] to the Marxist concept of production, which literally suggests a process and the application of tools to a raw material."[47] This process is a labor that, in its convergence with the "real object," creates its own history. He recognizes the "diversity of its moments,"[48] whose "forms of order... are the *'diachrony'* of a basic *'synchrony.'"*[49] The C Text analogy suggests that this "work of elaboration" is the labor by which the epistemological activities of the individual converge with a real object, the labor that produces the real foundations of society. But, like Marxist epistemologies, the grammatical analogy locates this labor against a temporal absence. The analogy defines "relation" as the process of temporal signification, the relation of a subject to its antecedent. While Langland does not, of course, free himself from what Althusser calls the "comforting fascinations" of the myth of origin, his realist epistemology recapitulates a materialist epistemology: "[K]nowledge never arises except as *a relation inside its real object between the really distinct parts of that object.*" But both realist and materialist theories of the production of knowledge stress the temporal aspect of the process itself. As I will suggest, the fourteenth-century realist theory of relation functions as a "discourse which cannot be maintained except by reference to what is present as absence in each moment of its order."[50] "Relation" in the C Text depends upon definitions of it as a temporal process that attempts to recuperate an absence. In revising his discussion of the relation between labor and reward, Langland's significant innovation is to introduce a temporal distinction, an index or record of the distance between an event and its beginning.

In this grammatical analogy, the poem locates the origins of epistemological and labor relations in a foundation that it identifies implicitly with truth itself:

> Relacioun rect... is a record of treuthe—
>   *Quia antelate rei recordatiuum est*—
> Folowynge and fyndynge out þe fundement of a strenghe,
> And styfliche stand forthe to strenghe þe fundement,
>
> . . . .
>
> As a leel laborer byleueth [with] his maister
> In his pay and in his pite and in his puyr treuthe,
> To pay hym yf he parforme and haue pite yf he faileth
> And take hym for his trauaile al þat treuthe wolde,
>
> . . . .
>
> And man is relatif rect yf he be rihte trewe.
>
> (C 3.344–55)

The passage is a comprehensive, if elliptical, survey of the roles that "truth" plays in fourteenth-century social theory. Truth is the foundation of mutual trust that underlies all labor relations, the alignment of individuals to a social ideal (being "rihte trewe") and also the abstract principle itself of social bonds, of which labor relations are just a metonymy ("As a leel laborer byleueth . . ."). As subsequent parts of the analogy make clear, all of these facets of truth are also analogies of the relation between God and man. Truth is the proper alignment of social and spiritual relations. These relations should be so intimately connected with "truth" that they recall it; they are a record of it. Reward in such relationships is legitimate because mercede is united with truth.[51] The new passage in the C Text defines the conditions under which Theology's injunction, that "mede may be wedded to no man bote Truethe" (C 2.139), might become true. Reward acquires its valence as mercede when it is introduced into "relacioun rect," when the relationships that precede it define its meaning. Mercede draws its value from relations prior to it, not from the relations that it creates. The grammatical analogy begins as a resolution of the problem of meed's meaning, but it is perhaps more important as an investigation into the nature of relations. Although Langland's use of the technical language of grammar has often been regarded as more obfuscating or ingenious than precise,[52] his discussion of direct relation, in particular, betrays his awareness of the sophisticated treatments of the category of relations in fourteenth-century logic and grammar.

Langland may have borrowed aspects of the analogy from the intensive scholastic debate over the nature of relation, which concerned itself with the "reality" of relations within the Trinity and between man and God.[53] The most obvious traces in the analogy, however, lead directly to treatises on grammar related to book 17 of Priscian's *Institutiones grammaticae,* which often circulated separately under the title *De constructione,* or with book 18 as *Priscianus Minor,* which was part of the advanced university curriculum in England through the fourteenth century.[54] The phrase in *Piers Plowman* "Quia antelate rei recordatiuum est" (Because it is a record of what has gone before) derives ultimately from *Institutiones* 17.56, where it describes the relation between a pronoun and its antecedent. Although the phrase became subjected to sophisticated scholastic glosses that related it to larger philosophical questions—none, however, as fully developed as Langland's—it remains firmly associated with grammatical treatises. Despite Amassian's and Sadowsky's assertion that the phrase is "a grammatical *and philosophical* commonplace," I have never found the phrase in anything other than a grammatical context.[55] Indeed, Vincent Ferrer, in his tract on the definitions of terms, relegates the phrase to the grammarians only,[56] and Petrus Hispanus says that his treatise on logic will treat only *relatio* "ad aliud," not as "antelate rei recordatio."[57] Langland's integration of the grammatical and philosophical categories of relation is virtually unprecedented and forges at least as rich an association as the fusion of legal, familial, and grammatical categories in the passage.[58] Both grammatical theory and scholastic theology in the late Middle Ages demonstrate the absolute dependence of the category of relation on an antecedent or a foundation. Langland's images of a society dependent for its coherence on a "lord antecedent" or the individual dependent for his salvation upon God the "graciouse antecedent" are not merely extensions of a grammatical trope; they disclose a strong belief that relations of all kinds contract their reality from foundations.

Relation itself is an empty category, both in the ethos of the poem and in contemporary theoretical definitions. David Aers argues that categories of social and familial relation in the poem are an unreified ideal, the product of suppressed and unfulfilled desires. The poem's attempts to replace its own vivid picture of a thriving contemporary society founded on new modes of material production with an "alternative social and ecclesiastical order" lead Langland to "develop a version of Christian community around the concepts of *kyndenesse* and fraternity." But, as Aers suggests, the dislocations and mobility that characterize fourteenth-century England, and that form so large a part of the ethos of the poem, make such totalizing visions of human solidarity merely utopian: such attempts to refigure the world betray the "emptiness in the terms 'kindness' and 'fraternity.'"[59]

Langland's deployment of such "empty" categories of unity may not be, as Aers suggests, simply the unconscious result of an evasion of the world of material production. The definitions of relation that appear in grammatical treatises along with the phrase from *Priscian Minor* suggest that the poem's use of "empty" categories of social relation is deliberate and systematic. Indeed, both grammatical and philosophical treatises interrogate the "emptiness" of the category of relation. Petrus Helias, the most influential commentator on Priscian, associates relation with absence: "[R]elatio dicitur habere recognitionem absentium, quia relatio semper fit ad rem absentem vel quasi ad absentem" (Relation is said to have the recalling of absent things, because relation always occurs with respect to something absent or as if absent).[60] But Helias's definition stops short of suggesting that absence is a fundamental property of relation itself; he implies, instead, that relation compensates for absence. Later grammarians draw out the implications of this and other early formulations of the nature of relation. Perhaps the most extended investigations appear in the modistic grammarians of the mid–thirteenth century. Thomas of Erfurt, attempting to reconcile Donatus's account of relative pronouns with Priscian's, associates Donatus's *qualitas infinita* with relative pronouns: "[M]odus significandi, qui vocatur relatio, sumitur a proprietate rei, quae est proprietas absentiae, et incertudinis" (The mode of signifying that is called relation is taken from the property of a thing, which is the property of absence and uncertainty).[61] Thomas's association clarifies the ontological status of *relatio:* it is no longer loosely connected with absence, but is now the category of absence and uncertainty itself. On the strictly grammatical level, this simply means that the referent is unknown or "infinite"—much like the interrogative *quis,* which Priscian also describes as "infinite."[62] But Thomas's definition of *relatio* also shows how grammatical categories become metaphysical categories; *relatio* is influenced by, and influences, scholastic treatments of the purely philosophical problem of relation. In a version of his *Summa* that circulated under the title *Absoluta,*[63] Petrus Helias shows how *relatio* is defined in accordance with Aristotelian categories: "[I]n relationis essentia non possit" (Essence cannot exist in relations).[64] *Relatio* becomes an increasingly precise definition of an "empty" category that lacks certainty, presence, and being.

The phrase from *Priscian Minor,* however, holds the key to one of the ways in which *relatio* is prevented from becoming a meaningless, ineffable category and also undergirds the poem's insistence that divine and kingly antecedents govern human culture. As Petrus Helias says, *relatio* is "ad antecedens";[65] it refers to what precedes it. Indeed, its only function is to recall that antecedent, a function that defines the category of *relatio* and gives it its meaning. Martin of Dacia's etymology of the phrase sums up its role neatly: "Dicitur enim *relatio* quasi *retrolatio.* Et relativum semper refert suum antecedens ut ipsum absens est" (Relation, indeed, is said to be just like a bringing-back. And a relative always refers to its antecedent, which is itself absent).[66] Implicit in Martin's definition is the notion of *relatio* as a concept involving action (a *latio,* a "bringing," from the verb *fero*).[67] Almost all treatises describe that act as a mental process, as *secunda notitia, secunda cognitio,* or (as in *Piers Plowman*) *recordatio.* Thomas of Erfurt offers perhaps the most succinct description of the extent to which *relatio* depends on a cognitive process:

> Recordatio enim nihil aliud est, quam cognitio secunda, ut si aliquid sit primo cognitum, postea oblitum, et iterum ad memoriam reductum; unde dicitur relatio, quasi antelatae rei recordatio.
>
> [*Recordatio* is nothing other than second cognition, such as when something is first known, and then forgotten, and then brought back a second time to the memory; whence it is said to be relation, as it is a record of a thing gone before.][68]

Scholastic discussions often call the memory's formation of mental images based on objects seen in the past *recordatio.*[69] Robert Kilwardby uses the term in an approximately physiological description of the way that memory makes the mind, which would otherwise digress and wander, present to itself.[70] The term sometimes finds its way into epistemological problems, such as whether one can have knowledge of things constructed from memory. Aquinas asks, for example, whether one can have knowledge of a gold mountain if one has seen a mountain and seen gold.[71] The occurrence of *recordatio* in scholastic treatises confirms its use as a technical term of memory, which is the apparent sense of Erfurt's quotation. But his equation of *recordatio* with *secunda cognitio* points to a use of the term in contexts that are more helpful in explaining the use of the term in *Piers Plowman. Secunda cognitio* and *secunda notitia,* which several grammarians give as an alternative gloss for *recordatio* but do not explain further,[72] have a primarily contemplative significance. The terms appear, often along with *recordatio,* in discussions of the way in which the mind can be drawn to think of God by a process of abstraction. William of Ockham illustrates this by comparing it to the way we recall images: "non in primam cognitionem simplicem et propriam creaturae, sed in secundam notitiam . . . vel in notitiam compositam propriam creaturae" (not in the first simple and particular cognition of the creature, but in the second notice . . . or in the composed, particular notice of the creature).[73] *Secunda notitia* is the knowledge of God constructed from the memories of what one has already seen: "[A]liquis cognoscens Deum ducitur per notitiam memorativum ad cogitandum de creatura prius visa vel cognita, sicut homo cogitando de Deo recordatur de aliquo sancto homine quem prius vidit" (Someone knowing God is led by the notice of memory to think of a creature earlier seen or known, just as a man, in thinking of God, is prompted *[recordatur]* by some holy man whom he has seen earlier).[74] This last example suggests the extent to which Ockham conceived of *secunda notitia* as a contemplative act: it functions by bringing before the mind an object of veneration that in turn raises the mind to the contemplation of higher things. *Secunda notitia* and *cognitio* are not the mere mechanical acts of recollection, nor are they a secondary, remote knowledge of things experienced in the past. They belong to an epistemological order higher than that of primary experience and begin with a fundamentally ethical act that assumes a certain disposition and habit of the mind. Ockham suggests that someone's *secunda notitia* of God might start from the memory of "aliquo sancto homine quem prius vidit."

Some grammatical treatises include this contemplative function of recollection in their discussions of *recordatio*. Petrus Helias begins a discussion of *relatio* by summarizing the standard explanation that it is the recall *(recordatio)* of things that have gone before. But he goes on to point out that what is recalled cannot necessarily be accounted for by simple grammatical principles:

> Ideo autem dixi "de qua fit sermo vel cogitatio," quia quandoque relatio fit ad rem de qua iam sermo precessit, quandoque itaque quod non precessit sermo sed tantum cogitatio, sicut contingit quandoque et maxime in legendis sanctorum quod fit relatio non ex eis de quibus fuit sermo sed de quo habita est cogitacio ut "igitur Beatus Martinus" et cetera.
>
> [Moreover, for this reason I said "about which talk or thought takes place," because when relation occurs with respect to a thing that has already been talked about, or not even talked about, but merely thought about, as happens sometimes—especially in reading about the saints—the relation does not arise from those things of which specific mention is made, but from that of which it is habitual to think, as "Therefore the Blessed Martin," etc.][75]

Helias introduces a hermeneutic element into the working of grammatical relation: what *recordatio* recalls depends upon one's predispositions, upon that which "habita est cogitacio." His choice of saints' lives provides an apposite illustration of the mode of contemplative reading that M. B. Parkes calls monastic *lectio,* which involves "rumination on the text as a basis for *meditatio.*"[76] Helias's invocation of such habits of reading in the context of saints' lives bears a striking resemblance to Ockham's description of someone thinking "aliquo sancto homine." *Recordatio* in both writers is an aspect of *meditatio,* a fundamentally ethical and spiritual exercise. Indeed, *Piers Plowman* elsewhere defines *recordatio* as a spiritual exercise: in passus 4 Reason refuses to have mercy unless "Religiouse Romeris *Recordare* in hir cloistres" (B 4.120). John Alford, disagreeing with Skeat, argues that the word here means essentially what Ockham and Helias have suggested: "[W]e may interpret *recordare* in a peculiarly monastic sense: 'to reminisce,' that is, to meditate upon the Scriptures."[77]

The occurrence of *recordatio* in a passage advocating the restoration of proper social relations may appear fortuitous here, and as only part of the sweeping reforms that Reason urges, but the association of the two ideas is hardly unprecedented. Indeed, Helias begins this passage by making *relatio* almost wholly dependent upon *recordatio:* "Relatio itaque est rei de qua precessit sermo vel cogitatio, recordatio" (Relation is the recollection of a thing about which talk or thought has already taken place).[78] The definition Helias subsequently gives to *recordatio* emphasizes its foundation in contemplative habits of mind, which begin with the recollection of saints and models of ethical living. *Piers Plowman*'s incorporation of *recordatio* into the discussion of social relations explains further how the poem can advocate the restoration of social relationships without articulating a clear program for that restoration. "Relacioun rect" is not an absolute affirmation of the value of political and social structure, but a reminder that social relations, like grammatical relations, are uncertain and have no intrinsic being. The true alignment of society depends upon individual negotiations. Even if treatises on grammatical relation sometimes betray an incipient interest in social relation, in the imaginative formation of a community composed of exemplary lives, they describe *recordatio* as an individual, solitary act.

Conscience's brief sketch of a harmonious society in his explanation of "[r]elacioun rect" is not actually a description of the society that exemplifies those bonds, but of a society's dependence on individual ethical choices. "Relacioun rect" is not precisely the same thing as "treuthe," despite Conscience's apparent equation of the two in C 3.344. What he actually says is that it is a *record* of "treuthe." As grammatical treatises show, relation is far from synonymous with truth, characterized as it is by uncertainty, infinity, and absence.

Relation does not impose order on grammar or society. It only acquires meaning through the action of one of its terms. The poem's metonymic image of the reciprocal relation between "maister" and "leel laborer"[79] is entirely subordinated to the servant's act of *recordatio*. The rectitude of their relation depends, initially, upon the servant's act of belief in the "antecedent," just as the subordinated clauses depend upon the antecedent verb "byleueth":

> As a leel laborer byleueth [with] his maister
> In his pay and in his pite and in his puyr treuthe,
> To pay hym yf he parforme and haue pite yf he faileth
> And take hym for his trauaile al þat truthe wolde .
>
> (C 3.348–51)

The act of *recordatio* or belief is not one of the consequences of "relacioun rect"; it is the means by which true relation is created. The laborer must induce in himself the proper ethical disposition and must align himself in accord with the source of truth. He becomes "relatif rect yf he be rihte trewe" (C 3.355); he is not the source of truth, but his act of belief in a source of noncontingent "puyr treuthe," his fulfillment of the injunction "*Credere in ecclesia,* in holy kirke to bileue" (C 3.357), places him in "relacioun rect."

The laborer is not the foundation of truth. He might be "trewe," but he is only true in relation to "puyr truth." His "truth" is literally the adjectival property, "trewe," dependent on a preceding substantive. "Relacioun," too, seeks out a substantive. One way of reading the passage, and the one Pearsall's punctuation emphasizes,[80] is to see Langland personifying "relacioun" itself as the seeker of a divine antecedent, replacing the "leel laborer" in the quest for truth:

So of ho[l]y herte cometh hope and hardy relacioun
Seketh and seweth his sustantif sauacion,
That is god, the ground of al, a graciouse antecedent.
(C 3.352–54)

Most critics argue that Langland here merges two classes of relation,[81] those of noun and pronoun, substantive and adjective. While there is at least one treatise that includes the relation of adjective and noun in its discussion of *relatio*,[82] most, following the lead of Priscian's *Institutiones*, place their main discussion of *relatio* in the section on pronouns. Indeed, one treatise discusses only adjectives as antecedents, classifying a relation in which a pronoun refers to a preceding adjective as *relativum accidentis*.[83]

Whether or not Langland's confusion of two classes of relation can be traced to a source, what is important is the way that he uses a single aspect of grammatical relation to discuss relation in general. His conversion of restricted, technical material into an allegory of social relations is not merely a feat of ingenuity. His reliance on general theories of relation current in the fourteenth century gives a theoretical underpinning to his argument that human society and individual piety must refer to a foundation to be meaningful.

The examples that Langland selects of "relacioun rect" in action are precisely those that appear in general discussions of relation. Underlying almost all general discussions of relation are the questions of the nature of relations within the Trinity and between Creator and creature.[84] The grammatical analogy in *Piers Plowman* discusses most extensively the last of these problems, but the end of the poem's discussion of relation alludes to the great problem of Trinitarian relations:

hic & hec homo askyng an adiectif
Of thre trewe termisonus, *trinitas vnus deus:*
Nominatiuo, pater & filius & spiritus sanctus.
(C 3.405–6a)

More specifically, the figures of father and son, master and servant that comprise the principal characters of the analogy are the principal examples that appear in scholastic discussions of relations between God and man. Aquinas, discussing kinds of relation, refers to those that constitute social bonds as "relativas habitudines": "[R]elativa quaedam sunt imposita ad significandum ipsus habitudines relativas, ut dominus et servus, pater et filius, et hujusmodi" (Certain relatives are imposed to signify relative conditions, as a master and slave, a father and son, and so forth).[85] The notion of "relative habitude," too, may influence the shape of the grammatical analogy in *Piers Plowman*. The implication that some relations depend upon convention and concessions of status lies behind the section on temporal kingship:

> A[c] relacioun rect is a ryhtful custume,
> As a kyng to clayme the comune at his wille
> . . . .
> So comune claymeth of a kyng thre kyne thynges,
> Lawe, [l]oue and lewete and hym lord antecedent.
> (C 3.374–79)

Langland's equation of "relacioun rect" with "ryhtful custume," which may be a translation of *habitudo*,[86] appears in similar forms in other discussions of the relation of dominion. Wyclif, for example, makes *dominium* equivalent to both *habitudo* and *relatio:* "[G]enus dominii, patet quod sit relacio, et per consequens habitudo: nam dominus et servus . . . dicuntur ad aliquid, et per consequens illud quo formaliter dicuntur huiusmodi est relacio" (The category of dominion includes relation, and therefore condition, for a master and a servant . . . are said [to be] toward something [i.e., to stand in relation to each other]).[87] Langland's discussion of relation may begin with terms from grammatical treatments of the topic, but the examples he uses and the shape his argument takes suggest that he situates his discussion within the larger philosophical discourse of relation.

One common feature of this discourse is the interrogation of the category of relation. One of the *objectiones* that Wyclif raises in the first book of *De dominio divino* impugns the legitimacy of lordship by associating it with *relatio:* "[D]ominium, si sit relacio, tunc non est activum nec cum tanta diligencia appetendum, cum sit res minime entitatis et per consequens minime bonitatis" (If dominion is a relation, it is neither active nor to be sought with such great diligence, for the thing [i.e., dominion] is of minimal actuality and minimal goodness). As he had pointed out earlier, lordship draws its legitimacy from a presupposition of right, not from the fact of relation. Wyclif calls this presupposition a "fundamentum,"[88] thereby raising one of the great questions of late medieval discussions of the nature of relations: where the fulfillment, or foundation, of relations lies.

Langland raises the same question. His substitution of a "hardy relacioun" seeking its foundation for the laborer seeking accord with his master is more than a synecdochic figure of the laborer's activity; it suddenly makes the nature of relation itself the subject of the passage. Like the laborer, relation is incomplete unless it refers to something beyond itself. The passage's definition of relation belongs squarely within the later Aristotelian tradition, which held that relation is an accident that inheres in only one term but refers to another *(ad aliud)*.[89] This conventional description perhaps influences Petrus Helias's definition of grammatical *relatio* as "ad antecedens"[90] and other grammarians' observations that *relatio* does not have the property of being.[91]

Langland's description of relation, and more precisely of "direct relation," as depending upon another term or antecedent bears a superficial resemblance to discussions of "direct relation" in grammatical treatises. Petrus Helias's commentary on Priscian, which is perhaps the *locus classicus* for the distinction between *relatio directa* and *indirecta,* says that the difference is determined by the relation of the "relativum" to its antecedent. In direct relation, the pronoun draws its case directly from its antecedent: "[E]st relatio directa quando relativum potest secum trahere casum ad quem refertur" (Direct relation is when a relative is able to draw along with it the case to which it refers).[92] The pronoun in indirect relation does not draw its case from its antecedent: "Indirecta vero relatio est quando relativum non potest secum trahere casum ad quem refertur" (Indirect relation, indeed, is when a relative is unable to draw along with it the case to which it refers).[93] Helias's use of *ad quem refertur* rather than the more usual *antecedens* perhaps reflects the terminology of the larger philosophical debate on relation, but neither his nor later grammatical treatises ascribe to the antecedent the absolute influence on the "relativum" that it seems to have in Langland. Indeed, Helias and the grammarians he influences define "direct relation" by the agreement of case alone, not by the agreement of "kind," "case," *and* "nombre," as Langland does.[94] Langland appears to be drawing from other sources than the tradition descended from *Institutiones* 17.56 for his discussion of direct relation. The closest approximation of the idea in grammar is the one we have just seen, where a pronoun in direct relation might "trahere casum" from what precedes it.[95] While grammatical treatises acknowledge the power that the antecedent wields over the relative pronoun, they concentrate either on the nature of the pronoun or on the ontological status of the general relation. They refer to the antecedent, for the most part, with such coy invocations as "ad aliquid" or "ad antecedens." The influence behind Langland's description of direct relation as something "Folowynge and fyndynge out þe fundement of a strenghe, / And styfliche stande forth to strenghe þe fundement" (C 3.345–46) is not grammatical but philosophical. Late medieval philosophical discussions of relation invariably discuss it in terms of the antecedent, arguing over the question of whether the relation altered the nature of the antecedent or whether relation was simply a mental category.[96] Both sides of the issue used terms that seem to have influenced this passage of *Piers Plowman,* but those on the realist side of the debate use the terms in precisely the same way that the poem does.

Like the nominalists, the realists define relation as something "ad aliud"; unlike them, they argue that this "aliud" is something real and that the whole relation depends on the reality of this referent. They emphasize the importance of this referent by calling it not a thing *(res),* but a foundation *(fundamentum).* Duns Scotus is typical in asserting that relation requires, among other things, a foundation firmly rooted in reality: "[F]undamentum reale quod scilicet sit in re et ex natura rei" (A real foundation is that which is in the thing and arises from the nature of the thing).[97] In his *Ordinatio* William of Ockham tersely says that Scotus believes that "relatio seipsa refertur ad fundamentum" (relation itself refers to its foundation).[98] Using a verb that recalls Petrus Helias's observation that a pronoun draws its case *(trahere casum)* from its antecedent, Henry of Ghent argues that the reality of the entire relation is drawn from its foundation: "relatio realitatem suam contrahit a suo fundamento" (a relation draws its own reality from its foundation).[99] Helias, like Langland, is discussing direct relation and restricts his discussion to grammatical phenomena. He stops short of explicitly metaphysical claims. Langland, however, incorporates assertions like Scotus's directly into his discussion. The foundation confers reality on the rest of the relation, which functions in part by signifying, calling attention to, the foundation; it is a "record of treuthe," "[f]olowynge and fyndynge out þe fundement." Langland's incorporation of this aspect of the philosophical discussion of relation further discloses his attempts to anchor human and divine institutions in stable beginnings. Relation is no longer an incomplete image of something that has gone before, a trace of one aspect of the antecedent (such as its case). It no longer depends on a beginning that has only a partial bearing on what follows, and that might be characterized as "accidental" in the first place.[100] The chief function of relation becomes the disclosing of its own antecedent; it signifies an absolute beginning, a foundation. Indeed, some philosophers argued that relation signifies nothing other than its foundation, as Richard Fitzralph argues in a discussion of relative nouns: "Nec sequitur quod talia nomina relativa significant aliquid aliud a fundamento sed quod consignificant aliquid aliud vel aliter saltem significant quam absolute" (It does not follow that such relative nouns signify something other than their foundation).[101] Relation only becomes intelligible and coherent when it refers to its foundation.

The abstruse and recondite nature of this grammatical allusion demonstrates the very difficulty of referring to foundations. That the poem insists on the capacity of grammatical technology to make its larger point about economic, social, and philosophical foundations only underscores its deeper insistence: that we must continue to come to terms with the practice of language and the practices to which language calls us, and has called us from the very beginning.

PRINCIPIUM

[First, foremost *(princeps)*, principle, a beginning beyond human agency]

Beginning Perfection

The Theology of Inception

This booke is begunne be Gods gift and grace, but it is not yet performid.

—Julian of Norwich

[W]er gedacht hat, beginnt erst zu denken und denkt erst.

—Heidegger, *Heraklit*

One of the most highly charged theological issues of the fourteenth century was the role that the will played in salvation. It is one of the issues that divided theologians, virtually defining who belonged to the relatively conservative tradition associated with Augustine, which argued for the primacy of grace, and who belonged to the group sometimes called the *moderni,* which argued that works played a critical role. What has not been noticed before is the extent to which this debate focuses on beginnings, concerned with the moment at which grace begins its work. As we will see in a moment, these discussions of beginning amount to a theology of inception that is just as acutely interested in defining the moment of beginning as are the logical treatises on incipit. But this discourse also affects the way works can be written, not just performed. In this chapter, we will be examining one example of the way in which a rather arcane theology of beginnings is linked to the production of a vernacular work, a work that also uses *grammatica* as a way to define a theology that not only participates in both sides of the debate but that is also interested in the language of beginning.

The theology of *Piers Plowman* has long perplexed its readers. Since the writing of the B Text, the poem's theological proclivities have been read in contradictory ways, as constituting a repository of patristic principles, as a flirtation with heterodox or proto-Reformation ideas, or (in the Reformation itself) as an unfortunate expression of conservative Catholic doctrine, even while its evident piety is endorsed. These different views may be explained by their different historical circumstances, but opinions about the poem's theology continue to diverge even today. Much of the confusion over the poem's theology may be irresolvable. *Piers Plowman* may not articulate a consistent theology because it borrows different concepts about beginning from opposing schools of theology.

On the whole, however, the poem's theology is voluntarist. Its most potent uses of beginning are derived from the semi-Pelagian notion, widespread in the fourteenth century, that the will is reponsible for inaugurating salvation. But *Piers Plowman* also has affinities with more orthodox—and contradictory—doctrines that held that only prevenient grace, a precondition for salvation instituted by God, can inaugurate the individual activity of the will. In this chapter, I show that the debate between "semi-Pelagian" and "orthodox" theologians over the circumstances of salvation is a debate about the delimitations of beginnings. *Piers Plowman* appropriates aspects of both sides of the debate, putting the radically different and opposed kinds of beginning to different purposes. For the most part, however, the poem explores the consequences of an individual will that is capable of inaugurating meaningful action.

GRACE AND THEOLOGICAL BEGINNINGS

When Will's search for Dowel reaches a dead end in passus 11 of the C Text, Dame Studie refers him to her cousin Clergie. Her recommendation of a figure that represents institutionalized learning is initially puzzling, for she has just rebuked her husband, Wit, for divulging too much about Dowel. The terms in which she recommends Clergie, indeed, emphasize the preeminence of Clergie's knowledge. He represents the highest of the disciplines:

> Y shal kenne þe to clergie, my cosyn, þat knoweth
> Alle kynne kunnynges and comsynges of dowel,
> Of dobet [and] of dobest—for doctour he is knowe
> And ouer skripture the skilfole and screueynes were trewe.
> (C 11.91–94)

Clergie's compendious knowledge makes him superior not only to Wit, the instincts of native intelligence, but also to Scripture, the praxis of biblical exegesis. His catalog of "kunnynges" makes Clergie the obvious source for the information about Dowel that Will seeks. Dame Studie's reference to "comsynges" (beginnings) might be a tacit acknowledgment of the stage of the search at which Will finds himself—merely beginning—but by associating Clergie with "comsynges," Dame Studie associates the theology of the poem itself with beginning.

But the beginnings that Clergie knows about are neither the inception of formal instruction nor the first elements of the knowledge of salvation. Clergie, or theology, is the final subject—the completion—of formal education, and the discipline of grammar, which inaugurates it, is usually associated with beginning. Grammar, not theology, is "the ground of alle." Clergie represents not the beginning that Will hopes to make, but the knowledge of beginnings. The passage highlights the important role that beginnings play in the theology of the poem. The "comsynges" of Dowel, Dobet, and Dobest are not the arbitrary points that mark the start of a new life, but the beginnings that play a recurrent role in the progress toward salvation. The poem's penitential theology depends fundamentally upon beginnings, suggesting that penance enables the sinner to make successive new beginnings. But Langland's association of the science of theology with beginning suggests that his conception of Clergie and of the theology of the poem itself is informed by one of the most significant controversies of fourteenth-century redemptive theology, which circles about what Robert Grosseteste elsewhere calls a "distinction of beginnings."[1] Like a scholastic *distinctio,* indeed, the poem separates out the different beginnings that are entailed in a theology of redemption, but makes no explicit attempts to resolve contradictory connotations or to assimilate them into an analytical framework.[2] Although the poem finally associates the most effective beginnings with the individual will, much of the poem's theological drama stems from the confrontation of the two kinds of beginning.

Langland's redemptive theology depends not so much upon defining the precise moment at which salvation begins as it does upon the recursive force of beginnings themselves. The poem's theology incorporates mutually contradictory accounts of the moment at which salvation begins, but is more engaged with the discursive force of these beginnings than with the validity of their claims for priority. Although the poem's theology bears the traces of the Augustinian claim that grace precedes works, its discursive practices themselves seem regulated more by the procedures of those virtually heterodox thirteenth- and fourteenth-century theologians who argue that the actions of the will precede those of grace. The poem frames the crucial issue of the efficacy of human effort, in other words, in terms of beginning. But locating beginnings in the poem's theological practices does not resolve that crucial issue; those beginnings do not amount to a theology of origin. The poem's theology is more radical than its political ideology. It correlates beginnings that resist attempts to reconstitute the origins of salvation or to determine the anteriority of any redemptive impulse. These disjunctive beginnings correspond, in fact, to what Said (following Foucault) has defined as secular, "gentile" beginnings, as opposed to origins or "sacred" beginnings.[3] Clergie's knowledge of "comsynges" represents the epistemological center of the poem's theology, the nonsacred beginnings that constitute *Piers Plowman*'s theology of redemption.

The disjunctiveness of the poem's theological beginnings descends from the mutually exclusive claims that contesting groups of theologians in the thirteenth and fourteenth centuries made about the means by which the sinner acquired salvation. Conservative theologians argued that divine grace is the necessary precondition for salvation. Because of the depravity of their wills, humans cannot perform works that will merit them salvation. These theologians, often termed "Augustinians," strenuously opposed the nominalists or *moderni,* often referred to today as "semi-Pelagians," men such as William of Ockham, Robert Holcot, Adam Woodham, and Gabriel Biel, who argued that a properly disposed will could merit grace.[4] Their opponents, indeed, portrayed them as championing the efficacy of the human will at the expense of divine grace. A frequently cited quotation of the most prominent of the Augustinians, Bishop Thomas Bradwardine, complains that the nominalists "cum Pelagio pro libera arbitrio contra gratuitam tuam pugnant" ([together] with Pelagius fight for free will against your grace).[5] Bradwardine may exaggerate the nature and the intensity of the conflict, but he does define the poles of the debate: the roles that grace and free will play in salvation.

Most of these theologians do not define the relation between grace and free will as fundamentally agonistic. The debate over them was largely a matter of establishing priority, a matter of establishing which of the two inaugurates salvation. Almost all discussions of the relation between grace and works involve a discussion of beginnings. Even theologians who fundamentally agreed over the relation between the two argued over how to demarcate the beginning of salvation. The debate, for the most part, prompted theologians to construct rival versions of the beginning of salvation. Conservative theologians argued that grace must begin redemption, since the human will is incapable of any independent good action. As Gregory of Rimini puts it: "Nemo potest habere ante primam gratiam actum aliquem libri arbitrii non culpabilem; igitur nemo de condigno vel de congruo potest mereri primam gratiam" (No one can have any act of the free will that is not culpable before initial grace; therefore no one, from worth *[condigno]* or from suitability *[congruo]* can merit initial grace).[6] Some theologians, indeed, argue that the will is so thoroughly incapacitated by its "natural" state of *acedia* that its inability to achieve good works is simply a sign of its enfeebled ability to begin much of anything at all. No human action can win merit unless it is preceded by an infusion of grace. No human action, indeed, can even begin a motion toward salvation: "[S]ine deo bonum opus . . . nec incipere nec perficere possit" (without God a good work can neither begin nor be perfected).[7] The inadequacy of the human will is often described in terms of its belatedness, its inability to inaugurate any beginning at all. One of the most distilled expressions of this idea is Bonaventure's, which goes further in both directions, describing the difference between humans and God as the absence and presence of being and the absence and presence of beginning *(principium)*: "creatura de se habeat *non-esse,* totum autem *esse* habeat aliunde: sic facta fuit, ut ipsa pro sua defectibilitate semper suo principio indigeret et primum principium pro sua benignitate influere non cessaret" (The creature should have from itself nonbeing, but its whole being it should have from elsewhere: thus it was made, so that it would always stand in need of its beginning on account of its own deficiency and so that the first beginning would not cease to influence on account of its own benevolence).[8] It is a beautiful, rhetorically balanced reflection of what the sentence describes: a beginning that continues to begin and to make other beginnings. And it throws into light the real question behind this debate: whether humans are ontologically capable of making beginnings at all. Most medieval theologians were neither as philosophically skeptical nor as eloquent as Bonaventure about the capacity to begin, even if they suggested that the capacity is weak and attenuated. Elaborating on Augustine's later, more conservative, voluntary doctrine, the fourteenth-century Dominican theologian Hugolinus de Urbe Veteri connects Augustine's earlier trope of the will as a "motus animi" to his apparently contradictory definition of the will as fundamentally passive:

> Deus praevenit voluntatem, ut recipiat gratiam, se solo movendo et iustificando voluntatem et infundendo gratiam. Probatur, quia nemo meretur primam gratiam, nemo incipit se sufficienter disponere ad primam gratiam, sed praevenitur "voluntas a domino," ut dicit Augustinus libro De praedestinatione santorum circa principium: "Nemo sibi sufficit ad incipiendum vel perficiendum."
>
> [God prevenes [comes before, overcomes] the will so that it might receive grace, with himself alone stirring and justifying the will and infusing grace. This is proven because no one wants to merit initial grace, no-one begins to dispose himself properly for initial grace, but "the will" is prevened "by the lord," as Augustine says in his book "On the predestination of the holy," near the beginning: "No one is sufficient of himself to begin *[incipiendum]* nor to come to completion."][9]

I shall discuss later, in connection with Patience's riddle and its definition of "Do wel," how the paradigm of fourteenth-century physics influences the terms that theologians use to demarcate the beginning of the will's actions. Hugo's description of the will appears to be more conventional, placing him among the opponents of voluntarism. In attributing the true beginning to a point beyond, and prior to, the will, he reiterates the topos used by conservative theologians since Augustine to describe the mediated and radically contingent actions of the will.

Augustine's important definition, actually a formulation of grace as a beginning, appears in Lombard's immensely influential *Sentences*. His distinction between "operating grace" and "cooperating grace"[10] appears in a close paraphrase of Augustine's argument that the initial inclination of the human will to do good works actually begins with the operation of divine grace. A prevenient grace achieves what a debilitated will cannot:

> Operans enim gratia praeperat hominis voluntatem ut velit bonum; gratia cooperans adjuveat ne frustra velit. Unde Augustinus... Cooperando Deus in nobis perficit, quod operando incipit, quia ipse ut velimus operatur incipiens, qui volentibus cooperatur perficiens. Ut ergo velimus operatur.
>
> [Operating grace prepares the will of a man so that he wants the good. Cooperating grace helps so that he does not wish it in vain. As Augustine [says]... Through cooperation God fulfills in us what he begins by operation, whereby he himself brings it about at the beginning that we are willing, and finishes off the work in cooperation with us who are [now] willing. Thus he works in us [so] that we are willing.][11]

The achievement of good works begins with the operation, not of the will, but of divine grace. Grace prepares the will, beginning its inclination toward good works. The achievement of "bona pietatis opera" might be achieved by a "cooperation" between the will and divine grace, but theologians in the tradition of Augustine insist that the movement toward salvation does not begin with the sinner. Most of these theologians emphasize grace's role in "preparing" the will of the sinner.[12] Only the infusion of grace can inaugurate salvation; it is "quod operando incipit." Even those theologians who were prepared to admit that *operatio* implied some degree of human agency were careful to preserve the absolute priority of grace. Wyclif, whose discussion of the priority of grace and the will in *operatio* rests on rather subtle distinctions between conditional and absolute priority, vehemently points out that it is only those "modern Pelagians" who assert that the human will can precede, and cause, grace:

> cooperacio gracie dei cum homine, si est, presupponit hominem tamquam eius causam: ymmo cooperacio, ut huiusmodi, presupponit operacionem. Hoc tamen esset hereticum, et sine colore prophane dictum, quod deo cooperante cum homine per

> graciam suam, prius naturaliter et principalius operatur homo quam deus per graciam; et hoc oportuit pelagianos illos modernos dicere.
>
> [The cooperation of the grace of God with man, if it exists, presupposes that the man is the cause of it: but rather, cooperation presupposes operation. But let this be heretical and spoken profanely without truth, that while God cooperates with man through his grace, man operates by natural law and as the primary agent before God works through grace; and yet this must be what those modern Pelagians are saying.][13]

Bradwardine defends the absolute priority of both grace and the divine will to the human will much more vociferously. He devotes three chapters of *De causa Dei,* his great work opposing the Pelagian heresy of the efficacious will, to arguing that the divine will is the supreme beginning: "[V]oluntas diuina fit primum principium liberum" ([T]he divine will is the first free beginning).[14] As he demonstrates with a quotation from Augustine, this first beginning inaugurates the actions of even human "liberum arbitrium" in attaining merit: "In bonis merendis causae principalitas gratiae attribuitur, quia principalis causa bonorum meritorium est ipsa gratia, qua excitatur liberum arbitrium" (The principle of the cause of good merits is attributed to grace, because the primary cause of good merits is grace itself, through which the free will is stirred).[15] Even when they describe the "operation" of grace as an act of divine will, Augustinian theologians attribute to the human will a distinctly secondary, belated role.[16]

The nominalists, on the other hand, emphasize the priority of the human will to grace. Like the Augustinians, they also describe priority in terms of beginning. It is probably misleading, in fact, to describe the conservative theologians as "Augustinian," since some of their opponents, the *moderni,* draw on the early Augustine to make their case for the priority of the human will. Alexander of Hales, for instance, uses Augustine's *De duobus animabus* to argue that the human will's natural anteriority makes it possible for the human to merit grace naturally:

> Si "voluntas est motus animi nullo cogente," ergo voluntas est libera, et ita sui gratia et non alterius; et ita sine gratia potest esse motus animi . . . et ita videtur quod voluntas semper ante

> gratiam. Adhuc, Augustinus: "Cetera cum possit homo nolens, credere non potest nisi volens"; et ita prius est volens quam credens. Unde prior est voluntas quam gratia.... Adhuc, "posse credere est natura hominum, sed credere est gratia fidelium"; et ita videtur quod naturaliter [quis] credere potest, et ita naturaliter mereri.

> [If "the will is the movement of the soul, with no one compelling," then the will is free, and thus grace is of itself and not of another. Thus the movement of the soul is possible without grace, and so it is evident that the will always precedes grace. Augustine says further: "Although man is capable of other things though unwilling, he cannot believe unless he is willing," thus the willing precedes the believing. Therefore the will is prior to grace.... Further, "It is the nature of man to be able to believe, but belief is the grace of the faithful"; and therefore it seems that anyone can believe naturally, and merit naturally.][17]

The motion of the will precedes the activity of grace, just as the will to believe precedes belief itself. The passage from the potential for belief to its actuality, the elision between possibility and certainty, is a characteristically semi-Pelagian rhetorical maneuver, typified in *Piers Plowman*'s discussion of Trajan's salvation. As Robert Adams and Pamela Gradon have pointed out, where traditional commentators treat the *vix salvabitur* text as "denoting the *difficulty* of salvation ... Imaginatif uses it to prove the *certainty* of salvation for the righteous.... early Pelagians such as Fasticulus had used the text in exactly the same way."[18] Despite the relative infirmity of the human will, it becomes, in the Pelagian scheme, the instrument of salvation itself because it inaugurates the process of redemption. The will derives its potency from its ability to make a beginning. What often distinguishes Pelagians from semi-Pelagians is the degree to which that beginning is regarded as efficacious.[19] Although semi-Pelagians might recognize the priority of human actions, the equivalence of the will and of beginning, they nevertheless admit the necessary operation of grace. No fourteenth-century theologian, indeed, denied altogether the superiority of grace to the will.[20] In fact, one of the more radical of the nominalists, Robert Holcot, also describes grace in terms of inauguration:

> Si est iustus, hoc non est nisi per gratiam tuam: quia nullus potest iustus fieri nisi te iniciante et incipiente bonum motum.
>
> [If a man is just, it is only through your grace, because no one can be made just except with you initiating and beginning a right motion.][21]

Holcot's *Super librum sapientiae* is a more conservative work than his commentary on the *Sentences,* but even here he implies that the sinner attempting to become "iustus" is the agent of beginning, although divine grace designates the site of beginning. The presence of grace marks a moment of beginning, but the sinner initiates that beginning. Even when nominalist theologians admit that the infusion of grace is necessary to salvation, they define it as a beginning that allows the sinner greater freedom to act. William of Ockham discusses the problem that Augustine's passage on operation and cooperation concerns: the extent to which charity informs the actions of the human will. Even after baptism, Ockham argues, the sinner must perform good works to complete his salvation. Although the sinner may be granted grace, he is not necessarily granted the two other theological virtues.[22] The sinner must acquire them for himself; the inception of grace places an even greater responsibility upon the sinner. Even the infusion of grace, Ockham suggests, is still a beginning, and one that does not dictate a necessary conclusion:

> [I]n operibus nature videmus frequenter quod deus dat alicui principium operationis & tamen non dat actualiter omnia necessaria ad illam operationem. Exemplum. deus creando hominem dat sibi principium respectu actus sciendi & volendi: quia intellectum & voluntatem. & tamen non oportet quod det sibi habitus per quos faciliter potest in talia opera.
>
> [In the works of nature we often see that God gives to something the beginning of the operation, yet does not actually give all things necessary for that operation. An example: by creating man God gives him the beginning with regard to the act of knowing and of willing: that is, the intellect and the will. Yet it is not fitting that he should give him the disposition *[habitus]* through which he easily could [achieve] in such works.][23]

Although Ockham traces the inception of the human will to the agency of God, he simultaneously insists that the will inaugurates man's independent obligation to perform good works. Indeed, this particular *quaestio* eliminates the role of cooperative grace altogether, suggesting that prevenient grace only inaugurates the action of the will, which achieves the potential contained within the beginning. The beginning that God imposes does not inevitably lead to the perfection of life and work. Arriving at that conclusion is not an easy task.

Most nominalist discussions of the human will attempt to prove that the individual can, indeed, inaugurate an effective, free beginning. Indeed, Bradwardine's assertion that only God makes a "primum principium liberum" is probably a direct response to this nominalist argument. William of Ockham is perhaps the most vociferous proponent of the primacy of the human will. He argues that, since every praiseworthy act demands the assent of the will, the beginning of every act is the will itself.[24] He cites with approval an "opinio Scoti" that the will begins human works: "[N]ullum est principium contingenter operandi nisi voluntas vel aliquid concomitans voluntatem" (there is no beginning of operating contingently except for the will or something accompanying the will).[25] In his *Reportationes* on the *Sentences,* he argues even more explicitly that the will is the beginning of meritorious works, that it is the "principium principale operationum meritoriarum" (the principal beginning of meritorious works).[26] Ockham's championing of the will rests as firmly upon an appeal to the importance of beginnings as does Bradwardine's championing of divine grace. Like Bradwardine, he argues that the beginning of salvation must be independent and free of influence. In responding to Thomas Aquinas's argument that God must infuse charity in the sinner since charity exceeds all natural human faculties,[27] Ockham defines the human will as a principle of inception as thoroughly as Bradwardine defines the divine will as the first beginning. Aquinas had argued, almost paradoxically, that charity must begin "ab aliquo principio," not within the human faculties. In order to allow man his freedom to act, however, God granted him charity as a "superaddition" to his natural will. Aquinas is forced to this conclusion by the dictum that a motion must have a proximate cause:

> [S]icut motus naturalis est ab aliquo principio intrinseco, ita motus voluntarius est ab aliquo intrinseco. Igitur si actus caritatis

> esset totaliter ab exteriori movente, non esset voluntarius.... Igitur est aliquis talis habitus creatus in nobis.
>
> [Just as a natural movement arises from some intrinsic beginning, so a motion of will arises from something intrinsic. And so, if the act of charity should arise completely from an exterior movement, it would not be voluntary.... Therefore there is some such disposition *[habitus]* created in us.][28]

Ockham's response ascribes even greater priority to the acts of the will. If anything were to precede a freely chosen act, he argues, then it cannot be described as free, nor, indeed, as an act of the will at all. The infusion of charity is still an antecedent act that prevents the human will from effecting a true beginning. As Ockham points out, Aquinas's own argument defeats itself:

> [Q]uando dicitur quod si [esset] ab aliquo exteriori principio, non esset actus meritorius, illud est contra se ipsum. Quia sicut nullus actus est voluntarius qui est totaliter a principio exteriori, ita nullus actus est voluntarius—secundum quod voluntarium distinguitur contra naturale—qui est totaliter a principio naturaliter agente. Igitur si actus caritatis esset a caritate et non a voluntate, non esset actus voluntarius.
>
> [When it is said that if it [were] from some exterior principle, it would not be a meritorious act; that contradicts itself. Just as no act is voluntary that arises in its entirety from an external beginning, so no act is voluntary—according to the distinction between voluntary and natural—that is in its entirety from the beginning acting according to nature. Thus if an act of charity came from grace and not from will, it would not be a voluntary act.][29]

Ockham's attempt to establish the efficacy of the human will leads him to discount any influences upon it at all. Even a natural beginning operating upon the tendencies of the will, he suggests, denies it the power to create its own beginnings. As it is with Bradwardine, the central issue for Ockham in the confrontation between divine will, or grace, and the human will is the point at which a truly free act begins. For Ockham, it begins with the human will, whose chief attribute is its freedom from prior influence. The will is itself a principle of beginning.

Clergie's knowledge of the "comsynges" of Dowel evokes this important theological issue, an issue that itself largely concerns the nature of the beginning of salvation. By associating beginning directly with Dowel, Langland discloses the tendencies of his own redemptive theology. A theology that stresses the necessity of prevenient grace would, as we have seen, associate grace, rather than the most basic level of good works—doing well—with beginning. As Adams has demonstrated, Langland's theology is essentially semi-Pelagian, stressing the efficacy of human works.[30] Like the nominalist theologians, Langland expresses the concomitant of human capability in terms of priority: "grace ne groweþ noȝt [til good wil yeue reyn]" (B 12.60). As Adams says of this passage, "[N]o neo-Augustinian could have written these lines. They concede that the Holy Ghost is the source of grace, but no one has ever questioned that . . . Imaginatif makes grace's growth conditional on preceding good will."[31] For the most part, Langland's evocations of grace and works place him on the side of theologians who championed the priority of the will.

But the polemical force of the category of beginning also affects the role of grace in the poem. At several important junctures, the poem clearly associates grace with a beginning that precedes any individual action. The clearest of these associations appears in the C Text. Indeed, the C Text revises Imaginatif's passage from passus 12 of the B Text to stress the temporal priority of grace to works: "Ac grace ne groweth nat til gode wil gyue reyne. . . . Ac Ar such a wil wexe worcheth go[d] sulue / And sent forth the seynt spirit to do loue sprynge" (C 14.24, 26). It is harder to use the C Text version as an example of the poem's semi-Pelagianism, as is the case with many of the other passages that had articulated a volitional theory of salvation in the B Text. The C Text is generally more theologically conservative than the B Text.[32] The C Text revision may bring the passage into line with neo-Augustinian sentiment, but it also exposes the contest over priority that largely informed the polemic on both sides of the debate concerning salvation by works. In the C Text, Langland equivocates, proposing dual beginnings for the infusion of grace: the work of the will and the instillation of charity by the Holy Spirit. The C Text passage is not simply a revised history that recounts an earlier, more authoritative origin; it encapsulates a conflict over priority that both sides of the debate believed was irresolvable.

In his semi-Pelagian commentary on the *Sentences,* indeed, Thomas Aquinas argues against precisely the relation between charity and will that Langland describes in the C Text passage. The initiation of charity by the Holy Spirit excludes any act of the will; if charity is granted by the Holy Spirit, he says, then it is an act that precedes human action, a "principium extrinsecus": "[S]i actus caritatis esset totaliter ab exteriori movente, non esset voluntarius" (If an act of charity were totally the result of an exterior movement, it would not be voluntary).[33] William of Ockham's discussion of Aquinas's critique only urges more strongly that charity must be an act of the will, which it cannot be if it is initiated solely by the Holy Spirit.[34] Langland's revision, which attempts to reconcile competing claims to priority, is a formulation that two of the most influential theologians of his age specifically rejected. By emphasizing the belatedness of the will, Langland denies its efficacy altogether.

By attempting to integrate a prevenient grace into a work that narrates the ability of the individual will to inaugurate its own salvation, Langland produces in the C Text an uneasy synthesis of two principles that Aquinas and Ockham argue are logically contradictory. Langland's refusal to resolve these contradictions with the scholastic rigor that usually accompanies the dissemination of the competing principles probably precludes any attempt to make him a champion of either side of the debate. Traces of the claims that both sides made remain in the poem. Robert Adams, for instance, who spearheads a scholarly consensus that has begun, in his words, to "tilt the balance in favor of a Langland who was . . . semi-Pelagian," nevertheless concedes that "those who argue for a more Augustinian view of the poem (i.e., the priority of grace to works) can make an effective case when dealing with certain passages in isolation or when dealing with the C version."[35] The debate over beginnings within the "Pelagian" controversy of the fourteenth century gives Langland the license to portray Dowel as the inception of salvation, even while he continues at particular points to associate grace with beginning. Indeed, Langland's interest in beginnings may at times outweigh his sense of obligation to one particular side of the debate over the priorities of salvation.

Even where Langland explicitly associates grace with the beginning of salvation, he incorporates the language or imagery of semi-Pelagian beginnings. The ending of the autobiographical passage in the C Text, for instance, includes both an acknowledgment of the inauguratory potential of grace and a suggestion that beginnings are radically voluntary.

> Ac ȝut, I hope, as he þat ofte hath ychaffared
> And ay loste and loste, and at þe laste hym happed
> A bouhte suche a bargayn he was þe bet euere,
> And sette al his los at a leef at the laste ende,
> Suche a wynnyng hym warth thorw wordes of grace.
> *Simile est regnum celorum thesauro abscondito in agro.*
> *Mulier que inuenit dragmam, etc.*
> So hope y to haue of hym þat is almyghty
> A gobet of his grace and bigynne a tyme
> That alle tymes of my tyme to profit shal turne.
> (C 5.94–101, Pearsall)

Langland's allusion to these passages does not resolve the conflict of salvific priorities. Both of these biblical passages are commonly interpreted as allegories of the role of either grace or works in salvation; they are interpreted in two mutually exclusive ways, each of which stresses either the role of grace or the necessity of good works. Indeed, these passages stem from a tradition as unresolved over the issue as this passage from *Piers Plowman*. The woman's discovery of the drachma, for example, is predominantly interpreted as the intervention of grace. Bede suggests that the woman's discovery of the drachma is an allegory of the discovery of the sinful man by the "sapientia Dei."[36] The exhibition of the coin to her friends is a manifestation of the operation of grace.[37] Similarly, commentators often equate the treasure hidden in the field to a grace that precedes human works. Paschasius Radbertus, for instance, points out that the treasure is discovered not by our own efforts, but by the demonstration of God's grace.[38] On the other hand, the parable's field can become the site of human endeavor itself, a figure of the "exercitium boni operis" or the "exercitium actionis." Commentaries that allegorize the field in this way relate the discovery of the treasure as an allegory of what man can do "per bonum operationem."[39] The same source may even perpetuate the conflicting interpretations. The *Glossa ordinaria*, which begins by comparing the man discovering the treasure to one "qui impetrat gratiam dei," suggests that the parable describes an incapacitated will, unable to act without the intervention of grace. At the same time, the *Glossa* itself interprets the ending of the parable as a voluntary, affective beginning; the man who sells everything he has in order to buy the field with the treasure in it "incipit ire: cum incipit diligere."[40] Despite its initial intimations of a prevenient grace, the *Glossa*'s interpretation of the parable is echoed in a passage of *Piers Plowman* that dramatizes a beginning: the ending of the poem itself. The last line constitutes, as Pearsall puts it, "the beginning of a new search."[41] That search commences with Conscience's crying out for grace, a gesture remarkably like the *Glossa*'s "impetrat gratiam": "And sethe he gradde aftur Grace tyl y gan awake" (C 22.386).

The poem's multifold associations of grace with voluntary, individual, beginnings suggest that the poem is less interested in clearly delineating an effectively Pelagian theology than it is with appropriating the traces of a debate largely about beginnings for its own discursive purposes—its analysis of the formative power of inception. The ending of the poem itself suggests that beginnings need not necessarily be generative; they can also be disjunctive and doomed, disrupting hierarchies and priorities. A beginning marks, indeed, what de Certeau has described as a tragic event: the passage from a spatial to a temporal order.[42] The passage in the poem from a theoretical definition of the order of salvation to its actual manifestation in time, its real beginnings, involves doomed attempts to conflate two orders of temporal priority.

The autobiographical passage from the C Text echoes difficulties theologians encountered in trying to establish, in practice, the priority of grace or of the will. One option led to extreme, "hard" determinism; the other led to radical voluntarism and a denial of God's omnipotence. The imposition of real beginnings also raises certain questions about their epistemology: At what point can they be said to start? Do they mark the ending of what comes before them? The dreamer's request for a "gobet" of grace to "bigynne a tyme" suggests that he is attempting to impose a radically disjunctive beginning, one that becomes fully voluntary despite its inception by grace, and one that marks a passage into the temporal order.

Indeed, the narrator suggests that it is not grace that begins an action; the presence of grace does not itself constitute a beginning. Grace may precede the action of the will, but it does not mark an inception.

What Foucault suggests about the problematic of origin is also true of the poem's disinclination to delimit the inception of grace: grace is the "return of that which has already begun."[43] A beginning can only be marked by the individual, not by the presence of something that precedes individual action. Such epistemological problems suggest the difficulty of disentangling in practice the priority of grace and works. Some theologians, indeed, attempted to resolve the problem by distinguishing temporal from causal priority (Thomas of Buckingham, Hugolinus de Urbe Veteri) or by arguing that grace could be conferred, under God's *potentia ordinata,* simultaneously with a good act (William of Ockham).[44] Wyclif, indeed, saw the introduction of time as one of the principal objections to voluntarist theology. A meritorious beginning is not possible (with one exception), since the achieving of merit demands motion, itself a function of time: "[N]ullus creatus spiritus citra Christum meretur in principio sui esse; meritum enim requirit mocionem obiecti, deliberacionem animi, et tercio conclusionaliter adhesionem voluntarium equitati, que non fiunt subito in instanti" (No created spirit apart from Christ deserves to arise from its own beginning; for worthiness requires motion of the object, deliberation of the spirit, and third, and finally, voluntary adherence to justice, things that do not happen in an instant).[45] The appeal to temporal order exposes some of the tensions and contradictions that underlie attempts to settle the priority of grace and the will. Beginning, in other words, is troubled by time. The tearing of the pardon marks a shift in the poem's treatment of historical beginning from one that concerns the origins of dominion over space to one that takes up more directly the problematic nature of time in the act of beginning.

Theological Beginnings and the Tearing of the Pardon

The ending of the autobiographical passage, indeed, marks several opposing trajectories. Nicolaus Gorran's interpretation of the parable of the hidden treasure recapitulates some of them, beginning with the "bonum operationem" of discovering the treasure and concluding with his suggestion that the man's selling of everything he owned represents the "temporalium abdicationem."[46] He begins, in other words, by advocating the performance of good works in the temporal realm—the field itself—and concludes by recommending a rejection of the temporal realm in which those deeds are performed. The parable suggests, that is, a lesson contrary to T. P. Dunning's influential argument that the poem advocates the proper use, rather than rejection, of *temporalia*.[47] In passus 5 of the C Text, the narrator attempts to link the two discourses of possession and salvation, asserting that the beginning of his soteriological career will be marked by the inception of a temporal order, an order that will transmute his misspent time to profit. Time takes on a value of its own that intersects with, but does not completely overlap, the values of eternity. The narrator's appropriation of time for personal profit, indeed, verges on usury, since usury is often defined as a selling of God's time for personal profit. Thomas of Chobham, for instance, says that the "fenetrator nihil vendit debitori quod suum est sed tantum tempus quod dei est" (the usurer sells nothing to the debtor that is his own—only time, which is God's).[48] By introducing a different order of time into a passage that is apparently about the necessity for a prevenient, sustaining grace, Langland makes final salvation dependent on a temporal beginning that inaugurates the formation of a secular subjectivity standing implicitly outside the economy of eternity and outside the scheme of grace itself.

The passage's collocation of a voluntary beginning and the prevenient beginning of grace portrays them as fundamentally disjunctive, one standing outside the capacities of the individual and one compelling the individual to locate himself outside the scheme of eternal redemption. The intimations of usury also suggest that the individual stands outside the field of permissible social practices; the man seeking to make a new beginning must alienate himself both from past practices (from the "tyme" he has "myspened") and from his fellow man (the profit motive has, at the end of the C Text autobiographical passage, dissolved the bonds of "treuthe" that are the constitutive principles of a community).

But as the pardon demonstrates, grace is mediated by written discourse itself, preceding, or as conservative theologians might say, "preventing," the individual from initiating his own salvation: the "wynnyng" of the mercantile *viator* in C 5 comes through "wordes of grace." The pardon itself constitutes a preordained code, establishing the principles that regulate the effective beginning of individual salvation according to the discursive practices of the *lex ordinata*.[49] Indeed, the formal, conventional ending of the "pardon passus" suggests that the good works that the rest of the passus apparently advocates cannot be undertaken unless they are preceded and enabled by grace:

> Forthy y consayle alle cristene to crye god mercy
> And marie his moder be oure mene to hym
> That god gyue vs grace here er we go hennes
> Suche werkes to worche the while we ben here
> That aftur oure deth day dowel reherce
> At þe day of dome we dede as he tauhte.
> (C 9.348–52)

At the same time, however, this ending does not resolve the difficult issues of the relation between Dowel and grace: the extent to which grace obviates the necessity for good works and the extent to which grace precedes the activity of the will. Grace in the pardon scene is implicated in the same problem that confronts the semi-Pelagian theologians: divine grace, which is necessarily more powerful than any human project, must somehow accommodate the necessity of voluntary beginnings. On a larger scale, the pardon scene marks the same passage that the brief autobiographical passage from the C Text marks: the passage from a spatial to a temporal order, or from a predisposed, external grace to a subjective beginning. Indeed, the pardon scene's attempt to establish an order of grace leads to what is perhaps the poem's scene of greatest disruption—the tearing of the pardon—and its most disjunctive beginning: the inception of the *Vita,* which scribes and early critics treated as the beginning of an entirely different poem.[50] As I shall argue, the passus following the pardon scene is largely concerned with the problems entailed in effecting a subjective, voluntary beginning. It self-consciously explores the potential of a disjunctive beginning for both inaugurating a new work and for initiating the work of salvation.

While Penn Szittya and Wendy Scase have demonstrated how the specifically antifraternal, antimendicant bent of debates over the relation between dominion and grace affects *Piers Plowman*'s treatment of voluntary poverty,[51] neither has discussed the extent to which the pardon passus, in particular, uses theories of dominion to interrogate the immanence of grace at all levels of a properly ordered society. The theory of dominion in the late fourteenth century, indeed, depended heavily upon grace. In many ways, the definitions of the function of grace in discussions of dominion parallel those of the debate over grace and free will in salvation. Indeed, men like Richard Fitzralph, Uthred of Boldon, and Wyclif figure importantly in both debates.[52] Dominion may become a simple index of salvation: as Gordon Leff points out, Wyclif's theory of dominion argues that possession is only legal when the possessor is in a state of grace.[53] One later Wycliffite sermon, indeed, reflects the simple equation between justifying grace and legal title: "Oonli he þat stondiþ in grace is verri lord of þingis, and whoeuer failiþ riȝt bi defaute of grace, him failiþ riȝtwise title of what þing þat he occupieþ."[54] The crucial injunction in *Piers Plowman*'s pardon to "have wel" implicates contemporary discourses on dominion and the distinctions they trace between different kinds of "having." Most instructive, perhaps, is Wyclif's argument in *De civili dominio* that only one kind of "having" is legitimate: one can only "have well" if one is in a state of grace. Having dismissed "natural" possession as unjust and civil possession as dependent on the fortuitousness of power, he concludes that the "tercio modo habendi, exellentissimo possibili, quoad genus, habent solum existentes in caritate vel gracia quidquid habent."[55] A more complex relation between grace and possession was traced by the most influential theorist of dominion in fourteenth-century England, Richard Fitzralph. His *De pauperie salvatoris* influenced Wyclif's own theories, yet it handles much more subtly the problematics of grace in operation. As Leff points out, the practical consequences of Wyclif's doctrine are "reduced to nullity . . . by the impossibility of knowing who was damned and who was saved."[56] Fitzralph carefully distinguishes between the jurisdiction of positive law, which governs "political" and "civil" possession, and divine law, which governs "original" or natural possession and dominion.[57] He tries to distinguish, in other words, between the human institution of legal property and original lordship. But as James Dawson points out, Fitzralph does not, therefore, discount the importance of the origins of dominion: "[H]e prefers to keep the Augustinian terminology that suggested that human lordship is somehow closely connected to and dependent upon original lordship."[58]

In other words, prevenient grace is as crucially important for Fitzralph's theory of dominion as it is for conservative doctrines of salvation. Fitzralph's insistence that grace must precede ownership is both functional and historiographic: no one can have dominion before he has justifying grace,[59] just as grace historically preceded dominion: "[H]omo primus in iustificante gracia erat creatus [et] gracia talis ipsum dominium primo homine, ordine causalitatis seu nature, precessit" (The first man was created in justifying grace, and such grace by order of causality or of nature came before dominion itself).[60] Grace, that is, precedes and inaugurates ownership. True ownership—dominion—can only be recovered by an infusion of grace, a process that recapitulates the process of the original conferring of ownership:

> [C]aritas sive gracia primo homini in origine sua sibi collata fuit previa causa dominii et causa cuiusque actus huius dominii... unde nullus de stirpe ipsius primi parentis seminalis filius, donec a peccato mundetur et graciam gratificantem receperit, istud dominium potest recipere seu habere.
>
> [Charity or grace was brought to the first man at his origin as the prevenient cause of the lord and the cause of every act of this lord... wherefore no seed-born son from the stock of that first parent is able to receive or have dominion until he is cleaned from sin and receives the gift of grace.][61]

Ownership depends as radically on a reconstruction of beginnings as salvation does; determining the point at which grace begins its operation is both crucial and controversial. The pardon passus is, essentially, constructed around the problematics of each sphere, around the conditions of "doing well" and "having well."

The passus may suggest that the pardon is problematic because the institutional operation of grace might not be sufficient to redeem members of entire classes, but it also preempts the initiative of the individual that is a fundamental aspect of semi-Pelagian doctrines of redemption. As Hugolinus de Urbe Veteri suggests, the social distribution of grace is not sufficient:

> Non requiritur gratia praecise, ut signum ipsium esse accepti deo, vel ut actus sit acceptus ad vitam aeternam. Petet, quia huiusmodi signum non est necessarium viatori nec umquam apparuit de communi lege sufficienter nec est necessarium deo, qui aeternaliter novit... qui sunt bene operantes.

> [Grace is not exactly sought as a sign of their being accepted by God, or that an act is accepted unto eternal life. It is sought because such a sign is not essential for the *viator,* nor is it ever sufficiently apparent from the common law nor is it necessary with God, who from eternity has known who are doing good works.][62]

Contrary to the Wycliffite *sermo ad status,* Hugolinus suggests that the order of society, or civil law itself, does not signify the flourishing or operation of grace. His recognition that the site of redemption is the *viator* himself and that his actions are a crucial part of his redemption, is characteristically semi-Pelagian. His implicit recognition that redemption is marked by a subjective beginning, by a renewal, echoes the language of voluntary beginnings.

The conflicts behind the pardon scene might be characterized, indeed, as a conflict between two different kinds of beginning, one corresponding to the prevenient beginning of the conservative theologians, the other corresponding to the voluntary, subjective beginning of the semi-Pelagians. Most of the passus sketches the consequences of a beginning that is external to the *viator,* and which determines his fate. The prevalent ideology of the passus—that salvation is communal, dependent upon the regulation of degrees of human dominion—is based primarily on an appeal to origins, to historical beginnings that precede and prevent individual beginnings. Salvation is primarily a matter of conforming to an order that has already begun. The pardon is inadequate, in other words, because it is based on what such famous semi-Pelagians as Ockham and the early Aquinas defined as a "principium extrinsecus," a beginning that prevents the will from imposing a beginning. Ockham's desire to formulate the will as a principle of beginning itself leads him to reject any extrinsic beginning, since it precedes the will's activity: "[N]ullus actus est voluntarius qui est totaliter a principio exteriori" (No act that is completely from an exterior beginning is voluntary).[63] Piers rejects the pardon because it is predicated on an exterior beginning, the antecedent conditions that preclude the "principium intrinsecus" of the will and that regulate the operation of a collective, prevenient grace.

Langland's association of the structure of society with the structure of a text links both society and the pardon with extrinsic beginnings in another way. As A. J. Minnis has pointed out, the distinction between the two kinds of beginning originates in prologues. It is a distinction that is applied with increasing refinement to important texts, describing two distinctly different approaches to a text. For most scholastic thinkers, the extrinsic beginning locates the text's specific place in the domain of knowledge; it defines the text in relation to other texts. The "principium intrinsecus," on the other hand, discloses the allegorical and spiritual content implicit in the text.[64] The ethical lesson of the pardon rests, according to this definition, on a "principium extrinsecus," since it is a text that defines the activity of salvation in relation to the text of society itself. It defines salvation as a fundamentally relational activity, depending upon the exterior conditions of production and possession. The allegorical, spiritual content of the pardon, too, is fundamentally economic and relational, reified in the pardon's system of "having." The pardon contains only a *principium extrinsecus,* excluding the subjective, ethical potential of the *principium intrinsecus* that is the will itself. Piers's dramatic rejection of the pardon suggests that it cannot be implemented by simply revising its terms, by inscribing an interior space for voluntary beginnings. Truth's supplementary inclusion of the merchants, indeed, suggests that the attempt to include interiority in the pardon's discursive order is inadequate; the secrecy of the letter is a parodic reflection of private redemptive beginnings. Divergence from the order of the *status* is exceptional, only possible as a covert activity.

Will's quest for salvation continues with the poem's most obvious rebeginning—the beginning of the *Vita,* which, as I argued in another chapter, attempts to supplant the poem's first beginning. Will begins again outside the site of communal redemption, in search of the beginnings that will resolve the fundamental theological questions of the poem. The poem's attempt to isolate the beginnings that produce the discourse of salvation is an example of what Foucault describes as *la pensée du dehors,* an attempt to describe the formative powers of a discursive practice by standing outside them. The poem, then, moves from an endorsement of a prevenient scheme of salvation to its "external conditions of possibility, toward that which enables the aleatory series of discursive events, and which determines limits."[65] The poem begins again, in other words, with a search for more effective beginnings. The beginning of the next passus, like the beginning of most passus of the poem, makes Will himself a liminal figure, standing outside the structure that articulates redemption.[66]

INCIPIENT PUNS: THE INAUGURATION OF DOWEL

The disjunction between passus 7 and passus 8 marks, as I have said, the transition between the part of the poem organized according to a spatial order to the part of the poem organized according to a temporal order. That transition is prompted by the failure of a structured scheme of redemption and the subsequent search for the beginnings that actually inaugurate salvation. Like most liminal states, the beginning of passus 8 is a "period of symbolic enrichment,"[67] collocating allusions to several kinds of radical, personal beginning. The beginning of the active search for the meaning of "Dowel," contained in the disjunctive, "secular" beginnings of the end of the pardon passus and the beginning of the next passus, inaugurates a series of definitions of "Dowel" as a voluntary and affective beginning. Despite its erasure of the tearing of the pardon, which seems to evade the acute disruption of the A and B Texts, the C Text's revision of the remainder of the passus actually makes its ending more disruptive. It erases the exchanges between Piers and the priest over the possibility of other beginnings that might resolve the problem of the pardon's inadequacy. The C Text ends with mere "jangling," the exchange of words whose only result is to disturb Will's sleep.

In the B Text, the exchange hints at conditions under which language might become productive. The priest scoffs at Piers's attempt to formulate an ethical code, condescendingly acknowledging Piers's learning:

> "What!" quod þe preest to Perkyn, "Peter! as me þynketh
> Thow are lettred a litel; who lerned þee on boke?"
> "Abstynence þe Abbesse myn a b c me tauȝte."
>
> (B 7.136–38)

Piers defends his learning by appealing to its origin, referring to it as an inception—referring to it, indeed, by an incipit. As Judson Allen has observed, *Abstinentia* is the most common incipit in homiletic *distinc-*

tiones. Langland seems to be "referring [not] to an ascetic virtue, but to a book, by its incipit."[68] The learning that authorizes Piers's actions derives its legitimacy and its power from its beginnings. The origins of his learning are intractably textual; its *dispositio* comprises a series of incipits, metonymic beginnings that stand for an entire linguistic order (the "a b c") or homiletic practice. In Piers's hands, those beginnings enable him to subvert the communal, materialist ideology of the pardon by deploying the text *"Ne soliciti sitis"* (B 7.131) and to challenge the priest's own scholarly diligence ("litel lokestow on þe bible"; B 7.137). But the "bookishness" of these enabling beginnings is not an incidental feature of this debate alone. The contexts in which Dowel is defined most clearly as a beginning are invariably academic debates. While the poem defines Dowel as a powerful voluntary beginning, it also does so in a specifically academic, intellectual, register.

The passus following the pardon scene associates not the faculty of the will but the character Will himself with beginning. He appears in a setting that recalls the three-day disputation (compare A 9.107–8) in which a university candidate establishes his status as *baccalarius principians* or *incipiens*. His encounter with the two friars at the beginning of the passus establishes his enterprise as specifically academic and, by demarcating the commencement of Will's objections, implicitly inaugural: "*'Contra!'* quod I as a clerc and comsed to disputen" (B 8.20). Anne Middleton has traced allusions to the ritual of inception at medieval universities and its "customary interlude of academic wit," which involves extended punning on the name of the candidate, in Will's encounters with Wit and Will later in the same passus. The putative *thema* for this disputation, Thought's citation of the verse "libenter suffertis insipientes cum sitis ipsi sapientes" (B 8.93), acquires a twofold intellectual reference: as Middleton says, its "appropriateness here is enhanced by the latent wordplay provisionally linking fools *(insipientes)* with beginners *(incipientes)*."[69] Several *Piers* manuscripts, indeed, make this wordplay more than latent, changing the reading of this well-known biblical text to *incipientes*.[70] The incipient pun motivates other writers to link fools with beginning. In a discussion of the *dixit insipiens* verse, Isaac de Stella, whose collection of Sexagesima sermons surveys the ways in which God is characterized by, and precedes, beginning, implicitly defines the fool as one who overlooks the connotations of his title:

> Dixisti enim, o insipiens, in corde tuo, extra cor tuum ipse: *Non est Deus,* quod tamen nec dicere omnino potuisses, si is quem negas non esset, sine quo nihil esse posset. Si ergo es ipse qui dixisti, procul dubio est is de quo dixisti. Quidquid enim est, aut principium est, aut de principio esse necesse est. Quare si de principio es, necessario est principium unde es; aut si principium ipse es, tunc quod esse negas, es.
>
> [For you have said, O fool *[insipiens],* in your heart, out of your heart you yourself have said: "There is no God," something you could not have said at all, if the one whose existence you deny did not exist. If, therefore, you yourself said this, far from uncertain is the one about whom you spoke. For whatever exists must either be the beginning or come from the beginning. Therefore if you are from the beginning, you must necessarily come from the beginning; or if you yourself are the beginning, then you are what you claim does not exist.][71]

Isaac characterizes the fool as denying origins and thereby denying his own beginning. Although his attack is a version of Anselm's ontological argument, he defines foolishness as a fundamental epistemological failure, as the refusal to adequately recognize beginnings. Bartholomaeus Anglicus argues that the pervasive effect of the divine beginning is so evident that even fools should find it difficult to reject the principle that God is the beginning of all things: God "is iknowe in þe effect of his workes and dedes in so muche as he is *principium* and cause of alle þinge, for vnnethe any foole doutiþ where God be oþir no."[72] In his commentary on Paul's passage in Romans about those who bear only the *form* of knowledge, Sedulius Scotus makes the intersection of fools and beginning even more insistently epistemological—indeed, pedagogical: "*Eruditor insipientium,* ut quid timorem Domini, qui est initium sapientiae, reliquisti?" (*Teacher of the foolish:* have you left behind the fear of the Lord, [which] is the beginning of wisdom?)[73] Associating a lack of wisdom with an ignorance of beginnings explains some of the symbolic force behind the designation of a student completing his theological training as an *incipiens,* but Sedulius Scotus also calls into question the whole project of secular learning, which neglects the true beginning of wisdom. Ymaginatif, indeed, criticizes the "kynde knowyng" of "olde lyveris" for its inadequacy, deploying against it the Pauline reversal of mundane epistemology: "Sapiencia huius mundi stulticia est apud deum" (The wisdom of this world is with God foolishness; B 12.138). The *incipiens* stands precisely at the intersection of wisdom and foolishness, leaving behind the ignorance of the unlettered fool, but beginning an enterprise that can equally be characterized as resolutely foolish.

The quibble over *incipiens* and *insipiens* appears at the point in *Piers Plowman* that marks Will's induction into the action of the poem itself. It characterizes his entire enterprise as simultaneously foolish and wise, a covert, learned pursuit of what ought to be glaringly apparent. His activity is, in every sense of the word, a beginning activity: it is both elementary and inaugural. The record of his poetic activity, the passus itself, is a beginning, implicitly like the document the *incipientes* at universities produced: the allusive, inaugural document called the *principium,* which interwove sophisticated commentary on a specific problem from the *Sentences* with references to the *incipiens*'s own life.[74] Will's *principium* is a self-reflexive commentary on poetic beginning itself, inaugurating the poem's most distinctive rebeginning (the *Vita*)[75] and inserting him into one of the most vexed of questions that circulates in commentaries on the *Sentences:* the extent to which the will is a beginning.

Langland's persistent, if not thorough, identification of the will with beginning concurs with the trajectory of the *Vita,* which largely narrates Will's search for Dowel. The crucial problem of his search is knowing how to inaugurate the redemptive activity of the will; he encounters successive attempts to determine precisely what inaugural actions constitute Dowel. The emergence of Will's search as one for an effective beginning averts the disruption that ends the preceding passus. Indeed, in the C Text, the passus beginning the *Vita* is incorporated into the passus that describes the castle of Kynde. The "jangling" that had ended the preceding passus threatens to disrupt the beginning of the search for Dowel, but Will forestalls it with a specifically academic intervention:

> I dorste meue no matere to maken hym to Iangle,
> But as I bad þoght þoo be mene bitwene,
> [To] pute forþ som purpos to preuen hise wittes,
> What was Dowel fro dobet and dobest from hem boþe.
>
> (B 8.123–26)

The procedures of learned disputation end this passus, as they begin it. Will's invocation of what one could call the university's technologies of knowledge sustains his own discourse, preventing yet another narrative disjunction. The search for Dowel, indeed, comes to be defined as the crucial academic activity of making distinctions. From this point on, Dowel will be defined only as the first member of a triad. This schematic tendency defines Dowel itself even more clearly as an inaugural principle.

The clearest definition of Dowel as a beginning comes from Wit's discussion of the castle of Kynde in the A Text, where he initially equates knowledge with power: "iche wiȝt in þis world þat haþ wys vndirstonding / Is chief soueryn ouer hymself" (A 10.71–72). The poem oscillates between metaphors derived from the schoolroom and the military siege, drawing an explicit connection between schoolchildren grappling with their first lessons and a ducal Dowel defending the territory of the heart from the incursions of sin:

> þanne is dowel a duc þat destroyeþ vices,
> And sauiþ þe soule þat synne haþ no miȝt
> To routen ne to resten ne ro[t]en in þin herte;
> And þat is dred of god, dowel it makiþ.
> It is begynnyng of goodnesse god for to douten.
> Salamon it seide for a soþ tale:
> *Inicium sapiencie timor domini.*
> . . . dred is such a maister
> þat he makiþ men meke & mylde of here speche,
> And alle kynde scoleris in scole to lerne.
> (A 10.71–73, 76–84)

The passage resolves the conflicting metaphors by presenting the *dominus* as a grammar master who coerces his students with the "betyng of þe ȝarde" (A 10.85). It returns to the inaugural site of learning, to "Grammer, þe ground of al" (B 15.372), a discipline that Dame Studie associates with both beginning and the same coercive methods that Wit describes: "Grammer for girles I garte first write, / And bette hem wiþ a baleys but if þei wolde lerne" (B 10.180–81). By claiming responsibility for the inception of all seven liberal arts, in fact, Dame Studie associates herself with the arcane science of beginnings. Her claims of pedagogical priority are the "signe" that Will is to use to introduce himself to Clergie, who knows, as Dame Studie says in the C Text, "Alle kynne kunnynges and comsynges of dowel, / Of dobet [and] of dobest" (C 11.92–93). And, as we will see in the two following sections, it is grammar that is the ground of some of the poem's most arcane interrogations of the act of beginning. Part of the reason for this, perhaps, is seen in the appearance of grammatical metaphors at just the points where the poem imagines the possibilities of intrinsic beginning. That is, metagramatical theory is the means by which the poem imagines or figures beginning as a science founded in language, already containing its objects of inquiry, the letters, syllables, and properties that constitute language. As Robert Kilwardby says, grammar is a science because it contains its own beginnings.[76] Understanding Dowel, for instance, involves deciphering what is already implicit in it, its intrinsic grammatical features that signify the possibility of a science of intrinsic beginning.

It is the "comsyng" of Dowel that is most clearly defined in the A Text's passage on the *inicium sapiencie*. Although the first half-line of 82, which I have omitted, appears to begin a discussion of Dobet ("For doute men doþ þe bet"), the remainder of this passage clearly discusses Dowel. Such elisions are characteristic of definitions of the three lives, but the A Text goes further than the other two texts in allowing Dowel to supplant the other two lives: "ȝif clene consience acorde þat þiself dost wel / Wilne þou neuere in þis world, [wy], for to do betere, / For *intencio indicat hominem*" (A 10.88–90).[77] By suggesting that doing well supersedes the necessity of willing to do any better, the A Text locates the crucial inception of the will only at the stage of doing well. The formative stage of the triadic scheme is the most important: intention both precedes and subsumes action.

Later revisions to the poem attempt to demarcate more clearly the inception of Dowel. The same passage in the B Text distinguishes between Dowel and Dobet by distinguishing between two kinds of "dred": "That dredeþ god, he dooþ wel; þat dredeþ hym for loue / And [dredeþ hym] noȝt for drede of vengeaunce dooþ þerfore þe bettre" (B 9.98–99). This distinction probably comes from sources such as Nicholas Lyra's gloss on Proverbs 9:10 ("The fear of the Lord is the beginning of wisdom," what John Fleming would call the "supertext" of this passage), which also contrasts two kinds of *timor,* the second of which is a kind of love. Each of the two is also described as a beginning:

> Perfecta charitas foras mittit timorem, timor vero filialis cum sapientia manet: propter quod est principium intrinsecum sapientie: timor vero seruilis est principium extrinsecum.
>
> [Perfect love casts out fear; fear truly remains related to wisdom; therefore it is the intrinsic beginning of wisdom: servile fear is certainly an extrinsic beginning.][78]

Each of the first two modes of doing well, in other words, constitutes a beginning, beginnings, furthermore, that this passage ultimately helps us to see in terms of a teleology of kinds of beginning, moving from the extrinsic to the intrinsic, from he who "dooþ wel" to he who "dooþ . . . bettre." But, at the same time, the conceptual sequence of the two lines from B 9, the way in which this brief narrative of doing well and doing better develops, tells us something important about the way in which Langland tends to imagine beginnings of any kind as insistent, perdurable, and efficacious. Where Nicholas of Lyra begins with "[p]erfecta charitas," for instance, the more "perfect" of the two stages here, and the one that obliterates the very beginning in fear by casting it out, Langland begins with the undifferentiated "dred" of God, which bifurcates in the next line into a "dred" "for loue" and a "drede of vengeaunce." Only then do we begin to understand what is implicit in that first "dred" of God, what we did not yet understand, but what nevertheless allows us to act, to do, at the very least, "wel." Each of these two lines, in other words, describes an incipient understanding of "dred," that is, as a form of doing that is predicated on the incipience of ultimate wisdom. This phenomenological rather than structural understanding of Proverbs 9:10, this tendency to describe first the intrinsic function of a mode of fear or of doing rather than its rank or status in a scheme that is fully disclosed at the beginning, is characteristic of Langland's sensitivity to the complexity of theological, and particularly soteriological, beginning. Even when Langland discusses the three modes of doing together he tends to invest them with an insistent incipience, seemingly reluctant to suggest a progressive development, the attainment of one mode following the completion or perfection of another. The A Text, for example, suggests that Dowel and Dobet are the coincident beginning of Dobest, not the fully realized conditions that must be fulfilled before doing best can even be said to begin: "dobest out of dobet & dowel gynneþ springe"

(A 10.127). The poem's interest in tracing the influence of purportedly imperfect modes on a state of perfection discloses its underlying ideology of beginnings, its interest in the persistence of beginning, not necessarily the completion of what is promised in the beginning. It is in this important sense that beginnings in the poem's theology can be said, echoing Hesiod's proverbial statement, to wield most of the power over what follows. This understanding of beginning is clear in a beautiful passage by John of Salisbury that meditates on the incipient nature of understanding, commenting also on the important verse in Proverbs 9:10:

> uoluntatis appetitus impletur, cum flos studii uergit in fructum; nam philosophiae finis sapientiae est. Sed nescio quonam pacto iam uersamur in fine illius cuius initium nondum agnoscimus, quod in rebus omnibus potentissima pars esse censetur. Verum tamen qui finem nouit, initium ignorare non potest, cum radix initii per multiplices uirtutis tramites usque ad coronam finis fructusque dulcedinam uiuacitatis suae soliditatis pertranseat. Ecce, inquit beatus Iob, timor Domini ipsa est sapientia.[79]

> [The desire of the will is satisfied when the bloom of study becomes fruit; for the end of philosophy is wisdom. But I do not know how we will reach the end of something whose beginning we do not yet know, since this is by common consent the most dominant part in all things. But he who knows the end cannot be ignorant of the beginning, since the root of the beginning passes through manifold paths of virtues till it reaches the crown at the end and the sweetness of the fruit and of its life force and of its solidity. Behold, says blessed Job, the fear of the Lord is wisdom itself.]

The pursuit of ethical perfection does not culminate in an obliteration of its initial stages nor efface the relict forms of its inception. Perfection depends, as John of Salisbury says, radically upon its beginnings. This passage suggests that beginnings are even more influential than the popular proverbs about their dictating conclusions suggest. Beginnings wield a persistent influence on conclusions, operating epistemologically, implicating the knowledge of their inception in the achievement of a conclusion: "initium ignorare non potest."

Much as Langland does, John of Salisbury refrains from defining dread as a solely affective function, preferring to trace the connection between wisdom and its beginning. *Timor* is *sapientia* itself; it becomes a figure of intellectual discipline, a kind of superego that coordinates more basic affects, such as the will: "uoluntatis appetitus impletur, cum flos studii uergit in fructum" (the desire of the will is satisfied when the bloom of study bears fruit). Both the will and *timor* are persistent and singularly powerful beginnings, but John points out that every beginning is the most powerful part of an enterprise, the literal root of action. The figure of organic continuity illustrates the role that beginnings play and clarifies a description of the three lives in the A Text that immediately precedes the passage about the beginning of Dobest that I have discussed: "of dred & [his] dede dobest arisiþ / Which is þe flour & þe fruyt fostrid of boþe" (A 10.121–22). The first two modes, Dowel and Dobet, are dynamic principles that continue to "foster" the third mode, beginnings that continue to exert their influence.

Beginning Passages: Dowel and Patience's Riddle

The poem's persistent interest in beginnings and its incipient formulation of a soteriology based on beginnings blur, from the outset, the divisions between the three modes. As I have suggested, the poem's attempt to formulate Dowel in terms of a powerful beginning (most notably, with the beginning of Christ's *facta* at the marriage feast in Cana[80] and the dread that enables at least the first two modes) forestalls any attempt to define the three lives as static categories. Most explanations of the three lives, however, derive from the influential arguments of Henry Wells, Nevill Coghill, and R. W. Chambers, who use the *ordinatio* of the B and C manuscripts, by now largely discredited, to divide the *Vita* into sections, each of which describes one aspect of a tripartite scheme.[81] Dunning's emphatic assertion about the properties of the three lives clearly reveals his underlying assumption that they are configured according to a static scheme: "the three 'lives' mentioned by Thought as Dowel, Dobet and Dobest, are not subjective but objective states of perfection or well-doing."[82] Recent studies that treat the three modes as more dynamic describe the scheme as either heuristic—in Robert Worth Frank's words, "a device for labelling divisions"[83]—or deliberately imperfect:

Dowel and Dobet are, as Middleton argues, "positive and superlative degrees of something intelligible only in its completed form, the superlative degree, Dobest."[84] Neither of these two recent approaches interrogates the poem's persistent association of Dowel with beginning, although Middleton's alignment of the first two modes with their terminus in the third, an explanation that points toward the implacability of ending or "perfection," is compelling. But the very difficulty of separating each of these modes into distinctive features is probably part of their larger significance.

The fluidity of Dowel, Dobet, and Dobest, the way in which one elides with another, ultimately refers us to an emerging ethics of beginning rather than an ontology of action. It is precisely because these modes cannot be defined apart from the ways in which they begin, apart from the ways in which each refers back to a prior attempt to make a good beginning, that it is difficult to represent them as incremental stages toward perfection. Dowel, for instance, continues to "foster" Dobest because it acts as a beginning. Each of the three modes, indeed, is itself associated with beginning, and the various schemas that characters in the poem invent only tend, overall, to nullify intelligible gradations and to link beginning and conclusion more insistently, leaving the two *termini* of each mode as the points that must be identified in order fully to understand the entire analogy.[85] Just as the terminist logicians do, in other words, we need to designate the outer and inner limits of each mode. But, as we have seen, that is precisely what each of the failed attempts in the poem has in common with the others. What we can say is that the poem associates each of the modes with beginning, and that that makes one of their crucial features their temporality, their entrance into time, even if we do not know precisely how (or when) to mark it. The section from the A Text that I have been discussing, for instance, defines "dobet" as "to suffre" (A 10.118), suggesting that one appropriate response to the passing of time is to endure it.

Clergie's definition of the three modes at his banquet and Patience's riddling explanation of the definition disclose the intractably temporal nature of Dowel, Dobet, and Dobest. Clergie seems to define them as the infinitive form of a verb, a part of speech that medieval grammarians argue represents the passage of time itself. Because they implicate time, verbs function as Dobet does, by "suffering"; enduring temporal change is a constitutive part of their nature. In order to understand why Clergie frames the three modes in this form, and the complicated relationship between action, beginning, and time that this passage invokes, we will need to refer to what might be called the deep structure of temporal language in the medieval theories of the verb.

Standard late medieval definitions of the verb describe it as a marker of mutability, a signifier that operates through the agency of time. It is, for the modistic grammarians of the thirteenth century and later, a "modus fluxus et fieri."[86] As the modistic grammarian Martin of Dacia argues, the verb embodies a continuum, describing only the transformation of one accident into another.[87] The difficulty that characters in *Piers Plowman* and the poem's later readers encounter when they try to establish the boundaries of Dowel, Dobet, and Dobest is the inevitable consequence of the fundamentally verbal nature of the three modes.[88] Each mode signifies more than a changed life; it signifies the activity of change itself. Their processual nature effaces distinctions between them. Each shades imperceptibly into the next, a series of accidents in a single continuum.

The exchange at Clergie's feast alludes to the verbal nature of Dowel, Dobet, and Dobest in yet another way. The A Text's definition of Dobet as "sufferance" is excised in the later versions, but passus 13 in the B Text integrates the equation more fully, and more elaborately, into the operation of all three modes. "Suffering" the passage of time is both an essential feature of the verb and an obligatory spiritual exercise.

Aristotle's assertion that the indication of time is a corollary function of the verb[89] encouraged later grammarians and logicians to define time as an increasingly integral part of the verb itself. Boethius, for example, largely repeats the Aristotelian definition, but adds the more emphatic statement that "verbum vim temporis in significationibus trahit" (the verb takes the force of time in significations)[90] and Aquinas points out that the actions implied by a verb must unfold in time:

> Curro vero cum sit verbum significans actionem, consignificat tempus, quia proprium est motus tempore mensurari; actiones autem nobis notae sunt in tempore.
>
> ["I run": since it is a word signifying action, it also signifies time, because it is obligatory that motion be measured by time; actions, indeed, are known to us within time.][91]

For the modistic grammarians, time had become an inalienable feature of the verb, as one *quaestio* on Priscian asserts: "Verbum non potest privari tempore" (The verb cannot be deprived of time).[92] The verb is an index of the passage of time, and grammars divide verbs into two classes that describe the only possible response to the passing of time: "agendi et paciendi" (acting and suffering).[93] Conscience's reply to Clergie's initial definition of Dowel (or, in the K.-D. B Text, Clergie's reply to Conscience's skepticism) situates his response in the second category, that of *paciendi:*

> Thanne passe we ouer til Piers come and preue þis in dede.
> Pacience haþ be in many place, and paraunter [knoweþ]
> That no clerk ne kan, as crist bereþ witnesse:
> *Pacientes vincunt &c.*
>
> (B 13.133–36)

What Conscience (Clergy) recommends is precisely the passivity that the verbal passive signifies. The underlying grammatical metaphor motivates a complex pun that shifts between two registers and two languages, linking a verbal mode with an ethical mode. The "pacientem" of a verb[94] may be linked, on a lexical level, with the "suffering" of Dobet in the A Text, but its metaphorical associations—the temporal implications of *paciendi*—emerge in the B Text. Conscience's passivity has a fixed term; it establishes temporal limits: "'Thanne passe we ouer *til* Piers come'" (emphasis mine). It is entirely appropriate that Conscience turns to Patience for guidance at this point, since Patience's fundamental nature is to "suffer," to "passe . . . ouer" things. He is a secular figure, characterized, like the Wife of Bath, by the authority of experience: "Pacience haþ be in many place." His riddle, indeed, suggests that the passage of time is a fundamental characteristic of Dowel, invoking such mysterious temporal figures as "þe Saterday þat sette first þe kalendar" (153), "þe wit of þe wodnesday of þe nexte wike after" (154), and "[t]he myddel of þe Moone" (155) that he suggests contain an intrinsic Dowel, "[in a bouste] faste ybounde." It answers, if it does not necessarily clarify, Clergie's obscure definition of Dowel by challenging him to solve it, to "Vndo it; lat þis doctour deme if dowel be þerInne" (157). We will attempt later to undo it ourselves, but we first need to think about the way in which

Clergie's definition helps to establish Dowel as the intrinsic subject of incipient time.

That definition demands a response diametrically opposed to the self-conscious passivity of his guests, who immediately yield to the authority of Piers Plowman, whose future "dede" will prove the validity of Clergie's assertions. Clergie's assertions, indeed, formulate Dowel as an active principle, something "fyndyng out," rather than "suffering." As might be expected from a character whose academic specialty is the science of beginnings—the knowledge of the "comsynges of dowel, / Of dobet [and] of dobest" (C 11.94–97)—Clergie draws on sophisticated grammatical theory to define each of the three modes as a principle of beginning.

> . . . dowel and dobet arn two Infinites,
> Whiche Infinites wiþ a feiþ fynden out dobest,
> Which shal saue mannes soule; þus seiþ Piers þe Plowman.
> (B 13.128–30)

As I have suggested, Dowel is defined against the incipient grammatical metaphor of verbal activity and passivity. The most authoritative discussion of this passage, Middleton's, uses Priscian to define the "infinites" as principally interrogative pronouns that signify "lack of completion, substance, and quality."[95] Although she relates Priscian's definition of the verbal infinitive to the themes of the passus, she does not argue that the verb in "Dowel" is itself an infinitive. But there are good reasons for thinking that Clergie's definition applies to the infinitive form of the verb "do."[96] On several other occasions the poem treats the construction "dowel" as an infinitive, and in accordance with the emergence of the infinitive in a distinctly learned register at Clergie's banquet, every occurrence is motivated by a pedagogical metaphor. Wit places all three modes in apposition with a series of infinitive forms (one of which is "do" with terminal *-n*) in a passage I have already discussed: "Dowel, my [deere], is to doon as lawe techeþ: / To loue . . . and to lene . . . To ȝyuen and to yemen . . . To helen and to helpen . . . to drede, and . . . to suffre" (B 9.202–7). The disputed passus 12 of the A Text clearly treats Dowel as an infinitive: "he cam not by cause to lerne to dowel . . . and bad me go do wel" (A 12.32, 36).[97] Incontrovertible evidence that the poem at least occasionally inflects Dowel as an infinitive form appears in the B Text, when Dame Studie cautions Will against "Experimentȝ of Alkenamye[,]

Nigromancie and perimancie": "If þow þynke to dowel deel þerwiþ neuere" (B 10. 217–18).[98]

Clergie's definition of Dowel as an infinitive links the abstract and quiescent features of learned discourse directly with the active, inceptive demands of salvation. Clergie's definition, that is, invokes both the uncertainty and indeterminacy of the verb and the specificity and inaugural power of nouns. Like Dowel, Dobet, and Dobest, the infinitive is both a verb and a noun, signifying, according to the Parisian grammarian Magister Jordanus, both *in vi verbi* and *in vi nominis.*[99] Although grammarians recognized that the infinitive lacked the *substantia* of the noun, they argued that it could function syntactically as a noun, acting as a provisional subject. Medieval syntactic theory describes the structure of any complete sentence as a motion—the *motus* that constitutes the function of the verb—between a *principium* and a *terminans,* both of which are some form of noun, since a noun represents *quies* or the *modus per se stantis.*[100] Since a sentence's subject is also its *principium,* the infinitive is the only verbal form that can signify beginning, although under certain constraints. As Pseudo-Albertus Magnus points out, citing Aristotle's *Physics,* the verb cannot normally begin the *motus.*[101] The infinitive, however, can function as the subject of a sentence because it represents a *principle* of beginning, the potential for action: one must consider

> aliam naturam in infinitivo per quam potest esse illud a quo actus egreditur, quia potest esse in ratione principii respectu actus, ut *legere est bonum.* Et sic potest supponere.
>
> [the infinitive as having another nature whereby it is able to be that from which an action sets out, since it can share the characteristic of a beginning with respect to action, as in "to read is good." And so it can act as the subject.][102]

As infinitives, then, Dowel and Dobet contain within them the principles both of unperfected action and of beginning itself, the potential to act. According to both this grammatical metaphor and the metaphor of adjectival comparatives in which Dowel is the first term of a series, Dowel is the beginning of the perfected life.[103] Since all three modes are constructed from infinitives, they also signify the passage of time, the "flux" of the verb; they are both agent and action, *principium* and *motus,* signifying the inception of action and the passage of time—in other words, both the "dede" of Piers Plowman and the "suffering" of Clergie's audience.

The inception of Christ's earthly career, the miracle at the wedding feast, offers a clear example of the relation between Dowel and beginning; indeed, the passage that describes it in *Piers Plowman* offers convincing evidence that the poem associates the verbal infinitive "do wel" explicitly with beginning:

> In his Iuuentee þis Iesus at Iewene feeste
> Water into wyn turnede, as holy writ telleþ.
> And þere bigan god of his grace to do wel . . .
> . . . .
> So at þat feeste first as I bifore tolde
> Bigan god of his grace and goodnesse to dowel.
> (B 19.108–10, 115–16)

But, as I have argued, it is not only Dowel that is defined in terms of beginning. Indeed, all three modes are cast in the infinitive, suggesting that they all represent the crucial principle of beginning. Despite—or because of—the poem's accounts of powerful voluntary beginnings, it does not clearly project the *terminus* of those beginnings. Langland's theology continues to incorporate an effective grace in the inaugural stages of salvation. Individual effort, or doing well, is a necessary part of salvation, but not its sufficient cause. Since Dobest, the perfection of life or of works, cannot be achieved solely by human agency, the poem does not recount the achievement of the perfect life. It ends, indeed, with the beginning of a search for Grace.

Patience's riddle, which purportedly answers Clergie's obscure definition, is in part an attempt to explain how a principle that is both a beginning and an activity can fail to achieve its objective. The riddle is a metonymy of the greater riddle of the poem itself: how one passes from the beginning that Dowel represents to the completion that Dobest represents. As a grammatical series representing the progress from a beginning to a completed, perfected state, Dowel, Dobet, and Dobest mirror the three stages by which any sentence (usually referred to as a "construction") attains completion or perfection. The first stage, which gauges the *motus* implicit in the sentence, establishes the degree of transitivity or intransitivity between the persons or acts referred to in the sentence.[104]

"Socrates legit bene," for example, is an intransitive construction, since "hoc adverbium *bene,* quod est secundum constructibile in ista constructione, dependet ad verbum, quod est primum constructibile" ("Socrates reads well." . . . the adverb "well," which is of secondary construction in this sentence, depends on the verb, which is of primary construction).[105] The second stage, essentially concerned with grammatical propriety, establishes the congruity of a sentence—the agreement of parts of speech and of significations.[106] The final stage, the complete construction, is reached when the sentence establishes its meaning in the mind of the hearer:

> signum perfectionis constructionis est generare perfectum sensum in animo auditoris, ita quod omnis illa contructio erit perfecta, quae perfectum sensum in animo auditoris generabit. . . . Nam ea magis perfecta est, quae magis quietat animum auditoris; et quae minus quietat, minus perfecta erit.
>
> [The sign of a perfect construction is to produce perfect sense in the mind of the listener, in such a way that each construction will be perfect, since it will produce perfect sense in the mind of the listener. . . . For the more it puts at ease the mind of the listener, the more perfect it is; and the less it puts it at ease, the less perfect it is.][107]

Much of the peripatetic activity of Will in the second half of the poem could be explained as the result of a spirit that "minus quietat," aggravated by a grammatical construction that achieves something less than perfect sense in his mind. Will's attempts to uncover the meaning of the series imitate, on some level, the progression of a construction like the Dowel series from imperfection to perfection. The *quies* that perfect comprehension bestows is a metaphorical echo of the rest that will come to Will himself when he achieves the perfection of Dobet, the final stage of redemption.

Like the Dowel series, the riddle's first two lines use an underlying grammatical metaphor to formulate the poem's larger problem: "Wiþ half a laumpe lyne in latyn, *Ex vi transicionis,* / I ber þer, [in a bouste] faste ybounde, dowel" (B 13.151–52). Beyond the problem of what these lines mean, however, lies a deeper problem: Dowel has nothing to do with the *vis transicionis,* since it is a clear example of what medieval grammarians called a minor *in*transitive construction.[108] As G. L. Bursill-Hall summarizes it, the "verb *transire*... refers to something which may 'transit' from one place to another quite different place.... the intransitive does not do this but remains in the same place."[109] The second element of the construction, the adverb "wel," continues to refer to the first element (the principium), "Do." It is not clear why Patience should suggest that this intransitive construction (which he may refer to as the "bouste") is bound "ex vi transcionis." These two lines encapsulate the fundamental problem that the Dreamer faces, of realizing the obligation to begin a new life, of beginning the attempt to reform, but being at the same time uncertain of how exactly to make that new beginning, and particularly of how to deploy it with a definite end in mind. In grammatical terms, Dowel continues to refer to the first constructible, the principium, which is merely the injunction "do," an act with infinite, uncertain reference. Yet the triadic construction of the three lives compels the Dreamer to make the transition from mere doing to completion, from the *principium* to the *terminus*. He remains bound in a life of pure beginning, a life of pure, undirected action with no possible end. This transitivity, the passage from Dowel to Dobest that is essentially the movement of becoming, is described by the other aspect of the infinitive verb, that which is the mode of flux and becoming, the signifier of *motus*.

Ben Smith has demonstrated that the enigmatic calendar references in this passage probably refer to the weeks of Creation and Redemption, and that the specific times here correspond to the first Sabbath and the Passion.[110] They mark the completion of the two great beginnings of human history. Skeat first pointed out that the "middel of the moone" refers to the paschal moon, by which, as R. E. Kaske suggests, "the two great periods are decisively separated and from which both draw their ultimate significance in the plan of salvation."[111] The rest of the riddle, in other words, shows the passage of time from the beginning of the world to its completion in the incarnation: it hints at the two greatest representatives of the "vis transicionis." The "middel of the moone" signifies the passage between them, the measurement of the *motus* between a principium and a terminus. A *motus* that finds its expression in a precise measure, the "middle," is also a common definition for the action of a verb: the means by which the *motus* that the verb represents is known, its specific temporal referent, is called its "measure." As an infinitive verb, "do" lacks this measure and cannot express a particular movement toward fulfillment. As part of an intransitive construction, it does not begin a motion toward any terminus: it can do nothing other than refer to itself. Dowel and Dobet cannot be clearly separated because they lack measure; they lack the temporal articulation of verbs in action. Patience's injunction, "undo it," which comes at the end of the passage, may be a glancing invitation to solve the riddle by undoing Dowel, by inflecting an infinitive form, making it something other than a continual beginning: a transitive action that can be measured.[112]

The problem that the riddle poses is precisely the same problem that confronts Will in his search for redemption: how one can begin a motion—a *motus animi*—toward perfection, how the will can inaugurate salvific action. Solving the riddle and uncovering the principles of Langland's theology are exercises that correlate the function of intrinsic beginnings. Despite the poem's continual association of beginnings with academic pursuits, it does not imagine the study of beginnings as a merely academic matter, for a beginning does not happen only in a university, a book, a *vicus,* or a dream. It happens wherever we are, whenever we act, however we choose to begin. We must begin, and must begin where we are.

We can now, if we choose, begin to read the poem.

Notes

Incipit: A Fourteenth-Century Incipit

1. The suggestion made in *Brewer's Dictionary* that the streets are named after parts of the liturgy used during the Corpus Christi procession is clearly wrong. Most of these streets are named in London records well before the Feast of Corpus Christi was introduced into England between 1310 and 1320; see Miri Rubin, *Corpus Christi: The Eucharist in Late Medieval Culture,* 200 n. 258. There is a reference to Paternosterstrete in 1307 in *Calendar of Early Mayor's Court Rolls, A.D. 1298–1307,* ed. A. H. Thomas, 256. There are a number of references to the production of books in the *vicus* of Paternoster Row. Sir John Oldcastle was accused of leaving a heretical work to be illuminated and bound by a limner living in Paternoster Row (David Wilkins, *Concilia Magnae Britanniae et Hiberniae,* 3:352); John de Grafton, a "parchemener" and "stationarius" mentioned in 1353 and 1366, is described as living in St. Paul's Churchyard (*The Royal Commission on Historical Manuscripts,* col. 27; PRO Minister's Accounts, 1092/3); Nicholas le Bokbindre, who died in 1306, lived in or near St. Paul's Churchyard (Reginald R. Sharpe, *Calendar of Wills Proved and Enrolled in the Court of Husting, London, A.D. 1258–A.D. 1688,* 1:175); Peter Bylton, who described himself in his will as a bookbinder, left behind a stock of books in his house in Paternoster Row and willed a furred gown to a "textwriter" who worked for him; and Michael of Ludgate Hill, on which St. Paul's stands, is described as early as 1223 as someone "qui vendit libros" and around 1243 as "venditor librorum" (both examples cited in Graham Pollard, "The Company of Stationers before 1557," 5; the preceding two examples are cited on 14 and 4 n. 3). In 1355 John de Bury, a "clericus," and his wife Lucy leased shops in "Paternoster rowe situate near the shops of John Malemakere and William Halford, scrivener" (Reginald R. Sharpe, *Calendar of Letter-Books Preserved among the Archives of the Corporation of the City of London at the Guildhall, Letter Book G,* 41). C. Paul Christianson has pointed out that when a royal patent was read publicly at St. Paul's in 1314, the audience was made up of canons, ministers, and "the many others writing there then." Between 1404 and 1410 at least nineteen of the twenty-nine tradesmen in Paternoster Row whose trades can be identified were involved with the production of texts (*A Directory of London Stationers and Book Artisans, 1300–1500,* 20–21, 31).

2. The name of Paternoster Row may have originated from the making of "paternosters," strings of beads used to count the recitations of the Lord's Prayer by anyone who did not know enough Latin to say the Divine Office. But there are relatively few of these "paternosterers," and almost none in Paternoster Row itself. Eilert Ekwall's comprehensive book lists only three paternosterers *near* Paternoster Row *(Street Names of the City of London)*. At any rate, the history of the street in the thirteenth century sees its transformation from its former name of Spurrier Lane into one named for an incipit, whether it was initially the incipit of a spoken or a written text.

3. For discussions of the various uses and forms of the incipit, see Jacques Lemaire, *Introduction à la codicologie*, 165–66; Morton Bloomfield, *Incipits of Latin Works on the Virtues and Vices, 1100–1500*, 1–6; D. C. Greetham, *Textual Scholarship: An Introduction*, 59; Samuel Berger, *Histoire de la Vulgate pendant les premiers siècles du moyen age*, 307; Ivan Illich, *In the Vineyard of the Text: A Commentary to Hugh's "Didascalicon,"* 8, 95–96. One example of the citation of a (vernacular) text by incipit in administrative records is by Edward I's Clerk of the Wardrobe; see Juliet Vale, *Edward III and Chivalry: Chivalric Society and Its Context, 1270–1350*, 19–20.

4. See Mary Carruthers, *The Book of Memory: A Study of Memory in Medieval Culture*, 86.

5. See the *Hereford Breviary*, ed. W. H. Frere and L. E. G. Browne, 3:li. A useful summary of musical practices in the liturgy can be found in Frank Harrison, *Music in Medieval Britain*, 46–103.

6. For discussions and examples, see Robert Adger Law, "'In Principio,'" and Morton Bloomfield, "The Magic of *In Principio*."

7. Martin Heidegger, *An Introduction to Metaphysics*, trans. Ralph Mannheim, 128.

8. Rita Copeland, *Rhetoric, Hermeneutics, and Translation in the Middle Ages: Academic Traditions and Vernacular Texts*, 81.

9. Maureen Quilligan, *The Language of Allegory: Defining the Genre*, 58.

10. Morton W. Bloomfield, *Piers Plowman as a Fourteenth-Century Apocalypse*, 32, cited in Quilligan, *Language of Allegory*, 60–61; emphasis mine.

11. Quilligan, *Language of Allegory*, 53.

12. Giorgio Agamben, *Infancy and History: The Destruction of Experience*, trans. Liz Heron, 49.

13. Pierre Aubenque, *Le problème de l'être chez Aristote*, quoted from Reiner Schürmann, *Heidegger on Being and Acting: From Principles to Anarchy*, trans. Christine-Marie Gros, 334 n. 5.

14. Augustine, *Tractates on the Gospel of John 1–10*, trans. John Rettig, 42.

15. Boethius, *The Consolation of Philosophy*, trans. Richard Green, bk. 3, pr. 3, p. 46.

16. Since there may be some readers who will cavil at this statement, I should point out two things: (1) No other Middle English poems with this form have survived, a form that is specifically different from other poems that could be said to contain multiple beginnings, such as *Troilus and Criseyde*, whose beginnings are all explicitly subordinate to the first one, and none of which would make an intelligible beginning were the ones before it to be lost, set as they are within an anticipated and emergent narrative. (2) No Langland scholar has yet managed to locate another medieval dream poem with *multiple* dreams.

Poems that *describe* dreams within them do exist *(The Nun's Priest's Tale)*, but they are scarcely like *Piers Plowman*, in which the narrator has a series of successive dreams, and in which the mere presence of the dream is a challenge, rather than an adjunct, to the manifest integrity and continuity of the poem. It is, at any rate, not my point to establish whether other poems like this were written. It should be clear that a poem like this violates the expectations of readers of medieval texts, whether reading now or six hundred years ago, and that this poem regards itself as having an exceptionally difficult time with beginning.

17. Hannah Arendt, *The Human Condition*, 177. Heidegger had earlier made the same observation, most lucidly in an essay on *physis:* "The Greeks usually hear two things in this word: on the one hand, *arché* means that from which something takes its egress and inception; on the other it means that which, *as* such egress and inception, at the same time reaches beyond whatever emerges from it, thereby dominating it. *Arché* means both inception and domination inseparably" ("On the Being and Conception of *physis* in Aristotle's *Physics* B, 1," trans. Thomas J. Sheehan, 227).

18. Steven Justice, *Writing and Rebellion: England in 1381*, 137.

19. See Henry Knighton, *Chronicon Henrici Knighton*, ed. Joseph Rawson Lumby, 2:138.

20. Justice, *Writing and Rebellion*, 16–17, 23–25.

21. Ibid., 16.

22. Ibid., 67. See, for instance, BL MS Harley 992, MS Harley 2259 ("Richard Strangway's Book"), manuscripts that, as I will be arguing in a forthcoming British Library book, are almost certainly the products of study in one of the Inns of Court.

23. Knighton, *Chronicon Henrici Knighton*, 138; emphasis mine.

24. Ibid.

25. Thomas Walsingham, *Chronicon anglie*, ed. Edward Maunde Thompson, 321.

26. Anne Middleton, "Acts of Vagrancy: The C Version 'Autobiography' and the Statute of 1388," 219.

27. *The Westminster Chronicle, 1381–1394*, ed. L. C. Hector and Barbara Harvey, 314.

28. For this portion of the petition, see ibid., 304.

29. Ibid., 342.

30. Thomas Favent, "Historia Mirabilis Parliamenti," ed. May McKisack, 24.

31. Ibid.

32. Slavoj Žižek, "The Spectre of Ideology," 21.

33. See, for instance, Hannah Arendt, *Human Condition*, 177–78, and *On Revolution*, 207–15. For further discussions of the formal nature of ideology, see Frederic Jameson, *Marxism and Form: Twentieth-Century Dialectical Theories of Literature;* Slavoj Žižek, *The Sublime Object of Ideology;* Terry Eagleton, *Ideology;* and Pierre Bourdieu, *Language and Symbolic Power.*

34. Augustine, *De civitate Dei*, 12.20.

35. Krzysztof Pomian, *L'ordre du temps*, 264; my translation.

36. For fuller discussions of each of these, see Lynn White, *Medieval Technology and Social Change*, 122–25; and Carlo Cipolla, *Clocks and Culture, 1300–1700*, 40 ff.

37. For one excellent and telling example, see Anne Middleton's thorough and subtle account of the motives behind the documentary excesses of the Cambridge Parliament in 1388, which responded to crises of labor relations by imagining forms of authentication and validation that would stabilize or renovate changing forms and relations of work ("Acts of Vagrancy," 208–317).

38. *The Shewings of Julian of Norwich,* ed. Georgia Ronan Crampton, 154.

39. Bloomfield, *Piers Plowman,* viii.

40. Robert Adams, "The Nature of Need in 'Piers Plowman' XX," 301.

41. Anne Middleton, "Narration and the Invention of Experience: Episodic Form in *Piers Plowman,*" 109.

42. John Milton, *Paradise Lost,* ed. Merritt Hughes, 8.25–51.

43. "It happens in many analyses that as one approaches their end new recollections emerge which have hitherto been kept carefully concealed" (Sigmund Freud, *From the History of an Infantile Neurosis,* 17:89).

44. Cf. J. LaPlanche and J.-B. Pontalis, *The Language of Psycho-Analysis,* trans. Daniel Lagache, 334.

45. Middleton, "Narration and the Invention of Experience," 101.

46. For editions and studies of the work of this group, also known as the "Oxford Calculators," see Curtis Wilson, *William Heytesbury: Medieval Logic and the Rise of Mathematical Physics;* William of Ockham, *Summa logicae,* ed. P. Boehner, G. Gál, and S. Brown; William of Sherwood, *Syncategoremata,* ed. J. R. O'Donnell; Walter Burley, *De primo et ultimo instanti,* ed. Herman and Charlotte Shapiro; Thomas Bradwardine, *Treatise on "Incipit" and "Desinit,"* ed. Lauge Olaf Nielsen; and Janet Coleman, "Jean de Ripa O.F.M. and the Oxford Calculators."

47. William of Sherwood, *William of Sherwood's Treatise on Syncategorematic Words,* trans. Norman Kretzmann, 113.

48. Petrus Hispanus, *Tractatus syncategorematum,* trans. Joseph P. Mullally, 59.

49. "To assign the first instant of the being of a thing . . . is not the same as to assign the last instant of a thing's being. . . . to assign the last instant in which a thing has being is not the same as to assign the first instant in which a thing ceases to be"; Walter Burley, *De primo et ultimo instanti,* 166. Thirteenth-century logicians saw this indeterminacy as a purely logical phenomenon, the consequence of having to locate a dividing point in just one segment; it could not, for various reasons, be common to both.

50. Cited in Bradwardine, *Treatise on "Incipit" and "Desinit,"* 17–18.

51. William of Sherwood, *Treatise on Syncategorematic Words,* 109.

52. Rupert of Deutz, *De Trinitate et operibus ejus, PL* 167, col. 331.

53. Michel Serres, *The Parasite,* trans. Lawrence R. Schehr, 177.

54. Jacques Derrida, *Of Grammatology,* 288.

55. As Pierre Bourdieu has observed of agrarian Algeria, the time of year devoted to plowing is charged with a repertoire of symbols of beginning: it is "an inaugural moment, when the year, like the house, which must remain open to the fertilizing light of the sun, opens up to the male principle which fertilizes and sows it" (*The Logic of Practice,* trans. Richard Nice, 241).

56. See A. D. Nuttall, *Openings: Narrative Beginnings from the Epic to the Novel,* 34.

57. Ibid., vii–viii.

58. Ibid., 208.

59. Ibid., 213.

60. Michel Foucault, *The Order of Things: An Archaeology of the Human Sciences*, trans. Alan Sheridan, 337.

61. Ibid., 328–29. Nineteenth-century recuperative projects could be even more idealizing: the attempt to reconstruct primitive Indo-European was a conservative exercise in comparison with projects that attempted to reconstitute the language of paradise itself. For a recent account, see Maurice Olender, *The Languages of Paradise: Race, Religion, and Philology in the Nineteenth Century*, trans. Arthur Goldhammer.

62. Foucault, *Order of Things*, 330.

63. From this perspective, as Deleuze points out, the urgent pressures of termination and inception that are painfully evident in this worry over the use of time are facets of the compulsions of notional limitation: "As a means of filling time, it makes no difference whether repetition is subordinated to the extrinsic identity of a dead matter or to the intrinsic identity of an immortal soul" (Gilles Deleuze, *Difference and Repetition*, trans. Paul Patton, 112). On the variety of times invoked, suppressed, and anticipated in this remarkable passage, see Middleton, "Acts of Vagrancy," 266–77: "With this patently fictive and after-the-fact tale of its beginning, Langland *in effect declares his work finished—as finished as it ever will be*" (275).

64. Foucault, *Order of Things*, 329.

65. R. Howard Bloch, *Etymologies and Genealogies: A Literary Anthropology of the French Middle Ages*, 44. "It is as if language, for Augustine, were transparent because its eternally subsistent object always draws words to their natural mark" (50).

66. Ibid., 54.

67. Petrus Hispanus, *Tractatus syncategorematum*, 259.

68. Ibid., 262. I have used the Latin text because the double force of *principium* does not come across in translation.

69. Derrida, *Of Grammatology*, 28, 72.

70. See Jacques Derrida, *Edmund Husserl's Origin of Geometry: An Introduction*, trans. John P. Leavey Jr., 87–88.

71. Derrida, *Of Grammatology*, 199. Hereafter cited in the text.

72. Bradwardine, *Treatise on "Incipit" and "Desinit."*

73. Ibid., 50.

74. Sigmund Freud, *Beyond the Pleasure Principle*, trans. James Strachey, 43.

75. Ibid., 24.

76. Deleuze, *Difference and Repetition*, 71.

77. Ibid., 114.

78. Ibid., 294.

79. Frantzen, *Desire for Origins*, 121.

80. Heidegger, *Introduction to Metaphysics*, 191.

81. Ibid., 128. In his commentary on Heraclitus, Heidegger says that the "*Logos* is the original *[ursprüngliche]* gathering" (*Heraklit*, 278).

82. Heidegger, *Heraklit*, 292.

83. Schürmann, *Heidegger on Being and Acting*, 122–23.

84. Ibid., 127.

85. Heidegger, *Heraklit,* 370.

86. It is on this point that I find Edward Said's work in *Beginnings* less useful in thinking about the nature of beginning. While Heidegger makes fairly fine distinctions in *kinds* of beginning *(Ursprüng, Anfang, Beginn),* these distinctions all point toward the immanence of beginning, as we have been seeing. Said's reliance on Foucault's basic distinction between origin and beginning has the effect of simplifying the underlying philosophical problems of both, making one pathologically fictive and the other restrictively and preclusively performative: "The *beginning* of writing . . . is not something to be pushed further and further back until a set of forces is identified as having determined that beginning. 'A book,' says Conrad in a late essay, 'is a deed, . . . [and] the writing of it is an enterprise.' . . . To begin to write, therefore, is to work a set of instruments, to invent a field of play for them, to enable performance" (Edward Said, *Beginnings: Intention and Method,* 24). A later essay of Said's makes it clear that his notion of beginnings is designed to exclude the more complex iterability of origins that we have seen in Heraclitus, Heidegger, and Deleuze: writing, for him, is the "irreducible intention to perform a specific activity with . . . originality as an irreplaceable action giving forth the writing"; this inceptive event is explicitly opposed to forms of iteration, repetition, and immanence: "Originality in one primal sense, then, has to be loss, or else it would be repetition. . . . originality is the difference between primordial vacancy and temporal, sustained repetition" (Edward Said, "On Originality," 132–33). While an attractive way of describing the act of writing metonymically (that is, partially), Said's study has the unfortunate effect of occluding the imperatives of beginning in the act of writing and runs the risk of not thinking through the problematics of beginning and writing "authentically," as Heidegger might say, precisely because Foucault's distinction does not allow us to think incipiently about beginning as the form of immanence.

87. Bonaventure, *Breviloquium,* 5.2.3.

88. Derrida, *Of Grammatology,* 316.

89. Steven Kruger, *Dreaming in the Middle Ages,* 34.

90. Geoffrey Chaucer, *Boece,* in *The Riverside Chaucer,* ed. Larry D. Benson, 3 pr. 3. This ambiguity is a feature of the Latin text also: "[T]enui licet imagine uestrum tamen principium somniatis" (Boethius, *Consolatio philosophiae,* ed. James J. O'Donnell).

91. Michel Foucault, "Dream, Imagination, and Existence," 51.

92. See Kimberly W. Benston, "Performing Blackness: Re/Placing Afro-American Poetry," 173.

93. Robert Adams, "Langland's Theology," 91.

94. David Lawton, "The Subject of *Piers Plowman,*" 19–20.

95. Ibid., 21.

96. Nick Gray, "A Study of Piers Plowman in Relation to the Penitential Tradition," 440.

97. Mary Carruthers, *The Search for St. Truth: A Study of Meaning in "Piers Plowman,"* 80. In arguing that "intellegere" is derived from "intus legere," Aquinas suggests that the course of all forms of understanding follows this movement from externality to interiority: "[H]uman knowledge begins with the outside of things as it were [and so] it is evident that the stronger the light of the understanding, the further can it penetrate to the heart of things" (*Summa theologica,* trans. Fathers of the English Dominican Province, 2.2, q. 8, art. 1). The earliest appearance of this etymology, and so of the injunction to read inwardly, may be in the *Book of Nehemiah (II Esdra)* (2:8): "Et legerunt in libro legis Dei distincte et adposite ad intelligendum." See the commentary on this passage in Nicholas of Lyra, *Postilla,* in *Glossa ordinaria, PL* 113, col. 42. Using a similar etymology, Anselm of Canterbury links the discovery of an inner law with the formation of the inner man or, more precisely, of a clean heart, the true beginning of the self: "[D]a mihi intellegere hoc: intus legem peto, ut cor mundum crees in me, Deus" (*Meditatio super Miserere, PL* 158, col. 837).

98. Joseph S. Wittig, "'Piers Plowman' B. Passus IX–XII: Elements in the Design of the Inward Journey."

99. For discussions of the development and uses of the distinction between extrinsic and intrinsic prologues, see R. W. Hunt, "The Introductions to the *Artes* in the Twelfth Century," 5:117–44; A. J. Minnis, A. B. Scott, eds. with David Wallace, *Medieval Literary Theory and Criticism, c. 1100–c. 1375: The Commentary Tradition,* 122–26, 130. The later medieval physics of motion, which we will see echoed in discussions of the treatises on incipit, is intensely interested in the possibility—or the impossibility—of intrinsic beginnings. Walter Burley, for instance, argues that the only intrinsic terminus possible is the end of a motion. Even an ending that makes another beginning possible is necessarily extrinsic to that second motion: "[N]ullum ultimum est intrinsecum motui nisi ultimum motus ex parte post vel aliquod mutatum esse acquisitum per istum motum. Unde nullum initium motus incipientis a quiete est intrinsecum illi motui. Tamen mutatum esse copulans partes motus adinvicem est intrinsecum utrique parti. Et tunc dico quod si terminata calefactione statim incipiat frigefactio, ultimum calefactionis et primum frigefactionis mensuratur eodem instanti. Et hoc est possibile quia ultimum calefactionis est instrinsicum calefactioni et principium frigefactionis est extrinsecum a frigefactione. Ideo ista posunt inesse eidem in eodem instanti. Quid autem sit principium motus incipientis a quiete videbitur in tractatu sequenti" (No extreme is intrinsic to motion except the extreme at the end of motion . . . or some changed state . . . acquired by this motion. Thus, no beginning of motion beginning from rest is intrinsic to that motion. But a changed state joining the parts of motion to each either is intrinsic to either part. And then I say that if, when heating is ended, cooling should immediately begin, the extreme of heating and the beginning of cooling are measured by the same instant. And this is possible because the extreme of heating is intrinsic to heating and the beginning of cooling is extrinsic to cooling. Therefore, these can be in the same [thing] at the same instant) (Walter Burley, *In physicam Aristotelis expositio et quaestiones,* bk. 5, fol. 166r; translated by Edith Dudley Sylla in "Fourteenth-Century Theories of Alteration," in *Infinity and Continuity in Ancient and Medieval Thought,* ed. Norman Kretzmann, 237). For an extended discussion of the designation of intrinsic and extrinsic limits in logic, see Norman Kretzmann, "Incipit/Desinit." Perhaps the most important medieval discussions of extrinsic and intrinsic limits appear in the *Sophismata* of the early-fourteenth-century Oxford logician Richard Kilvington (*The Sophismata of Richard Kilvington,* ed. Norman Kretzmann and Barbara Ensign Kretzmann).

100. Derrida, *Edmund Husserl's Origin of Geometry,* 95.

101. In more specifically literary terms, the same question of the extrinsic and intrinsic commencement of writing has been discussed by Pierre Macherey, in terms he describes as the *endroit* and *envers* of the text, inseparable concepts that together determine the "principle of coherence in the discourse" *(A Theory of Literary Production)*. Much of *Of Grammatology* is concerned with interrogating the claims of interiority that traditional linguistics (from Plato to Saussure) has made for a *langue* that excludes, or exteriorizes, writing. Saussure's claim, for instance, that writing is "unrelated to [the] inner system of language" rests on the assumption of a natural relation between sound and language that the whole of *Grammatology* demonstrates is untenable in at least its most intelligible form (30–35). And in his work on Husserl, Derrida cites approvingly Husserl's maneuver to resolve the contradictions of representing writing as the condition of the possibility of ideality and its objectivity as founded on the material grapheme by maintaining a phenomenological opposition between "*internal* or intrinsic *(innere)* historicity" and "external *(aussere)* history" (95). In his *De principiis naturae,* Thomas Aquinas attempts to distinguish between Aristotle's apparently contradictory claims that only intrinsic causes are principles *and* that *principium* "is properly said of extrinsic causes and 'elements' of those causes which are the part of the thing, that is of the intrinsic causes" (*De principiis naturae,* ed. John J. Pauson, 79–104). As most of his discussion suggests, the principal difficulty lies in distinguishing between an event whose first term merely marks a beginning and one that *induces* a beginning. In adopting the four Aristotelian causes, he argues that two, the material and the formal, are intrinsic while the other two, the efficient and the final, are extrinsic. He calls these the intrinsic and extrinsic principles, respectively, unlike Aristotle, who argues that only the first two causes are principles at all. In arguing that a subset of the material cause, privation, could be called (although only "per accidens") a third principle, Aquinas effectively collapses the distinction between causes and principles. Without explicitly acknowledging it, Aquinas's text demonstrates that both intrinsic *and* extrinsic principles need to be examined in explaining the emergence of any object (including a text). *Piers Plowman* pushes this logic further in a poem whose final cause (the intention of its maker) and efficient cause (the author's agency) can be said to be *intrinsic* principles, the very topic of the poem's unfolding meditation; and the formal cause (the ideality of the poem's form), the *extrinsic* (social, political) injunction to impose order, restrain narrative profligacy, or curb theological and political addresses—in short, its corollary function of *disruption*. Anne Middleton's brilliant article "Acts of Vagrancy" shows how all of these pressures operate against the backdrop of the restraints and injunctions of the 1388 Cambridge parliament and reactions against Lollardy (see esp. 259–74, 280–88).

INITIUM: INCIPITS AND THE INTENTIONS OF VERNACULAR WRITING

1. Cf. Elton D. Higgs, "The Path to Involvement: The Centrality of the Dreamer in *Piers Plowman,*" 2.

2. Samuel Moore, "Studies in *Piers the Plowman,*" 21.

3. W. W. Skeat, *The Vision of William concerning Piers the Plowman,* 2:li.

4. W.W. Skeat, *Langland's Vision of Piers Plowman: The Vernon Text,* xxv.

5. George Kane, *Piers Plowman: The Evidence for Authorship,* 46–50; Robert Adams, "The Reliability of the Rubrics in the B-Text of *Piers Plowman.*"

6. Kane, *Piers Plowman: The Evidence for Authorship,* 49.

7. Kane and Donaldson discount Skeat's suggestion that these two manuscripts, L and M, constitute a genetic group, because of the relatively few agreements between the two. But the opening *ordinatio* they share is, as far as I know, the only example among all *Piers Plowman* manuscripts of any attempt to rationalize the beginning of the poem or to impose an identical plan. See George Kane and E. Talbot Donaldson, *Will's Visions of Piers Plowman, Do-Well, Do-Better, and Do-Best,* 37–38; W. W. Skeat, *Piers Plowman,* part 4, 840.

8. In W the next passus is headed "Primus passus de dowel"; in M the scribe seems to have had some difficulty in determining where, precisely, the new prologue ended; he concludes the entire poem at passus 11 with an *explicit* that also concludes the prologue: "Explicit prologus de dowel dobeet & dobest."

9. "Explicit liber petri plouman" (MS Douce 323).

10. Kane's argument that *liber* at passus 10 of D has the restricted sense of a subdivision is a bit disingenuous: it is not as easy as he suggests to fix the "special meaning of the term *secundo libro*" (*Piers Plowman: The Evidence for Authorship,* 47 n. 10). D itself, like all other *Piers* manuscripts except H of B, uses *passus* for internal divisions. The other examples of the use of *liber* that Kane adduces, in fact, use it either as a synonym for *passus,* and then only once (in passus 1 in G of B), or apply it to the entire poem, as D does in its *explicit.* D's use of *liber* at passus 10 is deeply ambiguous, marking the start of a virtually independent work, but a work that its own *explicit* subordinates to the whole. For further discussion of the "book" of *Piers Plowman* see the beginning of the chapter "Thema."

11. BL, Add. 35287, fol. 1r. A later, obviously Protestant, hand has inserted *filius* above *Maria* and added an *e* to change the name to a genitive. A. C. de la Mare has pointed out to me that the phrase is fairly common as a scribal comment; but here it is clearly in a secretary hand much later than the hand of the manuscript itself.

12. See George Kane, *The A Version: Will's Visions of Piers Plowman and Do-Well,* 18.

13. MS Bodley 814. Other B manuscripts that use this method are W, Hm, Cr, L, Y, Bm, Cot, and C.

14. MS Bodley 851; emphasis mine. The C Text portion of Z is written in a different hand than the A Text—or Z Text—portion, with a larger *anglicana media/currens* and with secretary forms replacing a smaller *anglicana formata* on fol. 139 near the end of passus 8.

15. See Adams, "Reliability of the Rubrics," 208–31. John Alford argues that the "most trustworthy principles of organization are those embedded firmly in the text itself, such as the three dreams that make up the A version and the eight that make up the B and C versions" ("The Design of the Poem," 31).

16. For studies that treat the structure of the whole poem, see Robert Worth Frank, *Piers Plowman and the Scheme of Salvation: An Interpretation of Dowel, Dobet, and Dobest,* 3; J. V. Holleran, "The Role of the Dreamer in *Piers Plowman,*" 33–50; Elizabeth D. Kirk, *The Dream Thought of Piers Plowman,* 15 ff.; Higgs, "Path to Involvement," 1–34; Mary-Jo Arn, "Langland's Characterization of Will in the B-Text," 287–301; and James F. G. Weldon,

"The Structure of Dream Visions in *Piers Plowman*," 254–81. A few studies analyze smaller groups of dreams as parts of a larger thematic schema: John A. Burrow, "The Action of Langland's Second Vision"; Joseph A. Longo, "*Piers Plowman* and the Tropological Matrix: Passus XI and XII"; and Wittig, "'Piers Plowman' B. Passus IX–XII," 211–80.

17. Cf. George D. Economou, "The Vision's Aftermath in *Piers Plowman:* The Poetics of the Middle English Dream Vision," and Middleton, "Narration and the Invention of Experience." Weldon's article "The Structure of Dream Visions in *Piers Plowman*" is one of the few to argue for the formal integrity of each dream, but he places them in a "unified structure composed of interrelated yet contrasting *kinds* of dream visions" (254).

18. Weldon, "Structure of Dream Visions in *Piers Plowman*," 254. The portions of the waking intervals that echo the beginning of the poem and function as prologues to the subsequent dreams are as follows. In the A Text: 5.3–9; 9.1–2, 53–60; in the B Text: 5.3–9; 8.1–2, 63–70; 11.4–9; 13.1–21; 15.1–12; 18.1–5; 19.1–5; in the C Text: 5.1–111; 10.1–2, 61–67; 11.164–69; 15.1–25; 20.1–5; 21.1–5.

19. Rita Copeland, *Rhetoric, Hermeneutics, and Translation in the Middle Ages*, 222, 166–67. On *intentio*, which she observes is "often equivalent to a statement of the work's significance" in later exegetical structures, see also 76–90.

20. Edward Said, *Beginnings*, 41.

21. Rosemarie McGerr, *Chaucer's Open Books: Resistance to Closure in Medieval Discourse*, 19.

22. Marie Magdeleine Davy, ed., *Les sermons universitaires parisiens de 1230–31: Contribution à l'histoire de la prédication médiévale*, 45. Judith Davidoff lists the following poems that exemplify what she calls "circularity of diction": *Sir Gawain and the Green Knight; Pearl; Patience; The Awntyrs of Arthure at the Terne Wathelyne; The Avowing of Arthure; Sir Degrevant; The Parlement of the Three Ages; Death and Liffe; The Kingis Quair;* Bannatyne MS vol. 3, 296–300; Bannatyne MS vol. 4, 40–42; app. A in *The Chanson d'Aventure in Middle English*, ed. Helen Estabrook Sandison; Carleton Brown, ed., *Religious Lyrics of the Fourteenth Century*, 78–80; Judith M. Davidoff, *Beginning Well: Framing Fictions in Late Middle English Poetry*. The repetition of opening lines in the conclusions of *Patience, Pearl*, and *Sir Gawain and the Green Knight* is one sign of the influence of preaching manuals in their composition.

23. A. C. Spearing, "Verbal Repetition in *Piers Plowman* B and C," 734. Spearing cites Peter of Cornwall's amazed response to a sermon that returns ingeniously to its beginning: "Totus enim sermo ille quibusdam distinctionibus uaritatus et flosculis uerborum et sententiarum depictus et copiosa auctoritatum subiectione roboratus, a principio per tramites suos ad idem principium decurrebat et recurrebat" (The whole of that sermon was varied by certain distinctions and embroidered with flowers of words and sentences and strengthened by a copious underlay of authorities. By its paths it ran backward and forward from its beginning to the same beginning; 734).

24. Robert of Basevorn, *Forma praedicandi*, 310; emphasis mine. Some rhetorical treatises apply Horace's injunction that the parts of a work should observe proper proportions to the relation between the beginning and the end. The amplitude of a work derives from the concordance of beginning and end: "Pulchriter inveniat, inventaque honeste. / Fini principium sit par" (He should invent beautifully, and what is invented should be done so honestly. The beginning should be equal to the end) (Charles Fierville, "Notices et extraits des manuscrits de la Bibliothèque de Saint-Omer," 135, cited in Douglas Kelly, "Theory of Composition in Medieval Narrative Poetry and Geoffrey of Vinsauf's *Poetria nova,*" 124).

25. "Conclusio est oratio sententiam intentionis explicans" (The conclusion is an oration expounding the meaning of the intention) (Ludolf of Hildesheim, *Summa dictamine,* 1:31). See also Rosemarie McGerr's useful discussion of the two preceding passages and similar ones from sermon literature and *artes dictaminis* in *Chaucer's Open Books,* 19–26. While I wrote this chapter before her book appeared, I discuss several of the same prescriptive texts she does, and for complementary reasons. She argues that such anticipations of the ending come at the beginning because the conclusion of a work is its problematic moment, and I would argue, naturally, that it is precisely because the beginning is such a powerful moment that modes of inception become the important topic of compositional precept that they do. The involvement of an ending is, of course, only one of numerous modes of beginning, but so is the recapitulation of a beginning only one form of ending. At this level, this book and McGerr's are exactly complementary, telling both sides of the same compositional story. Where I differ from McGerr is in pursuing the problem beyond the domain of composition, as I think Langland does in manifold ways, making the problem of beginning a larger ethical, social, political, and religious one.

26. Cf. A. J. Minnis, *Medieval Theory of Authorship: Scholastic Literary Attitudes in the Later Middle Ages,* 20. In his *Ars componendi sermones,* Ranulph Higden implicitly distinguishes between the two terms *intentio* and *finis* by suggesting that the composition of a sermon requires rectitude of intention to reach its proper "finis": "Rectitudo intencionis requiritur scilicet ut propter finem debitum predicat quod tunc fit quando predicat ad dei glorificacionem, ad proximi edificacionem, et ad veritas insinuacionem" (Rectitude of intention is necessary to be sure in order that he might foretell the necessary end, which occurs whenever he preaches to the glory of God, for the edification of his neighbor and for the instillation of truth) (*The Ars componendi sermones of Ranulph Higden, O.S.B.,* ed. Margaret Jennings, 310).

27. *The Legendys of Hooly Wummen,* ed. Mary S. Sergeantson, p. 1, lines 21–24.

28. Bene of Florence, *Candelabrum,* ed. Gian Carlo Alessio, 211.

29. Walter Burley, *Expositio super de generatione et corruptione,* Oxford, All Souls College, MS 86, fol. 199v.

30. Minnis, *Medieval Theory of Authorship,* 153–54.

31. John Ashenden, *Summa judicialis de accidentibus mundi,* MS Bodl. 714, fol 1v.

32. "Nota etiam quod alius modus debet esse scientiae quae habet informare affectum secundum pietatem; alius scientiae quae habet informare intellectum solum ad cognoscendum veritatem. Ille qui erit ad informationem affectus, erit per differentias quae dictae sunt, quia precepta, exempla, exhortationes, revelationes, orationes introducunt pietatis affectiones" (Note further that there must be another mode of knowledge whose task it is to inform the affection according to piety, and another [mode of] knowledge whose task it is to inform the intellect solely in understanding truth. That which will be for informing the affection will be by different [means], which are dicta, because precepts, examples, exhortations, revelations, and orations induce the affections of piety) (Alexander of Hales, *Summa theologiae*, lib. I, tract, introd., q. I., c.iv, art. I, ad 2; I, p. 8b). Cited in James Simpson, "From Reason to Affective Knowledge: Modes of Thought and Poetic Form in *Piers Plowman*," 5.

33. Cf. the twofold division of formal cause in Robert Kilwardby's *Summa Priscianum:* "Causa formalis consistit in modo agendi et in ordinatione partium doctrinae.... Ordinatio partium doctrine in divisione patebit" (The formal cause consists in the mode of doing and in the ordering of the part of learning... the order of the part of learning will fall into a division) (quoted in Hunt, "The Introductions to the Artes in the Twelfth Century," 137 n. 2).

34. William Caxton, *The book of fame made by G. Chaucer.*

35. Cf. Hans Vaihinger, *The Philosophy of As-If: A System of the Theoretical, Practical, and Religious Fictions of Mankind,* trans. C. K. Ogden, 38–39. Said discusses the role of the "summational fiction" in the creation of beginnings and endings in *Beginnings,* 48–50.

36. For a discussion of the propriety of scribal attempts to resolve apparent lacunae in the *Roman de la Rose,* see David Hult, *Self-Fulfilling Prophecies: Readership and Authority in the First Roman de la Rose,* 34–55.

37. In at least one case, the *intentio* of the compiler is presented as the motive behind the imposition of order on a diverse gathering of material: the *Summa judicialis de accidentibus mundi* of John Ashenden begins, "Intencio mea in hoc libro est compilare sentencias astrologorum de accidencium prognosticacione que accidunt in hoc mundo ex corporum superiorum volubilitate" (My intention in this book is to compile the teachings of the astrologers on the prognostication of events that occur in this world by the influence of the superior bodies) (Bodl. MS Digby 225, cited in Malcolm Parkes, "The Influence of the Concepts of *Ordinatio* and *Compilatio* on the Development of the Book," 130). Other useful discussions of the effects of *compilatio* on the disposition of works can be found in A. I. Doyle and M. B. Parkes, "The Production of Copies of the *Canterbury Tales* and the *Confessio Amantis* in the Early Fifteenth Century," and A. J. Minnis, *Medieval Theory of Authorship*. An analogous case is Gui de Mori's recension of the *Roman de la Rose,* in which, as David Hult points out, "his immediate purpose was to supplement (and not to supplant) the *Rose* text.... While Gui expresses a clear desire to maintain the intended meaning ('entention'), he sees no contradiction in his plan to excise part of the original text and interpolate passages of his own composition" (Hult, *Self-Fulfilling Prophecies,* 35).

38. Bernard of Utrecht, *Commentum in Theodulum,* in A. J. Minnis, *Medieval Theory of Authorship,* 50.

39. Copeland, *Rhetoric, Hermeneutics, and Translation,* 186–202.

40. "If supplementarity is a necessarily indefinite process, writing is the supplement itself par excellence since it marks the point where the supplement proposes itself as supplement of supplement, sign of sign, *taking the place of* a speech already significant: it displaces the *proper place* of the sentence, the unique time of the sentence pronounced *hic et nunc* by an irreplaceable subject, and in return enervates the voice. It marks the place of the initial doubling" (Derrida, *Of Grammatology,* 281).

41. George Kane, "The Text," 180. G. H. Russell shows how the revisions of C 9.1–61 divulge, in a microcosmic instance, the impulses behind the revising of the B Text, the beginning of another poem: "Clearly, this was for the poet an area of his poem where his revising activity was urgently required, at times as repair, but conspicuously *as recreation*" (Russell, "The Imperative of Revision in the C Version of *Piers Plowman*," 239–40; emphasis mine). Russell's interest in the psychology of revision is perhaps another manifestation of the impulse to recover the poet's ideal *archetypus*.

42. Anne Middleton, "Making a Good End: John But as a Reader of *Piers Plowman*," 245.

43. Published in Kane, "The Text," 182.

44. Robert of Basevorn, *Forma praedicandi*, 309.

45. Geoffrey Chaucer, *The Book of the Duchess*, in *The Riverside Chaucer*, ed. Larry D. Benson, 1330–34.

46. T. P. Dunning argues that in the A Text Langland "makes *the right use of temporal goods* his theme.... the remainder of the poem develops from passus i and is concerned with the allegorical exposition of the same principles. The subject, then, may be said to be *Temporalia—sub specie aeternitatis*" (*Piers Plowman: An Interpretation of the A Text*, 6–7). Kaske argues that Holy Church's speech, principally concerned with the treasure that is Truth, contains the germ of the poem's design. For a further discussion of the relation between treasure and Truth, see James Simpson, "Spirituality and Economics in Passus 1–7 of the B-Text."

47. A. J. Colaianne, "Structure and 'Foreconceit' in *Piers Plowman B:* Some Observations on Langland's Psychology of Composition," 110.

48. Ibid., 106.

49. None of the standard classical rhetorical texts has a term for the archetypal work: the nearest to the idea is perhaps Horace, who refers to the conceived work merely as "materia": "Sumite materiam vestris, qui scribitis, / equam viribus" (Take material, you who write, equal to your strength) (Horace, *Ars poetica*, ed. and trans. Rushton Fairclough, 38–39). That the formulation of the concept was medieval and possibly originated with Geoffrey of Vinsauf is suggested by Conrad of Mure, who cites both the passage from Horace and the *Poetria nova* 43–36 as authorities for his discussion of "prehabita dispositione": "Prudens enim architectus non procedit inconsulte ad actum operandi, nisi prehabita dispositione architipa et mentali" (For the prudent builder does not proceed thoughtlessly to the act of working; rather, he has a preformed archetypal and mental formation) (Walter Kronbichler, ed., *Die summa de arte prosandi der Konrad von Mure*, 26). The Horatian passage does not embody the idea nearly as explicitly, and most of Conrad's discussion owes a direct debt to Geoffrey of Vinsauf. Colaianne's article is in many ways a disappointing execution of a useful idea. Several aspects of his article themselves suggest a lack of "foreconceit": despite his claims, there is a great deal of evidence for medieval compositional theory, as I have attempted to show. And the link Colaianne draws between digressive form and "lack of foreconceit" remains more speculative than it needs to be.

50. John M. Bowers, *The Crisis of Will in Piers Plowman*, 157.

51. Cf. Bernard of Utrecht, *Commentum in Theodulum*, in *Accessus ad auctores*, ed. R. B. C. Huygens, 65.

52. Anne Middleton, "The Audience and Public of 'Piers Plowman,'" 113. Elsewhere in the article she suggests that the poem abdicates from established traditions of *ordinatio:* "Clarity, explicit organization, and comprehensiveness of form were the entire purpose of the teaching compendia [the source for Langland's 'conceptual syntax'], and by Langland's time their internal order and self-explanatory prologues had achieved a high degree of articulation, both in Latin and in the vernacular. Though the existence of such works made Langland's composition possible, his poem is insouciant and enigmatic where his purported sources are systematic and explicit; they explain themselves where his work declines to do so directly" (112).

53. I.e., the category "cui parti philosophiae supponitur." See Judson Boyce Allen, *The Ethical Poetic of the Later Middle Ages: A Decorum of Convenient Distinction,* chap. 1; and Parkes, "Influence of the Concepts of *Ordinatio* and *Compilatio,*" 119–21.

54. *The Wars of Alexander,* ed. Hoyt N. Duggan and Thorlac Turville-Petre, lines 1–14.

55. The beginning entails an initial negotiation or denial of dynastic traditions: "[W]e can regard a beginning as the point at which, in a given work, the writer departs from all other works; a beginning immediately establishes relationships with works already existing, relationships of either continuity or antagonism or some mixture of both" (Said, *Beginnings,* 3). The category *cui parti philosophiae supponitur* is one aspect of the proprietary demands of beginning, as are the openings of *Sir Gawain and the Green Knight* and *Winner and Waster,* which situate the work within an explicitly dynastic context, and the prologue of Gower's *Confessio Amantis,* which is a declaration that demands are placed on a beginning, and an emulation of attempts to place works within the domain of philosophy: "This prologe is so assised / That it to wisdom al belongeth." On the uses of techniques such as the *divisio textus* in the *Confessio* to "transform traditional materials into a sustained ethical argument," see Rita Copeland, *Rhetoric, Hermeneutics, and Translation,* 202–20.

56. The extent of But's contribution is uncertain: Skeat was convinced that only the last twelve lines are But's (*The Vernon Text,* 141); R. W. Chambers suggests that But wrote the last twenty-four lines (Chambers, "The Original Form of the A Text of *Piers Plowman*").

57. Middleton: "Making a Good End," 255–60.

58. Ibid., 263.

59. Ibid., 246.

60. See David Hult's "Closed Quotations: The Speaking Voice in the Roman de la Rose."

EXORDIUM: MAKING BEGINNINGS

1. Bene of Florence, *Candelabrum,* 137–38.

2. Cf. Horace, *Epist.* 1.2, in *Satires, Epistles, and Ars poetica,* ed. and trans. H. Rushton Fairclough.

3. Cf. Cicero, *De inventione,* 1.20, in *De inventione, De optimo genere oratorum, Topica.*

4. "Expedit in principio predicatori ut quantum poterit deo inoffenso auditores reddat benivoles et attentos ad audiendum et sollicitos ad exequendum" (Ranulph Higden, *Ars componendi sermones,* 43). "Quod autem in proemiis siue prologis debeamus captare beneuolentiam et facere auditores attentos et efficere eos dociles" (In proems or prologues we must capture good will and make the listeners attentive and make them docile) (Thomas of Chobham, *Summa de arte praedicandi,* ed. Franco Morenzoni, 264).

5. Thomas of Chobham, *Summa de arte praedicandi,* 298.

6. Chaucer, *Boece,* bk. 3, pr. 3.

7. "Prius ergo debet illi qui dictare proposuit totam materiam in sue mentis armario premetiri" (First, therefore, he who proposes to write must premeasure the whole material in the cabinet of his mind) (Bene of Florence, *Candelabrum,* 211). "Circinus interior mentis praecircinet omne / Materiae spatium. Certus praelimitet ordo / Unde praearripiat cursum stylus") (Geoffrey de Vinsauf, *Poetria nova,* lines 55–57).

8. Cf. Cicero, *Topica.*

9. For discussions and examples of the placement of poetry under the study of ethics, see Minnis, *Medieval Theory of Authorship,* and Minnis and Scott, eds., *Medieval Literary Theory and Criticism, c. 1100–c. 1375.*

10. Oxford, Bodl. MS Rawl. D 328, fol. 144v.

11. John Chrysostom, Homil. 9, *Epist. ad Hebraeos,* quoted in Janus Gruterus, *Florilegii magni seu Polyanthae Tomus secund,* 523.

12. MS Bodl. 633, printed in *Florilegium morale oxoniense. Secunda Pars: Flores Auctorum,* ed. C. H. Talbot, Analecta Medievalia Namurcensia, 6 (Louvain: Nauwelaerts, 1956), 49. The phrase also appears in Gruterus, *Florilegii magni seu Polyanthae Tomus secund,* 523. Variants appear in Bene of Florence, *Candelabrum,* 4.16, p. 138, and in Eduardus Margalits, ed., *Florilegium prouerbium universae latinitatis,* 155. The phrase may be derived ultimately from Hesiod: see K. F. W. Wander, *Deutsches Sprichworter-Lexicon,* s.v. "Anfang" 17. It appears as "dimidium facti qui coepti habet" (half done he who has begun) in Horace, *Epistles,* 2.40, and in Seneca's *Epistles,* 34.3.

13. Pseudo–Cicero, *Ad C. Herennium de ratione dicendi (Rhetorica ad Herennium),* ed. and trans. Harry Caplan, 2.1.1.

14. Cf. Leslie Brisman, *Romantic Origins.* Said argues that the continuity of the work itself, its form, is entailed in the conceptual act of beginning itself: "What is really anterior to a search for method, to a search for a temporal beginning, is not merely an initiative, but a necessary certainty, a genetic optimism, that continuity is possible *as intended by* the act of beginning. Stretching from start to finish is a fillable space, or time . . . awaiting an author or a speaker to father it, to authorize its being. . . . The starting point is the reflexive action of the mind attending to itself, allowing itself to effect (or dream) a construction of a world whose seed totally implicates its offspring. It is . . . Husserl asserting the radical originality of consciousness which will support 'the whole storied edifice of universal knowledge'" (*Beginnings,* 48).

15. "Fundamentum bene dictandi a fonte sapientiae cognoscitur emanare, quia 'recte scribendi,' sicut ait Horatius, 'sapere est et principium et fons.' Unde qui rerum cognitione caret tanquam cecus ducitur et oberrat, deficiens in rebus, deficiens in sermone" (The foundation of writing well is known to proceed from the fount of wisdom, because "writing correctly," as Horace says, "is the beginning and fount of knowledge." Wherefore he who lacks the knowledge of things is led as if he were blind and he wanders, wanting in affairs, wanting in his speech) (Bene of Florence, *Candelabrum* 1.5, p. 6).

16. Ibid. The idea in the *Poetria nova* is essentially the same, if the underlying imagery differs slightly: "Praemetitur opus, seriemque sub ordine certe/ Interior praescribit homo, totamque figurat / Ante manus cordis quam corporis; et status ejus / Est prius archetypus quam sensilis" (Ernest Gallo, ed., *The "Poetria Nova" and Its Sources in Early Rhetorical Doctrine,* lines 45–48). John of Garland has a similar passage, even more obviously indebted to the *Poetria nova:* the material of the work consists of a beginning, middle, and end: "Preordinande sunt iste partes in mente, quia prius debet esse verbum in mente quam sit in ore" (Those parts must be prearranged in the mind, because the word first must be in the mind before it is in the mouth) (*Parisiana poetria,* ed. Traugott Lawler, cap. 3, p. 53).

17. The opening words of one treatise unambiguously identify the thema with the beginning: "Thema est principium sermonis" (The thema is the beginning of the sermon) (Pseudo-Aquinas, *Ars praedicandi,* fol. 4v).

18. A few fourteenth-century preaching manuals apply the recommendations found in the *Rhetorica ad Herennium* to the construction of sermons and suggest that a sermon should begin with a prologue that introduces the theme. Thomas of Chobham is one of the most faithful exponents of the application of principles of classical rhetoric to sermons, scrupulously following classical distinctions: a "prologus" is used in a sermon and not a "prefatio" because "prefatio . . . non usitate in rethorica" (the preface . . . is not used in rhetoric) (*Summa de arte praedicandi,* 263). He even transfers the traditional observation on beginnings to the prologue: "Et dicitur idem proemium, quia principium est quasi dimidium totius orationis" (And the same is said of the proem, because the beginning is comparable to half of the whole discourse) (264). Thomas's definition of the function of the exordium also comes directly from classical rhetoric (cf. 264), as does his enumeration of "vices" in *exordia* (cf. 272). Thomas furnishes an important example of the influence of classical rhetoric on at least one medieval genre and suggests that James Schultz's argument that Ciceronian doctrine did not influence medieval genres significantly should be amended to exclude sermons. See James A. Schultz, "Classical Rhetoric, Medieval Poetics, and the Medieval Vernacular Prologue," and G. R. Evans, "Thomas of Chobham on Preaching and Exegesis."

19. Thomas Waleys, *De modo componendi sermones,* 357. The identification of *thema* with *materia* is common even in rhetorical treatises. Some, however, define *thema* as unshaped, inchoate material: "'Thema' grecum est et dicitur aput Grecos quelibet informis materia" ("Thema" is Greek and among the Greeks is used of any sort of unformed material) (*An Early Commentary on the Poetria Nova of Geoffrey of Vinsauf,* ed. Marjorie Curry Woods, 16).

20. John of Wales, *Forma predicandi,* 340 n. 18.

21. Pseudo-Aquinas, *Ars praedicandi,* fol. 4v. The figure of the *thema* as a root is ubiquitous in preaching manuals; see also the diagram of the "arbor praedicandi" in the frontispiece to Thomas Charland, *Artes praedicandi.*

22. MS Anger 1582, fol. 132r, in Thomas Charland, *Artes praedicandi,* 113 n. 2. Cf. MS Arundel 275 83rb, 86r.

23. Cf. Allen, *Ethical Poetic of the Later Middle Ages,* 130. The eight kinds of artificial beginning allow one to begin, as Allen succinctly summarizes Geoffrey of Vinsauf's

treatment, "at the middle, or at the end, or one may begin with either a proverb or an exemplum drawn from beginning, middle, or end" (131). John of Garland's *Parisiana poetria* is another influential treatise that observes eight kinds of artificial beginning, comparing them to the branches of a tree: "Principium artificiale est quando inchoamus a medio materie vel a fine, et hoc possumus facere viij modis; vnde hoc principium viij habet ramos" (An artificial beginning is when we begin in the middle or at the end of the material, and we can do this in eight ways; therefore this beginning has eight branches) (*Parisiana poetria,* ed. Traugott Lawler, 53). The distinction between natural and artificial beginnings has a long pedigree, apparently beginning with Donatus's commentary on Virgil: cf. J. Brummer, ed., *Vitae Virgilianae,* 18; and see Minnis and Scott, eds., *Medieval Literary Theory and Criticism,* 18. Matthew of Vendome recommends only two kinds of beginning (with the figures of hypozeuxis and zeugma), but recognizes six altogether: "In exercitio disciplinae versificatoriae materia duobus modis inchoatur et elegantius potest inchoari. Sunt autem alii modi quatuor, quos . . . lippis et tonsoribus relinquimus" (In the exercise of the discipline of versifying the material is begun, and can elegantly be begun, in two ways. There are, however, four other ways, which we can relegate . . . to the bleary and the tonsured) (Matthew of Vendome, *Ars versificatoria,* 112).

24. John of Garland, *Parisiana poetria,* 53. Conrad of Hirsau also shows how the terms *ordo* and *principium* are virtually interchangeable, suggesting that the order of a book is something one finds at its beginning: "[R]equiritur etiam *ordo* in librorum principiis, utrum sit *naturalis* an *artificialis. . . . Naturalem* noueris *ordinem* cum liber iuxta geste rei seriem incipitur, *artificialem* ubi librorum principiis ordo debitus non tenetur" (Order is required in the beginnings of books, whether it is natural or artificial [order]. . . . You will recognize natural order when a book is begun in conformity with the sequence of events, artificial [order] when the order appropriate to the beginnings of books is not observed) (*Dialogus super auctores,* ed. R. B. C. Huygens, 18).

25. Allen, *Ethical Poetic of the Later Middle Ages,* 136. The "Assisi" commentary on the *Poetria nova* is an exemplary instance of this principle: "[D]ispositio [est] una que attenditur in ingressu materie, penes quantitatem que attenditur in progressu materie. . . . In quarum prima sciendum est quod . . . materie specialis dispositio quantum ad ingressum consistit in ordine" (The disposition [is] the one which is expected as the material unfolds. . . . With regard to the first of these it should be known that . . . the special disposition of the material with regard to beginning it consists of its order") (131–32; Allen's translation). As Allen suggests, "The order, or disposition, is that which one notices at the beginning of the text—I might almost say *as* the beginning of the text" (132).

26. Thomas Waleys, *De modo componendi sermones,* 361–62.

27. Boniface VIII, "Unam Sanctam," 2: col. 1246.

28. That is, particularly for Platonists, "Deum," "materia," and "forma" (Robert Grosseteste, *Hexaemeron,* ed. Richard C. Dales and Servus Gieben, O.F.M.). This portion of Grosseteste's work belongs to a long tradition within hexaemeral writing, dating back at least to Ambrose's attacks on the Manichaeans in his *Hexaemeron* (Ambrose, *Hexaemeron,* ed. Carolus Schenkl, 1.3), part of which Grosseteste himself cites in part. prima 9.2. Seventy years after Grosseteste wrote this, and almost a millennium after Ambrose's work was written, Boniface still charges the Manichaeans with this heresy.

29. See Grosseteste, *Hexaemeron*, 6. Adam Marsh, a student of Grosseteste's works, supplied his own rubrics, which often clarify the matter of each section. In this case, his rubric makes clear that the basis of Grosseteste's *distinctio* is linguistic: "Distinccio huius nominis 'principium,' ut manifestum sit quilibet intellectus huius nominis 'principium' coacervantur ipso cum dicitur *in principio* et cetera" (Distinction of the term "beginning," so that it might be clear whatever meanings of the term "beginning" are lumped together when "in the beginning" itself is said and [when] other things) (appendix, *Hexaemeron*).

30. I.e., "Dicitur enim principium in successione temporis et principium in ordine numerali, et principium in mole et magnitudine, principium quoque in mocione. Sed hii intellectus principii non privant 'esse ab alio simpliciter,' secundum quem intellectum tantum unicum est principium; sed inuunt hoc quod dicitur principium 'esse primum in suo genere,' et 'non habere prius in eodem genere.' Dicitur eciam ars 'principium' artificii, et 'principium' id ex quo fit facilius, et finis ultimus et optimus 'principium' eius quod est ad finem" (For *principium* is used of the succession of time, and *principium* of the sequence of number, and *principium* of weight and magnitude, and *principium* also of motion. But none of these meanings of beginning exclude [the sense of] "being from another simply"; according to which meaning there is only one beginning; but they suggest that the beginning is said of "being of the first of its kind" and "having nothing before of its kind." Art *[ars]*, too, is said to be the "beginning" of skill *[artificii]*, and "beginning" from which a thing can most easily be done, and the last end, and the best, [is called] the "beginning" of what happens toward that end) (Grosseteste, *Hexaemeron*, part. prima 10.1).

31. Ibid.

32. Ibid.

33. Ibid.

34. Cf. Charlton T. Lewis and Charles Short, *A Latin Dictionary* (Oxford: Clarendon, 1975), s.v. "ars."

35. John Wyclif, *The English Works of Wyclif*, ed. Frederic David Matthew, 447.

36. "[E]xordium nichil aliud est quam captacio beneuolencie" (the exordium is nothing other than the capturing of good will) (*Ars dictandi aurelianensis*, in *Briefsteller und formelbucher des elften bis vierzehnten jahrhunderts*, ed. Ludwig Rockinger, 1:108). The Baumgartenberg Formulary does not use the term *exordium* at all to define the second part of a letter: "nunc videndum est de epistole parte principali secunda, que est captacio beniuolencie" (now we must consider the second main part of the letter, which is the *captatio benevolentiae*) (*Formularius de modo prosandi*, in *Briefsteller*, ed. Rockinger, 2:744). Ludolf of Hildesheim makes the exordium an aspect of the *captacio beneuolentiae;* see *Summa dictaminum*, 1:367. Cf. also James J. Murphy, *Rhetoric in the Middle Ages: A History of Rhetorical Theory from Saint Augustine to the Renaissance*, 205–6.

37. *Rationes dictandi*, in *Briefsteller*, ed. Rockinger, 1:18. James Murphy points out that Rockinger mistakenly attributes the treatise to Alberic of Monte Cassino (*Rhetoric in the Middle Ages*, 220).

38. Cited in Allen, *Ethical Poetic of the Later Middle Ages*, 136.

39. Bonaventure, *Breviloquium*, prol., para. 5, in *S. Bonaventurae Opera Omnia*, vol. 1 (Milan, 1882), 5. 206; quoted in James Simpson, "From Reason to Affective Knowledge," 9.

40. A few *Artes praedicandi* simply state that the preacher must first capture the audience's good will, but do not link the capturing of good will specifically to the salvation of the will. Cf. Thomas of Chobham, *Summa de arte praedicandi,* 264; Ranulph Higden, *Ars componendi sermones,* 32.

41. Alain of Lille, *Summa de arte praedicandi,* cols. 113–14.

42. The word is, indeed, synonymous with "good will" in the Wycliffite Bible: "Charite is pacient, it is benynge or of good will," 1 Corinthians 13:4; "The benygnyte or good wille of God ledith the to penaunce," 1 Romans 2:4. The second version of the Bible replaces "benyngnete" in Psalm 64:112 with "good wille" (*The Holy Bible . . . in the Earliest English Versions,* ed. Josiah Forshall and Frederic Madden [Oxford, 1850]).

43. Benignity seems to be associated largely with nobility and "gentilesse": cf. the *Parson's Tale* 1.467: "Another is to be benygne to hire goode subgetz"; *Proceedings of the Privy Council* (c. 1420): "Many oþer gentill wordes my guid lorde . . . seide þere so benyngly" (*Proceedings of the Privy Council of England,* ed. Nicholas Harris Nicolas).

44. Cf. Bene of Florence, *Candelabrum,* 130, 135, 200.

45. Good will and the beginning of speech are associated elsewhere in *Piers Plowman.* In passus 3 Meed herself asks the king for permission to speak: "the kyng graunted hire grace with a good wille" (A 3.165).

46. Ranulph Higden, *Ars componendi sermones,* 32. He goes on to give an example of a "tale," taken from Gerald of Wales, that illustrates the thema: "[S]i thema sit: *fons ascendebat de terra* (Gen. 2:6), adduci potest illud quod narrat Giraldus Cambrensis in topographia Hibernie de quodam fonte in Cicilia, ad quem fontem accessit quis rubea veste indutus, statim educebatur aqua de fonte que tamen ad omnes alios viros manet invicta" (If the theme is "the fountain rose out of the earth," it is possible to adduce what Gerald of Wales narrates in his *Topography of Ireland* about a certain fountain in Sicily, to which fountain someone dressed in red clothes approached: immediately water was drawn from the fountain, which nevertheless remains unattainable for all others) (32–33).

47. James Simpson, "From Reason to Affective Knowledge," 19.

48. Bowers, *The Crisis of Will,* 97–189.

49. James Simpson, "From Reason to Affective Knowledge," 20.

50. Ibid., 14–19, 10–13.

THEMA: THE BOOK THAT MAKES ITSELF

1. Hugh of Saint-Victor, *Didascalicon,* col. 788.

2. Cassiodorus, *De artibus et disciplinis liberalium litterarum,* col. 1151. For a further discussion of the representation of grammar as the *radix* of a tree, see R. Howard Bloch, *Etymologies and Genealogies,* 89. Bloch refers to Theodulph of Orleans's *De septem liberalibus artibus in quadam pictura depictis,* which describes grammar sitting at the root of a tree, producing still more trees: "Huius Grammatica ingens in radice sedebat / . . . Omnis ad hac ideo procedere cernitur arbos."

3. For the *De arca,* see Carruthers, *Book of Memory,* 209–10; Chaucer's Parson says that "Penitence . . . may be likned to a tree" and proceeds to do so in lines 111ff. of his tale.

4. Gilles Deleuze and Félix Guattari, *A Thousand Plateaus: Capitalism and Schizophrenia*, 9. Much of the first chapter of *A Thousand Plateaus* is a useful discussion of the ways in which the rhizome undoes the formative image of the "root-book," the text that roots the book in the world: the "tree is already the image of the world, or the root the image of the world-tree. . . . This is the classical book, as noble, signifying, and subjective organic interiority. . . . The book imitates the world, as art imitates nature: by procedures specific to it that accomplish what nature cannot or can no longer do" (5).

5. Middleton, "Narration and the Invention of Experience," 94–95.

6. Middleton's observation that Langland nowhere "internally designates" his poem as a book ("Acts of Vagrancy," 288–89) is a trenchant claim for the provisional nature of Langland's work. Nevertheless, this passage suggests that at the very least Langland imagines his poem as an *alternative* to the books of doctrinal instruction and theology that might describe Dowel, a supplementary book that, like the Derridean supplement, turns out to be the trace of this originary plenitude, of the "bokes ynowe" that we somehow fail to locate in this book, a work designated a book by extension and implication.

7. James F. G. Weldon makes a similar point, dividing the dreams into "Dreams of Attachment," "Dreams of Detachment," and "Dreams of Spiritual Advance" ("The Structure of Dream Visions," 258). His division is useful, but it might be altered even on its own terms, as I have done here: the beginning of passus 8 suggests a greater detachment than Weldon recognizes.

8. For the intellectual context of this idea, see Wittig, "'Piers Plowman' B. Passus IX–XII."

9. Bowers, *Crisis of Will*, 138.

10. W. W. Skeat, *Piers the Plowman* (Oxford: Oxford University Press, 1886), 2.2, n. 2. Pearsall implicitly agrees with Skeat's interpretation: "The coarse woollen outer garment of a shepherd (a possible sense of *shep*) might be presumed to resemble that of a hermit. . . . L may be thinking of a shepherd as the simple, detached oberver familiar in pastoral tradition" (Pearsall, Prol. n. 2).

11. This is the B verse reading from the manuscripts WHmCrGOC2LMR.

12. See Steven Justice's *Writing and Rebellion* for a brilliant and thorough treatment of these concerns in the letters circulated by the rebels in 1381.

13. For the only discussion to date of this important circle of London grammarians see V. H. Galbraith, "John Seward and His Circle" and "More about John Seward."

14. *Rotuli Parliamentorum* (London, 1767–77), 2:273. The motive voiced by the lords and commons was that French had become "trop desconu en le dit roialme" (greatly unknown in the said realm). In practice, however, many pleas continued to be entered in French. While the targeting of Common Pleas records by the rebels was not likely the result of outrage over the use of English, it was only slightly less likely the result of their outrage over the continued use of French. It is much likelier that the attempt at reforming its language in 1362 and the 1381 rebels' attempt to destroy its symbolic efficacy was the result of its abuse at the hands of lawyers and the *mediocres*.

15. For references to accounts of these actions and to the training of common lawyers at the Temple, see T. F. Tout, *Chapters in the Administrative History of Mediaeval England: The Wardrobe, the Chamber, and the Small Seals*, 3:202, 369, and n. 6.

16. This is, of course, a stance equally charged with political consequences, but not one, I would argue, taken up as an explicitly repudiating gesture. I hope it is clear that Anne Middleton's acute observations in her article "William Langland's 'Kynde Name': Authorial Signature and Social Identity in Late Fourteenth-Century England" about the importance of designation and nomination in the larger project of the poem are an indispensable part of my conclusions here about the *kyndely* nature of incipient and intrinsic form.

17. There are other examples in the poem of the relation between the verb "shape" and the ethical disposition of the individual life: in B Passus 11 Ymaginatif discusses how the force of shame will reform drunkards: it will "shenden hym, and shape hym to amende" (424); the Samaritan points out to Will that the Holy Ghost is "grace withoute mercy / To alle unkynde creatures that coveite to destruye / Lele love or lif that Oure Lord shapte" (B 17.217–19); in the Prologue Will observes how "The Kyng and the Commune and Kynde Wit the thridde / Shopen lawe and leaute—ech life to knowe his owene" (Prol. 121–22). This last phrase may refer either to the duties of individuals within society (cf. E. T. Donaldson, *Piers Plowman: The C-Text and Its Poet,* 89) or to the property of individuals (cf. P. M. Kean, "Law, Love and *Lewte* in *Piers Plowman,*" 243).

18. Cf. Library of the Society of Antiquaries of London MS 687 (M), and the Duke of Westminster's Manuscript, Eaton Hall (W). This is the point, of course, at which many manuscripts divide the poem into a *Visio* and a *Vita.* Almost all C Text manuscripts mark the beginning of another *Visio* here, as in MS Douce 104 (D): "Explicit visio Willelmi W. de petro ploghman. / Et incipit visio eiusdem de do well." The "eiusdem" here and in X (Huntington Library MS HM 143) may refer to another vision "of the same kind," but the repetition of the name "Willelmi" in the incipit in other C Text manuscripts may simply mean that a second vision by "Willelmus" follows.

19. Bowers discusses Langland's use of this particular gesture in three of the poem's openings; see *Crisis of Will,* 145–46.

20. A. V. C. Schmidt's reading *(Vision of Piers Plowman)* seems preferable here, since, unlike K-D, it follows the reading of the vast majority of manuscripts,including the copy-text; there seems to be no compelling reason to emend the reading.

21. John Bowers points out in this connection that "twittering birds were associated in medieval literature with the vernal stirrings of natural energy... which paralleled and often stimulated a similar awakening in men, particularly in poets" (*Crisis of Will,* 144).

22. *Wynnere and Wastoure,* ed. Stephanie Trigg, line 44.

23. See Alfonso Maierù, *Terminologia logica della tarda scolastica,* 93 n. 155.

24. As in, for instance, Pseudo-Albertus Magnus's treatise on modes of signification: "principium effectivum imponens est intellectus agens, qui abstrahit res a conditionibus materialibus quae sunt esse nunc, hic et huiusmodi" (*Quaestiones Alberti de modis significandi,* ed. L. G. Kelly, q. 4, resp. ad 4, p. 21). As Umberto Eco and others say of Abelard's theory of grammatical origination, "[A] thing is meaningful because of the will that produces it as such" (Umberto Eco, R. Lambertini, C. Marmo, and A. Tabarroni, "On Animal Language in the Medieval Classification of Signs," 15).

25. Michel Serres argues that it is the act of designating intelligible patterns in the static, or noise, of the world that constitutes the only possible act of beginning. See *The*

Parasite. In *Rome: The Book of Foundations,* he argues that political beginnings emerge along with the inchoate forms of writing, animal husbandry, and civilization. His earlier book *Genesis* thinks about noise in terms of a Heraclitean flux or Bergsonian process, in which symbolic formations (money) and cultural formations (class) are the effect of the cessation of noise, which is the figure of a multiplicity, a turbulence, that is both prior to and produces representation, a recursive imperative that forces us continually to "return to the background noise" (*Genesis,* 91). See especially the last chapter, "The Birth of Time," 81–122. Giorgio Agamben points out that the management of the voice is not only the foundation of the *polis*—as Aristotle says, the human "alone has perception of good and bad and right and wrong and the other moral qualities, and it is partnership in these things that makes a household and a city-state" (*Politics,* ed. and trans. H. Rackham [Cambridge, Mass.: Harvard University Press, 1977], bk. I, sect. 2)—but also of ethics: "The space between voice and *logos* is an empty space, a limit in the Kantian sense. Only because man finds himself cast into language without the vehicle of a voice, and only because the *experimentum linguae* lures him, grammarless, into that void and that *aphonia,* do an *ethos* and a community of any kind become possible" (Agamben, *Infancy and History,* 9).

26. Curtius provides numerous examples from Latin poems. See Ernst R. Curtius, *European Literature and the Latin Middle Ages,* 85–86. Chaucer begins several dreams with the same gesture: ". . . never sith that I was born, / Ne no man elles me beforn, / Mette, I trowe stedfastly, / So wonderful a drem as I" (*The House of Fame,* in Geoffrey Chaucer, *The Riverside Chaucer,* ed. Larry D. Benson, 59–62); "Me mette so ynly swete a sweven, / So wonderful that never yit / Y trowe no man had the wit / To konne wel my sweven rede" (*Book of the Duchess,* 276–80).

27. A. C. Spearing points out, for example, how Lydgate attempts to situate himself among the pilgrims traveling to Canterbury, apparently taking the place of Chaucer: "[T]he nearer *The Siege of Thebes* gets to *The Knight's Tale,* the more of Chaucer's actual words Lydgate actually takes over. The reader begins to suspect that an ideal culmination of Lydgate's enterprise might be simply a recomposition of *The Canterbury Tales* analogous to the recomposition of *Don Quixote* imagined by Borges as the goal of his Pierre Menard" (*Medieval to Renaissance in English Poetry,* 108).

28. Several critics have discussed the perplexed relations in the poem between uncertain poetic authority and uncertain narrative definition. See J. A. Burrow, "Words, Works, and Will: Theme and Structure in *Piers Plowman,*" in *Piers Plowman: Critical Approaches,* ed. S. S. Hussey, 111–24; and Charles Muscatine, *Poetry and Crisis in the Age of Chaucer,* 71–109. Middleton discusses *Piers Plowman*'s complex relations between authorial self-presentation ("kynde name") and narrative definition ("kynde") in "William Langland's 'Kynde Name,'" 15–82; she discusses the emergence of modes of definition for the self and narrative in "Narration and the Invention of Experience," 91–122.

29. The relation between the "supplement" and the principle of plenitude is, Derrida suggests, a fundamentally imitative one: "[T]he substitute make[s] one forget the vicariousness of its own function and make[s] itself pass for the plenitude of a speech whose deficiency and infirmity it nevertheless only *supplements.* . . . The supplement adds itself, it is a surplus, a plenitude enriching another plenitude, the *fullest measure* of presence. It cumulates and accumulates presence" (*Of Grammatology,* 144).

30. Bowers, *Crisis of Will,* 139–40.

31. The Ilchester manuscript, however, includes part of the C Text's satire of Lollards, the "classification of beggars" from C 9, in its Prologue. Wendy Scase speculates that this section may have circulated "in an uninterpolated form during an early period of poem's history" (*"Piers Plowman" and the New Anticlericalism,* 150). Scase discusses the issue further in "Two *Piers Plowman* C-Text Interpolations: Evidence for a Second Textual Tradition."

32. Curtius, *European Literature and the Latin Middle Ages,* 468.

33. The following examples come from Ernst R. Curtius: Cicero, *De oratore,* 1.60: "Stilus ille multi sudoris est" (That pen is one of much sweat); Quintillian, *Institutio Oratoria,* 6.4.6: "ambitiosus declamandi sudor" (the eager /insistent sweat of declaiming); Jerome; Ennodius (ed. Hartel, 125.2); Einhard, preface to the *Vita Karoli; Poetae,* 4.266.25 and 1095.29; Alan's address to his book: "O mihi continuo multa sudata labore / Pagina" (Thomas Wright, *The Anglo-Latin Satirical Poets of the Twelfth Century* [London, 1872], 2:426); and an anonymous poet who commends to his patron "quae sudore meo de fonte bibi pegaseo" (what I have drunk by my sweat from the fount of Pegasus; *Neues Archiv der Gesellschaft für ältere deutsche Geschichtskunde,* 2.392.12) (Curtius, *European Literature and the Latin Middle Ages,* 468 n. 1). A more recent expression of the topos, in which sweat stands for intellectual effort, was noticed by Roland Barthes in his essay "Les Romains au Cinema," in *Mythologies,* 26–29.

34. Aegidius Romanus, quoted in Allen, *Ethical Poetic of the Later Middle Ages,* 91–92.

35. Allen, *Ethical Poetic of the Later Middle Ages,* 93.

36. Allen's suggestion that the identification of *forma tractandi* and *forma tractatus* in *Canticles* is rare or unusual is not entirely accurate. Indeed, some works that do not enact the ethical appeal Allen finds characteristic of *Canticles* and *Piers Plowman* nevertheless make the two kinds of formal cause equivalent. In the prologue to his *Modi significandi,* Boethius of Dacia argues that the *forma tractatus* is caused by the *forma tractandi:* "Est autem notandum quod forma tractatus causatur a forma tractandi; quia forma tractatus est forma rei operatae, forma tractandi est modus rei operandae sive modus agendi: Sed forma tractandi sive modus agendi causat et formalem dispositionem inducit in re operatae, sicut patet in malleatione" (Moreover, it is to be noted that the *forma tractatus* is caused by the *forma tractandi;* because the *forma tractatus* is the form of a thing that has been done, a *forma tractandi* is the mode in which a thing must be done or the mode of doing: but the *forma tractandi* or the mode of doing causes and induces a formal *dispositio* in the matter that has been handled, as is evident in hammering) (Boethius of Dacia, *Modi significandi, sive quaestiones super Priscianum maiorem,* ed. Jan Pinborg and Henry Roos, 86).

37. In a discussion of passus 9–12, Wittig shows, in some detail, how the poem's progress toward affective theology provides the structure of at least one of its parts: "Wit, the sincere spokesman for the soul's cognitive abilities, characterizes the three 'do's' and Sir Inwitte . . . as involving *affectus*—more than is within Wit's unaided power. He declares all this to Will, the reluctant *affectus,* who bears the responsibility of supplying precisely what Wit cannot. . . . it suggests why the dreamer's progress seems so spasmodic as long as his quest remains a merely intellectual one: information, which he is constantly receiving, can never replace reformation, which he would desperately like to avoid" (Wittig, "'Piers Plowman' B. Passus IX–XII," 226–27). James Simpson argues that the role of Will "shapes the most profound parts of the poem . . . in which Will, as the human will, having passed through the intellective faculties of his soul, seeks a more direct and experiential knowledge of God" ("From Reason to Affective Knowledge: Modes of Thought and Poetic Form in *Piers Plowman*," 7).

38. Joseph S. Wittig, "The Dramatic and Rhetorical Development of Long Will's Pilgrimage," 53.

39. Anne Middleton shows that the earliest owners of the poem were almost entirely clerical, and much early marginalia suggests that it was read for its doctrinal and edifying content. See "The Audience and Public of *Piers Plowman*."

40. Cf. Conrad of Hirsau, *Dialogus super auctores,* cited in Minnis and Scott, eds., *Medieval Literary Theory,* 43.

41. Trans. in Minnis and Scott, eds., *Medieval Literary Theory,* 19. The etymology also appears in Remigius of Auxerre, *In artem primam Donati,* ed. W. Fox, 2; Bernard of Utrecht, *Commentum in Theodulum,* 61; and Conrad of Hirsau, *Dialogus Super Auctores,* 43. Illumination figures prominently in discussions of beginning in rhetorical treatises, as in Geoffrey of Vinsauf: "The first peak of the work is not only luminous with light from the very end, but its glory is twofold: coming either from the end of the theme . . . or from the middle of it. Art draws from either an elegant beginning" (trans. James J. Murphy, in *Three Medieval Rhetorical Arts,* 37). This idea may lie behind part of the opening of *Piers Plowman:* the dreamer looks "into the eest an heigh to the sonne" (B Prol. 13). Unlike the illumination of rhetorical treatises, however, this illumination does not shed light on the poem's structure of beginning.

42. "Notandum quoque quare psalmus primus titulo careat, cum caeteri titulus habere videantur; ideo scilicet quia titulus omnium aliorum psalmorum esse consideratur" (It is also to be noted why the first psalm lacks a title, while he rest seems to have titles: plainly this is because [the first psalm] is considered to be the title of all the other psalms) (Bruno the Carthusian, *Expositio in Psalmos,* col. 639).

43. Peter Lombard, *Commentarium in Psalmos,* col. 60. See Cassiodorus, *Expositio psalmorum,* 97.27–28; Jerome, *Tractatus in librum psalmorum,* 1, 77.3–4.

44. "Materia autem hujus psalmi eadem est, quae et totius libri scilicet Christus integer" (the material of this psalm is the same as that of the whole book; that is, Christ, throughout) (Lombard, *Commentarium in Psalmos,* col. 59).

45. B 16.194, B 2.30, B 9.28, B 16.187.

46. See especially Statius's *Thebiad,* where Amphiaraus's prayer to Jupiter refers to him as *conditor* (founder) and "sator terraequae deumque," the sower/founder of the earth and gods, who also brings together the "effusum chaos in nova semina" (the diffusion of chaos in new seeds) (Statius, *Thebiad,* ed. J. H. Mozley 1:482–89). Virgil uses virtually the same tag for Jupiter: "hominum sator atque deorum" (sower/founder/progenitor of men and the gods) (*Aeneid,* ed. H. Rushton Fairclough [Cambridge, Mass.: Harvard University Press, 1978], 1:254). None of the studies of the figure of the plowman, as far as I know, has discussed the relation between the plowman and beginning. Important, and representative, studies are Barbara Raw, "Piers and the Image of God in Man"; Stephen

Barney, "The Plowshare of the Tongue: The Progress of a Symbol from the Bible to *Piers Plowman*"; Margaret Goldsmith, *The Figure of Piers Plowman: The Image on the Coin;* Malcolm Godden, "Plowmen and Hermits in Langland's *Piers Plowman*"; and Elizabeth D. Kirk, "Langland's Plowman and the Recreation of Fourteenth-Century Religious Metaphor."

47. "Arator... inchoatio bonum operum" (Rabanus Maurus, *De universo,* col. 504).

48. Derrida, *Of Grammatology,* 288.

49. Isidore cites a lost Roman comedy: "Vertamus vomerem / In cera mucroneque aremus osseo" (We turn the plowshare on the wax and we plow with a point of bone) (Curtius, *European Literature and the Latin Middle Ages,* 313).

50. Isidore of Seville, *Etymologia* 6.14, col. 242. The entry appears verbatim in Rabanus Maurus's influential *De universo;* cf. *PL* 111, col. 124.

51. Chaucer, *The Knight's Tale,* 886–87. Some critics suggest that the *Roman de la Rose* may be the source of the figure: "I won't keep you any longer on this subject; I should return to my story, since I must plow another field" (*The Romance of the Rose,* ed. and trans. Charles Dahlberg, 28215–16).

52. Schmidt glosses the word here as potentially carrying both meanings (The Vision of Piers Plowman).

53. "[T]hema ipsum quod deberet esse totius sermonis fundamentum..." (Thomas Waleys, cited in Thomas Charland, *Artes praedicandi,* 343). Waleys goes on, like many other writers of preaching manuals, to recommend that the *thema* be drawn from Holy Scripture.

54. *Commentarium in Joannem,* col. 829.

55. Ibid., col. 831.

56. For a brief discussion of this association, particularly with the office of preaching, see Barney, "The Plowshare of the Tongue," esp. 263–76.

Origo: Genealogy

1. Arendt, *Human Condition,* 224–25.

2. Thomas Walsingham, *Chronicon Anglie,* 321.

3. "[Q]uod initium eo modo antea nunquam fuit. Hoc ergo ut esset, creatus est homo ante quem nullus fuit" (*City of God,* bk. 12, chap. 20, cited in Hannah Arendt, *The Life of the Mind: Two/Willing,* 108–9).

4. I am deeply indebted here, as elsewhere in this book, to the crucial meditations of Hannah Arendt on freedom and human action and her insistent politicizing of beginnings. She is especially helpful in thinking through the ways in which political projects of all kinds are directed at the constraint of beginning and prevented from the forging of real initiatives themselves by the very perplexities of beginning. I would like to thank Allen Shoaf for suggesting that I think more thoroughly about Arendt's work on beginning. For Arendt, beginning is a thoroughly radical act that cannot, by definition, be constrained in any fashion. It is, as a consequence, the only truly human act, indeed the very expression of action itself. "The purpose of the creation of man was to make possible a *beginning:* 'That there be a beginning man was created, before whom nobody was.'... The very capacity for beginning is rooted in *natality,* and by no means in creativity, not in

a gift but in the fact that human beings, new men, again and again appear in the world by virtue of birth" (*Life of the Mind,* 217). See also *On Revolution,* 206–15. It is perhaps for this reason that the poem's genealogical figurations also represent its frustrations, the infinite deferral of a good beginning, real action, and true making, all of which are displaced by the very fashioning of a poem that can only become a genealogy of disappointed beginnings.

5. See M.-D. Chenu, "Les réponses de s. Thomas et de Kilwardby à la consultation de Jean de Verceil (1271)," 194; Anneliese Maier, *Zwei Grundproblem der scholastischen Naturphilosophie. Das problem der intensiven Grösse, die Impetustheorie,* 283; Thomas Aquinas, *In Aristotelis libros de caelo et mundo,* ed. Raymund M. Spiazzi, lect. 7; see also James A. Weisheipl, "Natural and Compulsory Movement" and "The Celestial Movers in Medieval Physics." Jody Enders's work has shown how thoroughly and alarmingly the inception of rhetoric unfolds at the scene of violence, whether it is in the horrific nature of the *imagines rerum* or the interpenetration of classical forensic rhetoric and techniques of torture. See her fascinating *Medieval Theater of Cruelty: Rhetoric, Memory, Violence.* I have argued that mnemotechnics begins as the scene of violent death in "Plague, Panic Space, and the Medieval Tragic Household," in *Domestic/Tragedy,* ed. Julie Carlson, *South Atlantic Quarterly* (spring 1999). More abstractly, Derrida links violence, inscription, and civilization in the section "Violence and the Letter," in his magisterial *Of Grammatology.* Elaine Scarry's *The Body in Pain* traces the instrumentality of language in torture and its displacement of the corporeal, a discussion I will be referring to later.

6. "[T]he history of Rome is one of its foundations. . . . The fork is the simple spot of its spiral, circling course, advancing by returns to its beginnings" (Serres, *Rome: The Book of Foundations,* 224). Arendt's analysis of foundational acts is perhaps less pessimistic, although she is as insistent as is Serres that the logic of beginning is implacably recursive. For her, however, this very recursiveness produces a kind of horizon of predictability, of law, that is suggested for her by the homologies between "principle" and "beginning" contained in both the Latin *principium* and the Greek *arché.* Her reading of Roman foundations, too, is derived from the more injunctive and hortatory Virgil, in whom she finds the possibility that the "historical significance" of "such legends . . . lies in how the human mind attempted to solve the problem of the beginning, of an unconnected, new event breaking into the continuous sequence of historical time" (*On Revolution,* 206). In *Piers Plowman,* however, the recursiveness of the beginning is a sign of the loss of time, of a fundamentally nostalgic rather than prophetic project, a figure of the belatedness of human action rather than a Virgilian historiography of the *magnus ordo.* Indeed, the perplexities of beginning implicate the inception of any act in what Arendt herself describes as a "measure of complete arbitrariness," a moment in which "it is as though the beginner had abolished the sequence of temporality itself, or as though the actors were thrown out of the temporal order and its continuity" (207).

7. Jürgen Habermas, *The Philosophical Discourse of Modernity: Twelve Lectures,* 250.

8. The best discussion of the way that genealogical projects in the Middle Ages organize these homologies is R. Howard Bloch's stimulating *Etymologies and Genealogies.*

9. Jacques Lacan, "The Subversion of the Subject and the Dialectic of Desire in the Freudian Unconscious," in *Écrits: A Selection,* 310, 311.

10. BL, MS Add. 35157 (U).

11. It is generally accepted that "frendes" here means "relatives": see E. S. Olszewska, "Middle English Fader and Frendes," 205–7.

12. Edward Said, "On Repetition," in *The World, the Text, and the Critic,* 117.

13. Good accounts of Langland's enterprise of poetic self-making here appear in George Kane, *Piers Plowman: The Evidence for Authorship,* 64 and n. 1, and in Middleton, "William Langland's 'Kynde Name.'"

14. MS Harley 992, fol. 14v.

15. Middleton, "Narration and the Invention of Experience," 108. She goes on to argue that a large part of the poem is concerned directly with loss, describing Piers himself as the "absent object of desire" who modulates the poem as "a kind of nostalgia, a lament for the lost order of time" (109).

16. Cf. Lauge Olaf Nielsen, "Thomas Bradwardine's Treatise on 'Incipit' and 'Desinit.'" Bradwardine's is apparently the latest example of a series of syncategorematic discussions of "incipit," derived from Aristotelian physics and beginning with William of Sherwood. See also Kretzmann, "Incipit/Desinit," 101–36; S. Knuuttila and A. I. Lehtinen, "'Plato in infinitum remisse incipit esse albus': New Texts on the Later Medieval Discussion on the Concept of Infinity in Sophismata Literature," 309–29.

17. Conscience's attack on Meed uses the same imagery. Meed, he suggests, lacks the understanding to turn to a new page: "thow art lik a lady that radde a lesson ones, / Was *omnia probate,* and that plesed hire herte— / For that lyne was no lenger at the leeves ende / . . . / Ac yow failed a konnynge clerk that kouthe the leef han torned" (B 3.338–41, 347).

18. Middleton, "Acts of Vagrancy," 275; first emphasis mine.

19. "Truth is best. . . . virtually all of *Piers Plowman* is an inquiry into its ramifications" (John Alford, "The Design of the Poem," 35). The fullest and best discussion of the poem's subjects of truth and epistemology is Mary Carruthers, *Search for St. Truth.*

20. Minnis, *Medieval Theory of Authorship.*

21. Rabanus Maurus, *De universo,* cols. 185–86.

22. It is perhaps typical of the influence of the principle of paternity that Langland should, ironically, appropriate this line from a hymn devoted to the Son—*Jesu salvator saeculi* (Skeat, *Vision of William concerning Piers the Plowman,* 2:244 n. 133).

23. *Athanasian Creed,* in *Breviarium ad usum insignis Ecclesiae Sarum.* Important discussions of the uncreated creator can be found in Augustine, *De Trinitate,* 4 and 5 c.6; Rufinus, *Commentarium in Symbolum Apostolorum,* col. 341; and Peter Lombard, *Sententiae,* Dist. 28, in which he distinguishes among the persons of the Trinity according to their relation to beginning: "Pater ergo principium est sine principio, Filius principium de principio, Spiritus sanctus principium de utroque" (therefore the Father is the beginning without beginning, the Son the beginning from the beginning, the Holy Spirit the beginning from both) (col. 90).

24. Or, as the C Text revision says, attributing to God an even greater generative role, "of al þat forth groweth" (C 10.151).

25. MS R.3.8 Trinity College, Cambridge; *Cursor mundi,* ed. Richard Morris, 1:25.

26. Peter Lombard, *Sententiae,* dist. 29, col. 90; emphasis mine.

27. These betrayals, moreover, are portrayed as individual moral failings, not a threat to the order as a whole: "ho-so passeth þat poynt is appostata of knyghthed" (C 1.98). It is dangerous, however, to read too much into the order of the argument at this point, since the C MSS X, U, I, and P offer conflicting lineations between lines 97–101.

28. Cf. B 19.111–14; [Richard of Saint-Victor], *Allegoriae in Evangelia,* cols. 751–54; Rupert of Deutz, *Commentaria in Evangelium Sancti Iohannis,* ed. H. Haake; and Bonaventure, *Opera omnia,* 6:239ff. Nicholas of Lyra, however, treats the feast at Cana as marking the inception of Christ's earthly career; he relates it to the incorruptible beginning with which the Gospel of John begins, the beginning that recounts the inception of the divine word: "Incorruptibilis verbi opus inchoans. quia ab hoc suum euangelium incepit dicens: In principio erat verbum &c. Solus verbum carnem factum esse. nec lumen a tenebris comprehensum fuisse testatur: quia alia euangelia non loquuntur de proprietatibus verbi... similiter describendo facta christi humanitus gesta incipit ab illo signo quia christus inuitatus ad nuptias deficiente vino aquam conuertit in vinum... & per hoc designatur quod in illis qui inuitatur christum ad nuptias spirituales per aggresum continentum virginale. debet deficere delectatio carnale. quod per vinum designatur vt aqua conuertatur nouo modo in vinum per christum mutando carnalem delectationem in spiritualem. & hoc modo incipiendo descriptionem operum christi ostendit suam virginitatem" (Nicholas of Lyra, *Postilla super Johannem,* in *Glossa Ordinaria* [Basle, 1489] D2v, col. b).

29. A. V. C. Schmidt, ed., *The Vision of Piers Plowman: A Complete Edition of the B-Text,* 204 n. 194.

30. Cf. *Middle English Dictionary,* ed. Hans Kurath and Sherman M. Kuhn, s.v. "but"; Skeat's glossary 2, s.v. "but."

31. B 2.30, B 9.28, B 16.187.

32. Cf. Bodl. Rawl. D 328, fol. 144v.

33. It is arguable that the passage also chronicles an incipient maternity, but Holy Church is presented in the poem more as a daughter than as a mother.

34. *The Chester Mystery Cycle,* ed. R. M. Lumiansky and David Mills, EETS, 1. The idea of God the Father as a being without beginning occurs elsewhere in the Chester Cycle: 2.1–2, 6.329–30. It also occurs in the York Cycle 1.1–2; in the Coventry Cycle, 1.4; and in the Wakefield Cycle, 1.7–8.

35. Julia Kristeva, "Credo in unum deum," 42.

36. As Thomas Aquinas argues, "[C]reation is not a change, but that dependence of created being on its source from which it is set forth" (*Summa contra Gentiles* 2, c. 18; *Compendium of Theology,* ed. Cyril Vollert, 1:99). He argues elsewhere that "God... does not act through a mediating action that is understood as proceeding from God and terminating in the creature. But His action is His substance, and whatever is in it is altogether outside the genus of created being by which the creature is really referred to God" (*De potentia,* q. 7, a. 10, in *Quaestiones disputatae S. Thomae Aquinatis,* vol. 2, ed. P. Bazzi [my translation]); see also *Summa theologica* 1, q. 13, a. 7, in Mark G. Henninger, S.J., *Relations: Medieval Theories, 1250–1325;* God is *"esse per essentiam,* not *esse participium"* (*Summa theol.* I, q. 104, a. 1, quoted in Henninger, *Relations,* 38).

37. The clearest articulation of his classification comes in his discussion of Vico's anticipation of his ideas in the *New Science:* "a. The... distinction between the gentile or

historical and the sacred or original—paralleling my distinction between beginning and an origin. . . . c. An acute awareness not only of genealogical succession . . . but also of parallelism, adjacency, and complementarity—that is, all those relationships that emphasize the lateral and the dispersed rather than the linear and sequential. . . . d. A central interplay between beginning and repetition, or between beginning and beginning-again" (Said, *Beginnings*, 357).

38. See Said, *Beginnings*, 6–13, for a general discussion of the problem of locating the beginning of an individual work in relation to other works.

39. Ibid., 50, 357.

40. The incarnation might be yet a further example of this kind of beginning; Langland synthesizes aspects of several beginnings to present the incarnation as an undoing of beginnings.

41. The partitions of this scheme have been much debated, and programmatic divisions cannot always be applied consistently throughout the poem. For attempts to do this, see Henry W. Wells, "The Construction of *Piers Plowman*," 123–49; Nevill Coghill, "The Pardon of Piers Plowman Considered from the B Text"; Henry W. Wells, "The Philosophy of Piers Plowman"; and R. W. Chambers, *Man's Unconquerable Mind*, 88–171. Robert Worth Frank has argued that the three lives are inseparable, indicating relative degrees of progress rather than stages of attainment: *Piers Plowman and the Scheme of Salvation*, 12, 34–44.

42. C 5.102–3.

43. See James H. Charlesworth, *The Old Testament Pseudepigrapha*, vol. 2, and O. F. Emerson, "Legends of Cain, Especially in Old and Middle English." Most commentators locate the conception of Cain in what Emerson calls a "period of transgression." See, for instance, Jerome, *Adversus Jovinianum*, 1.16, and Peter Comestor, *Historia Scholastica, Liber Genesis*, cap. 25: "Adam cognovit uxorem suam . . . sed non in paradiso, sed jam reus et ejectus" (Adam knew his wife . . . not in paradise, but when already guilty and ejected).

44. "[E]x cujus origine damnata, veluti massa une meritae damnatione tradita, fecit Deus alia in contumeliam vasa irae, alia in honorem vasa misericordiae" (From Adam's cursed beginning, as out of one mass given over to damnation, God made some in dishonor vessels of wrath and others in honor vessels of mercy) (Augustine, *Sancti Avrelii Augustini episcopi De civitate Dei libri XXII*, ed. Emanuel Hoffmann, 15:21).

45. *Cursor mundi*, ed. Richard Morris, 1, lines 1056–57 (MS R.3.8 Trinity College, Cambridge).

46. Commentaries on this verse, in fact, tend not to explicate it, assuming that the meaning is clear. Bruno Astensis, for example, merely points out that the result of evil conception is obvious: "Quem enim alium fructum diabolus concipere, vel parere potuit, nisi injustitiam, dolorem, et iniquitatem?" (For what other fruit could the devil conceive, or bring forth, unless injustice, sorrow, and iniquity?) ("Expositio in Psalmos," col. 719). I have not followed the K.-D. emendation here to "dolore[m]" because I believe the ablative form represents an attempt to reconcile the verse with the account of the conception of Cain "in cursed tyme." Both U and X of C have this reading; see Pearsall, 189 n. 211a.

47. Cain, they point out, means etymologically "possession," and Cain is the symbol of the earthly "exterior man." See Augustine, *De civitate Dei*, 15.17; Guibert of Nogent,

Moralium in Genesin, col. 79; John Wyclif, "De Officio Pastoralis," in *The English Works of Wyclif,* ed. Frederic David Matthew, 374. *Piers Plowman* seems to draw on this tradition, comparing the miscegenation between Cain's and Seth's offspring to those who "for coueetise of catel unkyndely be maried" (A 10.183).

48. Discussing *Ywain and Gawain,* line 559 (Ruth Mellinkoff, "Cain's Monstrous Progeny: Part II, Post-Diluvian Survival," 193). This belief was not limited to England: she observes, also, that the "favourite choice for the progenitor of the Saracens in the *chansons de geste* was Cain" (192).

49. Genesis 6:4.

50. Mellinkoff, "Cain's Monstrous Progeny," 192.

51. "Cain, quod interpretatur possessio, terrenae conditor civitatis . . . indicat istam civitatem et initium et finem habere terrenum" (Cain, which means "possession," the founder of the earthly city, indicates that that city has an earthly beginning and end) (Augustine, *De civitate Dei* 15:17).

52. "Thus grounded Caym thes four ordours, / That fillen the world ful of errours" (in Thomas Wright, ed., *Political Poems and Songs,* 1:225).

53. "[I]niquus Chaym, primogentius prothoplasti, quando poterat in alium vel in alios exercere, incepit istem proprietatem rerum introducere ac eam sumere sibi contra legem naturalem qua omnia debent ese communia" (Evil Cain, eldest son of the first man, when he was able to work his will on something else, or on other things, began to introduce the system of property and to claim it for himself against natural law, whereby all things ought to be in common) (Richard Fitzralph, *De pauperie salvatoris* 7, cap. 21, in John Wyclif, *Tractatus de civili dominio,* ed. R. L. Poole and J. Loserth, 3:177).

54. "The place of man and the place of God in the human generation that so dominates Genesis are easy to separate from one another: the place of man is in the body; the place of God is in the voice. . . . God's presence within the story of human generation is exclusively verbal. . . . The verbal enters the human phenomenon of generation by being placed before it and so coming to be perceived as its cause or agent" (Elaine Scarry, *The Body in Pain: The Making and Unmaking of the World,* 192–93).

CONDITORA: THE ARCHIVE OF GRAMMAR

1. Thomas Walsingham, *Gesta Abbatim Monasterii Sanctii Albani,* ed. Henry Thomas Riley, 3:308.

2. Middleton, "Audience and Public of *Piers Plowman,*" 109–10.

3. H and H2 add a line that makes this passage a virtual précis of the estates satire in the prologue: "And for flateryng freres alle foure orderys" (H2; cf. Kane, *A-Text,* 45, 47).

4. Edward Said, *Beginnings,* 34; emphasis in original. In Said's terms, the charter is a deliberate repudiation of a "dynastic ideology," offering "instead of a story a construction" (66). The charter's rebeginning is, despite or because of its purely materialist, cupidinous interests, analogous to the modern topos of beginning, declaring its own inception: "Beginnings inaugurate a deliberately *other* production of meaning—a gentile (as opposed to a sacred) one" (13).

5. See Tauno F. Mustanoja, *A Middle English Syntax. Part I: Parts of Speech,* 542.

6. E. Talbot Donaldson, "The Grammar of Book's Speech in *Piers Plowman,*" 267. Donaldson argues that after 2.95 the charter loses its prescriptive function and becomes "a prediction of future behavior of the grantees" (267).

7. I have used Schmidt's edition here, because I see little warrant for K.-D.'s emendations of these lines.

8. See *Fleta,* vol. 3, ed. and trans. H. G. Richardson and G. O. Sayles, 3.14. *The Charter of the Abbey of the Holy Ghost* introduces a charter in much the same way, also prefacing it with the word "begin": "Here begynniþ þe forseyd chartre. *Sciant presentes & futuri &c.*" (in Carl Horstmann, ed., *Yorkshire Writers: Richard Rolle of Hampole... and His Followers,* 1:338). See also John A. Alford, *"Piers Plowman": A Glossary of Legal Diction,* 140.

9. *Fasciculi Zizaniorum Magistri Johannis Wyclif cum Tritico,* ed. W. W. Shirley, 4.

10. See Robert Adams, "Some Versions of Apocalypse: Learned and Popular Eschatology in *Piers Plowman,*" 194–236. On the conjunction in medieval poetry, see Penn R. Szittya, *The Antifraternal Tradition in Medieval Literature,* 212–21.

11. "[C]arte humanitatis adinvente de hereditate civili perpetua sunt inpossibiles. Non enim durabit civile dominium nisi usque ad destruccionem Antichristi, vel ultimate usque ad diem iudicii" (human contrived charters concerning perpetual inheritance at civil law are impossible. For civil dominion will endure only as far as the destruction of the Antichrist, or ultimately until the Day of Judgment) (*De civili dominio,* in *The Latin Writings of Wycliffe,* ed. Reginald Lane Poole) 1.36. 83a, pp. 252–53.

12. Szittya, *Antifraternal Tradition,* 1986), 209; for citations see 209 n. 77 and 141 n. 68.

13. John Wyclif, *De civili dominio,* in *The English Works of Wyclif,* ed. Frederic David Matthew, EETS, 74.

14. See Scase, *"Piers Plowman" and the New Anticlericalism,* 88–96.

15. Wyclif and Lollard writers have the angel: see Wyclif, *English Works,* 122, 379–80, and Reginald Pecock's *The Repressor of Over Much Blaming of the Clergy,* ed. Churchill Babington, 323 (cf. Skeat, *Parallel Text,* 2:232). Some orthodox writers—including, perhaps, Langland, also use the angel: see John Gower, *Vox Clamantis,* bk. 3, chap. 5, lines 283–88. For orthodox writers who attribute the voice to a devil, see Uthred de Boldon, *De perfectione vivendi,* Cambridge, Corpus Christi College MS 103, fol. 322; and Ranulph Higden, *Polychronicon,* ed. Joseph Rawson Lumby, trans. John Trevisa, 5:130–31. See Scase, *"Piers Plowman" and the New Anticlericalism,* 90.

16. Uthred de Boldon, *De perfectione vivendi,* fol. 322.

17. See *De Donatione ecclesie sponse Christi,* MS Bodley 859, fols. 277r–288v, edition in C. H. Thompson, "Uthred of Boldon (A Study in Fourteenth-Century Political Theory)" (Ph.D. thesis, University of Manchester, 1936), 2 vols.

18. See Michel Foucault, "Nietzsche, Genealogy, History," in *Language, Counter-Memory, Practice: Selected Essays and Interviews;* Edward Said's distinction between "sacred" and "gentile" history makes a similar point (*Beginnings,* 349–50).

19. Guild of St. Mary, Norwich, in *English Gilds*, ed. Toulmin Smith, 14.

20. *English Works*, 390.

21. The tract's argument that it is not lawful to give away entailed property and that clergy's alms are not entailed culminates in an ironic account of the genealogy of entailing clergy, which replaces the legitimate genealogy of entailed property. See ibid., 391.

22. See "Of the Leaven of the Pharisees," ibid., 9.

23. "Twelve Conclusions of the Lollards," in *Selections from English Wycliffite Writings*, ed. Anne Hudson, 24; Latin text in *Fasciculi Zizaniorum*, 360.

24. Lineage is the true title to property, or, as R. Howard Bloch puts it, "A propre [belongs] to a lineage rather than to the individuals through whom it descends. And not only is the *propre* the equivalent of *heritage*, but it is synonymous with ancestry (nobility) itself. Property and genealogy are superimposed upon each other" (Bloch, *Etymologies and Genealogies*, 74).

25. Foucault, "Nietzsche, Genealogy, History," 82.

26. Middleton, "Audience and Public of *Piers Plowman*," 109.

27. James Simpson, *Piers Plowman: An Introduction to the B-Text*, 44.

28. "Women that hold of the King in Chief any Inheritance, of whatsoever Age they be, shall not . . . marry themselves without the King's Licence" (*The Statutes of the Realm*, 1.226). For disparagement, see Henry de Bracton, *De legibus et consuetudinis angliae*, ed. G. E. Woodbine, trans. S. E. Thorne, 2:257. Anna Baldwin discusses the marriage in *The Theme of Government in Piers Plowman*, 32–33.

29. "Mede is moilere, Amendes was here dame. . . . Amendes was here moder. . . . withouten here moder Amendes Mede may not be wedded" (C 2.120–23). The A Text is both less gender-specific and less insistent here. It has only "mede is molere of [m]endis engendrit" (A 2.83). The high incidence of scribal emendation in this line suggests that early readers did not see an important structural opposition emerging: many readings actually reconcile the two genealogies. See Kane, *A-Text*, 23.

30. Higden, *Polychronicon*, 2.269.

31. Cf. Henry de Bracton, *De legibus*, 1:18, 31, and William Blackstone, *Commentaries on the Laws of England*, ed. W. Hardcastle Browne, 1:447.

32. "Nostre Seigneur le Roy . . . voet . . . & fait muliere . . . le dit John" (*Rotuli Parliamentorum*, 3.342a).

33. Cf. Rabanus Maurus, in Thomas Aquinas, *Catena Aurea in Quatuor Evangelia*, ed. A. Guarenti, 7:16–18: "Homo autem ipse arbor bona vel mala dicitur, propter voluntatem bonam vel malam. Fructus autem sunt opera, quae nec bona malae voluntatis esse possunt, nec mala bonae voluntatis" (Man himself is called a good tree or a bad tree on account of a good or an evil will. The fruits are works, which cannot be good if of an evil will, nor evil, if of a good will); Bede, *In Evangelium S. Matthaei*, col. 38: "Per arborem intelligimus seu bonam seu malam voluntatem. Fructus autem opera, quae nec bonae voluntatis, mala nec malae esse possunt voluntatis bona, quae fit etiam bona, dum convertitur ad summum et incommutabile bonum, et impletur bono, ut faciat fructum bonum" (By the tree we understand a good or an evil will. The fruits or works cannot be evil if of a good will, nor good if of an evil will. The will becomes good when it turns itself to the highest and unchanging good, and is filled with goodness, so that it produces good fruit).

34. Cf. Pearsall, *C-Text,* 55 n. 27a.

35. Isaac of Stella, *Sermones,* col. 1751.

36. Cf. Carruthers, *Search for St. Truth;* and Alford, "Design of the Poem," 46. As a figure representing natural knowledge, Wit should be expected to champion genealogy.

37. Cf. Skeat, *Parallel Text,* vol. 2, glossary, s.v. "Bi-gon."

38. Lewis and Short, *Dictionary of Latin,* s.v. "emendo" and "mendum."

39. Cf. Simpson, "Spirituality and Economics," 83–103, and Frank, *Piers Plowman and the Scheme of Salvation,* 108 ff.

40. Richard Fitzralph, *Defensio Curatorum.*

41. "Genealogy does not pretend to go back in time to restore an unbroken continuity that operates beyond the dispersal of forgotten things. . . . On the contrary, to follow the complex course of descent is to maintain passing events in their proper dispersion" (Foucault, "Nietzsche, Genealogy, History," 81).

42. Holy Church's complaint in the A Text about Meed's growth, "Out of wrong heo wex" (A 2.21), may have something in common with antifraternal fears that the mendicant orders had grown to disproportionate dimensions; see Szittya, *Antifraternal Tradition,* 143–44, 224–25, 229–30.

43. See Alford, "Design of the Poem," 32–36; George Kane, *The Liberating Truth: The Concept of Integrity in Chaucer's Writings,* and James Simpson, "Spiritual and Earthly Nobility in *Piers Plowman.*"

44. For a magisterial treatment of the concept, see Richard Firth Green, *A Crisis of Truth.*

45. Robert Adams argues that the C Text division between meed and mercede consistently identifies meed with illegitimate reward and mercede with legitimate reward. His argument is both simpler and more persuasive than earlier attempts to grapple with the problem. See Robert Adams, "Meed and Mercede: The Evolution of the Economics of Grace in the *Piers Plowman* B and C Versions"; Samuel Overstreet, "*Grammaticus Ludens:* Theological Aspects of Langland's Grammatical Analogy"; John Alford, "The Grammatical Metaphor: A Survey of Its Use in the Middle Ages," 759–60; M. Amassian and J. Sadowsky, "Mede and Mercede: A Study of the Grammatical Metaphor in *Piers Plowman* C. IV. 335–409."

46. Adams, "Meed and Mercede," 220.

47. Louis Althusser, "Is It Simple to Be a Marxist in Philosophy?" in *Philosophy and the Spontaneous Philosophy of the Scientists,* 225.

48. Ibid., 227.

49. Louis Althusser and Étienne Balibar, *Reading Capital,* 67. In his discussion of the role of temporality in the construction of the anthropological Other, Johannes Fabian has urged a theory that will supplant a static epistemology, the formulation of a "*processual and materialist* theory apt to counteract the hegemony of taxonomic and representational approaches which [are] the principal sources of anthropology's allochronic orientation" (*Time and the Other: How Anthropology Makes Its Object,* 156).

50. Althusser and Balibar, *Reading Capital,* 35, 37, 69.

51. I am convinced by Mitchell's and Adams's identification of meed with indirect, mercede with direct, relations; other identifications have proved to be inconsistent and of-

ten incomprehensible. See A. G. Mitchell, "Lady Meed and the Art of *Piers Plowman*," 184–87, and Adams, "Meed and Mercede," 222–25.

52. Cf. Skeat's remark that the analogy is "barely intelligible and very dull reading" (*Piers Plowman: Part IV, Section I—Notes to Texts A, B, and C*, EETS, 67 [London, 1885], 70), and Samuel Moore's, that it is "quite unintelligible" ("Studies in *Piers the Plowman*," 192). Alford's survey of the use of grammatical analogies in the Middle Ages is a useful meditation on the associations the analogy in *Piers Plowman* elicits (Alford, "Grammatical Metaphor").

53. A useful discussion of the scholastic debate over the ontological status of relations, which was largely informed by the larger debate between the nominalists and the realists, is in Henninger, *Relations*. Important studies of the doctrine of relation in scholastic theology are J. P. Beckmann, *Die Relationen der Identität und Gleichheit nach J. Duns Scotus;* P. Duncoeur, "Le nominalisme de Guillaume Occam: La théorie de la relation," 5–25; and A. Krempel, *La Doctrine de la relation chez saint Thomas.*

54. Cf. R. W. Hunt, "Studies on Priscian in the Eleventh and Twelfth Centuries"; Hastings Rushdall, *Universities of Europe in the Middle Ages*, 1:443, 2:155; and Louis J. Paetow, *The Arts Course at Medieval Universities*, 61. Anne Middleton discusses the relevance of book 17 to the "two infinites" of B 13.127: "Two Infinites: Grammatical Metaphor in *Piers Plowman*."

55. Amassian and Sadowsky, "Mede and Mercede," 459; emphasis mine. I have found variants of the phrase in the following grammatical treatises: Sponcius Provincialis, *Summa de constructione*, BL, MS Arundel 514, fol. 65r, also BN, MS 15462 and Laon MS 465 (the last two edited in Charles Fierville, *Une grammaire latine*, 61); Alexander Villedieu, *Doctrinale*, 391; Thomas of Erfurt, *Grammatica speculativa*, ed. G. L. Bursill-Hall, 200–202, no. 39; Lambert of Auxerre, *De suppositionibus et de significationibus*, 8; John of Dacia, *Summa Grammatica*, vol. 1, pt. 2, pp. 470–71; Petrus Hispanus, *In summulas Priscianem minorem* and Peter Tataretus's commentary, 140; Martin of Dacia, *Modi significandi*, ed. Heinrich Roos, 46–47; *Regula confirmata per Priscianum de constructionibus*, BL, MS Harley 1610, fol. 29r; Petrus Helias, *Summa on Priscian Minor*, ed. James E. Tolson, bk. 1, 51; Bern, Burgerbibliothek MS cod. 467, fol. 44r; Antonius Aretini, *Novae regulae de constructionibus*, BL, MS Add. 22762, fol. 51v; Petrus Montagrana, *De relativiis*, BL, MS Add. 17903 fol. 1r; Vincent Ferrer, *Tractatus de suppositionibus*, ed. John A. Trentmann, 8, p. 169. The phrase appears in grammatical contexts in Thomas Aquinas's *Summa theologica*, q. 13 a. 1 ob. 3, and in *I Sententiarum*, in *Opera omnia*, ed. Stanislaus Edouard Fretté (Paris, 1873), vol. 7, d. 22, q. 1, a.1, ob. 3.

56. "Et licet hoc relativum de consideratione grammatici; tamen pertinet ad logicum tractare de ipso in quantum per ipsum variatur suppositio, appellatio" (And although this relative is the consideration of the grammarian, nevertheless it is worthwhile to treat it logically [in order to determine] to what degree supposition and appellation vary) (Ferrer, *Tractatus de suppositionibus*, 8, p. 169).

57. Petrus Hispanus, *Tractatus (Summule logicales)*, ed. L. M. de Rijk, 8.1, p. 185. Petrus's distinction between the logical and grammatical senses of *relatio* is one of the few occasions on which the two contexts are even mentioned.

58. "Just as grammar defines the rules of *recte loquendi,* so law defines the rules of right living. . . . grammar may be defined as the manifestation of law in the sphere of language. . . . 'Relacoun rect' is also 'ryhtful custume.' . . . Like God, the true source of all temporal power, the king is 'lord antecedent' in the political realm" (Alford, "Survey," 758–59); " *'indirect relation'* comments as aptly on family relations as on theological ones" (Overstreet, *"Grammaticus Ludens,"* 266).

59. David Aers, "*Piers Plowman:* Poverty, Work, and Community," 67, 69. Aers suggests that other unifying episodes in the poem betray underlying division. *Piers Plowman* excludes any mention of historical fraternities or guilds, and even such commemorations of corporate unity as Grace's apostolic gifts ("crafts") are "a utopian negation of the present world where the poet has to separate his language of 'fraternity' from actually existing 'fraternites'—at the grave cost of social and ethical emptiness" (70).

60. Petrus Helias, *Summa on Priscian Minor,* 1.88.

61. Thomas of Erfurt, *Grammatica speculativa,* 100. See also G. L. Bursill-Hall, *Speculative Grammars of the Middle Ages: The Doctrine of Partes Orationis of the Modistae,* 182–92, for a discussion of *relatio* and *demonstratio* as subaltern modes of signifying.

62. See Middleton, "Two Infinites," 176–77.

63. Richard W. Hunt, "The *Summa* of Petrus Hispanus on Priscianus *Minor.*"

64. Petrus Helias, *Absoluta,* BL, MS Royal 12 F xix, fol. 47vb. A treatise *De relativiis* by Petrus Montagrana subdivides grammatical relation into categories established "relativum accidentis," "relativum substantie identitatis," and "relativum substantie diversitatis" (BL, MS Add. 17903, fol. 1r).

65. Petrus Helias, *Summa on Priscian,* 17.31–32, p. 52.

66. Martin of Dacia, *Modi significandi,* 46.

67. Lewis and Short, *Latin Dictionary,* s.v. "latio," "fero."

68. Thomas of Erfurt, *Grammatica speculativa,* 200–202, no. 39.

69. Cf. William of Ockham, *Quaestiones in Librum quartum sententiarum (reportatio),* ed. Rega Wood and Gedeon Gàl, O.F.M., lib. 4, q. 14; Thomas Aquinas, *IV Sententiarum,* in *Opera Omnia,* ed. Stanislaus Edouard Fretté (Paris, 1879), vol. 7, d. 13.

70. The memory exerts a powerful, almost physical, restraint that allies it with the superego: "Dum enim anima quesitura in se quod in se deposuit, scilicet in memoria quasi claustro corporali, se a discursu cohibet et uagacione indeterminata, magis aliquo modo sibi presens efficitur, et facilius quod queritur inuenitur. Quia igitur intencio animi recordaturi alicuius rei quasi adducit ipsam in cellam talem ut ibidem ipsum reimetur et in eo quod querit inueniat, non in ipso spiritu corporeo qui tali cella continetur, ideo dicitur cella illa habere thesaurum memorie et formarum reposicionem" (When, in order to seek within itself what it has deposited in itself, that is, within memory as if in a bodily cell, the soul restrains itself from running about and from indeterminate wandering, it is by some means made more present to itself and that which is sought is more easily found) (Robert Kilwardby, *De spiritu fantastico,* ed. P. Osmund Lewry, O.P., 199, p. 103).

71. Petrus Thomae, *Quodlibet,* ed. M. Rachel Hooper and Eligius M. Buytaert.

72. "RELATIVUM nomen significat per modum referentis antecedens in secunda notitia est enim rei antecedentis recordatio" (Antonius Aretini, *Regulae de construction-*

ibus, BL, Add. 22762, fol. 51v); "Relatio est modus notificantis rem semper ut absens est, et secundum hoc ponitur sub secunda notitia") (Martin of Dacia, *Modi significandi*, 46). R. W. Hunt argues that the term *secunda notitia* is used in treatises later than Petrus Hispanus's commentary, most noticeably in the *Absoluta*, where it replaces *secunda cognitio* ("*Absoluta:* The *Summa* of Petrus Hispanus on Priscianus *Minor*," 106).

73. William of Ockham, *Quodlibeta septem*, ed. Joseph C. Wey, vol. 9, qq. 4, q. 3, c. 3.

74. Ibid., qq 4, q. 3, c. 2.

75. Petrus Helias, *Summa on Priscian Minor*, 17.83–84.

76. Parkes, "Influence of the Concepts of *Ordinatio* and *Compilatio*," 115. For fuller discussions of the relation between *lectio* and *meditatio*, see Fr. Vandenbroucke, "La lectio divina du 11e au 14e siècle," and Carruthers, *Book of Memory*, 162–65.

77. John Alford, "Some Unidentified Quotations in *Piers Plowman*," 393.

78. Petrus Helias, *Summa on Priscian Minor*, 17.83.

79. Both Alford and Overstreet implicitly equate "relacion rect," particularly as it is developed in the master/servant analogy, with order, propriety, and truth: "Social and linguistic order meet in the grammatical concept of 'relacion rect,' which Langland says, 'ys a recorde of treuthe.' [It] takes on spiritual significance. It becomes a condition of salvation" (Alford, "Grammatical Metaphor," 756–57); "*relacion rect* amplifies the growing theme of a patient *treuthe* which suffers now and is rewarded later" (Overstreet, "Grammaticus Ludens," 280).

80. Cf. Skeat's C Text 4.354, which has no comma.

81. "L. seems to speak indiscriminately of antecedent + relative pronoun and of substantive + adjective" (Pearsall, *C-Text*, 80 nn. 351–54). Amassian and Sadowsky ("Mede and Mercede") first argued this, on the strength of a fifteenth-century ME grammatical treatise (cf. S. B. Meech, "An Early Treatise in English concerning Latin Grammar"). Everyone following them, including Adams, has accepted this view.

82. Meech, "Early Treatise," 85.

83. Petrus de Montagrana, *De relativiis*, BL, MS Add. 17903, fol. 1.

84. The two most influential writers on the Trinity, Augustine and Peter Lombard, have extensive discussions of the nature of relations in their Trinitarian works. See Augustine, *De Trinitate*, ed. W. J. Mountain, 5.13–16; Peter Lombard, *Sententiae*, bk. 1, Dist. 26–32.

85. Thomas Aquinas, *Summa theologica*, 1a.13.7. Most commentaries on distinctions 28–32 of book 1 of the *Sentences* use the same analogies. See, for example, the commentaries of William of Ockham, Duns Scotus, and Gabriel Biel.

86. At least one grammatical commentary uses *habitudo* to define *relatio:* "[R]elatio est habitudo unius ad alterum" (Relation is the condition of one thing [as regards] another). Gerardus Hardewick, *Commentaria in summulas Petri Hispani* (Cologne, 1492), C.8va. Pierre Bourdieu's appropriation of the *habitus* as both a principle of psychic formation, or psychological discipline, and a principle of the external relations of production helps explain the obscuring in *Piers Plowman* of the difference between the individual's internally motivated efforts at belief and the worker's fulfillment of the externally compelled demands of manual labor: "[O]bjectified and internalized capital (properties and habitus) define . . . social class and constitute . . . the principle of the production of classified

and classifying practices"; "[T]he habitus is both the generative principle of objectively classifiable judgements and the system of classification *(principium divisionis)* of these practices" (Pierre Bourdieu, *Distinction: A Social Critique of the Judgement of Taste,* 114, 170).

87. John Wyclif, *De dominio divino,* ed. Reginald Lane Poole, 1.4.

88. Ibid., 20, 8.

89. "Relation realis non est ens per se, nec intervallum inter duo extrema . . . sed in uno et ad aliud" (Relation is not real of itself, and it is not the difference between two extremes . . . ; it exists, however in one [extreme] with reference to another) (John Duns Scotus, *Quaestiones super libros metaphysicorum Aristotelis,* 5, q. 11, n. 6). Cf. also Aquinas, *Summa theologica,* 1, q. 28, a. 1. A survey of the origins of the definition can be found in Henninger, *Relations,* 2–12.

90. Petrus Helias, *Summa on Priscian,* 17.31–32, p. 52.

91. "[I]n relationis essentia non possit" (Petrus Hispanus, *Absoluta,* BL, MS Royal 12 F xix, fol. 47vb).

92. Petrus Helias, *Summa on Priscian Minor,* 1.51. A slightly different account appears in the version of the *Summa* entitled *Absoluta:* "Directa relatio est quod in eodem casu est et quod secundum in eodem diccione trahitur id ad quod referta" (Direct relation is that which is in the same case, and that which accordingly is drawn into the same usage to which it refers) (BL, MS Royal 12 F xix, fol. 47vb). Other writers echo Petrus Hispanus's definition: Petrus Montagrana, *De relativiis:* "Directa illa dicitur que per similes casus fit. . . . Indirecta que per dissimiles casus fieri habet" (BL, MS Add. 17903 fol. 1v); Sponcius Provincialis, *Summa de constructione,* "Directa illa qui fit per similes casus. . . . Indirecta illa qui fit per dissimules" (direct relation is said to be that which occurs through similar cases. . . . Indirect [relation] is that which occurs through dissimilar cases) (BL, MS Arundel 514, fol. 68r).

93. Petrus Helias, *Summa on Priscian Minor,* 1.51.

94. John of Dacia does, however, relate the "nomen relatiuum" to these three categories, which themselves contain a beginning, constituting a kind of provisional, "accidental" foundation: "[N]omen relatiuum est principium constructionis, cuius principia actualia sunt modi significandi accidentales, qui sunt genus, casus, et talia" (The relative noun is the beginning of a construction, whose actual beginnings are the modes of accidental signifying, which are gender, case, and so forth) (*Summa grammatica,* vol. 1, pt. 2, p. 475).

95. An anonymous treatise on logic, however, uses the same verb to describe a relative noun's dual acquisition of meaning from its antecedent and its "suppositum": "[R]elativum relatum ad dictionem confuse significantem contrahit significationem suam partim a significatione sui antecedentis, partim a suppositione" (A relative related to an utterance whose significance is unclear [or mixed] draws its significance partly from the significance of its antecedent, partly from the supposition) (*Tractatus Anagnini,* 325).

96. See Henninger, *Relations.*

97. John Duns Scotus, *Quodlibet,* q. 6, n. 33. Henninger points out the reiterated references to "res" that underscore Scotus's "strongly realist theory of relations" (*Relations,* 69).

98. William of Ockham, *Ordinatio,* d. 30, q. 1 c, quoted in Gordon Leff, *William of Ockham: The Metamorphosis of Scholastic Discourse,* 229 n. 512.

99. Henry of Ghent, *Quodlibet,* 9, q. 3, fol. 349T.

100. See John of Dacia, *Summa grammatica,* vol. 1, pt. 2, p. 475.

101. Richard Fitzralph, *Summa,* 5.159va. Gordon Leff paraphrases this passage: "Relation . . . is not a self-subsisting entity which can be regarded for itself but refers to what Fitzralph calls its foundation" (*Richard Fitzralph, Commentator on the Sentences: A Study in Orthodox Theology,* 120).

Principium: Beginning Perfection

1. Grosseteste, *Hexaemeron,* 6.

2. On the *distinctio,* see Minnis, *Medieval Theory of Authorship,* 63, and Richard H. Rouse and Mary A. Rouse, "Biblical Distinctions in the Thirteenth Century."

3. See Edward Said, *Beginnings,* 174–75. "It is always against a background of the already begun that man is able to reflect on what may serve for him as an origin. For man . . . origin is by no means the beginning" (Foucault, *Order of Things,* 330).

4. This last group is occasionally referred to as the *moderni.* For discussions of the principal doctrines characterizing these two groups, see Gordon Leff, *Bradwardine and the Pelagians: A Study of the "De Causa Dei" and Its Opponent;* Heiko Oberman, *The Harvest of Late Medieval Theology: Gabriel Biel and Late Medieval Nominalism;* and William J. Courtenay, "Nominalism and Late Medieval Religion."

5. Thomas Bradwardine, *De causa Dei,* cited in Denise Baker, "*Piers Plowman* and Fourteenth-Century Theology," 718.

6. Gregory of Rimini, *Lectura super primum et secundum sententiarum,* vol. 6, ed. A. Damasus Trapp, O.S.A., and Venicio Marcolino, bk. 2, dist. 26–28, q.1, p. 32.

7. Ibid., bk. 2, dist. 26–29, q.1, p. 70.

8. Bonaventure, *Breviloquium,* 5.2.3.

9. Hugolinus de Urbe Veteri, *Commentarius in quattuor libros sententiarum,* ed. Willigis Eckermann and Venicio Marcolino, vol. 3, dist. 27, q. 1, art. 1, conc. 4, p. 428.

10. "*Operating grace* is an internal movement of the will or the intellect by God: *in nobis sine nobis.* It is also known as *excitans,* an involuntary movement of the will. *Co-operating grace* is the aid which God bestows upon one already incited by grace that he may do good; it is also called *adjuvans*" (Leff, *Bradwardine and the Pelagians,* 268).

11. Lombard, *Sententiae,* bk. 2, dist. 26, cols. 709–10. Distinctions 26–28 in commentaries on the *Sentences,* indeed, provide a *locus classicus* for discussions of the relation between free will and grace. The passage from Augustine's *De gratia et libero arbitrio* is as follows: "Et quis istam etsi parvam dare coeperat charitatem, nisi ille qui praeparat voluntatem, et cooperando perficit, quod operando incipit? Quoniam ipse ut velimus operatur incipiens, qui volentibus cooperatur perficiens. . . . Ut ergo velimus, sine nobis operatur; cum autem volumus, et sic volumus ut faciamus, nobiscum cooperatur; tamen sine illo vel operante ut velimus, vel cooperante cum volumus, ad bona pietatis opera nihil valemus" (And who would have begun to give even this small love except he who had prepared the will and brought to completion in cooperation what he had begun in operation? Therefore he brings it about at the beginning that we are willing, and finishes off the work in cooperation with us who are [now] willing. That, therefore, we are willing is brought about without us; but when we are [now] willing, and are willing to act, the work is effected in cooperation with us. But without him either bringing it about that we are willing, or cooperating when we are already willing, we are incapable of good deeds of piety) (Augustine, *De gratia et libero arbitrio,* 17.33, col. 901, cited by Denise Baker, "*Piers Plowman* and Fourteenth-Century Theology," 718). The passage, or close paraphrases of it, appears in Bradwardine, *De causa Dei contra Pelagium,* cap. 40, p. 366, cap. 42, p. 375; and in Durandus of Saint Pourçain, who argues, however, against the usefulness of the distinction: *In sententias theologicas Petri Lombardi,* lib. 2, dist. 26, q. 3, 151vb.

12. See, for instance, a twelfth-century commentary on the *Sentences:* "[V]oluntas hominis sola sine dei misericordia non sufficiat ad bonum. Sic enim e converso addici potest: Non est miserentis Dei solius, sola non impleat. Pro eo ergo dictum est, ut totum Deo tribuatur, qui hominis voluntatem bonam, et praeparat adjuvandum, et adjuvat praeparatem" (The volition of man on its own without the mercy of God is not sufficient unto good. This you can adduce from its opposite: without the mercy of God alone, on [its] own it will not be able to attain it. For this reason, therefore, it is said that the whole should be attributed to God, who prepares the good will of man by assisting, and assists by preparing) (Magister Bandini, *Sententiarum,* 2, dist. 26, col. 1054).

13. John Wyclif, *De ente librorum duorum,* ed. Michael Henry Dziewicki, 2, cap. 3; p. 151.

14. Bradwardine, *De causa Dei,* cap. 10, p. 197. The next two chapters contain a technical discussion of the divine inauguration of the will, as the headings indicate: "Quod primum principium necessarium verum incomplexum est Deo; & quod principium complexum primum simpliciter est de Deo: puta Deus est, Deus scit omnia, Deus vult omnia" (That the first, true, necessary, uncomplicated beginning comes from God; and that the first complex beginning simply comes from God: thought comes from God, God knows all things, God wishes all things) (cap. 11); "Ostendit quale sit illud primum principium" ([This chapter] discloses what that first beginning is) (cap. 12).

15. Ibid., cap. 40, p. 366.

16. As Bradwardine argues, uncreated, or divine, will always precedes created, human, will: "[I]n omni actione communi voluntatem increatae, et creatae, increata creatam naturaliter antecedit" (ibid., 2, cap. 29, p. 577).; see Leff, *Bradwardine and the Pelagians,* 94. Leff cites the wrong page for this quotation. For a general discussion of the *moderni,* particularly in relation to the poem, see Janet Coleman, *Piers Plowman and the Moderni.*

17. Alexander of Hales, *Glossa in quatuor libros sententiarum Petri Lombardi,* vol. 2, bk. 2, dist. 26, p. 241.

18. Adams, "Langland's Theology," 98; Pamela Gradon, "*Trajanus Redivivus:* Another Look at Trajan in *Piers Plowman,*" 108.

19. See, for example, Theophilus Reynaudus, *Apologia pro S. Valeriano,* col. 782.

20. Oberman suggests that most fourteenth-century theologians acknowledge grace as a necessary precondition for salvation: "[T]he habit of grace is required as the disposition for man's ultimate acceptation, that is, beatification by God" (*Harvest of Late Medieval Theology,* 168).

21. Robert Holcot, *Super librum sapientiae,* lect. 149; *In librum sapientiae Regis Salomonis praelectiones CCXIII,* lect. 150, p. 502. Later in the same *lectio,* indeed, he defines the inauguration of grace in terms that Nominalists specifically repudiate: "[G]ratia iusticie initium est: quia nisi gratia preveniat hominis voluntatem: saltem natura vel causalitate: homo iustus esse non potest" (Grace is the beginning of justice, because unless grace prevenes the will of man, at least in nature or causality, man cannot be just). Although he does not say so, Holcot is probably talking about the dispensation of grace under God's *potentia ordinata.* Elsewhere in *Super librum sapientiae* he articulates the characteristic semi-Pelagian dictum "Facientibus quod in se est Deus non denigrat gratiam" (lect. 28, 120).

22. William of Ockham, *In sententiarum,* 6, q. 3, art. 3. He seems to treat "caritas" and "gratia" synonymously in the *quaestio:* it begins, "vtrum infusa caritate infundantur virtutes moraliter" (whether, once grace has been infused, the virtues are morally infused) and concludes, "igitur gratia potest infundi sine talibus virtutibus" (therefore grace can be infused without these virtues).

23. Ibid., 4, q. 3, art. 3. Much of this passage does not appear in the Bonaventure edition. Ockham may have taken the passage from Pierre d'Ailly, who uses it in his *Quaestiones* on the *Sentences.* See *Quaestiones magistri Petri de Ailliaco cardinalis camarencis libros sententiarum,* 4, q. 3, art. 2 E. B1.

24. "[A]d eliciendum actum laudabilem concurrit voluntas; igitur nihil aliud a voluntate est sufficiens principium talis actus" (The will concurs in coaxing out a praiseworthy act; therefore, nothing other than the will is a sufficient beginning of such an act) (William of Ockham, *Quodlibeta septem,* vol. 2, q. 16, p. 182).

25. William of Ockham, *Scriptum in primum librum sententiarum,* ed. Gerard I. Etzhorn and Francis E. Kelley, 4, dist. 35, q. 2, p. 432.

26. William of Ockham, *Quaestiones in librum quartum sententiarum,* ed. Gerard I. Elzhorn and Francis E. Kelley, vol. 7, bk. 4, q. 13, p. 269. Anselm defined the importance of the will similarly: "Ex voluntate namque est radix et principium actionum quae sunt in nostra potestate" (For from the will is the root and beginning of actions that are in our power) (*Epistola* 133, col. 167).

27. Thomas Aquinas, *De caritate,* q. 1, a. 1, resp. J; see also William of Ockham, *Scriptum in librum primum sententiarum,* 3, bk. 1, dist. 17, q. 2, p. 468.

28. Thomas Aquinas, *De caritate,* q. 1, a.1, resp. J.

29. William of Ockham, *Scriptum in librum primum sententiarum,* 3, bk. 1, dist. 17, q. 2, p. 473. A similar passage from the commentary, which also identifies the will as an important beginning, is part of the first of four articles by which Ockham was condemned as a Pelagian at Avignon in 1326: "[N]ihil est meritorium, nisi quia voluntarium, et hoc, nisi quia libere elicitum vel factum, quia nihil est meritoriium, nisi quod est in nobis et in nostra potestate. Sed nihil est in nostra potestate, quod possiumus agere et non agere, nisi quia a voluntate tanquam a principio movente et non ab habitu" (Nothing is meritorious, except on the grounds that it is voluntary, and this too, unless it is freely elicited or done, since nothing is meritorious which is not in us and in our power. But nothing is in our power that we can do or not do unless it is so by our will as its first movement and not from a disposition) (A. Pelzer, "Les 51 Articles de Guillaume Occam censures en Avignon en 1326," cited in Leff, *Bradwardine and the Pelagians,* 189 n. 2).

30. See Adams, "Langland's Theology," 95–98, and "Piers's Pardon and Langland's Semi–Pelagianism."

31. Adams, "Piers's Pardon," 393.

32. See Britton J. Harwood, "*Liberum Arbitrium* in the C-Text of *Piers Plowman*." Adams points out that in the C Text Langland's views "remain influenced by semi-Pelagian thought, but he goes to great lengths to bring some of his earlier, more blatant statements into closer accord with the prevailing semi-Augustinian syncretism of the later fourteenth century" ("Piers's Pardon," 380 n. 39).

33. Thomas Aquinas, *De caritate,* q. 1, a.1, resp. J.

34. See William of Ockham, *Scriptum in librum primum sententiarum,* 3, bk. 1, dist. 17, q. 2.

35. Adams, "Langland's Theology," 96.

36. Bede, *In Lucae Evangelium expositio,* lib. 4, col. 522.

37. "Has autem convocat, dum per exhibitionem gratiae hominibus impensae, ad amorem sui vehementius accendit" (Moreover she calls them together, since through the exhibition of grace expended for men, she sets them more vehemently on fire for love of her [beloved]) (Zacharius Episcopus Chrysopolitani, *In unum ex quatuor,* lib. 3, col. 306). Zacharius's paraphrase of the passage makes Bede's sense clearer. Referring to the friends and neighbours as the nine angelic orders, Bede says, "Quae tanto supernae sapientiae juxta sunt, quanto ei per gratiam continuae visionis appropinquant" (In proportion to their proximity to the celestial wisdom they approach him through the grace of a continual vision) (Bede, *In Lucae Evangelium expositio,* lib. 4, col. 521). Zacharius's version also appears in the *Glossa ordinaria* and in Nicolaus Gorranus, *In Evangelio Lucae, Enarratio in Quatuor Evangelia* 2:294, col. a.

38. "Ubi manifeste ostendit quia in homine Christo, Deus est repertus, non nostra inventus peritia, sed ex sua demonstratus gratia" (When it is manifestly revealed that in the human Christ God is discovered, not revealed through our expertise, but revealed through his grace) (Paschasius Radbertus, *Expositio in Matthaeum,* lib. 7, cap. 13, col. 503).

39. Nicolaus Gorranus, *In Evangelio Matthaei, Enarratio in Quatuor Evangelia* 1:164, col. b.

40. *Glossa ordinaria,* vol. 5, fol. g4.

41. Pearsall, *C-Text,* 376 n. 386.

42. In a discussion of tragic models in Freud's work, de Certeau associates beginning with the transformation of the structural order of psychic principles into a series of successive events: "At the beginning, an order of agencies yields in topographical form, the 'moments' which will unfold in diachronic form with successive displacements of the 'hero.' Every play or story is the progressive transformation of a spatial order into a temporal series" (Michel de Certeau, "The Freudian Novel: History and Literature," in *Heterologies: Discourse on the Other,* 22).

43. Foucault, *Order of Things,* 332.

44. In his work on future contingents, in which he argues that God's will is prior in causality but not in time, Thomas Buckingham acknowledges that such an assertion creates "inconveniences" when one speaks of a particular instant in time, but not when one speaks of an instant of causality (see the edition of *De contingentia futurorum et arbitrii* *libertate,* conc. 11 ad. 3, p. 327). Hugolinus de Urbe Veteri argues for essentially synchronic effective causes of salvation—God, grace, and the will (see *Commentarius in quattuor libros sententiarum,* vol. 3, dist. 27, q. 1, p. 425). Ockham's argument that the will is an effective cause and that grace must be conferred, under the *potentia ordinata,* to a good act leaves him only one means of resolving the apparent contradiction: "quod propter istum actum confertur gratia non prius tempore sed simul" (*Sentences,* bk 4, qq. 8 and 9, quoted in Leff, *Bradwardine and the Pelagians,* 205).

45. John Wyclif, *De dominio divino,* ed. Reginald Lane Poole, bk. 3, cap. 4, p. 234.

46. Nicolaus Gorranus, *In Evangelio Matthaei, Enarratio in Quattuor Evangelia* I, 12.44, fol. 164b.

47. See T. P. Dunning, *Piers Plowman: An Interpretation of the A-Text,* 16 ff.

48. Thomas of Chobham, *Summa confessorum,* ed. F. Broomfield, 505; quoted in Le Goff, "The Usurer and Purgatory," in *The Birth of Purgatory,* 33. Le Goff includes examples from Peter Chanter: userers, who profit while they sleep, "vendit tempora dei" (quoted from John W. Baldwin, *Masters, Princes, and Merchants: The Social Views of Peter Chanter and His Circle,* 2:191 n. 13) and from a preaching handbook: "faciunt contra legem universalem, quia vendunt tempus, quod est commune omnium creaturarum" (they work contrary to universal law, because they sell time, which is common to all creatures) (*La Tabula exemplorum secundum ordinem alphabeti. Recueil d'exempla compilé en France à la fin du XII siècle,* ed. Jean T. Welter, 82).

49. For fuller discussion of the *potentia ordinata* as opposed to the *potentia absoluta* of the soteriology of the *moderni,* see Janet Coleman, *Piers Plowman and the Moderni,* 27–33, and Adams, "Langland's Theology," 109.

50. See my summary of the evidence in the chapter "Initium."

51. See Scase, "*Piers Plowman*" *and the New Anticlericalism,* 47–83, and Szittya, *Antifraternal Tradition,* 247–76.

52. Cf. Scase, "*Piers Plowman*" *and the New Anticlericalism,* 27 and n. 59.

53. Gordon Leff, *Heresy in the Later Middle Ages,* 2:549.

54. York, Dean and Chapter Library MS XVI.L.12, fol. 19v; cited in Anne Hudson, *The Premature Reformation: Wycliffite Texts and Lollard History,* 4.

55. John Wyclif, *De civili dominio,* ed. Reginald Lane Poole, bk. I, cap. 3, p. 17.

56. Leff, *Heresy in the Later Middle Ages,* 2:549.

57. Cf. Richard Fitzralph, *De pauperie salvatoris,* bk. 3, cap. 1, p. 382; bk. 4, cap. 2, p. 438. Richard Fitzralph's distinctions are based largely on Nicholas III's important bull *Exiit qui seminat.* Behind this discussion is a conventional distinction between *proprietas, possessio, usus fructus,* and *ius utendi* (6 Decr. tit. xii). Since my discussion concerns the conditions that ratify every kind of ownership, I shall use "possession," "dominion," and "ownership" interchangeably.

58. James Doyne Dawson, "Richard Fitzralph and the Fourteenth-Century Poverty Controversies," 336.

59. "... dominium non sequitur naturam specificam immediate, set mediante iusticia, que sine iustificante gracia non habetur" (dominion does not follow immediately from nature in its particular manifestation, but with the mediation of justice, which is not had without justifying grace) (Fitzralph, *De paupere salvatoris,* bk. 2, cap. 6, p. 344).

60. Ibid., bk. 2, cap. 6, p. 344.

61. Ibid., bk. 2, cap. 8, p. 348.

62. Hugolinus de Urbe Veteri, *Commentarius in quattuor libros sententiarum,* dist. 27, q. 1, art. 1 ad 3, p. 427.

63. William of Ockham, *Scriptum in librum primum sententiarum,* 3, bk. 1, dist. 17, q. 2, p. 473 (see note 29 above).

64. Minnis, *Medieval Theory of Authorship,* 30–33, 63–71. Minnis traces the distinction between extrinsic and intrinsic analysis to Cicero's *Topica;* commentaries on it and the *De inventione* refine the distinction considerably, Victorinus, for example, making it the difference between discursive formation and ethical impulse. As Minnis puts it, "The extrinsic art gives us knowledge alone; the intrinsic art shows us the reasons whereby we put into practice that which knowledge gives us" (30 and n. 134).

65. Michel Foucault, *The Discourse on Language,* in *The Archeology of Knowledge,* 229; I have quoted Said's translation, since it is more accurate than Smith's (*Beginnings,* 311).

66. His madness—his state of being "lik a lorel"—is another attribute that situates him at the site of liminality, as is his recurrent location in the wilderness. As Turner observes, the two traits are frequently likened to liminality. See Victor Turner, *The Ritual Process: Structure and Anti-Structure,* 95–100. Foucault, indeed, links madness to exteriority, the production of new discursive formations. As Said summarizes Foucault's larger project of uncovering the means by which notions of insanity have formed powerful new ways of constructing the self, "Discourse is precisely this exteriority given form, just as madness in Western society has been the exteriorization and confinement in asylums of a hidden silent self" (Said, *Beginnings,* 312). It may be that the significant disruptions and new beginnings in the poem can be linked to the poet's attempt to define the capacities of the (W)ill outside its usual constraints, whether those are prevenient grace or reason itself. The "exteriority" of the will, then, enables the "new discursive formations"—the beginnings—of the poem.

67. Turner, *Ritual Process,* 95.

68. Judson Boyce Allen, "Langland's Reading and Writing: *Detractor* and the Pardon Passus," 355 and n. 27. I have found this incipit in most of the alphabetically arranged *distinctiones* I have looked at: the next most common incipit seems to be *[liberum] arbitrium.* Cf. University of London Sterling Library MS 657, fol. 1; BL, MS Royal 5 C iii, fol. 81v.

69. Middleton, "William Langland's 'Kynde Name,'" 40.

70. Cf. Corpus Christi College, Oxford, MS 201, BL, MS Add. 35287; BL, MS Lansdowne 398 (M, R of B); BL, MS Cotton Vespasian B xvi; BL, MS Harley 2376; and BL, MS Add. 34779 (M, N, P2 of C). That this reading may not be the product of late scribal corruption is suggested by Donaldson's observation that R and F are "in some respect superior to other MSS," and that they represent a "stage in the B-Text slightly older than that represented by the rest of the B-MSS" (E. Talbot Donaldson, "MSS R and F in the B-Tradition of Piers Plowman"). If Middleton's claim that this wordplay extends back to the priest's scornful dismissal of Piers with the words *dixit insipiens* is correct, that would support my argument that the C Text systematically deletes the allusions to new beginnings at the end of C 19.

71. Isaac of Stella, *Sermons,* vol. 2, ed. Anselm Hoste and Gaston Salet, sermon 21, p. 54. The *dixit insipiens* verse often finds its way into Sexagesima sermons, since the Epistle for that Sunday is 2 Corinthians 11:19–33, which begins "Libenter suffertis insipientes . . ." The Sexagesima readings contain a constellation of themes that appear in *Piers Plowman:* the gospel reading is Luke 8:4–15, "Exiit qui seminavit," a parable with obvious importance for the poem. Like sermons with the Epistle as their theme, many of the gospel sermons from Sexagesima Sunday, including Isaac of Stella's, discuss beginnings, taking their cue from the image of the Word as seed. A particularly interesting conjunction of *Piers*'s important themes occurs in Nicholas III's bull *Exiit qui seminavit,* which allows friars use but not dominion of worldly goods. Its opening alludes to the themes of learning and foolishness in 2 Corinthians, observing that the seed of the Gospel is sown in "insipientes et ignaros, studiosos et desides" (*Corpus Iuris Canonici,* ed. Aemilius Ludwig Richter and Emil Friedberg, 5.12.3).

72. M. C. Seymour, ed., *On the Properties of Things: John Trevisa's Translation of Bartholomaeus Anglicus' De Proprietatibus Rerum, A Critical Text,* vol. 1, bk. 1, chap. 5, p. 47. Like Trevisa's translation, the Latin text does not pun explicitly, but it does associate foolishness with an agnosticism of beginning: "[C]ognoscitur in suo effectu, in quantum est omnium principium siue causa, quia Deum esse vix insipiens dubitat" (He is known in his effect, inasmuch as he is the beginning or cause of all things, and therefore [even] the fool scarcely doubts that God exists) (Bartholomaeus Anglicus, *De rerum proprietatibus,* lib. 1, cap. 5, p. 7).

73. Sedulius Scotus, *Collectanea in omnes B. Pauli Epistolas,* col. 28.

74. The *principium,* indeed, marked the end of a bachelor's study of the *Sentences,* which took the form of an introduction, itself called a *principium,* to each of the four books. See Gordon Leff, *Paris and Oxford Universities in the Thirteenth and Fourteenth Centuries: An Institutional and Intellectual History,* 166–67. A fifteenth-century commentary on the *Purgatorio* illustrates the link between reading the *Sentences* and beginning theological study: "Per Beatricem auctor intendit hic Sacram Theologiam, quam incepit studere, in qua profecit multum Parisius, in tantum quod legit Sententias, et factus fuit inceptor" (By Beatrice the author means here Sacred Theology, which he has begun to study, and in which the Parisian has far advanced, insofar as he has read the *Sentences,* and has been made an inceptor) (Giovanni da Serravalle, *Iohannis de Serravalle translatio et comentum totius libri Dantis Aldighieri, Purgatorio* 31.22–30). For discussions of the textual forms of the *principium,* see D. Trapp, "Peter Ceffons of Clairvaux" and "Augustinian Theology"; J. A. Weisheipl, *Friar Thomas d'Aquino: His Life, Thought, and Work,* 71–72, 99–104; Beryl Smalley, "Wyclif's *Principium*"; and William J. Courtenay, *Adam Wodeham: An Introduction To His Life And Writings,* 172–77.

75. For the argument that the first part of this passus, with its multiple, disruptive beginnings, constitutes Langland's *ars poetica principii,* see the chapter "Thema: The Book That Makes Itself."

76. Robert Kilwardby, *De ortu scientiarum,* ed. Albert G. Judy, cap. 52:165.

77. Although both Skeat and Kane have *indicat* at 10.90, Alford argues that the word should be *iudicat,* since the source of the quotation is a common canon law maxim. See John Alford, *Piers Plowman: A Guide to the Quotations,* 61.

78. Nicholas Lyra, *Postilla, Glossa Ordinaria,* vol. 3, fol. z2, col. b. His consequent rejection of the *principium extrinsecus* attributes limited initiative to the individual. His gloss on the *initium sapientie* verse in Job locates the beginning of salvation in the individual, but posits an immediate infusion of grace: "[P]rincipium accedendi ad deum per hoc quod anima ipsi deo totaliter subditur vt instinctum et voluntatem dei totaliter sequatur: et ista subiecto includit gratiam et virtutes infusas" (The beginning of the approach to God happens when the spirit is completely subjected to God himself so that it totally follows the prompting and will of God: and by its subjection it includes grace and infused virtues) (*Postilla,* vol. 3, fol. b4, col. b).

79. John of Salisbury, *Ioannis Saresberiensis Policraticus, sive De nugis curialium & vestigiis philosophorum,* vol. 5, bk. 9.

80. See B 19.108–23. Nicholas Lyra argues that the Gospel of John locates the inception of Christ's career at Cana: "[D]escribendo facta christi humanitus gesta incipit ab illo signo quia christus inuitatus ad nuptias deficiente[m] aquam conuertit in vinum" (In order to describe the deeds of Christ done in his human guise, he begins from that sign where Christ, invited to the wedding, turns water into wine) (Nicholas of Lyra, *Postilla, Glossa Ordinaria,* vol. 5, D2v, col. b).

81. See Wells, "Construction of *Piers Plowman,*" and "Philosophy of Piers Plowman"; Nevill K. Coghill, "The Character of Piers Plowman considered from the B Text," 108–35; and Chambers, *Man's Unconquerable Mind,* 88–171. Recent descendants of these four influential articles are too numerous to list; until very recently, almost every interpretation of Dowel, Dobet, and Dobest was an augmentation of an essentially static tripartite scheme. For a recent, skeptical, evaluation of the evidence that manuscripts offer for a disjunctive division of the three modes, see Adams, "Reliability of the Rubrics."

82. Dunning, *Piers Plowman: An Interpretation of the A-Text,* 173.

83. Frank, *Piers Plowman and the Scheme of Salvation,* 43.

84. Middleton, "Two Infinites," 173.

85. For a summary of the poem's contradictory schemes for the three lives, see Frank, *Piers Plowman and the Scheme of Salvation,* 40–43.

86. Pseudo-Albertus Magnus, *Quaestiones Alberti de modis significandi,* q. 13, arg. 6, p. 82. The same definition appears in Gentile de Cingoli, *Quaestiones supra Priscian Minori,* ed. Romana Martorelli Vico (Pisa: Scuola Normale Superiore, 1985), q. 7, p. 36; Michel de Marbais, *De modis significandi,* 181; and Siger de Courtrai, *Summa modorum significandi,* ed. G. Wallerand, 108.

87. Martin's own classifications of the verb, indeed, converge in a single continuum: "Hic autem motus est generatio vel corruptio vel alteratio accidens in accidens vel augmentum vel diminutio vel secundum locum mutatio. Quilibet istorum motuum habet se per modum fluxus sive per modum successionis sive per continui, *quod idem est*" (This motion is generation or corruption or alteration happening by chance or augmentation or diminution or changing of position. Any one of these motions happens by means of flux *[modum fluxus]* or by means of succession *[modum successionis]* or without interruption *[per continui],* which is the same) (Martin of Dacia, *Categoriae, Martini de Dacia opera,* ed. H. Roos, 14.5–9). I should note here that modistic and speculative grammars exert a more extensive and tenacious influence on subsequent pedagogical and theoreti-

cal grammar than Morton Bloomfield insisted was the case in his 1974 review of Bursill-Hall's work. Bloomfield asserted that speculative grammar "flourished for only about 40 years from 1280 to 1320 and was confined to parts of Central Europe" (*Speculum* 49 [1974], 104). His assertions are wrong for a number of reasons. First, the treatment of grammar as *speculativa* begins by the middle of the thirteenth century with Pseudo-Kilwardby and the immensely influential encyclopedist Vincent of Beauvais (see *The Commentary on "Priscianus Maior" Ascribed to Robert Kilwardby*, ed. K. M. Fredborg, N. J. Green-Pedersen, Lauge Neilsen, and Jan Pinborg; and Vincent of Beauvais, *Speculum Doctrinale*, 1.18). Second, modistic and speculative grammars were being disseminated as late as the early fifteenth century, and as far from Central Europe as England. John Seward, an important figure in a fascinating and forgotten coterie of London grammarians and scholars, wrote a modistic grammar probably based on Boethius of Dacia's *Modi significandi* sometime around 1400, which he dedicated to John Eyton, regent of theology in Oxford in 1387. Seward's circle describe themselves as meeting at Saint Paul's regularly to debate grammatical and metrical matters, and several of them presided over schools of grammar in the area around Cornhill, the one London locale with which Langland associates himself; Seward is described by his colleague William Relyk as teaching in Cornhill itself (see Galbraith, "John Seward and His Circle"; see also Cynthia Renée Bland, *The Teaching of Grammar in Late Medieval England*, 100). The popular, pedagogical address of modistic grammar is suggested by a metrical treatise written in 1322 by Johannes de Marvilla, the *Tractatus metricus de modis significandi*, printed in Rouen in 1500 (in *Expositiones modorum significandi*) and by Thomas of Erfurt's own *Fundamentum puerorum*, 105–6). Third, modistic grammar was still a provocative object for attack by the end of the fourteenth century in Paris, as indicated by Pierre d'Ailly's *Destructiones modorum significandi*, and as represented in Jean Gerson's *De modis significandi* (cited in Jan Pinborg, *Logik und Semantik im Mittelalter: Ein Überblick*, 117). Fourth, Bloomfield's argument that modistic grammar disappeared under the onslaught of nominalism is too categorical an assertion to be at all useful. In fact, such vociferous nominalists as William of Ockham assimilated features of modistic grammar, even using the concept of *modus significandi* (for a useful discussion, see Michael A. Covington, *Syntactic Theory in the High Middle Ages: Modistic Models of Sentence Structure*, 127–31), and Covington discusses an *Expositio Donati* written after 1350 that attempts to integrate "modistic metatheory" into a thoroughly nominalist ontology (128–30). Fifth, the teaching of speculative grammars in western European universities such as Bologna sometimes influenced the writing of even vernacular texts, as the work of Maria Corti and C. G. Alessio has shown in the case of Dante. See Maria Corti, *Percorsi dell'inventione: Il linguaggio poetico e Dante*, 79–81, 99–104; C. G. Alessio, "La grammaticale speculativa e Dante." That someone as learned as Bloomfield could have such a constricted view of the career of speculative grammar reminds us in what covert but persistent forms it continued to influence the conceptualization of grammar through the fourteenth century and how easy it is to foreclose its potential utility as an interpretive possibility for literary texts.

88. Indeed, the other popular definition of the verb describes it in terms of its lack of static, fixed qualities: it is "distant" from substance: "verbum . . . est distans a substantia." Cf. Priscian, *Institutiones grammaticae libri XVIII*, 1.1, Pseudo-Albertus Magnus, q. 7, arg. 1. Unlike the noun, the verb cannot be divided into smaller morphological units: "nulla pars significat seperatim" (no part signifies separately).

89. "Verbum... est quod consignificat tempus" (The verb is what signifies time); see R. H. Robins, *Ancient and Mediaeval Grammatical Theory in Europe*, 23. In virtually identical definitions, the two most influential grammarians of the Middle Ages, Donatus and Priscian, imply that the verb is delimited by its morphological function, which includes time (tense) and person or mood: "verbum est pars orationis cum tempore et persona" (Donatus, *Ars Grammatica*, 2.11); Priscian replaces person with mood (*Institutiones grammaticae libri XVIII*, 1).

90. Boethius, *In librum Aristotelis de interpretatione, Commentaria minora* (quoted in Bursill–Hall, *Speculative Grammars*, 197).

91. Thomas Aquinas, *Commentaria in Aristotelem*, 1:24.

92. Pseudo-Albertus Magnus, *Quaestiones Alberti de Modis*, q. 19, arg. 2, p. 138.

93. Pseudo-Grosseteste, *Tractatus de grammatica: Eine falschlich Robert Grosseteste zugeschriebene spekulative Grammatik*, ed. Karl Reichl, 45. With few exceptions, all grammatical treatises divide verbs into these two classifications, on the authority of Priscian (cf. *Institutiones grammaticae libri XVIII*, 1) and Donatus (cf. *Ars grammatica*, 2.11).

94. Cf. Pseudo-Grosseteste, *Tractatus de grammatica*, 45.

95. Middleton, "Two Infinites," 175.

96. The infinitive appears both with and without terminal *-n* in Middle English of the West Midlands; see Samuel Moore and Albert H. Marckwardt, *Historical Outlines of English Sounds and Inflections*, 125–26; Kenneth Sisam, *Fourteenth-Century Verse and Prose*, 290; and M. L. Samuels, "Dialect and Grammar," 217–18. Samuels points out at least one instance of a terminal *-n* that is metrically necessary (C 21.151). The Worcestershire MS, BL, Add. 35157 has at least one instance of the infinitive "do" without the terminal *-n*: "to louye thy lord leuest of alle, / Dey rather than do eny dedly synne" (C 1.143).

97. Anne Middleton has recently questioned the assumption that passus 12 is by Langland; see "Making a Good End."

98. I would like to thank Hoyt N. Duggan for the information on the infinitive forms of "dowel."

99. Magister Jordanus, *Summa* on *Priscianus Minor*, BL, MS Harley 2515, fol. 14v; for a similar definition from an anonymous twelfth-century grammatical treatise, see C. H. Kneepkens, "*Legere Est Agere:* The First Quaestio of the First Quaestiones-Collection in the MS Oxford, CCC 250," 126–29.

100. For discussions of the *motus* model of syntactic structure, see Covington, *Syntactic Theory in the High Middle Ages*, 48–82; Pseudo-Albertus Magnus, *Quaestiones Alberti de Modis Significandi*, xxiv–xxx; and Bursill-Hall, *Speculative Grammars*, 296–301.

101. Pseudo-Albertus Magnus, q. 18, arg. 7, opp. 1, p. 127.

102. Pseudo-Albertus Magnus, q. 18, p. 134. The *suppositio* is an earlier term for the grammatical subject. For another argument that the infinitive can be the *principium* of a *motus*, see Pseudo–Grosseteste, *Tractatus de grammatica*, 49.

103. Medieval grammatical theory may inform the articulation of Dowel, Dobet, and Dobest in at least one more way. A complete sentence begins with its inaugural elements, the parts of speech that constitute the *principium constructionis*, and terminates when it achieves complete intelligibility in the mind of the reader or listener, a state called *perfectio*. The ethical series of the three lives, then, can be compared to the linguistic passage of a sentence from its beginnings to its perfection.

104. See Thomas of Erfurt, *Grammatica speculativa*, 282–306.

105. Ibid., 282.

106. Ibid., 309.

107. Ibid., 316.

108. See G. L. Bursill-Hall, introduction to Thomas of Erfurt, *Grammatica Speculativa*, ed. G. L. Bursill-Hall (London: Longman, 1972), 109–13.

109. Ibid., 115. Thomas of Erfurt fully acknowledges the metaphorical force of the verb *transire*, if not quite as fully as Langland does: "Et sciendum, quod istae duae differentiae, transitivum et intransitivum, sumuntur in constructionibus metaphorice, id est, per quamdam similitudinem transitus realis. Nam aliquis dicitur realiter transire, quando transit de uno loco ad alium a primo diversum" (It must also be recognized that these two different kinds, transitive and intransitive, are taken metaphorically in their constructions—that is, through some similarity to a real transit. For someone is said to transit in real life, when he transits from one place to another that is different from the first) (ibid., 284).

110. Ben H. Smith, "Patience's Riddle, *Piers Plowman* B,XIII."

111. Skeat, *Piers the Plowman*, 2:196–97; R. E. Kaske, "*Ex vi transicionis* and Its Passage in *Piers Plowman*," 244.

112. The problem of measure is at the heart of the poem's investigation of the nature of salvation: to what extent must one rely on works to be saved? One figure in the poem warns the rich: "[T]he same mesure that ye mete, amys outher ellis, / Ye shulle ben weyen therwith whan ye wenden hennes: 'Eadem mensura qua mensi fueritis remecietur vobis.'" Measure becomes the characteristic mark of living according to sound economic principles, which are themselves a metaphor for the economy of salvation. In the A and B texts, for example, Conscience calls bribery and corruption "meed mesureless," but refers to wages legitimately earned as "mesurable hire." The problem of separating the two meeds, one legitimate and the other illegitimate, is almost as difficult to solve as the problem of discovering the beginnings of Dowel and Dobest, and, in a sense, both problems devolve to the problem of measuring actions. Meed, too, seems to be regulated by the rules of transitivity and intransitivity: in the C Text Conscience argues that the valence of meed depends upon the way in which it is given: "gilours giuen before and gode men at the ende / When the dede is ydo and the day endid." Paying someone before a task is performed would seem to be an intransitive act: it says more about the people involved in the transaction beforehand than it does about the task. Paying someone after a task highlights the importance of the task itself: the pay comes at the *terminus*, not the *principium*, of the action.

Bibliography

Abbreviations

AnnM	*Annuale Mediaevale*
ELH	*English Literary History*
JEGP	*Journal of English and Germanic Philology*
MLN	*Modern Language Notes*
Mae	*Medium Aevum*
MP	*Modern Philology*
MRS	*Mediaeval and Renaissance Studies*
MS	*Mediaeval Studies*
NM	*Neuphilologische Mitteilungen*
N&Q	*Notes and Queries*
PL	*Patrologia Latina*
RES	*Review of English Studies*
RTAM	*Recherches de théologie ancienne et médiévale*
YLS	*Yearbook of Langland Studies*

Editions of Piers Plowman

All citations from the poem, unless otherwise indicated, are from the Athlone editions, which like all editions are fallible, but are commonly assumed to be definitive.

Kane, George, ed. *"Piers Plowman": The A Version. Will's Visions of Piers Plowman and Do-Well.* London: Athlone Press, 1960.

Kane, George, and E. Talbot Donaldson, eds. *"Piers Plowman": The B Version. Will's Visions of Piers Plowman, Do-Well, Do-Better, and Do-Best.* London: Athlone Press, 1975.

Russell, George, and George Kane, eds. *"Piers Plowman": The C Version. Will's Visions of Piers Plowman, Do-Well, Do-Better, and Do-Best.* London: Athlone Press, 1997.

Other Editions Consulted, Cited, and Quoted From

Pearsall, Derek, ed. *Piers Plowman, by William Langland: An Edition of the C-Text*. Berkeley: University of California Press, 1979.

Schmidt, A. V. C., ed. *William Langland, The Vision of Piers Plowman: A Critical Edition of the B-Text*. London: Dent, 1978.

Skeat, W. W., ed. *The Vision of William concerning Piers Plowman: The "Vernon" Text; or Text A*. EETS, 28. London, 1867.

———, ed. *The Vision of William concerning Piers Plowman: In Four Parts—Part II. The "Crowley" Text; or Text B*. EETS, 38. London, 1869.

———, ed. *The Vision of William concerning Piers Plowman: In Four Parts—Part III. The "Whitaker" Text; or Text C*. EETS, 54. London, 1873.

———, ed. *The Vision of William concerning Piers Plowman: In Four Parts—Part IV, Section I—Notes to Texts A, B, and C*. EETS, 67. London, 1877.

———, ed. *The Vision of William concerning Piers Plowman, in Three Parallel Texts*. 2 vols. London: Oxford University Press, 1886.

Well-known medieval names are listed under their surnames unless the first name is considered more useful for identification (e.g., "Chaucer, Geoffrey," but "Isidore of Seville").

MANUSCRIPTS

Piers Plowman

A Text

Douce 323 (D)

Library of the Society of Antiquaries of London, MS 687 (M)

B Text

British Library, Add. 35287 (M)

Corpus Christi College, Oxford, MS 201 (F)

C Text

British Library, Add. 34779 (P2)

British Library, Add. 35157 (U)

British Library, Harley 2376 (N)

Bodley 851 (A and C) (Z of C)

Bodley 814 (B of B and C)

Douce 104 (D)

OTHER MANUSCRIPTS

British Library

Add. 17903. Petrus Montagrana, *De relativiis.*
Add. 22762. Antonius Aretini, *Novae regulae de constructionibus.*
Arundel 275.
Arundel 514. Sponcius Provincialis. *Summa de constructione.* Fols. 64v–68v.
Cotton Vespasian B xvi.
Harley 992. Treatise on Heraldry.
Harley 1610. *Regula confirmata per Priscianum de constructionibus.* Fols. 26–40v.
Harley 2259. Richard Strangeway's Book.
Harley 2515. Jordanus Magister, *Summa* on *Priscianus Minor.*
Lansdowne 398.
Royal 5 C iii. *De informacione predicatorum.* Fols. 52v–82.
Royal 12 F xix. Petrus Hispanus, *Absoluta.* Fols. 45–75v.

Oxford

All Souls College, MS 86. Walter Burley, *Expositio super de generatione et corruptione.*
Bodleian Rawl. D 328. Grammatical miscellany.
Bodley 714. John Ashenden, *Summa judicialis de accidentibus mundi.*

PRINTED SOURCES

Adams, Robert. "Langland's Theology." In *A Companion to Piers Plowman,* ed. John Alford, 87–114. Berkeley: University of California Press, 1988.

———. "Meed and Mercede: The Evolution of the Economics of Grace in the *Piers Plowman* B and C Versions." In *Medieval English Studies Presented to George Kane,* ed. E. D. Kennedy, Ronald Waldron, and Joseph Wittig, 87–114. Cambridge: Brewer, 1988.

———. "The Nature of Need in *Piers Plowman* XX." *Traditio* 34 (1978): 273–301.

———. "Piers's Pardon and Langland's Semi–Pelagianism." *Traditio* 39 (1983): 367–418.

———. "The Reliability of the Rubrics in the B–Text of *Piers Plowman.*" *MAe* 54 (1985): 208–31.

———. "Some Versions of Apocalypse: Learned and Popular Eschataology in *Piers Plowman.*" In *The Popular Literature of Medieval England,* ed. Thomas J. Heffernan, 194–236. Tennessee Studies in Literature, vol. 28. Knoxville: University of Tennessee Press, 1985.

Aers, David. *Community, Gender, and Individual Identity: English Writing, 1360–1430.* London: Routledge, 1988.

Agamben, Giorgio. *Infancy and History: The Destruction of Experience.* Trans. Liz Heron. London: Verso, 1993.

Alain of Lille. *Summa de arte praedicatoria. PL* 210. Paris, 1855. Cols. 109–98.

Alessio, C. G. "La grammaticale speculativa e Dante." *Letture classensi* 13 (1984): 69–88.

Alexander of Hales. *Glossa in quatuor libros sententiarum Petri Lombardi*. Vol. 2. Bibliotheca Franciscana Scholastica Medii Aevi, 13. Quarrachi: St. Bonaventure, 1952.

———. *Summa Theologica*. Quaracchi: College of St. Bonaventure, 1924.

Alford, John A. "The Design of the Poem." In *A Companion to Piers Plowman*, ed. John Alford. Berkeley: University of California Press, 1988.

———. "The Grammatical Metaphor: A Survey of Its Use in the Middle Ages." *Speculum* 57, no. 4 (1982): 728–60.

———. *"Piers Plowman": A Glossary of Legal Diction*. Cambridge: Brewer, 1988.

———. *Piers Plowman: A Guide to the Quotations*. Medieval and Renaissance Texts and Studies, 77. Binghamton: SUNY, 1992.

———. "Some Unidentified Quotations in *Piers Plowman*." *MP* 72–74 (1975): 390–99.

Allen, Judson Boyce. *The Ethical Poetic of the Later Middle Ages: A Decorum of Convenient Distinction*. Philadelphia: University of Pennsylvania Press, 1983.

———. "Langland's Reading and Writing: *Detractor* and the Pardon Passus." *Speculum* 59 (1984): 342–62.

Althusser, Louis. *Philosophy and the Spontaneous Philosophy of the Scientists*. London: Verso, 1990.

Althusser, Louis, and Étienne Balibar. *Reading Capital*. Trans. Ben Brewster. New York: Pantheon, 1971.

Amassian, M., and J. Sadowsky. "Mede and Mercede: A Study of the Grammatical Metaphor in *Piers Plowman* C. IV. 335–409." *NM* 72 (1971): 457–76.

Ambrose. *Hexaemeron*. Ed. Carolus Schenkl. Corpus Scriptorum Ecclesiasticorum Latinorum, 32. Leipzig: Freytag, 1897.

Anselm. *Epistola* 133. *PL* 159. Paris: Migne, 1903. Cols. 167–68.

———. *Meditatio super Miserere*. *PL* 158. Paris, 1853. Cols. 821–54.

Arendt, Hannah. *The Human Condition*. Chicago: University of Chicago Press, 1958.

———. *The Life of the Mind: Two/Willing*. New York: Harcourt Brace, 1978.

———. *On Revolution*. New York: Viking, 1963.

Aristotle. *Politics*. Ed. and trans. H. Rackham. Cambridge, Mass.: Harvard University Press, 1977.

Arn, Mary-Jo. "Langland's Characterization of Will in the B-Text." *Dutch Quarterly Review* 11, no. 4 (1981): 287–301.

Ars dictandi aurelianensis. In *Briefsteller und formelbucher des elften bis vierzehnten jahrhunderts*, ed. Ludwig Rockinger. Munich, 1863. Reprint, New York: Burt Franklin, 1961.

Athanasian Creed. In *Breviarium ad usum insignis ecclesiae Sarum*. Vol. 2. Ed. Francis Procter and Christopher Wordsworth. Cambridge, 1879.

Aubenque, Pierre. *Le problème de l'être chez Aristote*. Paris: Presses universitaires de France, 1962.

Augustine. *De gratia et libero arbitrio*. *PL* 44. Paris, 1865. Cols. 881–912.

———. *Sancti Avrelii Augustini episcopi De civitate Dei libri XXII*. Ed. Emanuel Hoffmann. Vindobonae, 1898. Reprint, New York: Johnson Reprint, 1962.

———. *Tractates on the Gospel of John 1–10*. Trans. John Rettig. Washington, D.C.: Catholic University of America Press, 1988.

———. *De Trinitate*. Ed. W. J. Mountain. Corpus Christianorum, Series Latina, 50–50A. Turnhout: Brepols, 1968.

Baker, Denise. "*Piers Plowman* and Fourteenth-Century Theology." *Speculum* 55, no. 4 (1980): 718.

Baldwin, Anna. *The Theme of Government in Piers Plowman*. Cambridge: Brewer, 1981.

Baldwin, John W. *Masters, Princes, and Merchants: The Social Views of Peter Chanter and His Circle*. Princeton, N.J.: Princeton University Press, 1970.

Bandini, Magister. *Sententiarum*. *PL* 192. Paris, 1880. Cols. 969–1112.

Barney, Stephen. "The Plowshare of the Tongue: The Progress of a Symbol from the Bible to *Piers Plowman*." *MS* 35 (1973): 261–93.

Barthes, Roland. *Mythologies*. Paris: Editions du Seuil, 1957.

Bartholomaeus Anglicus. *De rerum proprietatibus*. Frankfurt, 1601. Reprint, Frankfurt am Main: Minerva, 1964.

Beckmann, J. P. *Die Relationen der Identität und Gleichheit nach J. Duns Scotus*. Bonn: Bouvier, 1967.

Bede. *In Evangelium S. Matthaei*. *PL* 92. Paris, 1850. Cols. 9–132.

———. *In Lucae Evangelium Expositio*. *PL* 92. Paris, 1862. Cols. 301–634.

Bene of Florence. *Candelabrum*. Ed. Gian Carlo Alessio. Bibliotheca Scriptorum Latinorum Mediae et Recentioris Aetatis, 23. Padua: Antenore, 1983.

Benston, Kimberly W. "Performing Blackness: Re/Placing Afro-American Poetry." In *Afro-American Literary Study in the 1990s*, ed. Houston A. Baker and Patricia Redmond, 164–93. Chicago: Chicago University Press, 1989.

Berger, Samuel. *Histoire de la Vulgate pendant les premiers siècles du moyen âge*. Paris, 1893.

Bernard of Utrecht. *Commentum in Theodulum*. In A. J. Minnis, *Medieval Theory of Authorship: Scholastic Literary Attitudes in the Later Middle Ages*. 2d ed. Philadelphia: University of Pennsylvania Press, 1988.

———. *Commentum in Theodulum*. In *Accessus ad auctores*, ed. R. B. C. Huygens. Leiden: Brill, 1970.

Blackstone, William. *Commentaries on the Laws of England*. Ed. W. Hardcastle Browne. St. Paul, 1897.

Bland, Cynthia Renée. *The Teaching of Grammar in Late Medieval England*. East Lansing: Colleagues Press, 1991.

Bloch, R. Howard. *Etymologies and Genealogies: A Literary Anthropology of the French Middle Ages*. Chicago: University of Chicago Press, 1983.

Bloomfield, Morton W. *Incipits of Latin Works on the Virtues and Vices, 1100–1500*. Cambridge, Mass.: Mediaeval Academy of America, 1979.

———. "The Magic of *In Principio*." *MLN* 70 (1955): 559–65.

———. *Piers Plowman as a Fourteenth-Century Apocalypse*. New Brunswick, N.J.: Rutgers University Press, 1962.

———. Review of *Speculative Grammars of the Middle Ages* and *Thomas of Erfurt: Grammativa Speculativa*, by G. L. Bursill-Hall. *Speculum* 49 (1974): 102–5.

Boethius. *Consolatio philosophiae*. Ed. James J. O'Donnell. 2d ed. Bryn Mawr Latin Commentaries. Bryn Mawr, Pa.: Bryn Mawr College, 1990.

———. *The Consolation of Philosophy*. Trans. Richard Green. New York: Macmillan, 1962.

Boethius of Dacia. *Modi significandi, sive quaestiones super Priscianum maiorem*. Ed. Jan Pinborg and Henry Roos. Corpus Philosophorum Danicorum Medii Aevi, 4. Copenhagen: Gad, 1969.

Bonaventure. *Breviloquium*. Vol. 5. Paris: Editions Franciscaines, 1967.

———. *Opera omnia*. Quaracchi: St. Bonaventure, 1894.

Boniface VIII. "Unam Sanctam." In *Corpis Iuris Canonici*, ed. E. Friedberg. Leipzig, 1881.

Bourdieu, Pierre. *Distinction: A Social Critique of the Judgement of Taste*. Trans. Richard Nice. Cambridge, Mass.: Harvard University Press, 1984.

———. *Language and Symbolic Power*. Cambridge: Cambridge University Press, 1991.

———. *The Logic of Practice*. Trans. Richard Nice. Stanford, Calif.: Stanford University Press, 1990.

Bowers, John M. *The Crisis of Will in Piers Plowman*. Washington, D.C.: Catholic University of America Press, 1986.

Bracton, Henry de. *De legibus et consuetudinis Angliae*. Ed. G. E. Woodbine, trans. S. E. Thorne. Cambridge: Harvard University Press, 1968.

Bradwardine, Thomas. *De causa Dei contra Pelagium*. London, 1618.

———. *Treatise on "Incipit" and "Desinit."* Ed. Lauge Olaf Nielsen. *Cahiers de l'Institut du Moyen–Âge Grec et Latin* 42 (1982): 1–83.

Brisman, Leslie. *Romantic Origins*. Ithaca, N.Y.: Cornell University Press, 1978.

Brown, Carleton, ed. *Religious Lyrics of the Fourteenth Century*. Oxford: Clarendon, 1924.

Brummer, Jacob, ed. *Vitae Virgilianae*. Leipzig: Tuebner, 1912.

Bruno Astensis. *Expositio in Psalmos*. *PL* 164. Paris, 1854. Cols. 695–894.

Bruno the Carthusian. *Expositio in Psalmos*. *PL* 152. Paris, 1879. Cols. 637–1420.

Burrow, John A. "The Action of Langland's Second Vision." *Essays in Criticism* 15 (1965): 247–68.

———. "Words, Works, and Will: Theme and Structure in *Piers Plowman*." In *Piers Plowman: Critical Approaches*, ed. S. S. Hussey, 111–24. London: Methuen, 1969.

Bursill–Hall, G. L. *Speculative Grammars of the Middle Ages: The Doctrine of the Partes Orationis of the Modistae*. The Hague: Mouton, 1971.

Calendar of Early Mayor's Court Rolls, A.D. 1298–1307. Ed. A. H. Thomas. Cambridge: Cambridge University Press, 1929.

Carruthers, Mary. *The Book of Memory: A Study of Memory in Medieval Culture*. Cambridge: Cambridge University Press, 1990.

———. *The Search for St. Truth: A Study of Meaning in "Piers Plowman."* Evanston, Ill.: Northwestern University Press, 1973.

Cassiodorus, *De artibus et disciplinis liberalium litterarum*. *PL* 70. Paris, 1847. Cols. 1149–1219.

———. *Expositio psalmorum*. Corpus Christianorum, Series Latina, 97. Turnhout: Brepols, 1973.

Caxton, William. *The book of fame made by G. Chaucer*. London, 1483.

Chambers, R. W. "The Original Form of the A Text of *Piers Plowman*." *MLR* 6 (1911): 302–23.

———. *Man's Unconquerable Mind*. London: Cape, 1939.

Charland, Thomas. *Artes praedicandi, contribution à l'histoire de la rhetorique au moyen âge*. Publications de l'Institut d'Études Médiévales d'Ottawa, 7. Paris: Vrin, 1936.

Charlesworth, James H. *The Old Testament Pseudepigrapha.* New York: Doubleday, 1985.

Chaucer, Geoffrey. *The Riverside Chaucer.* Ed. Larry D. Benson. Boston: Houghton Mifflin, 1987.

———, trans. *The Consolation of Philosophy.* In *The Riverside Chaucer,* ed. Larry D. Benson. Boston: Houghton Mifflin, 1987.

Chenu, M.–D. "Les réponses de s. Thomas et de Kilwardby à la consultation de Jean de Verceil (1271)." In *Mélanges Mandonnet.* Bibl. Thomiste, 13. Paris: Vrin, 1930.

The Chester Mystery Cycle. Ed. R. M. Lumiansky and David Mills. EETS, s.s., 3. Oxford: Oxford University Press, 1974.

Christianson, C. Paul. *A Directory of London Stationers and Book Artisans, 1300–1500.* New York: Bibliographical Society of America, 1990.

Cicero. *De inventione, De optimo genere oratorum, Topica.* Cambridge, Mass.: Harvard University Press, 1976.

Cipolla, Carlo. *Clocks and Culture, 1300–1700.* London: Collins, 1967.

Coghill, Nevill K. "The Pardon of Piers Plowman Considered from the B Text." *MAe* 2 (1933): 108–35.

Colaianne, A. J. "Structure and 'Foreconceit' in *Piers Plowman B:* Some Observations on Langland's Psychology of Composition." *AnnM* 22 (1982): 102–11.

Coleman, Janet. "Jean de Ripa O.F.M. and the Oxford Calculators." *Medieval Studies* 37 (1975): 132–89.

———. *Piers Plowman and the Moderni.* Rome: Edizioni di Storia e Letteratura, 1981.

Comestor, Peter. *Historia scholastica, liber Genesis. PL* 198. Paris, 1855. Cols. 1053–1142.

Commentarium in Joannem. PL 175. Paris, 1879. Cols. 827–80.

The Commmentary on 'Priscianus Maior' Ascribed to Robert Kilwardby. Ed. K. M. Fredborg, N. J. Green–Pedersen, Lauge Neilsen, and Jan Pinborg. *Cahiers de l'Institut du Moyen–Âge Grec et Latin* 15 (1975).

Conrad of Hirsau. *Dialogus super auctores.* Ed. R. B. C. Huygens. Brussels: Latomus, 1955.

Copeland, Rita. *Rhetoric, Hermeneutics, and Translation in the Middle Ages: Academic Traditions and Vernacular Texts.* Cambridge: Cambridge University Press, 1991.

Corpus iuris canonici. Ed. Aemilius Ludwig Richter and Emil Friedberg. Graz: Akademische Druck– und Verlagsanstalt, 1959.

Corti, Maria. *Percorsi dell'inventione: Il linguaggio poetico e Dante.* Turin: Einaudi, 1993.

Courtenay, William J. *Adam Wodeham: An Introduction to His Life and Writings.* Leiden: Brill, 1978.

———. "Nominalism and Late Medieval Religion." In *The Pursuit of Holiness in Late Medieval and Renaissance Religion,* ed. Charles Trinkaus and Heiko Oberman, 26–59. Leiden: Brill, 1975.

Covington, Michael A. *Syntactic Theory in the High Middle Ages: Modistic Models of Sentence Structure.* Cambridge: Cambridge University Press, 1984.

Cursor Mundi. Ed. Richard Morris. EETS, 57, 59, 62, 66, 68, 99, 101. London, 1874–93.

Curtius, Ernst R. *European Literature and the Latin Middle Ages.* Trans. Willard R. Trask. New York: Pantheon, 1953.

Dahlberg, Charles. *The Romance of the Rose.* Hanover, N.H. University Press of New England, 1983.

Davidoff, Judith M. *Beginning Well: Framing Fictions in Late Middle English Poetry.* Rutherford, N.J.: Fairleigh Dickinson University Press, 1988.

Davy, Marie Magdeleine, ed. *Les sermons universitaires parisiens de 1230–31: Contribution à l'histoire de la prédication médiévale.* Etudes de Philosophie Medievale, 15. Paris: Vrin, 1931.

Dawson, James Doyne. "Richard Fitzralph and the Fourteenth–Century Poverty Controversies." *Journal of Ecclesiastical History* 34 (1983): 315–44.

de Certeau, Michel. *Heterologies: Discourse on the Other.* Trans. Brian Massumi. Minneapolis: University of Minnesota Press, 1986.

Deleuze, Gilles. *Difference and Repetition.* Trans. Paul Patton. New York: Columbia University Press, 1994.

Deleuze, Gilles, and Félix Guattari. *A Thousand Plateaus: Capitalism and Schizophrenia.* Trans. Brian Massumi. Minneapolis: University of Minnesota Press, 1987.

Derrida, Jacques. *Edmund Husserl's Origin of Geometry: An Introduction.* Trans. John P. Leavey Jr. Lincoln: University of Nebraska Press, 1978.

———. *Of Grammatology.* Ed. and trans. Gayatri Chakravorty Spivak. Baltimore, Md.: Johns Hopkins University Press, 1976.

Deutz, Rupert of. *Commentaria in Evangelium Sancti Iohannis.* Ed. H. Haake. Corpus Christianorum, Series Latina: Continuatio Medievalis, 9. Turnhout: Brepols, 1969.

———. *De Trinitate et operibus ejus. PL* 167. Paris, n.d. Cols. 199–1828.

Donaldson, E. Talbot. "The Grammar of Book's Speech in *Piers Plowman.*" In *Style and Symbolism in "Piers Plowman,"* ed. Robert J. Blanch, 264–70. Knoxville: University of Tennessee Press, 1969.

———. "MSS R and F in the B–Tradition of Piers Plowman." *Transactions of the Connecticut Academy of Arts and Sciences* 39 (1955): 177–212.

———. *Piers Plowman: The C–Text and Its Poet.* New Haven, Conn.: Yale University Press, 1949.

Donatus. *Ars grammatica.* In *Grammatici latini,* vol. 4, ed. H. Keil. Leipzig, 1864.

Doyle, A. I., and M. B. Parkes. "The Production of Copies of the *Canterbury Tales* and the *Confessio Amantis* in the Early Fifteenth Century." In *Medieval Scribes, Manuscripts, and Libraries: Essays Presented to N. R. Ker,* ed. M. B. Parkes and Andrew G. Watson, 163–210. London: Scolar, 1978.

Duncoeur, P. "Le Nominalisme de Guillaume Occam: La Théorie de la relation." *Revue neo–scholastique de philosophie* 23 (1921): 5–25.

Dunning, T. P. *Piers Plowman: An Interpretation of the A–Text.* Dublin: Talbot, 1937.

———. *Piers Plowman: An Interpretation of the A Text.* 2d rev. ed. Ed. T. P. Dolan. Oxford: Clarendon, 1980.

Duns Scotus, John. *Quaestiones super libros metaphysicorum Aristotelis.* In *Ioannis Duns Scoti . . . Opera omnia.* Lyons, 1639.

Durandus of Saint Pourcain. *In sententias theologicas Petri Lombardi.* Lyons, 1556.

Eagleton, Terry. *Ideology.* London: Verso, 1991.

An Early Commentary on the Poetria Nova of Geoffrey of Vinsauf. Ed. Marjorie Curry Woods. New York: Garland, 1985.

Eco, Umberto, R. Lambertini, C. Marmo, and A. Tabarroni. "On Animal Language in the Medieval Classification of Signs." In *On the Medieval Theory of Signs,* ed. Umberto Eco and Constantino Marmo, 3–41. Amsterdam: Benjamins, 1989.

Economou, George D. "The Vision's Aftermath in *Piers Plowman:* The Poetics of the Middle English Dream Vision." *Genre* 18, no. 4 (1985): 313–21.

Ekwall, Eilert. *Street Names of the City of London.* Oxford: Clarendon, 1954.

Emerson, O. F. "Legends of Cain, Especially in Old and Middle English." *PMLA* 21 (1906): 831–929.

Enders, Jody. *The Medieval Theater of Cruelty: Rhetoric, Memory, Violence.* Ithaca, N.Y.: Cornell University Press, 1999.

English Gilds. Ed. Toulmin Smith. EETS, 40. London, 1870.

Evans, G. R. "Thomas of Chobham on Preaching and Exegesis." *RTAM* 52 (1985): 159–70.

Fabian, Johannes. *Time and the Other: How Anthropology Makes Its Object.* New York: Columbia University Press, 1983.

Fasciculi Zizaniorum Magistri Johannis Wyclif cum Tritico. Ed. W. W. Shirley. Rolls Series, 5. London, 1858.

Fierville, Charles. *Une grammaire latine.* Paris, 1886.

———. "Notices et extraits des manuscrits de la Bibliothèque de Saint–Omer." *Notices et extraits des manuscrits de la Bibliothèque Nationale* 31, no. 1 (1884):135.

Fitzralph, Richard. *Defensio curatorum.* In *Dialogus inter militem et clericum,* ed. H. Milford. EETS, 167. Oxford: Oxford University Press, 1925.

———. *De pauperie salvatoris.* In *Iohannis Wycliffe: De dominio divino,* ed. Reginald Lane Poole, 257–476. London, 1890.

———. *Summa.* Paris, n.d.

Fleta. Ed. and trans. H. G. Richardson and G. O. Sayles. Selden Society, 72, 89, 99. London: Quaritch, 1955–84.

Foucault, Michel. *The Discourse on Language.* In *The Archeology of Knowledge,* trans. A. M. Sheridan Smith. New York: Pantheon, 1972.

———. "Dream, Imagination, and Existence." Trans. Forrest Williams. *Review of Existential Psychology and Psychiatry* 19 (1984–85): 31–77.

———. *Language, Counter–Memory, Practice: Selected Essays and Interviews.* Ed. Donald F. Bouchard, trans. Donald F. Bouchard and Sherry Simon. Ithaca, N.Y.: Cornell University Press, 1977.

———. *The Order of Things: An Archaeology of the Human Sciences.* Trans. Alan Sheridan. New York: Random House, 1970.

Frank, Robert Worth. *Piers Plowman and the Scheme of Salvation: An Interpretation of Dowel, Dobet, and Dobest.* Yale Studies in English, 136. New Haven, Conn.: Yale University Press, 1957.

Frantzen, Allen. *Desire for Origins: New Language, Old English, and Teaching the Tradition.* New Brunswick, N.J.: Rutgers, 1990.

Freud, Sigmund. *Beyond the Pleasure Principle.* Trans. James Strachey. New York: Norton, 1959.

———. *From the History of an Infantile Neurosis*. In *The Standard Edition of the Complete Psychological Works of Sigmund Freud*. Vol. 17, 7–122. Trans. James Strachey. London: Hogarth, 1955.

Galbraith, V. H. "John Seward and His Circle." *Mediaeval and Renaissance Studies* 1 (1941): 85–104.

———. "More about John Seward." *Edinburgh Bibliographical Society Transactions, 1938–45* 2 (1946): 385–86.

Gallo, Ernest, ed. *The "Poetria Nova" and Its Sources in Early Rhetorical Doctrine*. The Hague: Mouton, 1971.

Gentile de Cingoli. *Quaestiones Supra Priscian Minori*. Ed. Romana Martorelli Vico. Pisa: Scuola Normale Superiore, 1985.

Geoffrey of Vinsauf. *Poetria nova*. In Edmond Faral, *Les arts poétiques du XIIe et du XIIIe siècle*. Paris: Champion, 1924.

Gerardus Hardewick. *Commentaria in summulas Petri Hispani*. Cologne, 1492.

Giovanni da Serravalle. *Iohannis de Serravalle translatio et comentum totius libri Dantis Aldighieri*. Prati, 1891.

Glossa ordinaria. Basle, 1489.

Godden, Malcolm. "Plowmen and Hermits in Langland's *Piers Plowman*." *RES*, n.s., 35, no. 138 (1984): 129–63.

Goldsmith, Margaret. *The Figure of Piers Plowman: The Image on the Coin*. Piers Plowman Studies, 2. Cambridge: Brewer, 1981.

Gower, John. *Vox clamantis*. In *Complete Works of John Gower*, vol. 4, ed. G. C. Macaulay. London, 1902.

Gradon, Pamela. "*Trajanus Redivivus:* Another Look at Trajan in *Piers Plowman*." In *Middle English Studies Presented to Norman Davis in Honour of His Seventieth Birthday*, ed. Douglas Gray and E. G. Stanley. Oxford: Clarendon, 1983.

Gray, Nick. "A Study of Piers Plowman in Relation to the Penitential Tradition." Ph.D. diss., Cambridge University, 1984.

Green, Richard Firth. *A Crisis of Truth: Literature and Law in Ricardian England*. Philadelphia: University of Pennsylvania Press, 1999.

Greetham, D. C. *Textual Scholarship: An Introduction*. New York: Garland, 1994.

Gregory of Rimini. *Lectura super primum et secundum sententiarum*. Vol. 6. Ed. A. Damasus Trapp, O.S.A. and Venicio Marcolino. Berlin: De Gruyter, 1980.

Grosseteste, Robert. *Hexaemeron*. Ed. Richard C. Dales and Servus Gieben, O.F.M. Auctores Britannica Medii Aevi, 6. London: British Academy, 1982.

Gruterus, Janus. *Florilegii magni seu Polyanthae Tomus secund*. Argentorati, 1624.

Guibert of Nogent. *Moralium in Genesin*. *PL* 156. Paris, 1880. Cols. 31–338.

Gurevich, Aron. "The Merchant." In *Medieval Callings*, ed. Jacques Le Goff, trans. Lydia G. Cochrane. Chicago: University of Chicago Press, 1990.

Habermas, Jürgen. *The Philosophical Discourse of Modernity: Twelve Lectures*. Cambridge, Mass: MIT Press, 1987.

Harrison, Frank. *Music in Medieval Britain*. London: Routledge, 1963.

Harwood, Britton J. "*Liberum Arbitrium* in the C–Text of *Piers Plowman*." *Philological Quarterly* 52 (1973): 680–95.

Heidegger, Martin. *Heraklit.* Bd. 55, *Martin Heidegger: Gesamtausgabe.* Ed. Manfred S. Frings. Frankfurt: Klostermann, 1979.

———. *An Introduction to Metaphysics.* Trans. Ralph Mannheim. New Haven, Conn.: Yale University Press, 1959.

———. "On the Being and Conception of *physis* in Aristotle's *Physics* B,1." Trans. Thomas J. Sheehan. *Man and World* 9 (1976): 219–70.

Henninger, Mark G., S.J. *Relations: Medieval Theories, 1250–1325.* Oxford: Clarendon, 1989.

Henry of Ghent. *Quodlibet.* Paris, 1518.

Hereford Breviary. Vol. 3. Ed. W. H. Frere and L. E. G. Browne. London: Henry Bradshaw Society, 1913.

Higden, Ranulph. *The ars componendi sermones of Ranulph Higden, O.S.B.* Ed. Margaret Jennings. Leiden: Brill, 1991.

———. *Polychronicon.* Ed. Joseph Rawson Lumby. Trans. John Trevisa. Rolls Series, 40. London, 1865–86.

Higgs, Elton D. "The Path to Involvement: The Centrality of the Dreamer in *Piers Plowman.*" *Tulane Studies in English* 21 (1974): 1–34.

Holcot, Robert. *In librum sapientiae Regis Salomonis praelectiones CCXIII.* Basle, 1586.

———. *Super librum sapientiae.* Basle, 1489.

Holleran, J. V. "The Role of the Dreamer in *Piers Plowman.*" *Annuale Mediaevale* 7 (1966): 33–50.

Horace. *Ars poetica.* Ed. and trans. Rushton Fairclough. Cambridge: Harvard University Press, 1978.

———. *Satires, Epistles and Ars poetica.* Ed. and trans. H. Rushton Fairclough. Cambridge, Mass.: Harvard University Press, 1978.

Horstmann, Carl, ed. *Yorkshire Writers: Richard Rolle of Hampole . . . and His Followers.* 2 vols. London, 1895.

Hudson, Anne. *The Premature Reformation: Wycliffite Texts and Lollard History.* Oxford: Clarendon, 1988.

Hugh of Saint-Victor. *Didascalicon. PL* 176. Paris, 1874. Cols. 740–838.

Hugolinus de Urbe Veteri. *Commentarius in quattuor libros sententiarum.* Vol. 3. Ed. Willigis Eckermann and Venicio Marcolino. Wurzburg: Augustinus–Verlag, 1980.

Hult, David. "Closed Quotations: The Speaking Voice in the *Roman de la Rose.*" *Yale French Studies* 67 (1984): 248–69.

———. *Self–Fulfilling Prophecies: Readership and Authority in the First Roman de la Rose.* Cambridge: Cambridge University Press, 1986.

Hunt, R. W. "*Absoluta:* The *Summa* of Petrus Hispanus on Priscianus *Minor.*" In *The History of Grammar in the Middle Ages: Collected Papers,* ed. G. L. Bursill–Hall. Amsterdam: Benjamins, 1980.

———. "The Introductions to the *Artes* in the Twelfth Century." In *The History of Grammar in the Middle Ages: Collected Papers,* ed. G. L. Bursill–Hall. Amsterdam Studies in the Theory and History of Linguistic Science, 3d ser., vol. 5, 117–44. Amsterdam: Benjamins, 1980.

———. "Studies on Priscian in the Eleventh and Twelfth Centuries." *MRS* 1 (1941–43): 194–231; *MRS* 2 (1950): 1–56.

———. "The *Summa* of Petrus Hispanus on Priscianus *Minor*." *Historiographica Linguistica* 2 (1975): 1–23.

Illich, Ivan. *In the Vineyard of the Text: A Commentary to Hugh's "Didascalicon."* Chicago: University of Chicago Press, 1993.

Isaac of Stella. *Sermones*. *PL* 194. Paris, 1855. Cols. 1689–1876.

———. *Sermons*. Vol. 2. Ed. Anselm Hoste and Gaston Salet. Paris: Cerf, 1974.

Isidore of Seville. *Etymologia*. *PL* 82. Paris, 1850. Cols. 73–728.

Jameson, Fredric. *Marxism and Form: Twentieth-Century Dialectical Theories of Literature*. Princeton, N.J.: Princeton University Press, 1972.

Jerome, *Adversus Jovinianum*. In *Jankyn's Book of Wikked Wyves*, ed. Ralph Hanna III and Traugott Lawler. Athens: University of Georgia Press, 1997.

———. *Tractatus in librum psalmorum*. Corpus Christianorum, Series Latina, 78. Turnhout: Brepols, 1978.

Johannes de Marvilla. *Tractatus metricus de modis significandi*. In *Expositiones modorum significandi*. Rouen, 1500.

John of Dacia. *Summa grammatica*. Ed. Alfred Otto. Corpus Philosophorum Danoricum Medii Aevi, 1. Hauniae: Gad, 1955.

John of Garland. *Parisiana poetria*. Ed. Traugott Lawler. Yale Studies in English, 182. New Haven, Conn.: Yale University Press, 1974.

John of Salisbury. *Ioannis Saresberiensis Policraticus, sive De nugis curialium & vestigiis philosophorum*. Lyons, 1639.

John of Wales. *Forma predicandi*. In Woodburn O. Ross, "A Brief 'Forma Predicandi.'" *MP* 34 (1937): 337–44.

Jones, Evan John. *Medieval Heraldry: Some Fourteenth Century Heraldic Works*. Cardiff: Lewis, 1943.

Justice, Steven. *Writing and Rebellion: England in 1381*. Berkeley: University of California Press, 1994.

Justice, Steven, and Kathryn Kerby–Fulton, eds. *Written Work: Langland, Labor, and Authorship*. Philadelphia: University of Pennsylvania Press, 1997.

Kane, George. *The Liberating Truth: The Concept of Integrity in Chaucer's Writings*. London: Athlone, 1980.

———. *Piers Plowman: The Evidence for Authorship*. London: Athlone, 1965.

———. "The Text." In *A Companion to Piers Plowman*, ed. John Alford, 175–200. Berkeley: University of California Press, 1988.

Kaske, R. E. "*Ex vi transicionis* and Its Passage in *Piers Plowman*." In *Style and Symbolism in Piers Plowman: A Modern Critical Anthology*, ed. Robert J. Blanch, 228–63. Knoxville: University of Tennessee Press, 1969.

Kean, P. M. "Law, Love, and *Lewte* in *Piers Plowman*." *RES*, n.s., 15 (1964): 241–61.

Kelly, Douglas. "Theory of Composition in Medieval Narrative Poetry and Geoffrey of Vinsauf's *Poetria Nova*." *MS* 31 (1969): 117–48.

Kilwardby, Robert. *De ortu scientiarum*. Ed. Albert G. Judy. Auctores Britannica Medii Aevi, 4. London: British Academy, 1976.

———. *De spiritu fantastico*. Ed. P. Osmund Lewry, O.P. Auctores Britannica Medii Aevi, 9. Oxford: British Academy, 1987.

Kirk, Elizabeth D. *The Dream Thought of Piers Plowman.* New Haven, Conn: Yale University Press, 1972.

———. "Langland's Plowman and the Recreation of Fourteenth–Century Religious Metaphor." *YLS* 2 (1988): 1–21.

Kneepkens, C. H. "*Legere Est Agere:* The First Quaestio of the First Quaestiones–Collection in the MS Oxford, CCC 250." In *Studies in Medieval Linguistic Thought,* ed. Konard Koerner, Hans–J. Niederehe, and R. H. Robins. Amsterdam: Benjamins, 1980.

Knighton, Henry. *Chronicon Henrici Knighton.* Ed. Joseph Rawson Lumby. Rolls Series, 92. London, 1895.

Knuuttila, S., and A. I. Lehtinen. "'Plato in infinitum remisse incipit esse albus': New Texts on the Later Medieval Discussion on the Concept of Infinity in Sophismata Literature." In *Essays in Honour of Jaako Hintikka,* ed. E. Saarinen, 309–29. Dordrecht: Reidel, 1979.

Krempel, A. *La doctrine de la relation chez saint Thomas.* Paris: Vrin, 1952.

Kretzmann, Norman. "Incipit/Desinit." In *Motion and Time, Space and Matter,* ed. P. K. Machamer and R. G. Turnbull, 101–36. Columbus: Ohio State University Press, 1976.

Kristeva, Julia. "Credo in unum deum." In *In the Beginning Was Love,* trans. Arthur Goldhammer, 37–44. New York: Columbia University Press, 1984.

Kronbichler, Walter, ed. *Die Summa de Arte Prosandi der Konrad von Mure.* Zurich: Fretz and Wasmuth, 1968.

Kruger, Steven. *Dreaming in the Middle Ages.* Cambridge: Cambridge University Press, 1992.

Lacan, Jacques. "The Subversion of the Subject and the Dialectic of Desire in the Freudian Unconscious." In *Ecrits: A Selection,* trans. Alan Sheridan. New York: Norton, 1977.

Lambert of Auxerre. *De suppositionibus et de significationibus.* In *Logica (Summa Lamberti),* ed. Franco Alessio. Florence: La nuova Italia, 1971.

LaPlanche, J., and J.–B. Pontalis. *The Language of Psycho–Analysis.* Trans. Daniel Lagache. New York: Norton, 1973.

Law, Robert Adger. "*In Principio.*" *PMLA* 37 (1922): 208–15.

Lawton, David. "The Subject of *Piers Plowman.*" *YLS* 1 (1987): 1–30.

Leff, Gordon. *Bradwardine and the Pelagians: A Study of the "De Causa Dei" and Its Opponents.* Cambridge: Cambridge University Press, 1957.

———. *Heresy in the Later Middle Ages.* Manchester: Manchester University Press, 1967.

———. *Paris and Oxford Universities in the Thirteenth and Fourteenth Centuries: An Institutional and Intellectual History.* New York: Wiley, 1968.

———. *Richard Fitzralph, Commentator on the Sentences: A Study in Orthodox Theology.* Manchester: Manchester University Press, 1975.

———. *William of Ockham: The Metamorphosis of Scholastic Discourse.* Manchester: Manchester University Press, 1975.

The Legendys of Hooly Wummen. Ed. Mary S. Sergeantson. EETS, 206. London: Oxford University Press, 1938.

Le Goff, Jacques. *The Birth of Purgatory,* trans. Arthur Goldhammer. Chicago: University of Chicago Press, 1984.

Lemaire, Jacques. *Introduction à la codicologie.* Louvain–la–Neuve: Université Catholique de Louvain, 1989.

Longo, Joseph A. "*Piers Plowman* and the Tropological Matrix: Passus XI and XII." *Anglia* 82, no. 3 (1964): 291–308.

Ludolf of Hildesheim. *Summa dictaminum.* In *Briefsteller und Formelbucher des vierzehnten Jahrhunderts* I, ed. Ludwig Rockinger, 359–400. Munich, 1863.

Macherey, Pierre. *A Theory of Literary Production.* Trans. Geoffrey Wall. New York: Routledge, 1978.

Maier, Anneliese. *Zwei Grundproblem der scholastischen Naturphilosophie. Das problem der intensiven Grösse, die Impetustheorie.* Rome: Edizioni di storia e letteratura, 1951.

Maierù, Alfonso. *Terminologia logica della tarda scolastica.* Rome: Ateneo, 1972.

Margalits, Eduardus, ed. *Florilegium prouerbium universae latinitatis.* Budapest, 1895.

Martin of Dacia. *Categoriae. Martini de Dacia opera.* Ed. Heinreich Roos. Corpus Philosophorum Danicorum Medii Aevi, 2. Copenhagen: Gad, 1961.

———. *Modi significandi.* In *Martini de Dacia opera,* ed. Heinrich Roos. Corpus Philosophorum Danoricum Medii Aevi, 2. Copenhagen: Gad, 1961.

McGerr, Rosemarie. *Chaucer's Open Books: Resistance to Closure in Medieval Discourse.* Gainesville: University Press of Florida, 1998.

Meech, S. B. "An Early Treatise in English concerning Latin Grammar." In *Essays and Studies in English and Comparative Literature.* University of Michigan Publications, Language and Literature. Vol. 13 (1935): 81–125.

Mellinkoff, Ruth. "Cain's Monstrous Progeny: Part II, Post–Diluvian Survival." *Anglo Saxon England* 9 (1980): 193–97.

Michel de Marbais. *De modis significandi.* In *Notices et extraits des manuscrits de la Bibliothèque Imperiale XXII,* ed. Charles Thurot. Paris, 1868.

Middle English Dictionary. Ed. Hans Kurath and Sherman M. Kuhn. Ann Arbor: University of Michigan Press. 1952–.

Middleton, Anne. "Acts of Vagrancy: The C Version 'Autobiography' and the Statute of 1388." In *Written Work: Langland, Labor, and Authorship,* ed. Steven Justice and Kathryn Kerby-Fulton. Philadelphia: University of Pennsylvania Press, 1997.

———. "The Audience and Public of *Piers Plowman.*" In *Middle English Alliterative Poetry and Its Literary Background: Seven Essays,* ed. David Lawton, 103–23. Cambridge: Brewer, 1982.

———. "Making a Good End: John But as a Reader of *Piers Plowman.*" In *Medieval English Studies Presented to George Kane,* ed. Edward Donald Kennedy, Ronald Waldron, and Joseph S. Wittig, 243–66. Woodbridge, Suffolk: Brewer, 1988.

———. "Narration and the Invention of Experience: Episodic Form in *Piers Plowman.*" In *The Wisdom of Poetry: Essays in Early English Literature in Honor of Morton W. Bloomfield,* ed. Larry D. Benson and Siegfried Wenzel, 91–122. Kalamazoo: Western Michigan University, 1982.

———. "Two Infinites: Grammatical Metaphor in *Piers Plowman.*" *ELH* 39 (1972): 169–88.

———. "William Langland's 'Kynde Name': Authorial Signature and Social Identity in Late Fourteenth–Century England." In *Literary Practice and Social Change in Britain, 1380–1530,* ed. Lee Patterson, 15–82. Berkeley: University of California Press, 1990.

Milton, John. *Paradise Lost.* Ed. Merritt Hughes. New York: Macmillan, 1957.

Minnis, A. J. *Medieval Theory of Authorship: Scholastic Literary Attitudes in the Later Middle Ages.* 2d ed. Philadelphia: University of Pennsylvania Press, 1988.

Minnis, A. J., A.B. Scott, eds., with David Wallace. *Medieval Literary Theory and Criticism, c. 1100–c. 1375: The Commentary Tradition.* Rev. ed. Oxford: Clarendon, 1988.

Mitchell, A. G. "Lady Meed and the Art of *Piers Plowman.*" In *Style and Symbolism in Piers Plowman,* ed. Robert J. Blanch, 174–93. Knoxville: University of Tennessee Press, 1969.

Moore, Samuel. "Studies in *Piers the Plowman.*" *MP* 11 (1913): 177–93; 12 (1914): 19–50.

Moore, Samuel, and Albert H. Marckwardt. *Historical Outlines of English Sounds and Inflections.* Ann Arbor, Mich.: Wahr, 1990.

Murphy, James J. *Rhetoric in the Middle Ages: A History of Rhetorical Theory from Saint Augustine to the Renaissance.* Berkeley: University of California Press, 1974.

———, ed. *Three Medieval Rhetorical Arts.* Berkeley: University of California Press, 1971.

Muscatine, Charles. *Poetry and Crisis in the Age of Chaucer.* Wards–Phillips Lectures in English Language and Literature, vol. 4. Notre Dame, Ind.: University of Notre Dame Press, 1972.

Mustanoja, Tauno F. *A Middle English Syntax. Part I: Parts of Speech.* Helsinki: Société néophilologique, 1960.

Nicolaus Gorranus. *Enarratio in Quatuor Evangelia.* Lyons, 1692.

Nicholas of Lyra. *Postilla.* In *Glossa Ordinaria. PL* 113. Paris, 1879. Col. 35–61.

———. *Postilla.* In *Glossa Ordinaria.* Basle, 1489.

Nielsen, Lauge Olaf. "Thomas Bradwardine's Treatise on 'Incipit' and 'Desinit.'" *Cahiers de l'Institut du Moyen–Âge Grec et Latin* 42 (1982): 1–83.

Nuttall, A. D. *Openings: Narrative Beginnings from the Epic to the Novel.* Oxford: Clarendon, 1992.

Oberman, Heiko. *The Harvest of Late Medieval Theology: Gabriel Biel and Late Medieval Nominalism.* Cambridge, Mass.: Harvard University Press, 1963.

Ockham, William of. *In sententiarum. Opera plurima.* Lyons, 1496.

———. *Quaestiones in librum quartum sententiarum (reportatio).* Ed. Rega Wood and Gedeon Gàl, O.F.M. St. Bonaventure, N.Y.: St. Bonaventure, 1984.

———. *Quaestiones in librum quartum sententiarum.* St. Bonaventure, N.Y.: St. Bonaventure University Press, 1984.

———. *Quodlibeta septem.* Ed. Joseph C. Wey. St. Bonaventure, N.Y.: St. Bonaventure University Press, 1980.

———. *Scriptum in primum librum sententiarum.* Ed. Gerard I. Etzhorn and Francis E. Kelley. St. Bonaventure, N.Y.: St. Bonaventure University Press, 1979.

———. *Summa logicae.* Ed. P. Boehner, G. Gàl, and S. Brown. In *Opera Philosophica.* Vol. 1. St. Bonaventure, N.Y.: St. Bonaventure University Press, 1974.

"Of the Leaven of the Pharisees." In *The English Works of Wyclif,* ed. Frederic David Matthew. EETS, 74. London, 1880.

Olender, Maurice. *The Languages of Paradise: Race, Religion, and Philology in the Nineteenth Century.* Trans. Arthur Goldhammer. Cambridge, Mass.: Harvard University Press, 1991.

Olszewska, E. S. "Middle English Fader and Frendes." *N&Q* 218 (1973): 205–7.

Overstreet, Samuel. "*Grammaticus Ludens:* Theological Aspects of Langland's Grammatical Analogy." *Traditio* 40 (1984): 255–80.

Paetow, Louis J. *The Arts Course at Medieval Universities.* Urbana: University of Illinois Press, 1919.

Parkes, Malcolm. "The Influence of the Concepts of *Ordinatio* and *Compilatio* on the Development of the Book." In *Medieval Learning and Literature: Studies Presented to Richard William Hunt,* ed. J. J. G. Alexander and M. T. Gibson. Oxford: Clarendon, 1976.

Paschasius Radbertus. *Expositio in Matthaeum. PL* 120. Paris, 1879. Cols. 31–994.

Pecock, Reginald. *The Repressor of Over Much Blaming of the Clergy.* Ed. Churchill Babington. London, 1860.

Pelzer, A. "Les 51 Articles de Guillaume Occam censures en Avignon en 1326." *Revue d'histoire ecclesiastique* 18 (1922): 250.

Peter Lombard. *Commentarium in Psalmos. PL* 191. Paris, 1880. Cols. 61–1246.

———. *Sententiae. PL* 192. Paris, 1880. Cols. 521–962.

Petrus Helias. *Summa on Priscian Minor.* Ed. James E. Tolson. *Cahiers de l'Institut du Moyen–Âge Grec et Latin* 27–28 (1978).

Petrus Hispanus. *In summulas Priscianem minorem* and Tataretus's commentary. Venice, 1621.

———. *Tractatus (Summule logicales).* Ed. L. M. de Rijk. Assen: Van Gorcum, 1972.

———. *Tractatus syncategorematum.* Trans. Joseph P. Mullally. Milwaukee: Marquette University Press, 1964.

Pierre d'Ailly. *Destructiones modorum significandi.* In *Zwei Texte zur scholastischen Sprachtheorie in 14. Jahrhundert,* ed. Ludger Kaczmarek. Münster: Münsteraner Arbeitskreis für Semiotik, 1980.

———. *Quaestiones magistri Petri de Ailliaco cardinalis camarencis libros sententiarum* IV. Strasbourg, 1490.

Pinborg, Jan. *Logik und Semantik im Mittelalter: Ein Überblick.* Stuttgart: Fromman–Holzboog, 1972.

Pollard, Graham. "The Company of Stationers before 1557." *The Library,* 4th ser., 18 (1937): 1–38.

Pomian, Krzysztof. *L'ordre du temps.* Paris: Gallimard, 1984.

Priscian. *Institutiones grammaticae libri XVIII.* In *Grammatici latini,* vol. 3, ed. H. Keil. Leipzig, 1864.

Proceedings and Ordinances of the Privy Council of England. 5 vols. Ed. Nicholas Harris Nicolas. London, 1834–37.

PRO Minister's Accounts, 1092/3.

Pseudo–Albertus Magnus. *Quaestiones Alberti de modis significandi.* Ed. L. G. Kelly. Amsterdam: Benjamins, 1977.

Pseudo–Aquinas. *Ars praedicandi.* Strasbourg, n.d.

Pseudo–Cicero. *Ad C. Herennium de ratione dicendi (Rhetorica ad Herennium).* Ed. and trans. Harry Caplan. Cambridge, Mass.: Harvard University Press, 1954.

Pseudo–Grosseteste. *Tractatus de grammatica: Eine falschlich Robert Grosseteste zugeschriebene spekulative Grammatik.* Ed. Karl Reichl. Munich: Schoningh, 1976.

Quilligan, Maureen. *The Language of Allegory: Defining the Genre.* Ithaca, N.Y.: Cornell University Press, 1979.

Rabanus Maurus. *De universo. PL* 111. Paris, 1852. Cols. 9–614.

Raw, Barbara. "Piers and the Image of God in Man." In *Piers Plowman: Critical Approaches,* ed. S. S. Hussey, 143–79. London: Methuen, 1969.

Remigius of Auxerre. *In artem primam Donati.* Ed. W. Fox. Leipzig, 1892.

[Richard of Saint-Victor]. *Allegoriae in Evangelia.* In *Liber exceptionum. PL* 175. Paris, 1879. Cols. 751–54.

Robert of Basevorn. *Forma praedicandi.* In *Artes praedicandi, contribution à l'histoire de la rhetorique au moyen âge,* ed. Thomas Charland, 231–323. Publications de l'Institut d'Études Médiévales d'Ottawa, 7. Paris: Vrin, 1936.

Robins, R. H. *Ancient and Mediaeval Grammatical Theory in Europe.* London: Bell, 1951.

Roman de la Rose. 5 vols. Ed. Ernest Langlois. Paris: Firmin–Didot, 1924.

Rotuli parliamentorum. 6 vols. London, 1767–77.

Rouse, Richard H., and Mary A. Rouse. "Biblical Distinctions in the Thirteenth Century." *Archives d'histoire doctrinale et littéraire du moyen âge* 42 (1974).

The Royal Commission on Historical Manuscripts. 9th report, pt. 1. London, 1883.

Rubin, Miri. *Corpus Christi: The Eucharist in Late Medieval Culture.* Cambridge: Cambridge University Press, 1991.

Rufinus. *Commentarium in symbolum apostolorum. PL* 21. Paris, 1878. Cols. 335–86.

Rushdall, Hastings. *Universities of Europe in the Middle Ages.* Rev. ed. by F. M. Powicke and A. B. Emden. Oxford: Oxford University Press, 1936.

Russell, G. H. "The Imperative of Revision in the C Version of *Piers Plowman.*" In *Medieval English Studies Presented to George Kane,* ed. Edward Donald Kennedy, Ronald Waldron, and Joseph S. Wittig, 233–42. Woodbridge, Suffolk: Brewer, 1988.

Said, Edward. *Beginnings: Intention and Method.* New York: Basic Books, 1975.

———. "On Originality." In *The World, the Text, and the Critic.* Cambridge, Mass: Harvard University Press, 1983.

———. *The World, the Text, and the Critic.* Cambridge, Mass.: Harvard University Press, 1983.

Samuels, M. L. "Dialect and Grammar." In *A Companion to Piers Plowman,* ed. John Alford, 201–21. Berkeley: University of California Press, 1988.

Sandison, Helen Estabrook, ed. *The Chanson d'Aventure in Middle English.* Bryn Mawr College Monographs. Monograph Series 12. Bryn Mawr, Pa., 1913.

Scarry, Elaine. *The Body in Pain: The Making and Unmaking of the World.* Oxford: Oxford University Press, 1985.

Scase, Wendy. *"Piers Plowman" and the New Anticlericalism.* Cambridge: Cambridge University Press, 1989.

———. "Two *Piers Plowman* C–text Interpolations: Evidence for a Second Textual Tradition." *N&Q* 34 (1987): 456–63.

Schmidt, A. V. C., ed. *The Vision of Piers Plowman: A Complete Edition of the B–Text.* London: Dent, 1978.

Schultz, James A. "Classical Rhetoric, Medieval Poetics, and the Medieval Vernacular Prologue." *Speculum* 59 (1984): 1–15.

Schürmann, Reiner. *Heidegger on Being and Acting: From Principles to Anarchy.* Trans. Christine–Marie Gros. Bloomington: Indiana University Press, 1990.

Sedulius Scotus. *Collectanea in omnes B. Pauli Epistolas. PL* 103. Paris, 1864. Cols. 9–270.

Selections from English Wycliffite Writings. Ed. Anne Hudson. Cambridge: Cambridge University Press, 1978.

Serres, Michel. *Genesis.* Trans. Geneviève James and James Nielson. Ann Arbor: University of Michigan Press, 1995.

———. *The Parasite.* Trans. Lawrence R. Schehr. Baltimore, Md.: Johns Hopkins University Press, 1982.

———. *Rome: The Book of Foundations.* Trans. Felicia McCarren. Stanford, Calif.: Stanford University Press, 1991.

Seymour, M. C., ed. *On the Properties of Things: John Trevisa's Translation of Bartholomaeus Anglicus' De proprietatibus rerum, A Critical Text.* 3 vols. Oxford: Clarendon, 1975.

Sharpe, Reginald R. *Calendar of Letter–Books Preserved among the Archives of the Corporation of the City of London at the Guildhall. Letter Book G.* London: Corporation of London, 1905.

———. *Calendar of Wills Proved and Enrolled in the Court of Husting, London, A.D. 1258–A.D. 1688.* 2 vols. London, 1889–90.

The Shewings of Julian of Norwich. Ed. Georgia Ronan Crampton. Kalamazoo: Medieval Institute, 1994.

Siger de Courtrai. *Summa modorum significandi.* Ed. G. Wallerand. *Les oeuvres de Siger de Courtrai.* Les Philosophes belges, 8. Louvain: Institut supérieur de philosophie de l'Université, 1913.

Simpson, James. "From Reason to Affective Knowledge: Modes of Thought and Poetic Form in *Piers Plowman.*" *MAe* 55 (1986): 1–23.

———. *Piers Plowman: An Introduction to the B–Text.* London: Longman, 1990.

———. "Spiritual and Earthly Nobility in *Piers Plowman.*" *NM* 86 (1985): 467–81.

———. "Spirituality and Economics in Passus 1–7 of the B–Text." *YLS* 1 (1987): 83–103.

Sisam, Kenneth. *Fourteenth Century Verse and Prose.* Oxford: Clarendon, 1970.

Skeat, W. W. *Langland's Vision of Piers Plowman: The Vernon Text; or Text A.* EETS, 28. London, 1867.

———. *Piers Plowman,* part 4. EETS, 81. London, 1885.

———. *Piers the Plowman.* 2 vols. Oxford: Oxford University Press, 1886.

———. *The Vision of William concerning Piers the Plowman.* Oxford: Oxford University Press, 1886.

Smalley, Beryl. "Wyclif's *Principium.*" *Oxford Studies Presented to D. Callus.* Oxford Historical Series, n.s., 16 (1964): 253–96.

Smith, Ben H. "Patience's Riddle, *Piers Plowman* B,XIII." *MLN* 76, no. 8 (1961): 675–82.

The Sophismata of Richard Kilvington. Ed. Norman Kretzmann and Barbara Ensign Kretzmann. Oxford: Oxford University Press, 1990.

Spearing, A. C. *Medieval to Renaissance in English Poetry.* Cambridge: Cambridge University Press, 1985.

———. "Verbal Repetition in *Piers Plowman* B and C." *JEGP* 62 (1963): 722–36.

Statius. *Thebiad.* Ed. J. H. Mozley. Cambridge, Mass.: Harvard University Press, 1982.

The Statutes of the Realm. London, 1810.

Sylla, Edith Dudley. "Fourteenth–Century Theories of Alteration." In *Infinity and Continuity in Ancient and Medieval Thought,* ed. Norman Kretzmann. Ithaca, N.Y.: Cornell University Press, 1982.

Szittya, Penn R. *The Antifraternal Tradition in Medieval Literature*. Princeton, N.J.: Princeton University Press, 1986.

Tabula exemplorum secundum ordinem alphabeti. Recueil d'exempla compilé en France à la fin du XII siècle, la. Ed. Jean T. Welter. Paris: Occitania, 1926.

Theophilus Reynaudus. *Apologia pro S. Valeriano. PL* 52. Paris, 1894. Cols. 757–836.

Thomas Aquinas. *De caritate*. In *Quaestiones disputatae S. Thomae Aquinatis,* ed. P. Bazzi. Turin: Marietti, 1953.

———. *Catena Aurea in Quatuor Evangelia*. Ed. A. Guarenti. Rome: Marietti, 1953.

———. *Commentaria in Aristotelem*. In *S. Thomae Aquinatis opera omnia,* ed. Roberto Busa. Stuttgart: Fromman–Holzboog, 1980.

———. *Commentum in lib. I-IV sententiarum*. In *Opera omnia*. Ed. Stanislaus Edouard Fretté, 7–11. Paris, 1873–74.

———. *Compendium of Theology*. Ed. Cyril Vollert. St. Louis: Herder, 1947.

———. *De potentia*. In *Quaestiones disputatae S. Thomae Aquinatis,* vol. 2, ed. P. Bazzi. Turin: Marietti, 1953.

———. *De principiis naturae*. Ed. John J. Pauson. Textus Philosophicus Friburgenses, 2. Louvain: Nauwelaerts, 1950.

———. *In Aristotelis libros de caelo et mundo*. Ed. Raymund M. Spiazzi. Turin: Marietti, 1952.

———. *Summa contra Gentiles*. Turin: Marietti, 1946.

———. *Summa theologica*. Trans. Fathers of the English Dominican Province. New York: Benziger, 1947.

Thomas Buckingham. *De contingentia futurorum et arbitrii libertate*. In Bartholomew R. de la Torre, O.P., *Thomas Buckingham and the Contingency of Futures: The Possibility of Human Freedom*. Notre Dame, Ind.: University of Notre Dame Press, 1987.

Thomas Favent. "Historia Mirabilis Parliamenti." Ed. May McKisack. *The Camden Miscellany,* 3d ser., 14 (1926): 1–27.

Thomas of Chobham. *Summa confessorum*. Ed. F. Broomfield. Analecta medievalia Namurcensia, 25 (1968).

———. *Summa de arte praedicandi*. Ed. Franco Morenzoni. Corpus Christianorum, Series Latina: Continuatio Medievalis, 82. Turnhout: Brepols 1988.

Thomas of Erfurt. *Fundamentum puerorum*. In *Metrificale Marka z Opatowca I traktaty gramatyczne XIV I XV wieku,* by Ryszard Gansiniec. Wroclaw: Zaklad Norodowy im. Ossolinskich, 1960.

———. *Grammatica speculativa*. Ed. G. L. Bursill–Hall. London: Longman, 1972.

Thomas Waleys. *De modo componendi sermones*. In *Artes praedicandi, contribution à l'histoire de la rhetorique au moyen âge,* ed. Thomas Charland. Publications de l'Institut d'Études Médiévales d'Ottawa, 7. Paris: Vrin, 1936.

Tout, T. F. *Chapters in the Administrative History of Mediaeval England: The Wardrobe, the Chamber, and the Small Seals*. 6 vols. Manchester: Manchester University Press, 1920–33.

Tractatus Anagnini. In *The Origin and Early Development of the Theory of Supposition, Logica modernorum* 2.2, ed. L. M. de Rijk. Assen: Van Gorcum, 1967.

Trapp, D. "Augustinian Theology." *Augustiniana* 6 (1956): 269–72.

———. "Peter Ceffons of Clairvaux." *Recherches de théologie ancienne et médiévale* 24 (1957): 105–7.

Turner, Victor. *The Ritual Process: Structure and Anti-Structure*. Chicago: Aldine, 1969.

Vaihinger, Hans. *The Philosophy of As-If: A System of the Theoretical, Practical, and Religious Fictions of Mankind*. Trans. C. K. Ogden. London: Routledge, 1968.

Vale, Juliet. *Edward III and Chivalry: Chivalric Society and Its Context, 1270–1350*. Woodbridge, Suffolk: Boydell, 1982.

Vandenbroucke, Fr. "La lectio divina du 11e au 14e siècle. *Studia monastica* 8 (1966): 267–93.

Vendome, Matthew of. *Ars versificatoria*. In *Les arts poétiques du XIIe et du XIIIe siècle: Recherches et documents sur la technique litteraire du moyen âge*, ed. Edmond Faral. Paris: Champion, 1958.

Villedieu, Alexander. *Doctrinale*. In *Extraits de divers manuscrits latins pour servir à l'histoire des doctrines grammaticales au Moyen Âge*, ed. Charles Thurot. Paris, 1869.

Vincent Ferrer. *Tractatus de suppositionibus*. Ed. John A. Trentmann. Grammatica Speculativa, 2. Stuttgart: Fromman-Holzboog, 1977.

Vincent of Beauvais. *Speculum doctrinale*. Bibliotheca Mundi, vol. 4. Douai, 1624. Reprint, Graz: Akademische Druck- und Verlaganstalt, 1964–65.

Walsingham, Thomas. *Chronicon Anglie*. Ed. Edward Maunde Thompson. Rolls Series, 64. London, 1874.

———. *Gesta Abbatim Monasterii Sanctii Albani*. Ed. Henry Thomas Riely. Rolls Series, 28. London, 1869.

Walter Burley. *In physicam Aristotelis expositio et quaestiones*. Venice, 1501.

———. *De primo et ultimo instanti*. Ed. Herman and Charlotte Shapiro. *Archiv für Geschichte der Philosophie* 47 (1966): 157–73.

Wander, K. F. W. *Deutsches Sprichworter-Lexicon*. Leipzig, 1867–80.

The Wars of Alexander. Ed. Hoyt N. Duggan and Thorlac Turville-Petre. EETS, s.s., 10. Oxford: Oxford University Press, 1989.

Weisheipl, James A. "The Celestial Movers in Medieval Physics." *The Thomist* 24 (1961): 286–326.

———. *Friar Thomas d'Aquino: His Life, Thought, and Work*. Garden City, N.Y.: Doubleday, 1974.

———. "Natural and Compulsory Movement." *New Scholasticism* 29 (1955): 50–81.

Weldon, James F. G. "The Structure of Dream Visions in *Piers Plowman*." *MS* 49 (1987): 254–81.

Wells, Henry W. "The Construction of *Piers Plowman*." *PMLA* 44 (1929): 123–49.

———. "The Philosophy of Piers Plowman." *PMLA* 53 (1938): 339–49.

The Westminster Chronicle, 1381–1394. Ed. L. C. Hector and Barbara Harvey. Oxford: Clarendon, 1982.

White, Lynn. *Medieval Technology and Social Change*. Oxford: Oxford University Press, 1962.

Wilkins, David. *Concilia Magnae Britanniae et Hiberniae*. Vol. 3. London, 1737. Reprint, Brussels: Culture et Civilization, 1964.

William of Sherwood. *Syncategoremata*. Ed. J. R. O'Donnell. *MS* 3 (1941): 44–93.

———. *William of Sherwood's Treatise on Syncategorematic Words*. Trans. Norman Kretzmann. Minneapolis: University of Minnesota Press, 1968.

Wilson, Curtis. *William Heytesbury: Medieval Logic and the Rise of Mathematical Physics*. Madison: University of Wisconsin Press, 1960.

Wittig, Joseph S. "The Dramatic and Rhetorical Development of Long Will's Pilgrimage," *NM* 76 (1975): 52–76.

———. "*Piers Plowman* B. Passus IX–XII: Elements in the Design of the Inward Journey." *Traditio* 28 (1972): 211–80.

Wright, Thomas, ed. *Political Poems and Songs*. Rolls Series, 14. London, 1859.

Wyclif, John. *De civili dominio*. In *The Latin Writings of Wycliffe*, ed. Reginald Lane Poole. London, 1885.

———. *De dominio divino*. Ed. Reginald Lane Poole. London, 1890.

———. *The English Works of Wyclif*. Ed. Frederic David Matthew. EETS, 74. London, 1880.

———. *De ente librorum duorum*. Ed. Michael Henry Dziewicki. London: Wyclif Society, 1909.

———. "De Officio Pastoralis." In *The English Works of Wyclif*, ed. Frederic David Matthew. EETS, 74. London, 1880.

———. *Tractatus de civili dominio*. Ed. R. L. Poole and J. Loserth. London: Wyclif Society, 1904.

Wynnere and Wastoure. Ed. Stephanie Trigg. EETS, 297. Oxford: Oxford University Press, 1990.

Zacharius Episcopus Chrysopolitani. *In Unum ex Quatuor*. *PL* 186. Paris, n.d. Cols. 11–620.

Žižek, Slavoj. "The Spectre of Ideology." In *Mapping Ideology*. London: Verso, 1994.

———. *The Sublime Object of Ideology*. London: Verso, 1989.

Index

Medieval Cultures

Volume 25
David Rollo
Glamorous Sorcery: Magic and Literacy in the High Middle Ages

Volume 24
Steve Ellis
Chaucer at Large: The Poet in the Modern Imagination

Volume 23
Edited by Barbara A. Hanawalt and Michal Kobialka
Medieval Practices of Space

Volume 22
Michelle R. Warren
History on the Edge: Excalibur and the Borders of Britain, 1100–1300

Volume 21
Olivia Holmes
Assembling the Lyric Self: Authorship from Troubadour Song to Italian Poetry Book

Volume 20
Karen Sullivan
The Interrogation of Joan of Arc

Volume 19
Clare A. Lees
Tradition and Belief: Religious Writing in Late Anglo-Saxon England

Volume 18
David Matthews
The Making of Middle English, 1765–1910

Volume 17
Jeffrey Jerome Cohen
Of Giants: Sex, Monsters, and the Middle Ages

Volume 16
Edited by Barbara A. Hanawalt and David Wallace
Medieval Crime and Social Control

Volume 15
Kathryn Kerby-Fulton and Denise L. Despres
Iconography and the Professional Reader:
The Politics of Book Production in the Douce "Piers Plowman"

Volume 14
Edited by Marilynn Desmond
Christine de Pizan and the Categories of Difference

Volume 13
Alfred Thomas
Anne's Bohemia: Czech Literature and Society, 1310–1420

Volume 12
Edited by F. R. P. Akehurst and Stephanie Cain Van D'Elden
The Stranger in Medieval Society

Volume 11
Edited by Karma Lochrie, Peggy McCracken, and James A. Schultz
Constructing Medieval Sexuality

Volume 10
Claire Sponsler
Drama and Resistance: Bodies, Goods, and Theatricality in Late Medieval England

Volume 9
Edited by Barbara A. Hanawalt and David Wallace
Bodies and Disciplines: Intersections of Literature and History in Fifteenth-Century England

Volume 8
Marilynn Desmond
Reading Dido: Gender, Textuality, and the Medieval "Aeneid"

Volume 7
Edited by Clare A. Lees
Medieval Masculinities: Regarding Men in the Middle Ages

Volume 6
Edited by Barbara A. Hanawalt and Kathryn L. Reyerson
City and Spectacle in Medieval Europe

Volume 5
Edited by Calvin B. Kendall and Peter S. Wells
Voyage to the Other World: The Legacy of Sutton Hoo

Volume 4
Edited by Barbara A. Hanawalt
Chaucer's England: Literature in Historical Context

Volume 3
Edited by Marilyn J. Chiat and Kathryn L. Reyerson
The Medieval Mediterranean: Cross-Cultural Contacts

Volume 2

Edited by Andrew MacLeish

The Medieval Monastery

Volume 1

Edited by Kathryn L. Reyerson and Faye Powe

The Medieval Castle

D. Vance Smith is assistant professor of English at Princeton University. He has published articles on the medieval masculine body, *Piers Plowman,* Chaucer, medieval historiography, medieval economics and the Middle English romance, and plague and memory in the Middle Ages. He has a book on the economic anthropology of the medieval English household and the Middle English romance forthcoming from the University of Minnesota Press.